Economic Origins

of Antisemitism

Economic Origins
of Antisemitism

Poland and Its Jews in the
Early Modern Period

Hillel Levine   ← Main entry

Yale University Press
New Haven and London

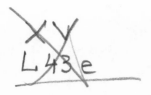

Designed by Sylvia Steiner.
Set in Garamond Book type by The Composing Room of Michigan, Inc.
Printed in the United States of America by BookCrafters, Inc., Chelsea, Michigan.

Library of Congress Cataloging-in-Publication Data

Levine, Hillel.
  Economic origins of antisemitism : Poland and its Jews in the early modern period /
  Hillel Levine.
    p.   cm.
  Includes bibliographical references and index.
  ISBN: 0–300–04987–0
  1. Antisemitism—Economic aspects—Poland.   2. Jews—Poland—Economic
conditions.   3. Jews—Poland—History.   4. Poland—Ethnic relations.   I. Title.
DS146.P6L48   1991
943.8'004924—dc20   90-26565
                         CIP

The paper in this book meets the guidelines for permanence and durability of the
Committee on Production Guidelines for Book Longevity of the Council on Library
Resources.

10   9   8   7   6   5   4   3   2   1

In memory of my dear grandparents,
my living bridge to the best of East European Jewry:
Jacob Peretz (1898–1967), of Grodno,
my teacher of Jewish history and Jewish living,
and
Sheina Gorodetzky Peretz (1900–1974), of Kobrin,
who in demonstrating the vast worlds of memory
that can be contained in a small paper bag
gave me my earliest and most profound instruction
in the social sciences.

Contents

Illustrations

Preface

This book presents an analysis of Poland and its Jews, from the period of that country's greatest territorial expansion and political strength in the sixteenth and seventeenth centuries through the period of its dissolution at the end of the eighteenth century. The formulation "Poland and its Jews" is not a casual one. Although Jews have resided in Poland for a millennium, most often they have been viewed as sojourners. The book focuses on the degrees of resourcefulness with which Jews and others reacted and interacted in relation to what were often elusive and conflicting forces. I shall try to avoid either sentimentalizing Poland's Jews or emphasizing their suffering, both of which distance us from that resourcefulness and its equivocal implications.

It is important to acknowledge what this book is not. My late teacher, the eminent Jewish theologian Abraham Joshua Heschel, characterized Polish Jews as being able to perceive the infinite by doing the finite, as "matching the material with the spiritual," as being adept at the "poetry of rigorism." This book presents little detail of Polish Jews' perceptions of the infinite, of their deep spiritual lives, and of their creativity. Neither does it capture that finite material history—the history of communal institutions, of rabbis and rogues, of leaders and movements. Many other books must be written to present those histories. But if not about the material and spiritual per se, this book is about the not-so-poetic rigors that Polish Jewish spirituality had to transcend.

This work is not free of the fashions of the marketplace of ideas and the spirit of the times. I have been the beneficiary of the revival of interest in comparative history and of attention to the areas where different aspects of modernization fail and to the reactions that such failures precipitate. This has been an important corrective to the triumphal way in which the modern world had previously been

xi

experienced and studied. Another great but departed teacher, Joseph Levenson, in his *Trilogy: Confucian China and Its Modern Fate,* distinguished between that which is "merely" of historical significance and that which is "truly" of historical significance. The difference is not only one of intonation. From the perspective of failed modernization, and of the migration of people and ideas to which this failure led in the nineteenth and twentieth centuries, the experiences of early modern Polish Jews are truly significant. And with the decline of the Soviet empire and the reconceptualization of East-West relations that are dramatically taking place, another chapter is added to the history of failed modernization, which must be seen in a new light. Some of the forces unleashed in these great revolutions for democracy, nationalism, and decentralized polities and economies in the Soviet Union and in its former satellites are threatening indigenous Jews, many of whom are the East European descendants of Poland's Jews. The ironies and patterns are not just significant; they are frightening.

The general rules of transliteration of the *Encyclopedia Judaica* are followed for Hebrew and Yiddish. Anglicized spelling of place names, as given in *Webster's Geographical Dictionary,* has been adopted. No political judgments about national boundaries are intended. Where a place name appears in Jewish sources in a somewhat different form, it is provided as well. The terms *gentry, nobility, aristocracy,* and *lords* are used interchangeably; *magnate* is used to indicate someone who has amassed land, wealth, and power.

I express my gratitude to the library staffs at Harvard University, Yale University, Boston University, Hebrew College, the Hebrew University and National Library in Jerusalem, the Jewish Historical Institute in Warsaw, the Czartoryski Museum, the New York Public Library, YIVO (Institute for Jewish Research), the Library of Congress, the British Museum, the Balliol Library, Bar Ilan University, and the Ozar Haposkim Institute.

I am deeply appreciative of the support for my research for this book from the National Endowment for the Humanities and the International Research and Exchange Board. Additional travel money came from Boston University faculty research funds. The Harvard Russian Research Center provided a stimulating environment in which to write.

The book has also benefited from several generations of inquisitive students. To my students at Harvard, Yale, and Boston universities, at several institutions in Poland where I lectured in 1984–1985, and in the People's Republic of China in 1989, I owe a debt of gratitude. Teachers, friends, and colleagues have commented on parts or all of the book, and I have profited from their learnedness. I thank them all: Orli Albeck, David Arnow, Yisrael Bartal, Brigitte Berger, Peter Berger, Eugene Black, Laurel Brake, Alina Cała, Leon Chernyak, Robert Cohen, Sidra Ezrahi, Yaron Ezrahi, Eric Fay, Talya Fishman, Ivriya Gal, Reuven Gal, Gao Wang Zhi, Ronald Garet, Charles Grench, Gu Xiaoming, Ze'ev Gries, Magdalena Gubala-Ryzak, Lawrence Harmon, Irving Janis, Marjorie Janis, Jacob Katz, David

Kazhdan, Monika Krajewska, Stanisław Krajewski, Shulamith Levine, Betty Lifton, Robert Lifton, Frances Malino, Mildred Marmur, Jean Morse, Stephen Morse, Hilda Nebenzahl, Yizhak Nebenzahl, Steven Ozment, Richard Rabinowitz, Emily Rose, Joanne Rose, Sylvia Rothchild, Samuel Schafler, Vera Schwarcz, Benjamin Schwartz, Steven Shaw, Ilana Silber, Michael Silber, Adin Steinzaltz, David Szonyi, Ara Tchividjian, Daveda Tenenbaum, Isadore Twersky, Anita Weiner, Eugene Weiner, Elie Wiesel, Zhao Fu San, and Anna Żuk. A special appreciation goes to Jerzy Jedlicki, of the Polish Academy of Sciences, who more than a decade ago brought to my attention vexing issues in Polish historiography that have been crucial to this study. Halina Nelken of Cambridge, Massachusetts, generously shared with me illustrations from her forthcoming book *Images of Lost Worlds,* reproduced here with the author's permission. Thanks also to Reuven Hecht for permission to print photographs from his collection. I have greatly benefited from Mildred Marmur's excellent editorial advice and her warm friendship. I would like to thank the staff of Yale University Press, particularly Charles Grench, Otto Bohlmann, Sylvia Steiner, and Richard Miller, the manuscript editor, who shared with me his good sense of style. Their wise counsel guided me through the last stages of this project and left its mark on this book. Blessed is the day when John Carter became my administrative assistant. My good fortune continues in working with Lauri Slawsby. Their care and skill are reflected on every page.

In bringing the research of several years and the engagement of many more years to conclusion, I look backward and forward. My dear friends have provided significant encouragement. I joyously acknowledge the special friendship of professors Sidra Ezrahi and Yaron Ezrahi. This book and my life have been much enriched by their devotion and our discourse, spanning decades and continents. In the inner- and outerworldly odysseys that accompanied the writing of this book, my parents, Harold and Shirley Levine, my wife, Shulamith Levine, and my children, Hephzibah Nehamah, Tiferet Ahavah, and Haninah Zephaniah Peretz, bore with me and at times joined me along the way. The joy that they brought to my life made these journeys less dangerous.

Boston, Massachusetts
December 31, 1989

Economic Origins
of Antisemitism

Introduction

The View from the Broken Bridge:
A Tale of Two Revolutions

Our anniversary-prone society has commemorated the bicenten-
nial of the French Revolution with great fanfare. Yet there has been less celebration of the revolution that occurred in Poland at the same time and that attempted
to bring about the same broad-reaching reforms and national regeneration, often
using the same terms of discourse. Both revolutions generated intense debate on
the position of Jews and Judaism within the new societies that were to emerge
with the onset of the modern era.

The French Revolution, succeeded by violence, dictatorship, and conquest,
spread its message as far east as the Russian Empire. That meeting of East and West
also precipitated the spread across Europe of the forces of political and social
reaction, given formal expression at the Congress of Vienna in 1815. For France's
forty thousand Jews, the revolution was followed by setbacks and disappoint-
ments. The increasing secularization of postrevolutionary society and the extrica-
tion of Christianity from the civic sphere created a vacuum to be filled by new
rationales for rejecting the Jew, more pernicious than the traditional theological
ones. The Dreyfus case and Vichy collaboration took place on the very soil producing millennial dreams of liberty, equality, and fraternity. The roots of modern
totalitarian movements—always inimical to Jews and Judaism—can be traced to
the French Revolution.[1] And yet that revolution is seen as having borne the seeds
of freedom and opportunity for the people of France, including its Jews. As such, it
is considered paradigmatic of Jewish entry into the modern world.[2]

1. Connections between the Enlightenment, the French Revolution, and modern anti-
semitism are suggested in Talmon, *Rise of Totalitarian Democracy;* Ettinger, "Jews and
Judaism"; Hertzberg, *French Enlightenment and the Jews.*
2. Simon Dubnow is representative of those historians who emphasize the revolution's

By comparison, the effects of Poland's revolution have received far less notice. Scant attention has been paid to the earliest experiences of modernization and the political events that affected approximately one million Polish Jews, living in what by the sixteenth century was (and continued to be until the Holocaust) a Jewish settlement area of unique density and intensity. The descendants of those eighteenth-century Polish Jews subsequently populated the major centers of Jewish life in the nineteenth and twentieth centuries and shaped the major Jewish responses to modernity. Poland's "bloodless revolution," its constitution of May 3, 1791, drawing inspiration from the Western Enlightenment, attempted to impose modernization from the top.[3] It was issued in the very season of the French constitution, the Declaration of the Rights of Man, and the American Bill of Rights, which together provided the legal moorings and a climate of opinion for Jewish participation in the modern world unfolding in the West. But the Polish constitution excluded Poland's Jews from its purview and actually had the effect of abrogating rights that they had enjoyed for six centuries. Half the world's Jews, at that moment residing in Poland, were now left out of public law and were legislatively defined as nonpersons.

The Polish revolution was of short duration and of limited benefit; it intensified the meddling of Poland's neighbors, the partition and annexation of the land, the political annihilation of the Polish state, and the economic decline of most Poles along with a growing awareness of their own backwardness.[4] Rather than spurring Poles to greater accomplishment, this awareness evoked in them zealous defensiveness, expressed in new ideologies depicting Poland's role in bridging East and West and in messianic fantasies describing its glorious future. But the administrative implications for Jews of being defined as nonpersons were explored in Poland as well as elsewhere, then and later.[5] For Polish Jewry, this revolution was the beginning of the end.

------

legal, administrative, and political changes contributing to this entry. Others, such as Heinrich Graetz, emphasize the influence of the Enlightenment, particularly as it developed in Berlin. Developments in both France and Germany influenced, and served as reference points for, policies toward Jews in Poland. For one effort to balance the factors, see Katz, *Out of the Ghetto,* and *Toward Modernity.*

3. Wandycz, *Lands of Partitioned Poland,* 9.

4. The reasons for the failure of the Four-Year Sejm and for the efforts to transform Poland in the eighteenth century are complex and controversial. Jerzy Jedlicki speaks of the "complex of backwardness" that develops among Poles in the eighteenth century as they observe the more successful early stages of modernization unfolding elsewhere. See Jedlicki, "Native Culture and Western Civilization."

5. Poland's neighbors, whose policies in the second half of the eighteenth century toward their Jews and those in the Polish territories that they annexed were erratic, nevertheless included Jews in their public law. Catherine II in 1786 issued a decree granting Jews full rights in accordance with their estate and making discrimination against them illegal. Although these privileges, "a landmark in the history of modern Jewry," preceded by five years the civil equality for Jews declared by the French National Assembly, they were in actuality never enforced. Richard Pipes, "Catherine II and the Jews," 13. Joseph II's edicts

This book is about the beginning of that beginning of the end, about Poland and its Jews in the world of early modern Europe and their relation to the forces that would transform Western Europe, but not Poland, during the early stages of modernization. There is much to learn from the successes of modernization, as well as from its failures. And if those failures shed some unwanted light on the situation of Jews in those countries where modernization succeeded, all the better. For in examining the incipient stages of modernization where it was stillborn, we gain deeper insight into elusive dangers where it proved to be viable.[6]

Modernity, whatever else it may imply, is a period that has its own history. One can analyze where it leads to observable transformations or to irresolvable conflicts and frustrated expectations, both in the East and in the West.[7] It was Leopold von Ranke, the great German historian of the last century, who characterized modernization as the "spirit of the occident subduing the world." But it was not only the Western Enlightenment or "functional rationality" that made Eastern observers glance westward with envy at the early modern transformations and made Western observers glance eastward with scorn and condescension at what they defined as backwardness. More often, it was Western consumer goods—the signs and the instruments of "wealth and power"—that in the East inspired visions of Manchesters on the Vistula or, some years later and with greater success, gave rise to the Manchesters of Singapore.[8] Among many observers of Western modernization there was little interest or appreciation for the intellectual, social, and political revolutions that were the matrices of those technological innovations in the West.

More recent studies of modernization emphasize "small changes" in indigenous social, political, economic, and intellectual forms that occur with apparent fortuitousness and with little relation to anything that can be initially identified as modern.[9] Under the influence of these small changes, movements, ideologies, and

---

of 1782 and 1789, however much they encroached upon the inner lives of Jews, granted them privileges and included them in public law. And even Frederick II's edict of 1750 and subsequent legislation, though often restrictive, never eliminated Jews from the social categories to which rights were attached.

6. Dumont, *Homo Hierarchicus*, 16, 237–38. Dumont makes a similar argument from a negative example regarding what Westerners, committed to equality, can learn about themselves from examining Indian society and its caste system, where equality does not develop.

7. Modernization as a concept has fallen out of fashion among some social scientists. For a summary statement on the sizable literature on modernization, see Berger, Berger, and Kellner, *Homeless Mind,* 8ff.

8. For comparative perspectives on how the "non-West" viewed the West during the early stages of modernization, see Schwartz, *In Search of Wealth and Power.*

9. See North and Thomas, "Growth of the Western World," 10–12, which suggests that the cumulative effect of "small changes" in secondary institutions in response to disequilibrium caused by expanded market sizes and price changes led to a restructuring of fundamental institutions in Western Europe in such a way that individuals were encouraged to

rituals are themselves likely to be reshaped, whether or not they succeed in maximizing the slight advantage that one region develops over another at a particular point.[10] For, as we now know, incipient modernization leads in more than one direction: as much as it may result in new modes of producing and, occasionally, in new modes of thinking, it often ends in failed modernization, economic stagnation, and political instability accompanied by anti-Western sentiments, despair and resentment, shame and blame.[11]

Here Ranke's unilinear and unidirectional nineteenth-century perspective clashes with our "postmodern" outlook and experiences. The awareness of backwardness—no less belligerent for all of its defensiveness—shapes its own theories and its own theodicies. Modernization is as much a problem of the proliferation of new modes of thinking as it is a problem of the dissemination of technology.[12] Whether people observing the early stages of modernization attribute the changes taking place around them to machines or to capital accumulation, to newly assumed worldly orientations or to the lost cargo of the ancestors, these interpretations are real in their consequences.[13] And though people are likely to measure themselves against the accomplishments of others, they may not be interested in emulating what others have done to achieve success. The East learns about the West (and the West about the East) through images that, as Peter Gay puts it, provide "a bit of reality with a mass of prejudice, a morass of clichés kept from drying out entirely in a thin trickle of fact."[14]

In early modern Poland members of the aristocracy—by far the most powerful group—though mindful of transformations occurring in the West and interested in some of the results, had their own way of doing things. In their pursuit of Western power and wealth they wanted industry without commerce, investment without capital accumulation, profitability without the development of

---

strive for greater economic productivity. See also Rosenberg and Birdzell, *How the West Grew Rich, Economic Transformation of the Industrial World,* and Landes's review, "To Have and Have Not."

10. Thane, Crossick, and Floud, eds., *Power of the Past,* 2.

11. For the political uses of these emotional responses to failed modernization in relation to German history before World War II, see Stern, *Politics of Cultural Despair;* Herf, *Reactionary Modernism.*

12. Bellah, "Meaning and Modernisation." Wiener, *British Culture,* points to the ongoing significance of meaning in the process of modernization. Attitudes of the English aristocracy, inimical to the industrial spirit, lose their social significance at a critical moment and allow for the growth of industry. Yet they surface at a later point, contributing to economic decline.

13. In the cargo cults that developed in Melanesia under Western colonialism, the natives viewed the imported products of Western technology as cargo promised to them by their ancestors which now was usurped by the colonialists. They had little understanding of, and appreciation for, the technology or the social, political, and economic forces that contributed to the production of that cargo. These cargo cults often provided the early foundations of rebellions against colonial rule. See Worseley, *The Trumpet Shall Sound.*

14. Gay, *Freud, Jews, and Other Germans,* viii.

human and natural resources, patriotism without participation, loyalty without an offer of security, unity without integration. They were inattentive to the small changes that were taking place in Poland and to the opportunities to catapult these into long-term benefits. Most important, many Polish publicists, envisioning a Poland endowed with that power and wealth sought to spur economic change without social change, to achieve productivity without altering the feudal structure of society and without surrendering gentry claims to serf labor. This book will explore where the Jews of Poland fit into early modern Polish society and Poland's vision of its future, and how these Jews were used to reconcile rather than resolve Poland's contradictions, to inhibit rather than reverse its decline, and to assign blame rather than analyze its failures.

At the time of these revolutions in the West and the East, in the late eighteenth century, the image of Polish Jews in such Western outposts as Berlin was one of unkempt masses, rigidly traditional in their values, wholly immune to change, and dangerously otherworldly. There was agreement on the basic "facts" about Poland's Jews among different observers of them, both within Poland and beyond it; among enemies of the Jews, eager to exclude and isolate them; among those imbued with the ethos of the Enlightenment, for whom the "amelioration" of the Jews was the acid test of Enlightenment verities; and among Jewish publicists trying to define the position of Jews in a world in flux. There was disagreement as to the causes of the problems of Polish Jews and as to the prognosis. Their enemies saw Polish Jews as demonstrating universal, quintessential, and unalterable flaws in the Jewish personality; their apologists flatly rejected the intractability of these problems. For Jewish enlighteners in particular, the conditions and circumstances of Poland's Jews had to be viewed within the context of the generally low level of civilization in Poland. They suggested that many of Poland's Jews had raised themselves to a higher level of existence than that which their Polish neighbors had achieved. These Jews along with others could be further improved through the availability of proper education and the granting of civic rights. It was particularly those most oriented toward acculturation and assimilation who were made most anxious by this image and reputation of Polish Jews lest it impinge on their own struggles in the West for political rights, economic opportunities, and, most important, social acceptance.[15]

15. See, for example, Friedlaender, *Aktenstücke*, 20, 114, and *Über die Verbesserung*, xlvi–xlviii. For a review of the information available in France regarding Polish Jews, see Frydman, "French Reports," 1:23–32. Some disciples of the short-lived Polish Enlightenment likewise made unfavorable comparisons between Polish Jews and West European Jews, such as the venerable Moses Mendelssohn. These Polish enlighteners, however, did not examine or acknowledge the different opportunities available to Jews in the West that contributed to their more positive image. This is illustrated by the following remark in a Polish memoir: "For us who are accustomed to our Itziks and Moskes who sit in the stores and get the masses drunk, it is a wonder to see people from that nation and faith in other lands who are so useful and educated." Cited in Ringelblum, "Hasidism and Haskala," 130.

An early commentator on Poland's failure to undergo the early stages of modernization and on the backwardness of its Jews was Solomon Maimon (1753–1800), one of the more brilliant and exotic of those Eastern European Jews who arrived in Berlin during the 1780s. Born in Lithuania, Maimon received an extensive talmudic education in his youth and then broadened his intellectual horizons by studying Jewish mysticism, or Kabbala. For a time he even visited the court of a Hasidic master. After moving to the West, he had contact with Moses Mendelssohn and his disciples in Berlin, among whom this Polish Jew—crude in manner and appearance—was received with mitigated enthusiasm. He became an avid participant in discussions on the educational needs of the Jews in his native country with these promulgators of the Jewish Enlightenment, or Haskala. The industrialist Isaac Daniel Itzig suggested that Maimon translate a history of the Jewish people. Through this work Jews would learn of the glorious moments of their past, when they lived in harmony with their Gentile neighbors and would perceive the depths to which they had now declined. Itzig's son-in-law, David Friedlander, a banker, recommended a book on natural religion. If Jews knew of "the eternal God who always acts through eternal and wise laws," their lot would improve. The sage Mendelssohn, however, was not enthusiastic about the suggestion. According to Maimon, he believed that "whatever was undertaken in this line, though it would do no harm, would be of little use."[16] It is not evident why Mendelssohn did not share his disciples' optimism for what would cure the ills of Polish Jews. Maimon's account leaves unclear whether Mendelssohn was more critical or more compassionate; whether he truly believed, based on personal experience or reputation, that those Polish Jews were utterly resistant to innovation, or whether he knew that their real problems stemmed from more than just the paucity of historical models for good relations with their neighbors or the need for a keener orientation to cosmological forces.

Maimon ultimately enjoyed greater success in his philosophical studies than in his efforts to launch joint educational projects with the Berlin Jewish enlighteners, the Maskilim. His *Versuch über die Transzendentalphilosophie,* on Kant's thought, particularly the *Critique of Pure Reason,* was praised by Kant and had a lasting effect on post-Kantian German philosophy. Maimon dedicated this work to Poland's "enlightened" king, Stanisław Poniatowski (1732–1798), making an effusive entreaty on behalf of his coreligionists in Poland.[17] Even better known at the time was his vastly popular autobiography, in the tradition of Jean-Jacques Rousseau's *Confessions.* This memoir, published serially in 1792 and 1793, became favored reading in German salon circles, which found in it both amusement and confirmation of their perception of those who came to be known as *Ostjuden.*[18]

Maimon opens his autobiography with a touching description of his early childhood. His grandfather, as was common enough in his day, was an *arendar,* a

16. Maimon, *Sefer Hayyei,* 213–14; Altmann, *Moses Mendelssohn,* 362–64.
17. Maimon, "Dedication to the Polish King."
18. For the history of the publication of this work, see Lahover's introduction to Maimon,

leaseholder for an estate of Prince Radziwiłł, who came of a family known for its Calvinist attachments.[19] The estate, in a small village on the Neman River, included houses, fields, and the inevitable tavern that was at the center of all such estates across Poland. Maimon describes the dire neglect of these estates, reflecting the state of entrepreneurialism in Poland. The gentry landlord—the *porez,* a character in Hebrew and Yiddish literature remembered for his bombast, capriciousness, and harshness—refused to make capital improvements or even to maintain the physical plant, though such neglect jeopardized his assets and profits. In accordance with the Polish gentry's economic thinking of the time, the lord was more deeply concerned to preserve strained cash reserves for imported commodities, particularly coveted luxury items. Maintenance expenditures of the estate's physical plant were left to his Jewish lessee, in this case Maimon's pious grandfather. Though he too could have ultimately reaped the benefit of an efficient estate, he refused to make needed repairs because they were part of the lord's contractual obligation. As Maimon comments, his grandfather "could not tolerate any innovations; all matters had to be conducted in the old manner," even if a Jewish leaseholder's contract with his gentry landlord was unenforceable.[20]

Maimon reports the comic and pathetic situation of a bridge that had fallen into disrepair longer ago than anyone could remember. It would damage the carriages of gentry travelers and their heavily laden entourages, who would often vent their spleen on the Jewish manager and his family. It was a regular occurrence, therefore, that when such a carriage passed by, Maimon's family, anticipating the worst, would follow well-rehearsed evasive measures and escape into the forest. If the lord and his party wanted to avenge their mishap, they would not find any members of Maimon's family to punish. They would have to satisfy themselves by ransacking the house and, as they often did after slaking their thirst, spilling out the grandfather's liquor supply in the tavern.[21] Solomon Maimon asks

---

Sefer Hayyei, 22–25. Two studies point to the complex relations that developed between German Jews and East European Jews: Aschheim, *Brothers and Strangers;* Wertheimer, *German Policy and Jewish Politics.*

19. Although Maimon does not identify exactly who this Prince Radziwiłł was, it is likely to have been Karol Radziwiłł (1734–1790), who we know about from other Jewish sources. See chapter 1 for an assessment of Polish Protestantism as a counterexample to Weber's efforts to link religious changes to a spirit of capitalism.

20. Maimon, *Sefer Hayyei,* 61.

21. For vivid descriptions corroborating Maimon's account of the lavish manner in which members of the Polish aristocracy in the last years of the Polish state comported themselves, see Bain, *Last King of Poland,* 93–114; Mączak, "Money and Society," 82ff. Members of the gentry were known to travel through the countryside with their own house furnishings—beds, tapestries, and the like—as part of their efforts to maintain a splendid style of living without cash expenditures. The requisite labor to support such maneuvers was not considered an expenditure. Indeed, serfs often provided that labor. Although hotel facilities in early modern Poland were primitive, the reluctance of the gentry to spend cash thwarted improvements. This reluctance was not an expression of frugality or of the

the obvious question: Why didn't his grandfather repair the bridge? "If my grand-father would simply have given up adjudicating with someone who was stronger than he was and would have suffered the wrongdoing and repaired the bridge with his own money, he would have spared himself all of these afflictions. But he persisted in making claims on the basis of the contract that he had, and the estate agent simply laughed at his troubles."[22]

This pastoral reminiscence of childhood, evocatively projected with slapstick, abruptly takes on a haunting quality as Maimon shudders at memories of "other difficult afflictions which I cannot pass over in silence." He describes his grandfather's relationship with the village Russian Orthodox priest, illiterate and boorish, who would imbibe at all hours in his grandfather's tavern. When the grandfather refused to continue his unlimited credit line, the priest contrived a blood libel, an incident not at all uncommon in eighteenth-century Poland. The priest conspired with a hunter to sneak into the tavern a sack containing the body of a murdered village child. The sack was discovered, and Maimon's grandfather was arrested. In accordance with juridical procedure, he was tortured in order to extract a confession that he had murdered a Christian for ritual purposes. The grandfather was close to death when the village officials found the hunter and proceeded to torture him. He admitted to the priest's plot. The grandfather was vindicated and set free. (The priest was never punished for his murderous scheme.) Maimon's grandfather instituted an annual celebration of his deliv-erance as a personal holiday of Purim, and Maimon's father wrote a poem in Hebrew to commemorate the event. The tavern probably remained the same, with or without the Russian Orthodox priest. The bridge was never repaired.

What is the "bit of reality," the "thin trickle of facts," in this depiction of Polish Jewry? Recent studies of modernization of consciousness as well as major trends in Jewish historiography would consider it a valuable intergenerational portrait of "traditional society," as shaky as Maimon's grandfather's bridge, and a credible image of premodern Polish Jews. The story includes a grandfather who manages enterprises without the entrepreneurial spirit; who fosters ad hoc re-sponses rather than long-term solutions; who is sufficiently proud to press his legal rights through the Polish courts, as hopeless as this action might be, but lacks the power to enforce his contract with the lord by any other means; and who is threatened by innovation and is reluctant to make investments. The landlord in the tale is absent, negligent, and contentious; the father is pious and learned yet

---

concern to accumulate capital for investment. It does reflect the crisis precipitated by low levels of monetary circulation in the Polish economy and gentry concerns to be able to satisfy appetites for expensive luxury items. Polish aristocrats traveling abroad in this period were often puzzled by the sober and unostentatious way of life that they discovered among their counterparts in the West, who were obviously far wealthier. It was only in the second part of the eighteenth century that a small, reform-minded group of Polish gentry, calling for commerce and industry in Poland, became equally impressed by what was being done with that wealth in the West.

22. Maimon, *Sefer Hayyei,* 58.

aware of the larger world and somewhat enamored of the new. And in the midst of all this the ever-present tavern, mainstay of the village economy, meeting place and battleground of Jews and Poles, doorway to the outer world of travel and commerce, and entrance to the cavernous inner world of demonic activity.[23] The inability of our Polish-Jewish disciple of Kant to "pass over in silence" those recollections beckons us to pause for a moment at the village tavern, peering through its window for the elusive sets of relationships that we want to analyze.

When Solomon Maimon was growing up in mid-eighteenth-century Poland, as much as 85 percent of rural Jewry—estimates would have it—was involved in some aspect of the manufacturing, wholesaling, or retailing of beer, mead, wine, and grain-based intoxicants like vodka. But the *propinacja,* as both the site and the institution of the trade in alcohol came to be called—after the small hovel that generally served as drinking room, hostel, barn, and storage room for this enter-prise—has its counterparts in peasant society, where drinking not only is a favor-ite pastime but becomes the opportunity to display, examine, strengthen, and: confirm communal bonds.[24] Imbibing, like praying, may be the practice of indi-viduals, but it is not only a solitary act. Though it may indeed function, as Marx would harangue us into believing about religion, as an opiate of the masses, it does far more than soothe and foster forgetfulness.

The Jewish tavern, the *kretchme* or *shenk* (Yiddish, Polish, and Russian cognates attest to its geographic distribution), was found in even the smallest village in seventeenth- and eighteenth-century Poland. Its social dimensions went beyond those of the German *Gasthaus,* a meeting place where the locals could have recreation—in the dual sense of passing the hours as well as engaging in imaginative creation around the *Stammtischen* of a fantasy social order that accorded those locals a dignity unavailable in daily life. The Jewish inn served additional functions to those of the wayside rest place for travelers through the provinces. There, sitting around at the geographic and social periphery of the community, necessity and hardship loosened the conventional structures, bring-ing together native and foreigner, gentry and burgher, clergy and laity, and, if our reports are accurate, human being and work animal for refreshment and rest.

The tavern, like its Jewish owner, was an intrusion of the "other" into the countryside; that which is "other" to the world of everyday life may have different valences including good and evil, life and death. For the villagers of the pre-modern world, anything that is foreign is suspected of having special connections with the devil. Anything that is not integral to the coherence of local culture is impure and dangerous.[25] The Jew's presence and function in the village evi-denced such associations. The Jewish innkeeper was assisted by a family member

23. Opalski, *Jewish Tavern-Keeper.*
24. H. H. Ben-Sasson, Baron, Kahanah, and Gross, *Economic History of the Jews,* 136; LeDonne, "Indirect Taxes in Catherine's Russia," 173–207; Horn, *Regesty dokumentów,* vol. 1, nos. 137, 172, 185, 227, 240; Katz, *Goy Shel Shabbat,* 70–83; Pipes, "Catherine II and the Jews," 3–20; Smith and Christian, *Bread and Salt.*
25. Douglas, *Purity and Danger;* Banfield, *Moral Basis of a Backward Society.*

who appeared equally strange in the eyes of the serf client, or by a peasant woman servant whose alliance with the Jew aroused suspicion. He sat behind his counter. Across that barrier of social separation and melded fate, he dispensed drink of uneven quality in exchange for the peasant's coins of uncertain value. In the simple act of pushing the overflowing cup across the counter and collecting a few coins, the Jew had little understanding of the complex economic interests in whose service he acted.[26] The serf, noisily plopping down his last coins on the counter and extending his emptied grail in his calloused, unsteady hand to the Jew for one more drink, likewise had little understanding of the economic forces, more powerful than his inner impulses for the gratification provided by alcohol, to which he was surrendering. They were the forces of the serf economy and of a monetary system that functioned to impede his accumulation of surplus profit by which he might improve his family's standard of living. He could resist that system through backbreaking toil to earn payment in kind and through fiscal ingenuity to retain some cash reserves. The drink was both the effect and the cause of that broken resistance and degradation. The Jew, as the primary representative of this system, as the monetizer of unmarketable grain, could avert facing his contribution to the plight of the serf—"a Goy," he might mutter with self-righteousness, "drunken sloth is the essence of the Gentile." This role of the Jew in purveying drink confirmed and dramatized the Jew's position as middleman between wheat field and market, between agriculture and industry, between the local community and the mysterious outside world, between the absent landowner and his local agents who dispensed land, arranged work schedules, collected rents and taxes, and adjudicated and disciplined. The Jew was the bridge between the netherworld of demonic and destructive forces and the other world of spiritual and inebriated elevation. The Jew spanned the growing gap between abstract monetary exchange of commerce and personal reciprocity of the feudal economy, between the reality of the declining estates of the déclassé nobility, contemptuous of entrepreneurialism, innovation, or hard work, and their sanguinity that despite their financial problems "there will be a jingle," that with the assistance of the Jew they would continue to hear the reassuring sound of coins exchanged for grain and usable to import the luxury items of which the lords were so fond.[27] The Jew was the *faktor* of the gentry landlord and the confidant of the peasant. Yet he was suspected in his business affairs, religious matters, and family involvements by both lord and serf; as such, this shared resentment toward the Jew fostered a modicum of solidarity among other Poles. Like the *Korn Jude*

26. The social role of the monetizer has been studied by Georg Simmel in his 1889 essay "Zur Psychologie des Geldes." He gradually expanded this analysis into a book, *Philosophie des Geldes (The Philosophy of Money,* trans. Tom Bottomore and David Frisby [London, 1978]). It is difficult to ignore Simmel's polemical overtones, as he aims his analytical and rhetorical powers against Marx. Whereas Marx's notion of *Kapital* has been most influential in the history of ideas and in world history, Simmel's notion of money deserves more attention among social theorists as well as among Jewish historians.
27. Macząk, "Money and Society," 88.

Fig. 1. *Korn Jude*. This silver and alloy coin (Germany, 1694) depicts a "wandering Jew" with walking stick in hand carrying a sack of grain over his left shoulder. A devil perched on the sack punctures it.

depicted on German coins of this period—traversing the well-gleaned fields with an overflowing cornucopia-shaped sack on his back and a devil perched at its rim—the Jewish innkeeper was conveniently available for blame when gentry-produced grain shortages led to starvation of the serfs.

The propinacja provides, then, a valuable prism through which a complex set of social, psychological, economic, and political relations can be viewed.[28] The call for increased productivity was sounded all over Europe in the eighteenth century. On the eve of Poland's revolution, discussion of the propinacja elicited an unusually broad consensus among conservative gentry and reformers, Polish nationalists and Russian bureaucrats, and even some Jews: the propinacja, upon which the sustenance of so many of Poland's Jews was wholly dependent, was deemed the unproductive occupation par excellence. By extension, Poland's Jews themselves were considered unproductive. Rare was the publicist who recognized and declared the problems that Jews would have, within the feudal economy in which they functioned, in building merchant ships rather than taverns, in financing factories rather than stills.[29] This claim that the Jews were not productive, as it develops in Poland, became central to the attitudes and policies oriented toward Jews in Russia for a century and more. To analyze the claim—rather than simply making defensive and apologetic counterclaims about Jewish productivity—it is important to understand the economics of the propinacja within the context of the economy of Poland and, beyond that, within the context of the economy of Europe in the early modern period.[30] The Jew and the "jingle" will provide a deeper understanding of the *politics of productivity,* the process by which different segments of Polish society in this period defined what was economically useful. In trying to elicit those concepts of productivity, I shall draw from modes of economic thinking, venerable and new, that shaped the public discourse on what is, and what is not, productive. We will hear echoes of scholasticism and the Enlightenment, physiocracy and cameralism, as they provide epistemologies, logical structures, and ideologies, in the concepts of productivity that they shape and in the evaluation of the productivity of others that they prompt. Seen from this perspective, the propinacja and the reactions that it precipitates emerge as significant and representative—in more than a statistical sense—of Jewish economic activities and of Polish-Jewish relations.

28. For a fuller methodological statement on how institutions may be viewed as microcosms of larger systems and used as keys to social epistemologies, see Foucault, *Birth of the Clinic.*
29. Max Weber, in his occasional scattered observations on early modern Jews, asked why they did not build factories. As we shall see, his analysis of their pariah status (their "double ethic") and the inadequacies of their rationalism does not provide much more context for understanding the problems of Jewish entrepreneurialism than did late eighteenth-century Polish publicistic writings.
30. The economics of the Whiskey Rebellion in the early years of the United States are quite similar. The surplus corn of farmers west of the Appalachian Mountains again became marketable as grain rather than as alcohol after one technological improvement: the construction of the Erie Canal. See Rorabaugh, *Alcoholic Republic,* 77–92.

Fig. 2. *Inn in Polesie.* This wood engraving by S. Baranowski, of a Jewish innkeeper behind the counter, appeared in *Kłosy,* 1874. It is based on a painting by Antoni Piotrowski (1853–1924).

Fig. 3. *Inn, Jewish Proprietor and Peasant Patrons.* The Jewish innkeeper with pointed beard and nose stands behind the counter lined with bottles of vodka. This wood engraving appeared in *Kłosy* and is based on a painting by Władysław Grabowski (1850–1885).

The eminent historian of Polish Jewry Bernard Weinryb pointed in the 1930s to the "tragic internal contradiction" of Jewish studies.[31] Jewish historiography, he suggested, tends to place a heavy emphasis on ideas. The research that has been done on economic history, however, does not draw correlations to intellectual history except in a doctrinaire manner, generally appropriating Marxist methodology. This has led to distortions and has provided little illumination of the mutual relations between economic and spiritual history.

More than half a century later, Weinryb's concern is still apt. The study of Jews and Judaism has enjoyed a momentous renaissance in the post–World War II period following the destruction of its major research sites in Europe. And though such subfields as economic history are beginning to develop, there are few examples of the synthesizing work for which he calls. As more attention is being paid to the history of Polish Jewry, his warnings are particularly appropriate. With the recent intensification of interest in that history both among Polish historians in Poland and among Jewish historians outside of Poland, efforts must be made to overcome this problem. The different training of scholars—Polish historians familiar with Polish history, Jewish scholars trained in the history of Judaism— accounts in large measure, but not altogether, for this difference in perspective.[32] Among historians of Poland there is the tendency to see Jewish involvement anecdotally rather than systemically, to understate the extent of that involvement or exaggerate its conviviality. Jewish historians in the early decades of this century did significant research on communal and economic history. A promising generation of their disciples—the walls of the Jewish Historical Institute in Warsaw to this day are lined with the master's theses of young historians murdered during the Holocaust—would likely have fulfilled the need for this type of study. In the work completed by Jewish historians, however, insufficient attention has been paid to the links between patterns of thinking and patterns of activity, including economic activity. Whether the sacred aura associated with Polish Jewry, the otherworldly characterizations of the Polish Jew, is a cause or a consequence of that historiographic trend is not clear.

The record of their activities corresponds in some ways to the shadowlike presence of Poland's Jews in the past and their eerie disappearance from the present. To no small degree, the problems are influenced by the fortuitousness with which documentation has survived. The experience of doing archival research in Poland is more often one of frustration than of serendipity. The researcher pores over large archival collections on Polish life relating to periods in which there is good reason to believe that Jews were present and active, often hardly finding their trace. Undoubtedly, much material reflecting on a millennium of Polish Jewish history has survived the military and political vicissitudes of the twentieth century; with the changes taking place in Eastern Europe, this material will be better catalogued and more accessible. Our knowledge of Polish

31. Weinryb, "Economic and Social History of the Jews of Germany."
32. Trunk, "Polish Jewish Historiography," 247–68; Hundert and Bacon, *Jews in Poland and Russia.*

Jewry will be dramatically increased. Several excellent case studies in recent years present newly uncovered archival material and are rich in detail and compelling in their interpretation. Yet the generalizability of the realities that these studies reflect remains difficult to establish. The writing of that history becomes more like the archaeologist's excavation of a long-lost civilization, inferring the shape of the vase from a suggestive potsherd or two, speculating about complex social processes from the imagined artifact. On the side of Jewish intellectual history as well, what is derived from the interrogation of the evidence may appear to be too abstract. The judicious use of multiple comparisons—Jews and non-Jews in Poland; Polish, Central, and Western European Jews; East and West; Reformation and Counter-Reformation; medieval and early modern; social and intellectual history—designed through the equally judicious use of social science tools may compensate in part for the silence of the archives and move us farther along the path leading from description to analysis. A delicate lens is needed, one that can direct the abundant background light of well-chosen and synthesized theory and comparative historical material into the darker recesses of the historical stage on which Poland and its Jews interact. I shall try to synthesize secondary literature in diverse fields together with primary sources, mindful of the blessed accidents by which these sources give fleeting insights into lost worlds. The composite portrait, the systemic analysis of roles and functions of Polish Jews, is likely, therefore, to be imprecise in many details. But key elements of the more general picture that emerges should guide the search for prospective revision of details.[33]

In the past two decades it has been fashionable—by now it has become almost passé—to cite anthropologist Clifford Geertz in prolegomena to historical methodology: scholars embrace "interpretive" science, they search for "deep interpretation," and they embrace "thick" description, trying to hear the "said" of social discourse. This interpretive approach will provide a challenge and at times a checklist for what I would like to attempt. For example, to assert the truism that Jews in early modern Poland were middlemen is to offer little more than a description. To examine the economic, political, and cultural forces that shaped their position is to present an explanation. But to use material derived from these multiple comparisons to analyze Jewish perceptions of being middlemen, to explore how this situation was perceived by others and how, in turn, that perception affected the thinking and the activities of the Jews, is to move into the sphere of deep interpretation.

Perception is determined not only by the cognitive capacity or philosophical acumen of individuals. It relates to the collective meanings that are made socially available as well. And society is constituted of more than hierarchies of power, sets of social interaction, and structures of economic relations repeated and formalized. Society is available to be the object of reflection and analysis as well as manipulation, embodying the subjective and intersubjective interpretations of its

33. Scriven, "Maximizing the Power of Causal Investigations," 68–84.

participants. To link consciousness to historical narrative and social structure, I shall avoid the dogmatic formulations of the "materialistic" or "idealistic" school that Bernard Weinryb criticizes. Rather, I shall use the notion of the plausibility structure suggested by Peter Berger. This interpretive strategy is particularly apt, for it relates the impact of a discrete set of ideas, images, or symbols to the social process by which a consensus about what is plausible gets established among "right-thinking" people (and, perhaps, among "right-thinking" historians). And insofar as this strategy leads to underdeterminism rather than overdeterminism of causal relations, it is the side on which I prefer to err.[34]

But here is where interpretive science falters, misdirected perhaps by its own images as they become analytical tools in trying to tap the "said" of social discourse or in tracing the boundaries of the plausibility structure.[35] Interpretive science pays insufficient attention to differentials in power, the ability of one group to make its definition of the situation the context for interaction with other groups and therefore socially significant, even where the private meanings of the less powerful groups demonstrate amazing endurance. The calmness and reasonableness of a scholarly discourse does not capture the agitation in the processes which that method seeks to describe, particularly in regard to intergroup relations. Rather than a "said," we have to capture the shouting, ranting, and shoving, the well-institutionalized but no-less-violent coerciveness by which one group forces its meaning upon another. We also must grasp the disparate meanings at the disposal of the other group that are among its means to resist and frustrate the intentions of the first group.[36] This awareness of methodological flaws can save us from historiographic biases.

While trying to tap into the discourse between Poles and Jews, and even between Poles and the Western world, as it takes place through an early stage of modernization, and while paying careful attention to the form and texture of the "said," I shall also pay attention to the power differentials. I shall focus on the order that unfolds in sixteenth- to late eighteenth-century Poland—order in the dual sense, as Max Weber reminds us, of sets of social structural relations and meanings. The Polish gentry had the power to shape that order, in which Polish Jews attained limited degrees of freedom and security within the conflicts of Polish society. The Jews, and for that matter even the serfs, were by no means powerless. But however significant were the roles they played for the maintenance and transformation of Polish society, they, like Maimon's grandfather, tended to react to situations and

34. Berger, *Sacred Canopy,* 126.
35. Geertz, "Thick Description," 27.
36. This problem comes as something of a surprise in view of the ethnographic traditions from which this school of the social sciences emerges. In the study of colonialism, the power differentials in the social discourse between native and colonizer, and the way in which they might determine forms of behavior, are salient. The issue of differences in power must be raised repeatedly as both a problem and an opportunity to weigh factors carefully and introduce nuance rather than to posit an overdetermined circularity—of the cat-chasing-its-tail variety—between institutional structures and symbolic meanings.

opportunities rather than to take direct and creative initiatives. By providing this detailed context for the activities of Polish Jews, by reducing the indeterminacy of their actions while attempting to probe their motives and the meanings that they attach to different situations, I shall try to derive a better understanding of what prompted certain activities and reactions and inhibited others. Against this examination of their activities, motives, and meanings, I shall reassess the image of Polish Jews, provided by Maimon and others, as otherworldly and staunchly resistant to change as they stood at the threshold of the modern world.

In chapter 1, I consider the Polish gentry's concept of social order in the early modern period, as it developed in reaction to the Protestant Reformation and to the increasing political centralization taking place elsewhere in Europe. How did this concept of order conceal those institutions of order comprising Polish feudalism, as unacknowledged by their gentry architects as by foreign observers who romanticized Poland's "lack of order"? How did this order provide the molds in which Polish Jewry shaped, conceptually and organizationally, its social, intellectual, and religious order? And why did Polish Jews, the beneficiaries of centralized monarchical authority and the bearers of urban culture, drift en masse into the village and rural domain of decentralized gentry authority?

Chapter 2 focuses on the role of the Jewish arendar, comparing it to the role of the court Jew and Jewish merchants in the West from the middle of the seventeenth century and noting the different ways in which Jews were deemed "useful" in the West and in the East at the very moment when economic conditions in these two areas began to diverge.

In Chapter 3, I compare aspects of the shared legacy of medieval scholasticism, as they were refracted through the thinking and historical experiences of the Protestant West, of the Polish gentry under the influence of the Counter-Reformation, and of Poland's Jews. I use this comparison in trying to understand a range of attitudes and policies relating to commerce, the valuation of currency, entrepreneurial motives, and economic development. Efforts to identify the religious sources of capitalism have been as inexhaustible as they appear to be irresolvable. I identify elements of Judaism that may have provided Polish Jews with a special propensity or cognitive base for their role in bridging the gentry's bifurcated economies of the wheat field and the market with the early stages of the commercial and industrial revolutions in the West.

In chapter 4, I consider the propinacja as the gentry's device to reconcile internal contradictions and uncontrollable forces impinging on Polish feudalism. In examining the role of the Jew in the feudal economy in general and in the propinacja in particular, we can begin to understand why the Jews could not have been effective agents of protocapitalism, notwithstanding their innate abilities and their spiritual or cognitive propensities. Against this background, I analyze the eighteenth-century publicistic discourses influenced by the Western Enlightenment and French physiocracy and social dramas, such as the infamous blood libel, and their relationship to Jewish economic activities. This analysis points to a new way in which Polish Jewry proved to be "useful" and to what this reputation reflects of Polish perceptions of and capacities for productivity. I attempt to demonstrate how the selective perceptions of these new ideas and new realities in the West, as they were understood by different segments of the Polish gentry in the second part of the eighteenth century, intensified the awareness of backwardness and provided a new rhetoric of reform and vocabulary for linking Poland's economic and political decline to the Jews.

In Chapter 5, I reconstruct the events surrounding the efforts to initiate constitutional reforms made during the Four-Year Sejm (1788–1792), and focus on the legal and administrative transactions negotiated between the monarchy, gentry, clergy, burghers, and Jews. I question what these abortive efforts implied for Polish Catholic and Jewish visions of their independent and interdependent futures. The different Jewish reactions to the Four-Year Sejm and the decline of the Polish state present modes of thinking that become important in the programs of Hasidism and the Jewish enlightenment and that shape Eastern European Jewry in the nineteenth century.

By juxtaposing motives, roles, and actions of Poles and Jews, I seek insight into the causes and consequences of failed modernization. I shall try to understand the economic and emotional foundations of Solomon Maimon's grandfather's tavern, as well as its monetization of unmarketable grain and its suppression of entrepreneurialism, and the bridge, in whose repair neither he nor his gentry landlord would invest, and to discover where the broken bridge, with its contentiousness and recriminations, did lead.

Chapter 1

"For Lack of Order Poland Stands": Religious, Political, and Economic Foundations of Polish Society

By 1648, members of the Polish nobility had reason to be proud. Compared to its closest neighbors, their country was secure, powerful, and prosperous. The Muscovite kingdom was backward and isolated; the Ottoman Empire manifested signs of disintegration; the Holy Roman Empire was a medley of loosely coordinated principalities, a medieval remnant living on past glories; in Brandenburg-Prussia, there was little to indicate the economic, cultural, and political developments that would unfold during the next century and a half.[1] A glance farther to the West would have revealed decimated populations and devastated economies, the price of more than a century of religious wars that Poland had successfully avoided.[2] During this same period of strife in the West, the Polish nobility had emerged as the dominant economic and political force within its country, broadly based and intensely active. Poland came to be called the "republic of the *szlachta*" (nobles).

That the Polish lords failed to see the first signs of change in the relative rates of development between East and West is, therefore, not difficult to understand. They had their own interpretation of things. They owned vast lands that produced grain for the war-torn West.[3] The millions of peasants that they had enserfed

1. Harris, *Absolutism and Enlightenment,* 158–231.
2. Gierowski, "International Position of Poland," 220.
3. Glamann, "European Trade, 1500–1750," 430. Glamann indicates that the sixteenth-century inflation "of unprecedented proportions spurred commerce by creating capital accumulation and encouraged trading ventures because of the disparity in price levels within Europe." Also see Braudel and Spooner, "Prices in Europe from 1450–1750," 4:445. Poland's economic position began to decline relative to the Muscovite empire as well, though politically and militarily it remained stronger than its eastern neighbor for several more decades. Russian grain began at this time to appear on Dutch markets at a fraction of

provided a seemingly unlimited and controllable supply of labor.[4] And Poland's export surplus (30–40 percent between 1500 and 1600, thanks in part to the country's reserves of precious metals) permitted lavish imports of manufactured goods like textiles and tools from the West, and of spices, jewels, furs, and narcotics from the East.[5] Gentry landlords whose estates bordered on rivers or land routes could tax the vigorous trade with the West that moved through Poznań and Lissa, as well as the shipments and exports to Russia and Turkey that were transported through Cracow and Lwów to Mogilev, Smolensk, and Königsberg. The economy of Poland's internal towns, populated largely by Germans and Jews whose ancestors had migrated eastward during the Middle Ages, had come increasingly under gentry control; even with activities diminished from their early sixteenth-century levels, these towns continued to function as centers of trade and crafts.

In looking over their shoulders with smugness at the countries of the West, members of the Polish gentry may have been aware of, but did not pay much attention to, the development of new ideas and incipient forces of reconstruction. At the same moment, Western princes, lords, savants, and clerics were making

---

the cost of Polish grain despite the long and hazardous journey and high transportation costs. The growth in the demand for raw materials such as flax and hemp in the Baltic trade, which could be supplied by Russia but not by Poland, increased the economic advantage of Russia over Poland in Western markets. See Wójcik, "Poland and Russia," 116. For a summary of the research on the history of prices within Poland, see Hoszowski, "Revolution of Prices in Poland," 2:7–16, and "Central Europe," 85–103. In accordance with the reasoning of economic historians who focus on the alleged price revolution of sixteenth-century Europe, the Polish gentry had conditions that might have generated capital accumulation. Serf labor ensured a sufficient gap between price inflation and wages; price differentials across Poland should have spurred trade in internal markets.

4. Braudel, *Capitalism and Material Life*, 66–120, esp. 84. Braudel sees this relationship of the grain-growing regions to economic development in the West as a form of capitalism through intermediaries. He emphasizes the active role of those, like the Polish gentry, who fostered this trade, noting that the grain growers were "actors and participants" rather than "victims." In regard to Poland, it is difficult to identify any form of capitalism in the grain-growing regions, where coerced labor and surplus extraction prevailed. But emphasizing that members of the gentry were actors rather than victims is an important counterposition to what dependency theorists as well as many Polish landlords suggested about economic relations between East and West in the early modern period. For a summary of this argument, see Wallerstein, *Modern World-System.* I explore in later chapters what the case of Poland and its Jews implies for dependency theory.

5. Glamann, "European Trade," 509. The rise in price of precious metals made it economically feasible to apply new technologies to mines in Poland and elsewhere in Central Europe that had been abandoned in earlier centuries because of the difficulty in extracting ore. Attman, *Bullion Flow* 72ff.; Mączak, "Money and Society," 5:69–104. But the quantities of what was largely silver and lead had only shortterm and spotty effects on the Polish economy and could not counter the effects that waves of precious metal, coming from the New World, were having on prices across Europe.

adjustments to the new economic realities ensuing from the discovery of the New World and were beginning to take secular positions on the very issues that had hitherto incited holy wars. New conceptions of state and civil society, of political stability and religious tolerance, and of productivity and commerce began to circulate. Some Western publicists perceived the foundation of the state's wealth in its access to natural resources; others attributed greater importance to the profitability of a state's trade. The first were impressed by the seeming strength of the Spanish Empire, enriched in the second part of the sixteenth century by gold and silver from its New World colonies. The second noted with astonishment how much of this wealth was already stored in the coffers of Holland. That small country, endowed with few natural resources of its own, through assiduous and carefully planned foreign trade and through the nourishment provided in part by Polish grain, was able to amass wealth and translate that wealth into power.[6] The fate of other countries as well in this turbulent era would provide a focus for reflections on the wealth of nations. England, for example, siphoning off its share of profits from New World metal and Polish grain, would soon finance the first stages of industrialization.[7]

In the mid-seventeenth century, most of the Polish nobility saw no pressing need to learn those lessons offered by the recent experiences of Spain, Holland, Venice, or France. With few exceptions, the most reflective lords discussed only minor changes in domestic policy, and they made few realistic provisions for their implementation: their gold supplies and grain sales, which created what they confidently perceived as an advantageous position in international trade, seemed assured. But there were urgent lessons that members of the Polish nobility were prepared to learn from two changes that we now associate with the early processes of modernization.

Religious "Lack of Order": The Polish Reformation and Counter-Reformation

The century of religious dissension culminating in the wars of 1618–1648, which plagued Poland's western neighbors, did not leave Poland altogether unscathed.[8] The Reformation had made early and significant inroads, spreading as far east as the Vistula valley and perhaps farther. Yet the tremors of religious reform, from Lutheranism to the more radical antitrinitarian sects, were neither as strong nor as enduringly influential in Poland as they were in the West. What was it about Polish society and culture in the sixteenth and early seventeenth centuries that helped neutralize the impact of the Reformation? And what in Poland impeded the influence of another movement spreading from the West later in the

6. Goudsblom, *Dutch Society,* 10–24; Schama, *Embarrassment of Riches,* 15–125, 289–370.
7. Stone, *Causes of the English Revolution,* 67–72.
8. *New Cambridge Modern History,* 2:377ff, 5:559ff.

seventeenth and eighteenth centuries—whose success, some would suggest, was related to the diffusion of Protestantism—namely, modernization?[9]

Protestantism declined primarily because of those same social forces in Poland that hindered collective action generally. Even members of the nobility drawn to the new religious ideas often were more concerned with their personal freedom than with religious reform; they failed to provide material support for the creation of a new church and its ancillary institutions. At the same time, the abiding conflicts between the nobility and the burghers prevented them from collaborating in forming a united reformed church. The peasants' apathy and low level of education impeded their mobilization under the banner of religious reform. Seeking peasant support, the new sectarian Protestant clergy radicalized the social message of their religious doctrines, becoming critical of serfdom. Jan Przypkowski, for example, though not calling for the abolition of servitude, freed his serfs to fulfill his personal obligation to love the "creatures of one Creator." Other gentry believers, such as Jakub Niemojewski, sold their estates to assist their poor brethren. These radical doctrines, which called into question gentry privilege or otherwise undermined the compliance of the serfs with their subordination, were particularly threatening to potential and actual fellow travelers among the gentry, further weakening the impact of the Reformation.[10]

The religious ideologies that developed concurrently among Protestants in the West, connecting religious passions to entrepreneurial incentives, did not seem to develop the same affinities in Poland. Calvinism did not take root among the urban tradesmen and craftsmen as it did in Holland and England. And even among the few Polish Calvinists, predestination was never stressed as it was among Calvinists in the West. The Lutheranism of the lower middle class provided no stimulus for economic development. Strong residual attachment to magical conceptions, some of pagan origin that nonetheless had been accommodated by Catholicism, did not lend plausibility to transmundane concepts of the deity.[11] Neither could the austere conceptions of predestination and personal

9. The literature on Protestantism and modernization is vast and controversial. The Weberian thesis emerged out of Max Weber's controversy with Werner Sombart, who suggested Jewish propensities for capitalism. Neither referred specifically to Protestantism or Judaism in Poland in the early modern period. Weber, *Protestant Ethic*. For astute analyses of the critical literature on Weber, see Eisenstadt, "Protestant Ethnic Thesis," 297–320; Nelson, *On the Roads to Modernity*. Herbert Lüthy, in his important contribution to the literature on the Protestant ethic underscores the importance of examining the religious and organizational impact of the Counter-Reformation rather than making vague assumptions about Catholicism or interpolating a reaction from what we know about the Protestant Reformation. *From Calvin to Rousseau*, 34–36. Although Lüthy says little about the Jews and even less about Poland, his approach has important implications for Poland and Polish Jews.

10. Tazbir, "Fate of Polish Protestants," 212.

11. In the early seventeenth century among the other profitable enterprises of the Jesuits was the sale of "Jesuit tablets" as protection from the plague. Tazbir, *Piotr Skarga*, 97. Skarga reluctantly used such techniques as blessing the nets of fishermen and providing

salvation rival the popularity of church-purveyed indulgences and beliefs in the salutary effects of confession.[12]

The Polish Brethren, a Protestant sect whose members were largely of gentry descent, were not the most likely candidates to adopt the principles of dogged work, thrift, and the systematic accumulation of wealth associated with the rise of capitalism. One utopian community, established in Raków by some gentry who sold their estates, issued a catechism dedicated to King James I of England and promoted toleration, even a measure of skepticism, years before John Locke's *Letter on Toleration* and the deists appeared in the West. Whereas this theological radicalism in England nurtured the growth of liberal politics, in Poland it had virtually no influence.[13] Rather, it was transformed into a vague humanism, which sought to make serf life easier but by no means to abolish it. In part as a response to persecution, most of the Protestant sectarians withdrew from the arena of public affairs and thereby further limited their worldly effect. Their religious thought dwelled upon the image of exile and notions of alienation. Yet unlike that of the English Puritans in their Genevan exile, the revolution of these Polish "saints" led not to sustained thinking or action in regard to worldly issues, nor to disciplined politics, but to occasional intrigues.[14] Their economic doctrines, in contrast to those of Dutch merchants or Genevan patricians, did not emphasize an active and productive life, nor did their theological musings discern a sign of grace and God's favor in commercial success.[15] There is little evidence that these Protestant sectarians used their special relations with the like-minded spiritualists in England and Holland, with whom they were trafficking in religious ideas, to establish preferential commercial ties. Nor did they lend support to scientific experimentation, as did German pietists, whose efforts to impose system and rigor in all spheres of life led to their involvement in early empirical science.[16] The Polish sectarians had but a limited interest in, and influence on, worldly matters. Their social radicalism did not transform the institutions of Polish society. There is some evidence, however, that this religious ferment made an impression on Jewish savants in Poland and in surrounding countries.[17]

Paradoxically, the disinclination of the politically active segments of sixteenth-century Poland to act in consort contributed to national unity. Religious ferment and reform were ultimately ineffectual in weakening the authority of the

---

farmers with cures for their sick cattle in his effort to win back heretics to the Catholic church. Ibid., 46.

12. Keith Thomas emphasizes the gap between the period when beliefs lose their plausibility and that time when technological solutions to problems develop. See *Religion and the Decline of Magic.*

13. Kot, *Socinianism in Poland,* 219.

14. Walzer, *Revolution of the Saints,* 232.

15. Kot, *Socinianism,* 213.

16. Merton, "Puritanism, Pietism and Science," 574–606.

17. H. H. Ben-Sasson, *Jews and Christian Sectarians,* 369–85.

Roman Catholic church, the one institution that lent order to Polish society and culture. Instead, the church emerged from this period strengthened. The religious strivings among the gentry, which had prompted some affiliation with Reformation faith, soon yielded to practical considerations. The efforts of Polish kings, from the late sixteenth century on, to retain central authority, and of the gentry to retain control over serf labor, were better served by the continued influence of the Roman Catholic church than by divisive Protestant sects. Even before the arrival at the end of the sixteenth century of the forces of the Counter-Reformation, the Jesuits, there was a long queue of gentry before the confessionals of their father confessors. The interlude of weakened allegiance to Rome in Poland left its mark, however. Having given up the costly practice of paying tithes to the church, the gentry now routinely passed on that cost to the peasantry.[18]

Catholicism developed a new vitality across class lines. In the wake of the Counter-Reformation, local shrines sprang up across Poland and became the centers of new and emotionally satisfying religious cults. The increasingly popular Marian worship, at the site of the Black Madonna in the Jasna Gora monastery in Czestochowa, is but one example. Though the nobility did not distinguish itself in its personal piety, Polish Counter-Reformation Catholicism had an important influence even on this sector of Polish society. The Jesuits in particular expanded their educational network and influenced the children of the nobility.

What may have been the most enduring effect of the Polish Counter-Reformation and its Jesuit agents was the way in which it strengthened the foundations of that Sarmatianism that in the seventeenth and eighteenth centuries would provide the order and coherence unavailable from other sources.[19] Sarmatianism—not unlike the genealogical myths of other peoples, such as the Aryanism of the Germans or the Third Rome of the Russians—posited primordial common origins for the Poles, who were alleged to have descended from the ancient Sarmatians. This proud and independent people once inhabited lands into which gentry colonization was now expanding. The myth of Sarmatia in its early form served two purposes: it fostered the Polonization of diverse populations, particularly within the gentry estate, and the spread of a national culture; and it combatted the residual influence of the Reformation. In the hands of the Jesuits, Sarmatianism developed in other directions. It popularized and bolstered the belief that disasters occur as a result of heresy; and insofar as the outsider was seen as the importer and instigator of that heresy, it stoked xenophobic sentiments.

But by the seventeenth century, this conservative doctrine had become the nobility's canon of belief and code of behavior, legitimating the privilege and freedom that the gentry claimed as members of an exclusive caste.[20] The tribal was replaced by the senatorial, if not the imperial, despite the weakness of the Polish monarchy, which made that image difficult to sustain. The leaders of those

18. See Tazbir, *Piotr Skarga.*
19. See Cynarski, "Shape of Sarmatian Ideology," 6, for an excellent typology of the different phases of development of this archetypal myth.
20. Ibid., 10–12.

clans that supposedly had resisted the domination of the Roman Empire now saw themselves as the descendants of its elite. The restored Roman Catholicism, which distinguished the Polish nobility from the gentry of other Slavic peoples, took on a degree of political sentimentalism. Sarmatianism, at the same time, focused gentry attention on the East and provided modes of consciousness, historical myths, and ideologies for resistance to the new and the innovative. Thus in Poland, the seeds of a powerful ideology of antimodernization were sown before there were any serious modern stirrings.

The Counter-Reformation, Sarmatianism, and the political and economic problems following the period from 1648 to 1660—which in Polish historiography came to be known as the Deluge—increased intolerance for religious diversity. By the middle of the seventeenth century, most of Poland's Protestants had been converted back to Catholicism or forced into exile. The simultaneous decline in Polish arts and sciences from the levels attained in some areas during the Renaissance may be related to the religious orientation promoted by the Polish Counter-Reformation.

The combination of intolerance and the use of religion to promote national and social integration can be seen in the efforts to subordinate Russian Orthodox and Tatar minorities along the eastern border by coerced conversion to the Uniate church. The Uniate Compromise which forced these Orthodox to accept the authority of the Pope while allowing them to preserve their eastern liturgy and to follow their own priests, was a frequent source of tension with Moscow.[21] The resurgence of Catholicism, together with the popular piety and xenophobia that accompanied it, also had a decisive influence, as we shall see, on the fate of Poland's most unassimilable minority, the Jews.[22]

Political "Lack of Order": Polish Reactions to Centralized Absolutism

The myopic optimism of the Polish nobility was nurtured by the nobles' precarious victory over the political order to which their cousins in the West were increasingly subjected: centralized absolutism. It had not always been that way. The *corona regni poloniae,* as it had existed as early as the fourteenth century and through the second part of the sixteenth century, had been a powerful empire, far more centralized than any of the governments of Poland's neighbors. Yet this precocious absolutism notwithstanding, Poland in the seventeenth and eighteenth centuries did not develop the *Polizeiordnungskultur* that became so common in Europe; it was "the one major country which failed to

---

21. Gieysztor et al., *History of Poland,* 255.
22. The deal that Polish prelates thought they were making in 1759 with Jacob Frank, a Jew who claimed to be the messiah (he promised to lead the Jewish masses to the baptismal font but in fact attempted to establish a millennial movement under his leadership), was similar to the "tolerance" manifested toward the Uniates.

produce an Absolutist State in the region."[23] Its political history, from centralized monarchy to decentralized aristocracy, moved in the direction opposite to most European countries and hence provides the counterexample to the successful attainment of political absolutism in the early modern period.[24] The Polish nobility, so prone to idealizing decentralization, had emerged from an alliance of clans with emotional attachments. Its members enjoyed the benefits of political consolidation and economic strength, primarily as a result of the establishment of a stable monarchy. But this nobility, in fact, never abandoned some of its clanlike qualities. Despite the growing economic differentiation between a small class of wealthy magnates with huge estates and a sizable lower gentry, including many who became landless, there was no formal hierarchy, no division of authority with ranks and titles comparable to that which developed within the aristocracies of other European countries.[25] Primordial sentiments and ideologies could not compensate for these unmanageable social structural arrangements, such as growing disparities in wealth.

The king, whose main role was to represent the unity of Poland's territories, was elected (at least in theory) from among the clan leaders. Hence his position was weak. Yet when the Polish monarchy was strong, from 1386 until the end of the Jagiellonian dynasty in 1572, the king was always the grand duke of Lithuania, a hereditary title; the institution of the Polish monarchy was thus indirectly strengthened and stabilized, preserving a modicum of Polish central authority and absolutism. The Treaty of Lublin (1569), however, in revising the administrative relations between Poland and Lithuania, altered Poland's internal balance of power. Following the death of Sigismund Augustus (1520–1572), new monarchs were indeed elected by the gentry. This realization of the ideal left the monarchy an unwieldy institution.[26] The king became little more than a factional leader with limited revenues.[27] Sectors of the population that might have lent support to the king, such as the burghers and the Jews, were weakened because of their inability to own land. The respective jurisdictions of regional gentry councils (diets) and the jurisdiction of the monarch were never clearly defined, a situation that generated continuous conflict and impeded collective action.

This propensity for decentralization affected the Polish masses as well. Hereditary serfdom was legislatively imposed upon freemen, yeomen, and peasants in 1497 by King John Albert. He was forced to buy support for his military campaign against the Turks from the nobles, who evoked lapsed privileges and demanded that they be ratified by the king. This action provided the legal foundation for the renewal of a form of feudalism that had prevailed across Europe in the

---

23. Anderson, *Lineages of the Absolutist State,* 3; Raeff, *Well-Ordered Police State.*
24. Wójcik, "Poland and Russia," 117.
25. Anderson, *Lineages of the Absolutist State,* 3–4.
26. Wyczański, "Problem of Authority," 107ff.
27. Mączak, "Structure of Power," 122ff. See Zagorin, *Court and the Country,* for a comparison of how centralizing and decentralizing forces developed in England.

Middle Ages. But the economic base fostering the growth of this new institution of Polish serfdom developed more gradually over the following century.[28] With the rise in the price of grain all through the sixteenth century, the nobility sought to reassert the duty of peasants to spend time at corvée labor. Exaggerating the legal basis of certain rights, the gentry tied peasants more closely to the soil.[29] The expansion of serf labor in agriculture contributed to the serious reduction of both artisans and small tradesmen as economic factors: artisans compelled to work the land could no longer produce manufactured goods; indigenous crafts were further stymied because of these limits on the economic activities of the merchants, which made it impossible for those artisans who resisted enserfment to achieve economies of scale. Indirectly, the redistribution of income in favor of the gentry which reenserfment entailed limited the peasant demand for domestically produced manufactured goods, reducing revenues of small tradesmen and peddlers and increasing gentry demand for luxury imports. But Polish merchants were constrained from exporting domestic goods by the gentry, who were eager to preserve abundant supplies and thereby keep down their personal expenditures even at the cost of reducing national revenues and, willy-nilly, reducing the gold reserves needed to satisfy their appetites for foreign delicacies. Serious and prolonged currency problems added to the risks of artisans and merchants; political decentralization had an adverse effect on stabilizing currencies, as it had on standardizing laws and administrative measures. Polish manufacturing during the sixteenth century moved in the direction of a "downward spiral," as Harry Miskimin writes. "The ebullience and energy so apparent in England . . . in this same period were not to be found under the political conditions of Poland."[30]

What really set the tone for internal Polish order, however, and what contributed a sense of intrigue to its politics and limited the possibility of collective action, was the infamous *liberum veto*. Here, too, in the administrative procedures of Polish representative bodies, we see the influence of the gentry's archetypal myth of Sarmatianism. In spite of the needs for making collective decisions and for mobilizing Poland's leaders to avert danger and to confront crises, the gentry was inspired by the myth of everlasting rebellion that members enacted in the use of the veto, since unanimity was required for any proposal brought to the Polish diet. The delegates, elected by local and regional dietines, arrived with their instructions and were obliged to vote accordingly; that obligation eliminated the possibility that the assembly could be deliberative and rendered the diet impotent. Even the taxation measures, necessary to raise an army, were subject to this veto and consequently were rarely promulgated.

By the end of the seventeenth century, with the increasing use of the veto, diets were rarely brought to a successful conclusion. The ability of each member of the gentry to obstruct the passage of any proposal prompted the magnates either to seek control of the lower gentry and dietines or to act independently of

28. Miskimin, *Economy of Later Renaissance Europe,* 60.
29. Ibid., 58.
30. Ibid., 105, 162.

the parliament. The magnates accomplished these goals through unilateral action or through the confederations, generally constituted of smaller magnate groups, in which the veto was temporarily canceled and in which decisions could thereby be made. But the abrogation of this procedure, legitimated by tenaciously held myths, called forth strong indignation among other members of the gentry, often mobilizing conspiracies against the confederations that resulted in political chaos and paralysis.

The lower gentry, who had become déclassé, sometimes used the veto threat as a source of livelihood by selling their vote. Thus the monarchy and central authority were weakened, as déclassé nobles contributed to the relative power of their patrons, the magnates, who became strong enough to challenge the king and to undermine the forces of centralization. By the end of the seventeenth century, and in the eighteenth century, the liberum veto also weakened and eventually paralyzed central bodies by providing legal channels for foreign intervention. Interested parties could cancel pending legislation by bribing a member of the gentry to exercise his veto. The election of Polish kings in particular was accompanied by foreign influence peddling; the elector of Saxony, Frederick Augustus (1670–1733), was able to procure the Polish throne for himself through his conversion to Catholicism and with the financial assistance of his court Jew, Bend Lehmann.[31]

Poland's geopolitical position at the juncture between East and West, where two supranational communities overlapped, made it a likely site of conflict. Poland had long been viewed by the Latin West as a somewhat primitive outpost of civilization, useful at one time for repelling Tartar and Turkish invasions and later for providing an obstacle to Russian territorial ambitions. The Slavic East viewed Poland—in language Slavic but in religion Roman Catholic—as a traitor to the Slavic nation and the Orthodox church, and as a station through which the West's coveted technology and culture passed on their way to the East.

During Poland's periods of strength, particularly the sixteenth century, it expanded at the expense of both its eastern and western neighbors. But with the consolidation of central institutions in the Prussian, Russian, and Hapsburg empires after 1660, Poland's international position was weakened. As a buffer zone, it became integral to what the French called the "system of anarchy." Poland's regional situation thus was consistent with, and even supportive of, its weak internal order.

Poland was surrounded by empires whose collective resentment toward Poland was exceeded only by their territorial ambitions in regard to each other. The "system of anarchy" may have created an equilibrium in which a Polish state, weakened from within and from without, had to be maintained. But this support was by no means favorable to its long-term stability. Poland's more centralized neighbors utilized the conventional means that states have at their disposal for weakening another state, such as making threats, counterfeiting and debasing

31. Stern, *Court Jews,* 77–82. Stern's description of the gentry during the "elections" provides a vivid illustration of gentry lack of order.

currency, and imposing tariffs, as well as one means special to the Polish situation—intriguing, through manipulation of the liberum veto in the parliament and the diets.

Poland provided an opportunity for intervention by taking on religious issues that it could not defend in the international arena. The last of the Jagiellonian kings in the sixteenth century fostered a degree of religious tolerance. Later, Polish kings and the gentry—under the strong influence of the Counter-Reformation, with their Jesuit education and Sarmatianism—engaged in rampant persecution of Protestants and Orthodox who did not accept the Uniate compromise. Throughout Europe this action aroused indignation, which provided an excuse for threatening gestures and for interventions and ultimately served to rationalize the carving up of Polish territory. Neighbors to the east, west, and south proclaimed concern for the welfare of their coreligionists. Particularly the so-called enlightened despots, such as Frederick II and Catherine II, harbored little tolerance for the religious intolerance of others.[32]

It was precisely at this moment that many members of the Polish gentry, especially the magnates, began to make a virtue out of their dilemma and difficulties regarding order. Unable to achieve coordinated action, they scorned political unity; waxing eloquent in praise of their "golden freedom," they attributed Poland's condition, which they persisted in viewing as favorable, to the inimitable Polish anarchy.[33] They refused to allow the rise of powerful states around them to

32. The diminished role of religious institutions in the absolutist state was part of the attempt of the absolutist monarchs to create new centers of authority by subordinating the old. The personal pieties of absolutist monarchs notwithstanding, there was a growing sense that the church should be placed within the confines of the state. *Raison d'état* dictated a new tolerance, as long as it was consistent with empire building. Frederick II allegedly claimed that all religions are equally good if they teach men obedience. A new emphasis on population as a national resource prompted seemingly liberal and tolerant positions such as the following, attributed to the Prussian absolutist monarch: "If Turks or Pagans come to people my country, I would build them mosques or temples." Harris, *Absolutism and Enlightenment,* 218. To whatever degree religious tolerance was implemented in practice in the new absolutist states of Central and Western Europe, it established new legal standards for the treatment of minority religious groups such as the Jews. See Katz, *Out of the Ghetto,* 28–103. Moreover, it heightened expectations of members of these groups. In the case of Jews, it spurred their participation in the larger society while adding to their existences a measure of frustration. See Meyer, *Origins of the Modern Jew.*
33. I review the publicistic literature of this period in chapter 4. Sigismund III (1566–1632), who made an unsuccessful effort to establish *absolutum dominum,* became the focus of the Zebrzydowski rebellion between 1606 and 1609. See Gieysztor et al., *History of Poland,* 198; Davies, *God's Playground,* 1:360. Members of the gentry used issues of religious tolerance to combat the king's efforts to strengthen centralized authority. We even find coalitions of Protestants and Orthodox. There are no records of Jewish involvement or of Jews' seeking religious toleration rather than ad hoc solutions to their problems. Whereas the centralizers of the eighteenth century, such as Frederick II and Joseph II,

challenge their optimism and their sense of invulnerability. Their own interpretation of Poland's apparent strength and its endurance during Europe's Hundred Years War was echoed in a common saying, *nierządem Polska stoi* (for lack of order Poland stands).[34] This slogan was elevated to the status of a transcendental truth, chanted as an incantation, and reaffirmed through repetition during the next century and a half, particularly by the conservative gentry. This cherished belief about Poland's unique situation is a succinct expression of the Sarmatianism and messianism that would so influence Polish society and culture in the early modern period. Such ideologies obviated the need for deeper analysis.[35]

The gentry's belief in Poland's chosenness—and, to an increasing extent, in their chosenness among the chosen, in the unique prerogatives of their own estate—bolstered their optimistic sense of Poland's position relative to other countries. It was not dissimilar to the chiliasm of their contemporaries in England or the messianism of Dutch Calvinists. It was very different from them, however, in what it actually prompted. For those imbued with this thinking, it placed Poland above the laws of nature that pietists and messianists in the West were beginning to harness for the glory of God and the welfare of their countries. For the Polish gentry, the rewards of more systemic reflection were deemed to be meager. The Polish sense of apocalyptic election did not impart a sense of responsibility for worldly actions and of civic consciousness, as it did in England. Polish messianism became more exclusive as it became less worldly.[36]

This identification of Poland's unique order of "lack of order" coincided with another search for order. The "European mind," in Alexander Koyré's sweeping characterization,[37] tried to restore some sense of order following the "revolution" set in motion a century before by Nicolaus Copernicus, whom Poland later claimed as its favorite son. The "new philosophy," as John Donne wrote, "Calls all in doubt . . . / 'Tis all in pieces, all coherence gone, / All just supply, and all Relation: /

---

espoused some degree of religious tolerance as a means of weakening the Catholic church and elevating the state, Sigismund III, whatever his personal beliefs, was happy to enlist Jesuit support in opposing heretics. On the other hand, the Jesuits soon realized that an alliance with the gentry and the magnates, rather than with the monarchy, would be more useful in routing residual Protestantism and strengthening Catholicism. The fusion of Catholicism with Polish national identity was set at this early date. It would inhibit the development of the conception of a religiously pluralistic society or of a non-Catholic citizen.

34. Gieysztor et al., *History of Poland,* 240; Davies, *God's Playground,* 1:360. A more literal translation is "Poland stands by unrule." At an early date this motto was repeated by Polish writers such as Krzysztof Opaliński (1610–1656) and Stanisław Dunin-Karwicki (1610–1724) with overtones of criticism.

35. Cynarski, "Shape of Sarmatian Ideology," 5ff.

36. See Pocock, *Machiavellian Moment,* 343.

37. Koyré, *From the Closed World,* v, 3–4, 273–76.

Prince, Subject, Father, Son are things forgot."[38] This sense of "all coherence gone" scarcely impinged on the consciousness of smug Polish gentry, glorifying the integrative powers, the spiritual and social sources of solidarity, in Poland's lack of order. But the gentry's organization of this lack of order contrasted and soon came into conflict with anxious political reactions to that disintegration and sense of lost order as they developed elsewhere in Europe. The "Well-Ordered Police States," centralized and absolutist polities, through efficient organization and careful analysis, created new institutions and concepts of coherence, resulting in new attainments in planning and productivity.[39] The institutional devices to control production and distribution, with which the Polish lords sought to maintain Poland's advantageous situation, clashed with economic and political realities of the new centralized states, over which the Polish gentry had no control. With the passing of the eighteenth century, as disparities in the wealth and power of Poland and the West grew, glorification of their lack of order required all the more conviction.

Jewish Complacence

Toward the mid-seventeenth century, Polish Jews might well have displayed complacence. From a backwater of the medieval Jewish world, Poland in the early modern period rapidly became the center of one of the most populous and most creatively intense Jewish populations. It provided refuge for Jews of venerable communities in the West who had to flee persecution during a century of instability and decline, particularly between 1618 and 1648.[40] And the foundations of that center, as they were laid in this period, were so firm that for the next three centuries, despite the many reversals in the situation of Poland, Polish Jewry continued to proliferate demographically and intellectually, within its borders and beyond to the newer centers of Jewish life in the West and in the East.[41]

Both Polish Jews and Jews abroad viewed Poland as a rather secure place for

38. John Donne, "The First Anniversary: An Anatomy of the World," cited in Kuhn, *Copernican Revolution,* 194.

39. See Raeff, *Well-Ordered Police State.*

40. Shulvass, *From East to West,* 19–24.

41. The demography of Polish Jewry is speculative and subject to scholarly controversy. Adjustments must also be made for Poland's shifting geographic boundaries, which affect the bases of comparisons. The best estimates place the Jewish population in 1500 at thirty thousand out of a total population in Poland and Lithuania of five million. By 1576 the Jewish population had grown to 150,000 out of 7.5 million. In 1648 the Jewish population was estimated at 450,000, declining by 100,000 in the ensuing years of peasant rebellions and foreign invasions. Most of the Jews continued to settle in small villages along the Baltic in the east rather than in the towns of western Poland. Many German Lutherans in Poland successfully opposed Jewish settlement. Based on the census of 1764, estimates of the Jewish population of Poland range from 750,000 to 900,000, or about 10 percent of the Polish population. See Mahler, *Yidn in amolikn Poiln;* Baron, *Social and Religious History,* 16:207–11, 413–15; Weinryb, *Jews of Poland,* 308–20.

Jewish habitation.[42] In a popular etymology of their country's name, *po lin,* (here rest), Jews saw a divine mandate for Jewish settlement; God's chosen people would enjoy in this land a respite from their long wandering in exile and while waiting to be redeemed.[43] Their sense of security was shaken, but by no means shattered, by occasional Cossack attacks, urban riots, and the regular indignities to which Jews were subjected by zealous clergy, violent adolescents, and drunken peasants.

Jewish self-confidence and optimism derived in no small measure from the intense sense of order, based on Jewish traditions, that Polish Jews were able to institutionalize by the sixteenth century. A rabbi and communal leader of that period, Moses Isserles, reflecting on this order, commented: "For in truth, of all the precepts brought in the Tora, most of them are for the needs of the body and the ordering of people among themselves . . . [for] the purpose of ordering of the state and [providing] physical needs."[44]

The special relationships of Polish Jews with powerful Polish monarchs contributed to their sense of security. That sense of security also may have been bolstered by their own assessment of what others observed: "Allmost all trade is in theire handes."[45] Yet, as this Dutch visitor to Poland accurately perceived, trade may not have enlisted the admiration of their fellow Poles, who "esteem[ed] it sordide."[46] Polish Jews, despite the negative assessment of trade prevailing in Poland, may have staked their security, as did other Jewish communities in the early modern period, on their productivity and the valuable service that they rendered to the powerful parties in Polish society who benefited directly from Jewish trade. To give expression to their sense of security based on utility, Polish Jews could have borrowed the somber words of the thirteenth-century German scholar Asher ben Yehiel: "What other benefits do the nations derive from defending us and allowing us to live among them unless it be to their advantage to collect from us taxes and imports?"[47] In the early modern period this idea was reiterated in the more enthusiastic words of Rabbi Simeon Luzzatto's defense of mid-seventeenth-century Venetian Jews: "How profitable are the Jews!"[48] That

42. Weinryb, *Jews of Poland,* 51.
43. Ibid., 18.
44. Rama, *Torat Haola* (Prague, 1570) 3, 38, 102; cited in Y. Ben-Sasson, *Mishnato Haiyunit Shel Harama.*
45. Until at least the end of the seventeenth century, an increasing proportion of trade was in the hands of non-Catholic Poles and foreigners, including Italians, Germans, Armenians, and Scots. See Hundert, "Role of the Jews," 249.
46. Talbot, ed., *Relations of the State of Polonia,* 68. Some years later, another foreign traveler reported that "nothing can be bought or sold without the intervention of a Jew." Cox, *Travels,* 119. A similar image of Jewish enterprise emerges from other travel account, presented in Frydman, "French Reports," 1:14–30.
47. Cited in Baron, *History of the Jews,* 12:198.
48. Luzzatto, *Maamar al Yehudei Venezya,* The same argument is made in Wolf, ed., *Menasse ben Israel's Mission.* For a comparison, see Ravid, "How Profitable," 159–80. At

utility might lead to greater tolerance was not a wholly fatuous dream of Polish Jews, as they surveyed the experiences of some of their cousins in the West.

But the structural basis for that security changed from the sixteenth to the eighteenth century. The consolidation of the first Jewish communities in Poland had corresponded to the period in which the power of the Polish monarchy was increasing.[49] This singular development left its stamp on the legal status and political orientation of Polish Jews for centuries, long after memories of a powerful king and effective centralized authority had ceased to fit the real situation. From the end of the sixteenth century, an increasing number of Jews moved into the domain of the gentry. What prompted this move, and its consequences for Jewish security, is of utmost interest.

Despite this shift in the preponderance of power and authority from the monarchy to the nobility, and despite the limited means at the disposal of the monarch to enforce and implement special privileges that had been granted to Jews, Polish Jews continued to make annual payments for these royal privileges and to present hefty gifts at coronations. As the Dutch traveler, as early as the end of the sixteenth century, observed, "Extraordinarily, the kinge can exacte nothing uppon any subiecte, but onely on the Jews."[50] The confidence that Jews invested in charters led to undignified spectacles of negotiation and extortion. Profiting from concessions made to Jews for the most fundamental human and communal rights compensated the monarchy, in some measure, for its inability to administer taxation and elicit greater support from the gentry. But it only postponed the crisis. In this area, as in others, the gentry could enjoy its lack of order while passing on the costs, to Jews and to other vulnerable populations in Polish society, for whatever minimum degree of coordination and increasingly ineffectual centralized authority the monarchy did provide. The same efforts by which a seemingly powerless but resourceful Polish minority group, the Jews, sought to bolster its security by contributing to a centralized "order" allowed the gentry to avert confronting Poland's political problems until it was too late.

It was the monarchy, in its efforts to develop an efficient mechanism for taxing Polish Jews, that encouraged the expansion of the *kehillot* (sg. *kehilla*),

---

the very moment in Venice that the duties of civic virtue and republicanism were being debated and that the citizen-soldier, rather than the citizen-merchant, was being vaunted, Luzzatto's defense of the nonsoldiering Jews missed an important point. See Pocock, *Machiavellian Moment,* 181ff. Luzzatto and others who sought a basis for Jewish security in the utility of Jews might have been reminded by the transaction reported in the biblical book of Esther between Haman and the Persian king Ahasuerus that they cannot fully rely on kings or on the calculation of economic utility made by others. There is always the chance that someone will make a convincing argument to a gullible ruler that "therefore it profiteth not the king to suffer them" (Esther 3:8).

49. In spite of this royal support of Jewish settlement, Polish kings preserved local prerogatives *de non tolerandis Judaeis,* where they had been established. Weinryb, *Jews of Poland,* 132; Goldberg, *Jewish Privileges.*

50. Talbot, ed., *Relations,* 58.

units of community and polity.[51] Through the sixteenth century, local and regional communal structures federated into the Council of Four Lands.[52] It may not be historical coincidence that around 1580, at the very time when the monarchy as a centralizing institution of Polish society began its decline, this supracommunal structure began to function as the central institution of Polish Jewry. The Council of Four Lands may have compensated, at least in part, for decreasing Jewish security, the consequence of political decentralization and fragmentation.[53] In the century and a half preceding the Chmielnicki massacres of 1648 and the ensuing wars, Polish Jews had created the greatest networks of communal and educational institutions of any Jewry since the decline of the Jewish community of Babylon. This council, through its federated structures, sought to direct, regulate, and protect far-flung Jewish communities, otherwise subjected to different domains of authority and the conflicting interests of diverse segments of Polish society. The extant records convey a degree of success that varied with time and place, not only because of external factors but also because the council was often preoccupied with intracommunal feuds and personal squabbles.

Even in the midst of the Deluge, around 1650, Nathan of Hanover presented reflections of the well-structured life of Polish Jewry in somewhat hyperbolic and idealized terms: "All these pillars upon which the world stands were found in the land of Poland."[54] There were some efforts made to draw mundane political and social lessons from the murder of one hundred thousand to two hundred thousand Jews and the destruction of hundreds of communities, notwithstanding the elegiac needs of Nathan's contemporaries and the efforts to draw religious and moral lessons from the catastrophe.[55] Yet insofar as these lessons pointed to problems in Jewish relations with the gentry or the serfs, Jews registered some awareness of the problems but made no sustained attempt to change these situa-

51. Among their other functions, the kehilot were empowered to tax individuals—by criteria often internally generated—and to transmit moneys to the coffer of the ruler. A modicum of self-government was characteristic of Jewish diasporas but was particularly well developed in Poland. See Finkelstein, *Jewish Self-Government;* Baron, *Jewish Community.*

52. Although important research has been done on the origins of the council, the reconstruction of its records, and its relationship with local councils, many questions remain. See Dubnow, "Council of Four Lands," 250–61; Mahler, *Toledot Hayyehudim Befolin;* Weinryb and Dubnow, *Pinkas Hamedina;* Halpern, *Yehudim Veyahadut,* 37–194, and his assemblage and reconstruction of the *Pinkas Vaad Arba Arazot,* soon to be superseded by Israel Bartal's new edition.

53. The degree of decline in the king's authority, at least in the seventeenth century, is a subject of controversy among contemporary Polish historians. See the excellent essays of Wyczański, "Problem of Authority," and Mączak, "Structure of Power."

54. Nathan of Hanover, *Yeven Mezula,* 82ff.

55. See demographic studies cited in note 41 for problems in establishing more precise estimates.

tions.[56] A bit more than a century later, by which time the economic and communal lives of Polish Jewry had suffered a precipitous decline, Dov Ber of Bolechow, a traditional Jew with Enlightenment proclivities, would bemoan the contemporary Jewish condition. Referring particularly to the Polish gentry's recent dissolution of the Council of Four Lands, he wrote: "These traditions were beneficial to the congregation of Israel over a period of eight hundred years or more. And it represented for Israel a small redemption and a bit of honor that by the heavenly compassion upon us, God in his mercy did not abandon us, as it is written in the Torah of Moses, 'and even in the land of your enemies, I have not abandoned nor despised you.'"[57] This communal order, these structures of governance that Jews were able to organize for themselves, were viewed as a sign that in spite of all appearances, God had not abandoned the Jews. Jewish chosenness and salvation is evidenced here not by birth, as it was among the Polish Sarmatian gentry, nor by individual entrepreneurial success, as it was by the English Protestant "saints," but by the capacity, when unimpeded by others, to establish collective order. And although Dov Ber overstates the authority vested in this institution—as attested by the breaches of order reported on every page of the *pinkasim* (the record books of the council) as well as by the registries of regional and local communities—the success was impressive. Dov Ber's expression of messianic fervor for administrative structures and the security that he ascribes to governance, might be paraphrased to contrast with the more familiar boast of his fellow Poles: "Because of order, the Jews have been able to endure." We must try to understand the role of this Jewish order within the various dimensions of the inimitable Polish order, including patterns of economic organization, action, and thinking.

Order, Lack of Order, and Antiorder

There is ample reason to suspect the accuracy of the Polish gentry's somewhat vainglorious interpretation of what saved Poland. It is doubtful that Poland could fundamentally be characterized by lack of order and that such a lack of order could have the positive consequences that members of the gentry attributed to it. But in making their proud assertion grist for our historical mill, we must raise basic questions of interpretation. Are we not overdetermining the implications of their words about order and lack of order? What focused images of their thinking actually come through to us across the centuries and over the linguistic and cultural barriers that separate them from us? What characteristics,

56. The elegiac literature such as the *Yeven Mezula* or the *Megillat Eifa,* ed. M. Weiner (Hanover, 1855), registers some awareness of the social strain that precipitated the slaughter. But the conclusions tend to point to traditional theodicies and messianic explanations rather than calling for any sustained worldly action. For a summary and an analysis of these reactions, see Ezrahi, *By Words Alone,* 96ff.; Mintz, *Ḥurbran,* 102ff.; Roskies, *Against the Apocalypse,* 48ff.

57. Dov Ber, *Memoirs,* 80–83. Dov Ber vastly exaggerates the longevity of the council; it was established no earlier than the end of the sixteenth century.

purposes, and meanings of the gentry do we have the right to deduce from their use of one unfortunate slogan, popular as it may have been in a particular period, and to what extent can we infer some correspondence between the structures by which they perceived and those by which they acted? Can plummeting through the different levels of this image lead us to valid and reliable interpretations of gentry intentions, motives, and self-perceptions that we can compare with other perspectives so as to understand, if only a bit better, what "really" happened?

In accordance with my interpretive approach, we must take the Polish gentry at their word that they appreciated what they experienced and identified as a lack of order, that they were not made anxious by "all coherence gone" and did not partake of the pall of gloom that some historians say descended upon Europe toward the end of the Middle Ages. We take them seriously as individuals with observations and feelings but not always as experts with solutions; we are attentive to them as native informants, even as chroniclers of the opinions of their contemporaries, recording what they and others believed, but not as able analysts of their own situation. As Max Weber put it, "Conduct, especially social conduct and quite particularly a social relationship, can be oriented on the part of the actors towards their idea of the existence of legitimate order."[58] Lack of order seems to be their "idea" of that "legitimate order" to which members of the Polish gentry oriented their behavior. But we are not limited by their perception that Poland indeed did lack order, nor obligated to concur with their judgment about Poland's ability to stand on its own. And we certainly are not bound to accept the causal relationship that they so much wanted to believe existed between the structure of Polish society and the state of this orderless republic of nobles, about whose viability they tried hard to convince one another. By the time some confronted the crisis, it was too late.

Here we encounter more than a problem in historical interpretation. Order and words about order have special symbolic powers, difficult and compelling to decode. For more than other words, words about order, as Kenneth Burke has eloquently informed us, signify their meaning and the opposite of their meaning.[59] The concept of order must be viewed as a center from which many related considerations radiate. Both command or authority and structure or community are related to a cycle of terms implicit in the idea of order. Moreover, order as a polar term implies corresponding ideas, not only of disorder or lack of order, but also of antiorder.[60] This interpretive approach to concepts of order underscores the functionality of concepts of antiorder in establishing and perpetuating order. It points to the way in which certain collectivities remedy their difficulties in

58. Weber, *On Law in Economy and Society,* 2ff.; Little, *Religion, Order and Law.*
59. Burke, *Rhetoric of Religion;* Duncan, *Symbols and Social Theory,* 257ff.
60. Several other social scientists and literary analysts come to a similar conclusion from somewhat different perspectives. See, for example, Turner, *Ritual Process;* Girard, *Violence and the Sacred.* While some of these theories move dangerously close to a type of sociological Manichaeanism, they point to insidious tendencies which should not be overlooked.

establishing authority by assigning blame; their difficulties in lending coherence to their actions by expressing indignation, often leading to murderous rage; their difficulties in fortifying community by imposing segregation, victimization, and scapegoating.[61]

Members of the Polish gentry were not unique in having to face the crisis of social order and meaning on the eve of the modern period. The authority of religion, law, and the state, the prerogative of the individual and the collectivity, and the value and legitimacy of certain economic endeavors were addressed in new concepts of order that developed across Europe. The Polish lords went about solving this problem in their inimitable fashion. During the same period, when thinkers in the West from Machiavelli and Hobbes to Mandeville and Adam Smith were trying to resolve vexing dilemmas of human freedom and the commonweal, captured in such images as the multiheaded Leviathan or the hidden hand or in formulations of individual sin leading to collective virtue, the Polish lords were translating historical fictions into legal claims to serf labor, legitimating these rights with a dubious prescription as to what makes Poland "stand."[62] In upholding their "golden freedom" as an unequivocal, unqualifiable, and ultimate value and endowment, they resisted coordination and refused to relinquish their individual autonomy; they made political choices in relation to one concept of the collective good, even when the cost of their "golden freedom" was foreign domination. At a moment when in the West profound struggles for freedom were also taking place, when royal absolutism, as well as its "well-ordered police state" and other devices of public administration, was precipitating a reaction and thereby inadvertently strengthening liberal traditions of natural law, the Polish lords flaunted their personal freedom, depriving other Poles of the same. And at the same time as more citizens in the West were enjoying such liberties as the rights to acquire and own private property, legitimated as an effective means to "taming the passions," the Polish lords reveled in their freedom—a freedom that implies impulsiveness. Yet they persisted in believing that they inhabited a world governed by immutable laws; insofar as those laws proved to be an unreliable guide to changing situations, the frequent response of the Polish gentry was to attribute blame rather than to seek new explanations. And that blame often supplied the emotional foundations of an imagined antiorder.

In examining gentry responses to the Reformation and to absolutism, we have gained more of a sense of what this lack of order connoted. The failure of the Reformation, after some promising starts, enabled Poland to avert catastrophic religious wars. But it also deprived that country of some of the salutary effects of new spiritual, intellectual, and political challenges that benefited even some countries like France, which remained predominantly Catholic. The Polish lords' idealization of primordial chaos and spontaneity encouraged them to dissociate themselves from the real consequences of their actions or to manipulate others so

61. Robert Lane, *Political Ideology,* uses the apt phrase "high-tension morality."
62. Pocock, *Machiavellian Movement;* Hirschmann, *Passions and the Interests;* Dumont, *From Mandeville to Marx.*

as to reconcile disparities between the ideal and the real. Their idealization of the clan, the simple egalitarian social order, made them resistant to participating in, much less according legitimacy to, that order, which involved both social differentiation and hierarchical integration.

The denial of order and the projection of an antiorder are common responses to overwhelming contradictions that cannot be ignored or reconciled. We might call it saving appearances, paraphrasing the famous Platonic formulation of saving the phenomena.[63] It is in relation to this mode of conceptualizing order that we must examine the Polish gentry's response to the changing economic organization of the early modern world and their persistent efforts to preserve serf labor even after it proved to be unmanageable and unprofitable. What really made Poland stand was the gentry's use of antiorder to save appearances of Polish feudalism. With the ingenuity and the anxiety of Ptolemaic astronomers, they added epicycle to epicycle, creating new conditions under which hypotheses were to be deemed plausible, independently of their connection with reality. And when these efforts to save the system of coercive labor ultimately failed, they attributed the responsibility for that failure to others.

In 1648, Polish nobles might have looked westward and judged themselves fortunate, but they did not perceive the forces that, during the next century and a half, would lead them on a downward spiral. Nor did they take note of the incipient forces of modernization that would transform the war-shattered, economically depleted, and spiritually exhausted countries of the West into thriving mercantile and industrial states. By the second half of the eighteenth century, Poland was deeply affected by the cumulative results of years of peasant rebellion, economic stagnation, and political feuding, as well as by scheming neighbors. Less visible and susceptible to control, and more insidious, were shifts in international markets and waves of inflation. As Poland was disintegrating from within and being carved up from without, the virtues of its much-heralded and romanticized lack of order—the decentralized polity and autarkic economy controlled by an independent-minded and often impulsive feudal aristocracy—became less clear. Yet even the increasingly painful awareness of political and economic decline did not eliminate gentry efforts to confront current problems with old explanations instead of implementing new and appropriate courses of action. Peasant rebellions and low productivity did not prompt serious consideration of other modes of labor organization; they did raise questions about where to search for more docile serfs.

Gentry thinking sought to make vulnerable segments of the population account (and even compensate the Polish lords) for the growing gap that they experienced between perception and reality. With the exception of a small reform-minded portion of the gentry, which was influenced by the Western Enlightenment and whose equivocal position was not strengthened by the violence and intrigues that constituted the framework of its country's politics, most members of

63. Barfield, *Saving the Appearances,* 48–52.

the Polish gentry persisted in seeing their interests served by this lack of order. Though uncompromising in asserting their traditional prerogatives, including their entitlement to serf labor, nobles, up to the final partition of the lands of Poland and the complete loss of Polish sovereignty in 1795, continually exalted their contribution to Poland's ability to stand. They were joined in this by foreign enthusiasts. Observers from opposite sides of the eighteenth-century political spectrum, such as Jean-Jacques Rousseau and Edmund Burke, were charmed by such catch phrases as "golden freedom" and "republic of the nobility."

When Jews on the eve of the 1648 Deluge looked westward at their co-religionists, it was with a sense of concern at what they saw in those western lands, on the one hand, and with pride at what they had accomplished in Poland, on the other. By the end of the eighteenth century, however, the differing situations and differing directions of movement of Jews in the West and in the East were becoming clear. Jews in the West were taking their first halting but by no means irreversible steps toward full citizenship, already having demonstrated "how profitable are the Jews" and having achieved a modicum of economic integration and cultural participation in what would become modernized societies in Central and Western Europe and North America. At that same time, Polish Jews were moving closer and closer to their fate in the failed modernization of Poland—subordination and alienation. Were Poland's Jews "profitable"?

Methodological Musings and Historiographic Debates on Polish Feudalism

Whatever truth there was to the nobles' claim *nierządem Polska stoi,* slogans and idealizations could not conceal the real order over which the gentry had begun to preside in the early modern period: the enserfment and subordination of millions. With varying degrees of success, Polish feudalism bridged the wheat field and the market, the natural and the commercial, the reciprocal and monetary economic orders. We may appreciate the ingenuity of that bridge by examining, as Herbert Lüthy suggests, the enormity of the gap:

What we have here, in fact, are two archetypical images of society so radically different, so mutually exclusive, and each so "self-evident" to those whose imagination it shaped, that a dialogue seemed altogether impossible between the exponents of the one or the other doctrine, without either one ever glimpsing the deep cause of their perpetual misunderstanding. The economy is the wheatfield or the olive grove, where the fruits ripen under the sun and where God is present as the Giver of all good things, distributing His portion to the cultivator, the lord, and the cleric, according to His justice. Such justice is not that of *Do ut des* because the cultivator himself did not "make" the fruit, he has merely served it as a humble agent in the accomplishment of the miracle of harvests, and he is not the sole proprietor. Chrematism, on the other hand, is the market where anonymous buyers and sellers face each other and communicate with each other only by means of abstract signs; where possessions are merely merchandise passing from hand to hand representative of the sums of money which they have cost or will bring; where nothing grows, if not the profit of the intermediaries; and where God is no longer present, or at most, present only in the tables of laws: a code of commercial morality and honesty, the impersonal "rule of equity."[64]

Polish feudalism in this period emerged as a powerful institutionalization of order, by no means limited to its manifest economic functions of production and distribution. It fostered structures of social interaction, realms of economic enterprise, and modes of exchange, however fraught with conflict; it adumbrated patterns of meaning, as riddled as they were by deep contradictions and diverse significances for its different participants, including Jews. But this feat of social engineering had some not-so-hidden costs: Not only noble serf owners who shaped this distinct but unacknowledged order became brutalized by their failing efforts to recognize and reconcile market opportunities with production problems; rather, as Arcadius Kahan observes, "the whole body politic became dehumanized and permeated by elements of lawlessness."[65] We must clearly focus on the contours of Polish feudalism—the forces that sustained it and the beliefs that legitimated it—and on the built-in conflicts and contradictions that led to its declining profitability and plausibility. Examining the order of Polish feudalism along its two dimensions of structure and meaning will help understand that which is most often overlooked in analyses of this institution: how Polish Jews

64. Lüthy, *From Calvin to Rousseau,* 93. Marc Bloch is critical of this bifurcation as applied to the feudalism of the "Great Days of the Middle Ages," calling it a "pseudo-dilemma," a "lazy solution whose apparent simplicity would soon be explored by a more searching inquiry." He suggests that we ask, rather, "whether in this level of society, so very remote in all respects from ours, the instruments of exchange may not themselves have fulfilled functions very different from those of today or yesterday." Bloch, "Problem of Gold," 230ff. But this bifurcation, regardless of antecedents, is quite glaring in the case of Polish feudalism precisely because of the modes of exchange that Bloch analyzes in relation to medieval feudalism. Indeed, Bloch concedes that even in those periods of the Middle Ages when there was a more stable monetary supply, "far fewer payments in fact took the form of specie than one would be inclined to infer from a causal and incautious reading of the documents. Payments were rather replaced by goods or a few days work. Money was mentioned only to serve as a measure of value" (236). The economy of the market can be further subdivided in relation to modes or motives of acquisition. Georg Simmel, *Philosophy of Money,* distinguishes between the taking of booty and methodical acquisition. Karl Polanyi emphasizes the difference between production for use and production for gain.
65. Kahan, "Notes on Serfdom," 99. Antoni Mączak, "Vicissitudes of Feudalism," speaks of the pervasive and enduring influences of the peculiar form of feudalism that developed in Poland. Anderson, *Lineages of the Absolutist State,* 195; Kula, *Economic Theory of the Feudal System,* 186, Topolski, "Causes of Dualism," 7, asserts that "wars and internal chaos deepened by the predatory conduct of the gentry created conditions for the maintenance and development and impunity of that particular form of noneconomic compensation exacted by the gentry for their falling incomes."

both fostered and resisted Polish feudalism, and how they served the forces of social order and prompted the imagination of antiorder.

In response to these inferences regarding an institution as complex as Polish feudalism, an unlikely coalition of historians and methodological purists might join with the historical voices of the Polish lords in chanting "lack of order." They would direct us to the archives, warning us that abundant evidence of significant variations in the organization of the Polish countryside and village life in the early modern period awaits our consideration. They would challenge the very possibility of making generalizations about the order of Polish history, about feudalism in Poland, and about regional processes having to do with vague differential patterns of development between East and West.

But mustering historical details does not prove disorder and randomness. Those same archives contain aggregate data on how land division shaped the countryside, statistics on patterns of labor organization and surplus extraction, and codes and manuals of laws, charters, privileges, customs, and administrative advice that indicate an institutional dimension rather than uncoordinated repetition.[66] We sense the semblance of formalized order, as uneven, incomplete, and at times contradictory as the evidence for that order may be. This is not to deny the dangers of synthetic work or the methodological inadequacies of such concepts as the second serfdom, neoserfdom, or refeudalization.[67] Regional variants, as well as the different peasant obligations that we find on gentry, magnate, church, or monarchical estates, do make it difficult to generalize, even when we limit our focus to that feudalism which developed in Poland.[68] But I make no claim that the concepts introduced ever existed in history in their pure forms. Rather, I use them heuristically, for the purposes of analysis as ideal types, as Max Weber suggests. And if it is the case, as Eric Voegelin would lead us to believe, that "the order of history is the history of order," our concepts of that order in Polish history, which become a bit fuzzy when subjected to the heterogeneity of historical detail, attain sharp focus from the history of idealized order.[69] That order is manifest in the autarky with which the lords sought to resist autocracy, in their meld of the economic forces and social organization of the Wheat field and the market, and in the functional and symbolic use they made of the Jews. These were

66. A good example of a study that tries to balance generalizations with an awareness of serious variations in region and period while acknowledging the serious gaps in the extant archival record can be found in Mączak, "Money and Society," 69, 87, 98–99.
67. See Kamiński, "Neo-Serfdom in Poland-Lithuania," 253–68; Makkai, "Neo-Serfdom," 225–238.
68. Topolski, "Causes of Dualism," 10–12, presents a lucid summary of the rich Polish historical writing on "the causes of the formation of the manorial economy based upon statute labour" and defends the position that a few significant variables can be chosen for emphasis in analysis, independently of these differences and their influence on structures and functions of Polish feudalism. For a survey of the implications of regional differences for Polish Jewry, see Ettinger, "Legal and Social Status"; Goldberg, *Jewish Privileges*; Rosman, "Polish Magnates and the Jews."
69. Voegelin, *Order and History*, vol. 1.

the building blocks with which the Polish lords constructed their lack of order and by which they believed that their country endured. And if, as indicated by the most convincing studies of the success and failure of economic development, "small changes" at the right moment do count, there may be a different type of historical detail for which we must search in trying to understand why the Polish gentry was unable to take advantage of fleeting opportunities.

Historians are divided about fundamental issues in regard to the origins of Polish feudalism. Some contend that the rise of Polish feudalism must be related to global forces in early modern Europe. At the very moment of the reorganization of agriculture in the West, in that region east of a line drawn from Hamburg to Venice, a second serfdom, one that was not merely the continuation of medieval feudalism, became institutionalized.[70] Others underscore the indigenous roots of East Central European feudalism in general and Polish feudalism in particular, which were preserved through the eighteenth century and which "strongly coloured capitalist relationships even after its demise."[71]

The two perspectives are by no means mutually exclusive. Quite the contrary. The serfdom that emerged in early modern Poland must be viewed and analyzed not only in relation to other modes of serfdom that arose elsewhere at other times; it must be compared with, and where possible even linked to, contemporary conditions in other countries which accelerated the levels of productivity and stimulated economic development. Comprehending the effect of international forces on local responses, including choices made by the Polish lords, is necessary if we are to understand the growing divergence between East and West in the early modern period, the way that Jews contributed to this divergence, and, in turn, the impact that the different patterns of development had upon Jews in Eastern and Western Europe.[72] In making a judgment among a variety of alter-

70. Braudel, *Wheels of Commerce;* Topolski and Rutkowski, "La genèse du régime;" Topolski, "Causes of Dualism"; Wallerstein, "From Feudalism to Capitalism"; and *Modern World-System.*

71. Kahan, "Notes on Serfdom"; Kula, *Economic Theory of the Feudal System;* Mączak, "Structure of Power."

72. For a more recent survey of indigenous and exogenous factors in the growth of Polish feudalism, and a sharp critique of Anderson and Wallerstein in particular, see Topolski, "Sixteenth Century Poland." The more ideologized sides of this discussion, best represented by the dependency theorists, take on neo-Marxist overtones which I will try to avoid. For some comments on dependency theory and the role of Jews in economic development between East and West, see Levine, "Judaism and Mercantilism." The macro- and microeconomies of Polish feudalism have been insightfully analyzed in typological terms by the contemporary Polish economic historian Witold Kula, who acknowledges the problems of using models and making generalizations. The interpretation presented here is influenced by his approach but adds one group invisible within Kula's model of Polish serfdom: the Jews. The invisibility of the Jews in Polish historiography has unfortunate precedents, though in the case of Kula, it is most likely explained by the political climate of post–World War II Poland in which Kula wrote his *Economic Theory of the Feudal System.* In another of Kula's works on methodology in economic history, he does underscore the

native interpretations of the past, and in forging a path between historiographic debates that are only partially salient to an understanding of Jewish history, my goal is not so much to resolve issues in a controversial secondary literature as it is to choose those interpretations which shed new light on Jewish activities.

The Political and Economic Roots of the Second Serfdom

Contemporaneous developments in Western and Eastern Europe, including the rise of centralized absolutism, trade, and monetary problems, contributed to the genesis and ultimate impact of Polish feudalism. Its distinct features, however, are related to perceptions and propensities of the Polish lords and to their access to the large number of Jews they incorporated into this system.

The development of Poland's agrarian feudalism neither preceded, as in the West, nor was accompanied by, as in the East, the development of political centralization within the framework of an absolutist state.[73] The rise of Poland's feudalism, as we have seen, corresponded to, and perhaps is a primary manifestation of, the decline in its centralized authority at an early date. The power, wealth, and insubordination of the magnates contributed to these processes.

But shifts in the distribution of power do not sufficiently account for the development of this particular order. Economic factors giving rise to feudalism may be more difficult to observe but are no less important to consider. Studies of the rise of the earlier medieval feudalism in Europe emphasize the low level of monetization, an unreliable coinage system related to the decreasing centralization of authority and control over the mints, and a high interest rate. These factors discouraged investments, including those for agricultural labor and for improvements. Low monetary circulation likewise shrank trade and thereby contributed to the decline of towns and urban centers.[74]

The rise of the second serfdom in early modern Poland succeeded a period in the fourteenth and fifteenth centuries in which interregional trade and transshipment of goods across Poland was relatively widespread, establishing a favorable balance of trade.[75] The value of currency, the velocity of monetary circulation, and international rates of monetary exchange did complicate the terms of trade

---

importance of analyzing the economic roles and functions of Jews in Polish history. *Problemy i metody historii gospodarczej,* 76–77.

73. Anderson, *Lineages of the Absolutist State,* 195; Topolski, "Causes of Dualism," 74. Whether or not we accept Anderson's ideologically tinged theory of the origins of the modern absolutist state as a transmutation of feudalism, we must consider this anomaly that he suggests in the development of Poland, a country at the crossroads of East and West.

74. Usher, *Deposit Banking,* 193ff.; Bloch, "Problem of Gold," 186ff.

75. Schipper, "Economic History of the Jews in Poland-Lithuania," 155–203; Bogucka, "Monetary Crisis," 137–52; Mączak, "Money and Society," 70ff; Hundert, "Jews, Money and Society," 261–74.

for Poland in the sixteenth century and after, increasing antagonisms particularly between Jews and burghers.[76] But were there not domestic policies, more readily and directly controllable by the Polish lords, that would have strengthened the economic position of the country? At the moment when the magnates and lords could have created necessary institutions and taken advantage of opportunities to enlist coerced labor were there not other small changes and special economic opportunities for them to exploit? Did members of the nobility seek to reimpose coerced labor based on their reading of economic opportunities, or did this decision have deeper roots?[77]

The trade legislation passed by the magnates and the gentry at national, regional, or local convocations generally served their short-term self-interest, leading to profits and, most important, to control, rather than to productivity. Although many Polish lords maintained a variety of commercial pursuits, their scorn of trade was exceeded only by their passion for its profits and goods and their exaggerated confidence in their ability to control the terms of trade on domestic and international markets. Often, they sought to influence the price of Polish goods without regard for foreign market prices. The *taksa*, or fixed prices, for example, was a device for insulating trade from the influences of supply and demand. Measures referred to in the Polish publicistic literature as "containing the borders," as we shall see, were an expression of the gentry's efforts to control trade. The desire to impose autarkic structures on Poland was given expression at the moment when entrepreneurs in countries like England and Holland were trying to extend their nations' borders by building up merchant fleets and promoting international trade. Members of the gentry who were resourceful and powerful enough would exempt themselves from such restrictions. But these measures, when aimed at the merchants, eroded the economic base of the towns,

76. Szelągowski, *Pieniądz i przewrót cen,* 53–63. With the subordination of the Teutonic order to the north following the battle of Grünwald in 1410, Polish merchants were able to trade through Danzig without paying tax; following the Peace of Torun in 1466, Polish merchants had still greater access to Danzig and western Prussia. Poland's Levantine trade indeed was interrupted in the second half of the fifteenth century with the loss of Black Sea trade routes. But trade with countries contiguous with the Black Sea and the Mediterranean increased by way of the Baltic ports. With the new markets for Poland's timber and agricultural goods increasing from the end of the fifteenth century, conditions were certainly favorable for intensified import and export activity in Poland.

77. Bloch, *Land and Work in Medieval Europe,* 186, reminds us that monetary phenomena may be viewed "as a seismograph that not only registers earth tremors but sometimes brings them about." Bogucka, "Monetary Crisis," 138, underscores a trend in Polish historiography to see the monetary crisis as a result, and not only as a primary cause, of broader economic problems in early modern Poland. This trend is more important than it might at first appear. Marxist historians were not the first to pay special attention to the problems of capital. Within the Polish context accusations against speculators and coin clippers—code words for Jews—made their way uncritically into the domain of historical explanation. Hence a more sophisticated analysis of monetary problems is significant in countering these stereotypes.

"making it almost impossible for townsmen to make a living";[78] and when aimed at the peasants, they weakened autonomous peasant communities and independent initiative.

Thus there are similarities between the conditions that generated earlier medieval feudalism and the effects of the policies and actions of the sixteenth-century Polish nobility. But the same economic conditions that gave rise to serfdom might have led to a different pattern of development had the Polish lords supported policies favoring profits from commerce and rewards for achievement in undertaking risks and rendering services, rather than attempting to generate secondary revenues through tolls, taxes, and warehousing fees, over which they enjoyed monopolies as a result of their social position.[79] This did not happen. Whenever and wherever there were trade opportunities, edicts were issued that curtailed trade, particularly exports, but never effectively controlled the importation of foreign luxury items for the gentry's pleasure.[80] The declining effectiveness of the Polish monarchy and the rise of the magnates inhibited the promulgation of well-coordinated administrative, fiscal, and political measures that might have spurred economic growth, similar to the measures that were promoted by the centralized and absolutist states in the West.[81] The Polish burghers sought privileges comparable to those of the nobility instead of competing through new economic initiatives, as did the burghers in the West.

Historical actors as well as latter-day historians have underscored one particular "small change" contributing to the rise of the second serfdom: international grain prices. This factor provided the most manifest economic incentive for Poland's expansion beyond its eastern borders, enserfing large numbers of semi-nomadic Slavic and Tatar peasants, partly by the lure of participation in the momentary boom in grain profits, partly by force, and partly by the absorption of their leaders into the Polish aristocracy.

The increased rate of urbanization and the surge in population in Western countries created serious food shortages, from which Poland could have profited.[82] It is questionable, however, whether Poland fulfilled its potential as the

78. Miskimin, *Economy of Later Renaissance Europe,* 58.
79. Szelągowski, *Pieniądz i przewrót cen,* 73–74.
80. In 1524 Sigismund I (1467–1548) restricted the movement of Polish merchants in an effort to keep good currency in Poland and combat counterfeit coinage. In 1527 the Sejm in Cracow promulgated severe punishments against gentry or commoners who crossed the border, particularly into Silesia. At the Sejm of 1565 measures were passed prohibiting Polish merchants from traveling abroad and encouraging foreign merchants to settle in Poland. Trade was to center on fairs and warehouses located in towns, but not in rural areas. Ibid., 41–42, 85–87. Szelągowski questions whether these edicts were indeed aimed against the merchants, given the fact that the gentry active in trade had the most to lose from such restrictions. He provides an unlikely explanation that these policies testify to a transition from a regional to a national economy and early signs of mercantilism.
81. Mączak, "Money and Society," 69–71.
82. Wallerstein, in emphasizing the links in economic development between East and West, points to the incentives to increase grain production for Poland, a peripheral area in

breadbasket of Europe during the early stages of Western urbanization and industrialization, when circumstances for Polish profits were optimal.[83] The Polish
nobles succeeded, by the end of the sixteenth century, in generating no more
than 2.5 percent of Poland's total annual yield, three million bushels for export.
To do this, they had to use their "relatively unbridled power" to enserf the
peasants and brutally drive back to the land various segments of Poland's population—artisans, small traders, and other urban dwellers, among them the Jews—
whose economic positions were already weakened by gentry trade policies.
Religious tensions undergirded class conflict, fostering peasant rebellion and
ultimately complicating Poland's international standing. This extensive, rather
than intensive, farming did not improve the techniques and management of agriculture, nor did it contribute to any economy of scale. The long-term profits of
this arrangement are even more questionable. Had Poland, in tandem with the
West, increased its urbanization, removing labor from food production and
reserving more grain for internal consumption, those three million bushels of
grain would not have been available for export. Although satisfying less than 1
percent of Western European demand for grain, they were sufficient to save
Amsterdam and a few cities of the West from the large-scale starvation that under
conditions of shortage attend the lower classes, and from the food riots that
occasionally result from such conditions. Adequate grain supplies in the West
contributed to the growth of cities and to the availability of a labor force, and they
fostered a quantum leap in productivity and efficiency.[84]

But neither low productivity of the land nor low morale among the serfs
signaled danger to the Polish lords. According to their economic calculations,
land and labor were considered abundant, if not unlimited. The profits from grain
surpluses sold on international markets led to a greater concentration of wealth

---

relation to the developing European economy. One need not be an enthusiast of dependency theory, and certainly not a neo-Marxist, to appreciate the significance of the economic partnership, rather than exploitation, that joined the agrarian regions of Eastern
Central Europe with the newly developing affluent cities of the West. Indeed, this is
precisely the way Sarmatianism expressed the complementarity of Poland to the West. And
although there were victims of the trade between Western centers and Eastern peripheries,
the Polish gentry who willfully created the second serfdom and tenaciously sought to
preserve it were certainly not among them, as Braudel, *Wheels of Commerce,* urges us to
remember. See Miskimin, *Economy of Later Renaissance Europe,* 58.

83. Miskimin, *Economy of Later Renaissance Europe,* 58. Kahan, "Notes on Serfdom," and
Topolski, "Causes on Dualism," question the productivity of serfdom and therefore its
profitability. But for the short term in the sixteenth century, and precisely for those
peasants recruited into this mode of labor contract, there were economic incentives, in
addition to the gentry's use of force, to transform yeomen into serfs.

84. Miskimin, *Economy of Late Renaissance Europe,* 58–64. Topolski, "Sixteenth Century Poland," 84, argues that the small percentage of Western European grain needs supplied by Poland had only a speculative effect on grain prices rather than responding to
critical needs. Regardless of whether anyone in the West would starve without Polish grain,
its positive effect on Western commerce and industry is clear.

and land ownership in the hands of the magnates. Many small manors, however, were linked to internal markets rather than to exports.[85] By the second quarter of the seventeenth century, the profitable trend of increasing exports of Polish grain reversed itself. This reversal was the result of complex international changes, including price fluctuations and improved yields of other granaries that could supply Western Europe.[86]

The long-term and somewhat ironic effect of the second serfdom is that the export of Polish grain, during the early stages of the Western commercial and industrial revolutions, contributed to political stability in the West. It benefited agriculture and food provision, thereby supporting Western urbanization and undercutting the further marketability and profitability of Polish grain. Moreover, Poland's domestic instability in the seventeenth century created difficulties in the production and transportation of its grain, worsening its position in the international economy.[87] Harry Miskimin emphasizes that "out of self-interest," "the nobles successfully contrived to crush Polish economic development in order to reserve for themselves the rich grain trade and to assure adequate supplies of agricultural labor for the maximum exploitation of their estates."[88] Having done little in this period to bolster economic development, these lords now sought to devise techniques for profiting from economic decline; their inability to take advantage of "small changes" forced them to look for benefit in "backwardness."

The Social Architecture of the Second Serfdom

Let us now consider the social structures and idealized forms of the feudal estate. How it functioned as a microeconomy within the internal Polish economy and within the global macroeconomy was affected by local traditions, by its size or its land tenure, by its proximity to markets and river transport, by the number of peasants enserfed, by the degree to which an estate was under crown, church, or noble hegemony, and by the power and efficiency of the estate's managers. But Poland's second serfdom manifested a fairly common pattern of social relations. In examining this pattern, I shall try to establish the connections between the wheat field and the market, the "peculiar shape" that feudalism took on in early modern Poland, and the consequences for Polish Jews.[89]

Across the Polish countryside in the sixteenth century feudal manors began to spring up. In the center of the estate was the home of the lord. It might have been a hut, only slightly more elegant than those of the peasants, or a large palace. If the estate was large enough, there were houses of lower or déclassé gentry who

85. Topolski, "Sixteenth Century Poland," 78–84.
86. Braudel, *Capitalism and Material Life,* 66–120, esp. 84. The Polish gentry, in assessing the reversals in their economic situation after 1625, would hardly have agreed with the measure of initiative that Braudel attributed to them.
87. Kula, *Economic Theory of the Feudal System,* 129–33, 151.
88. Miskimin, *Economy of Later Renaissance Europe,* 60.
89. Ibid., 57.

provided various services in the lord's court. Some estates included a village, or even a town, where artisans and tradesmen received concessions. Invariably, an estate included a church, or at least a chapel, with attending clergy, who were often relatives of the lord; as common a sight on the Polish landscape as the estate church was the propinacja, or tavern.

In good years, the lord would sell surplus grain, feed for draft animals, and seed for the following year's planting. If his holdings were sufficiently large and he himself resourceful, he could transport grain to international markets like Danzig, where the prices were considerably higher than at local or regional markets. He could profit additionally by offering shipping and marketing services to smaller landlords. On the lord's bookkeeping ledgers, revenue from such services would be registered solely as profit since peasant labor would not be considered an additional expense. He could attempt to profit further by reducing his peasants' land plots and by forcing them to purchase produce over which he maintained a monopoly, such as salt, herring, and alcohol. In bad years, the lord could demand a larger proportion of his peasants' crops, often actually profiting from crop short-ages. He placed no particular value on capital accumulation, requiring only that it serve his needs for immediate consumption, nor on capital improvement, such as the repair of broken bridges. He used whatever means available to evade paying taxes to the monarch and tithes to the church.[90]

Distribution within the economy of the wheat field was based wholly on reciprocity, not on exchange.[91] But the lord met his own needs by utilizing the surplus cash that he siphoned off from the closed system of circulation within his autarkic estates. He alone was able to reach beyond the natural economy and gain access to the market, within which distribution was based on monetary exchange.

Yet the lords, as head of an idealized institution constructed upon self-serving fictions, was occasionally overwhelmed by hard realities. The fiction of a decentralized economy composed of small autonomous and autarkic productive units was predicated on the belief in the absolute power of the lord and the powerlessness of the peasants. The reality was far more complex, however rich, powerful, and capable as an administrator the lord might have been, he had little control over such exigencies as drought, plague, or war, which could hamper the productivity of his estates, and even ruin him. Neither could he do much to

90. Mączak, "Money and Society," 84ff.
91. Polanyi, Arensberg, and Pearson, ed., *Trade and Market,* 64–94. Although Polanyi's work has come under criticism and there is evidence against the late date that he established for the development of markets in Europe, his dichotomy between reciprocity and exchange is useful in understanding the second serfdom and the way in which it embeds economic relations in social relations as well as in religious definitions. Indeed, by paying attention to the religious and philosophical roots of Polish feudalism, I am able to make a similar argument in chapter 3 without Polanyi's evolutionary determinism. Simmel, *Philosophy of Money,* 142, likewise suggests that "exchange was at first necessarily exchange-in-kind, an exchange between direct values."

Fig. 4. *Peasants Dancing at an Inn* (1819). Oil painting by Michał Stachowich (1768–1825).

control international market prices other than to jockey himself into the most favorable position, as he saw it, in relation to those market forces. Moreover, his seemingly unlimited supply of what he viewed as free labor had hidden costs. Factoring out labor costs from his accounting ledgers often provided the lord with misleading information as to the profitability of his various investments; regardless of his accounting system, it was difficult for him to ascertain his precise financial position relative to the Western monetary markets in which he so much wanted to participate. Another hidden cost of this "free" labor was the lord's own helplessness; with no labor market to speak of, lord and peasant were altogether dependent upon each other.

Under the corvée system, the peasants owed a number of days a year in labor services to the lord. This number varied from estate to estate. In addition, the peasant had to make a certain monetary payment for the right to live in his estate and to till a small strip of land to sustain himself and his family. The terms of enserfment for the peasant in most parts of Poland became more severe from the sixteenth through the eighteenth century, with fewer opportunities to pay rent in lieu of contributing labor. Although having few formal legal rights, the peasant was far from powerless. He could escape, as often happened, leaving the lord shorthanded in field labor. He could also destroy the lord's resources by starting a fire or engaging in some other dramatic and obvious act, or by committing covert sabotage, the consequences of which the peasant was often enough accused. In addition to growing the agricultural produce needed to feed his family, the peasant also tried to accumulate some surplus with which to purchase manufactured goods, such as steel scythes or glassware, not readily available on the estate. Another item for which the serf needed cash reserves—an item of growing importance—was alcohol. Moreover, he needed money to pay cash dues to nobles, taxes to the state, and tithes to the church.

The serf's demand for these cash payments provides a suggestive illustration of the contradictory effects of the lord's economic policy. The lord subverted his own concept of reciprocity within a natural economy. Although the lord mandated cash payments from his serf as a means of extracting cash surplus in a system averse to free monetary circulation, this demand, from a member of a population whose access to the monetary economy was severely impeded, required and encouraged the serf to maintain some market relationship to generate cash. With great ingenuity, the serf concealed this cash from the landlord's agents, whose task it was to confiscate such "illegally" acquired surpluses. Having met the payments imposed on him, he worked even harder to generate an even larger cash surplus, thus further undermining gentry controls on surplus extraction and on monetary circulation.[92]

92. Estimates of the respective yields of serf and gentry plots indicate that the peasants worked their own plots more efficiently than those of their lords. Under different circumstances this peasant initiative and industriousness might have been channeled into entrepreneurialism. Furthermore, the ability of the serfs to generate a cash surplus was impressive in view of the shortage of small silver coins, the great and rapid devaluation of

The lord's efforts to maintain coerced labor and the sense of a natural economy without monetary exchange had implications beyond the feudal estate. They adversely affected the economic position of the towns. Peasants with access to town markets, the lords believed, might be tempted to siphon off and monetize larger portions of the agricultural yield; towns were also known to harbor fugitive serfs and thereby to weaken the labor supply.[93] The effect of their efforts on Poland's landscape and demography was visible. Even cities like Warsaw were reduced in size until the second half of the eighteenth century. The nobility began to enlist townspeople, including artisans and tradesmen, into feudal contracts similar to those they maintained with the peasants.[94] It is here that we discover the first instance of Jews making their entry into the domain of the feudal estate. And it is here that our attention is drawn to what is but one of the stark contradictions of this feudal order.

Jews in the towns were already in close alliance with the gentry, particularly where they sought protection from the burghers. But at the same time, they were perceived by the lords as harmful. Jewish merchants participating in the market economy, largely peddlers selling simple manufactured goods in backpacks or on carts, for whom no peasant wheat field was too remote, would provide cash to the peasants for their surplus grain or exchange agricultural produce for goods that were not fabricated on the estates, which were deemed self-sufficient by the gentry landlords. In monetizing the surplus grain of the serfs, the Jews performed a service not only to the serfs but also to the gentry, who needed their serfs' cash payments in addition to their coerced labor. Yet the monetization of peasant produce by Jews, made necessary by noble landlords' demands on the peasants to make cash payments, was perceived by those same nobles as the Jews' efforts to loosen the bonds by which the gentry sought to enserf the peasants. How did the nobility solve its "Jewish problem" within the social architecture of the second serfdom?

The Paradoxes of Polish Feudalism

Describing, even in detail, the internal relations and outer boundaries of an institution explains far less than what we would care to know about the participa-

---

those coins, and their low silver content, the result of minting policies or coin clipping. See Mączak, "Money and Society," 87; Bogucka, "Monetary Crisis," 141–43, 152.

93. This is a clear illustration of money and the loosening of feudal bonds, of chrematism and the abstraction of social relations. The extraeconomic relationships between different types of money, patterns of social relations, and modes of cognition are considered in chapter 4, based on Georg Simmel's fascinating study *The Philosophy of Money*. Simmel analyzes the relationship between money and freedom (297). Mączak, "Money and Society," 94–95, indicates that there was more serf mobility, socially and spatially, than we might expect from Kula's model. "Village Shylocks" (as he calls them), for example, could profit handsomely from the cash needs of their fellow serfs.

94. See Goldberg, *Jewish Privileges*, and "Between Freedom and Bondage," 107ff.

tion of different sets of historical actors. What meaning did the Polish nobles ascribe to their actions? What rationality did they experience in their institutions? And to what extent were they aware of contradictions in which they were involved and which they imposed on others?[95]

The lords viewed both the self-sufficiency that they sought to institute and the nonmonetary exchange that they sought to impose within the confines of the feudal estate as involving issues of principle and of entitlement rather than merely concerning practicality and exigencies. Their belief in autarky and reciprocity was legitimated and bolstered by a good measure of indignation, particularly when these beliefs were attacked or undermined, when the very means of control and exchange became unmanageable and unprofitable.

Monetary expenditures were seen as more than impediments to profitability. Members of the gentry were particularly intent on not paying for labor, which they considered a natural resource. In a late sixteenth-century manual on good management practices prepared for the feudal lords and their managers, this attitude was underscored: "It is not only harmful but also shameful to buy with money, as a result of neglectfulness, what could be had without expense."[96] In view of the low level of monetary circulation in Poland during this period and the unreliability of the coinage—both situations becoming graver through the seventeenth and eighteenth centuries—this management without expense was indeed economically advantageous. But why this reluctance to buy with money? The evocation of shame inclines us to suspect that its roots may be deeper than managerial styles or economic exigencies.

The efforts of the gentry to connect these two "archetypical images of society," and their bifurcated economies of the wheat field and the market, as Witold Kula reminds us, were implicitly paradoxical: The Polish gentry sought "to maximize the naturalization of production with the aim of maximizing commercialization."[97] Only by producing in the noncommercial, nonmonetary sector, by exploiting feudal relations and labor, and by maintaining the autarky of the natural sector as rigidly as possible did the feudal landlords have confidence that a profit could be derived and cash money generated, enabling them to participate in the commercial sector. Production, they believed, had to be confined to the idealized natural economy of the feudal estate, based on the personal relations of service, honor, and responsibility in accordance with God's justice, and as interpreted particularly to the cultivator by the lord and reinforced by the cleric. They claimed venerable principle and independent value for the relationship between lord and laborer first established by the feudal contract, rather than for the relationship based on money paid, established in freely negotiated contracts, and formulated in "markets where anonymous buyers and sellers face each other and communicate with each other only by means of abstract signs . . . and where God

95. See Weber's discussion of patrimonialism, *Economy and Society,* 1:231ff.
96. Gostomski, *Gospodarstwo,* ed. S. Inglot (Wrocław, 1951), 106, cited in Kula, *Economic Theory of the Feudal System,* 141.
97. Kula, *Economic Theory of the Feudal System,* 141.

is no longer present" or, at most, was represented in impersonal rules.[98] The use of money, the lords correctly suspected, weakens the personal relations between people and increases individual freedom.[99] The Polish gentry could not give free rein to this "extension of the succession of values by valueless things," as Georg Simmel describes monetary exchange.[100] This approach to personal exchange made a virtue out of what otherwise would have been their dilemma, for the level of monetary circulation in the Polish countryside was rather low.

The use of money in the natural economy, though vital to the exchange of petty goods and services, was thought to interfere with the reciprocity and *philia* upon which the feudal contract was based.[101] Organic imagery and familial models of social organization were used by Polish feudalism's enthusiasts and publicists to describe the demesne. This imagery, drawing a measure of authoritativeness from scholastic conceptions of autarky, would often be elaborated independently of active social realities and degrees of hierarchy and disharmony.[102] Models of social relations founded on mechanical images of solidarity and development, which began to prevail in the West, did not influence gentry thinking in Poland in this period.[103] Starting in the latter part of the sixteenth century, this familial and organic model of social relations was legitimated by Sarmatian patriarchal ideals and theories of Polish nationality. And as such new ideologies as physiocracy and cameralism drifted toward Poland from the West, arguments from these ideologies were selectively appropriated, in accordance with the legitimation they lent to the reality and meaning of the second serfdom.

The monetary economy included the ports of entry and the less distant markets for exchange in towns, as well as seasonal fairs. The lords' successful agricultural and financial management of the natural economy increased the scale and potential of their profit. On the basis of the Polish experience of the sixteenth and early seventeenth centuries, the Polish nobility, long after there was evidence to the contrary, assumed that there was a growing demand for Polish grain on international markets. Their economic expectations took on a taken-for-granted quality: they needed to avoid production and marketing problems in exporting grain so as to realize profits sufficient for importing manufactured goods from the

98. Lüthy, *From Calvin to Rousseau,* 93. See an analysis of this transition from status to contract in Maine, *Ancient Law,* 156–65, 422–25.
99. Simmel, *Philosophy of Money,* 297.
100. Ibid., 142.
101. Polanyi, Arensberg, and Pearson, *Trade and Market,* 76ff.; Mączak, "Money and Society," 87.
102. Walzer, "Symbolism in Political Thought," 193ff.
103. The intensified efforts of the Polish gentry to convert the Russian Orthodox serfs to Catholicism, even to the point of allowing for the type of arrangement involved in the Uniate compromise, might have had at least as much to do with the idealized social relations of the natural economy, *philia,* as it had to do with efforts to control the serfs.

West and luxury items from the East and West. Only thus could they maintain their comfortable standard of living.

Commercialization, the ability to monetize surplus into profit by participating in international markets, required some means to narrow the increasing gap between the Polish nobility's own perceptions of productivity and the economic realities determined by forces far beyond its own managerial skills and powers of imagination to shape. How did the nobles manage this gap between their high economic expectations and the more modest standard that quotidian realities could sustain? The nobles expressed awareness of this gap in the charges of *dezolacja*, "diminution in productive potential," which were not necessarily based on any evidence of wanton destructiveness but rather on the estate owners' sense of productive potential, their peculiar bookkeeping system, and the lack of consensus between landlords, serfs, and managers on the terms of productivity.[104] They often pressed these charges against their serfs, against their managers, and particularly against one sector of Poland's population from among whom the managers of the second serfdom were being recruited: Poland's Jews. For the management of estates, of gaps and contradictions, and of accusations of sabotage, we are beginning to see where the Jews fit into the contours of Polish feudalism.

Within these realities, Jewish modes of thinking and social relations occasionally enabled Jews to spot "small changes"; confronting a "challenge in the form of social or legal discrimination, they may well have been forced or stimulated to greater effort and discipline."[105] As a result of these circumstances, they may have been able to generate for themselves and for their landlords some short-term profits. But within the framework and against the contradictions of Polish feudalism, rarely could these Jews, whatever their entrepreneurial skills and their motives, turn small changes into productive forces.

Poland in the early modern period was by no means unique in the conflict that it faced between two concepts of order: one based on the natural economy, the other based on chrematistics. The ways in which Poland's gentry avoided the "pitched battle array with banners flying" that the nobility of other countries confronted had unique dimensions in its well-ordered lack of order.[106] To understand the devices by which Poland's nobles persisted in their efforts to preserve the order of feudalism, its structures and meanings, even as that institution lost its profitability and its plausibility, we must try to follow the logic by which those lords acted and by which they interpreted their situation. Maximizing "the naturalization of production with the aim of maximizing commercialization" is the stark paradox that sums up Kula's model of Polish feudalism. How the gentry did try to increase that naturalization—"by means of the *arenda*"—how the gentry used the Jew to assure themselves that "there will be a jingle," and the equivocal

104. Kula, *Economic Theory of the Feudal System,* 36.
105. Lüthy, *From Calvin to Rousseau,* 30.
106. Ibid., 98.

consequences will provide us with an interpretive entrée into the system of involvement of Jews in Poland's early modern economy. The difficulties in understanding the history of Poland and Polish Jews from anecdotes or case studies about this Polish landlord or that Jew are now clear. We require more systemic analysis of Jewish roles and functions, particularly insofar as they pertained to that shame-surrounded task, "to buy with money."

Chapter 2

From "Serfs of the Royal Chamber"
to "Serfs of the Many Chambers"

Poland in the early modern period did not lack the centralizing order developing elsewhere in Europe; but as a consequence of the efforts of the nobility, Poland's centralized authority was increasingly undermined and at times actively resisted. What was the position of Poland's Jews in the sixteenth through the eighteenth centuries, as more and more of them came under the direct or indirect control of feudal lords? And what effect did this have on the patterns of political and economic integration of Jews elsewhere?

In the sixteenth century, the security of Polish Jews was influenced by a fragile balance between centrifugal and centripetal forces operative within the Polish Republic and by a balance between diverse perceptions of Jews as being useful but pernicious outsiders to Polish society. For example, I have already hinted at the equivocal influence of Jews on the rise of the second serfdom that resulted from the initial position of a sizable Jewish population at the periphery of the feudal estate: Jews monetized the surplus grain that the serfs produced within the natural economy. With cash, the serfs could make their obligatory payments to the nobility but could also sidestep the reciprocity on which the lords based the natural economy. And, if sufficiently resourceful, the serfs could altogether escape the clutches of the feudal estate. Jews, by making cash available to the serfs, both fostered and resisted the conditions and the terms for the consolidation of that institution.

The situation of Poland's Jews became more and more precarious as these balances affecting Jewish security were increasingly upset by factors inherent to Polish society and gentry culture, as well as by political scheming carried out in St. Petersburg, Berlin, and Vienna and by economic transactions in Danzig, Amsterdam, London, and Madrid. This growing precariousness, experienced by Polish

Jewry in the mid-seventeenth century, was followed by a general pattern of deterioration in their political and economic conditions through much of the eighteenth century. It coincided with a period of new opportunities for Jews in the West. Those Jews were being readmitted into countries and city-states from which they had been expelled or excluded for centuries; small Jewish communities were being expanded and fortified under polities that were becoming increasingly centralized, with monarchies that were becoming more absolutist, and with economies that were fostering commerce domestically and internationally.[1] Yet although the conditions of Jews in the West and in Poland from the mid-seventeenth century on appeared to move along diverging trajectories, elusive connections may have made them more interdependent than is commonly recognized.[2] Against this background we must view the range of functions of Jewish initiatives within the political economy of Polish feudalism and understand how the Jews themselves interpreted these function. Specifically, we will examine how Jews bridged two looming gaps: in Poland's domestic relation, the discrepancies that were developing between the natural and monetary economies; in Poland's foreign relations, the position that Poland could assume between the patterns of political and economic development in the East and West.

The transformation that followed in the political situation of Polish Jews from the domain of centralized authority to that of smaller political provinces is similar to a transition whose significance the eminent Jewish historian Salo Baron underscores: the declining centralization of the Holy Roman Empire, beginning in the High Middle Ages, and its effect upon Jews.[3] Their status changed from "serfs of the royal chamber" to "serfs of many chambers." The less effectively that popes or emperors were able to intervene on behalf of Jews, the more subject the Jews became to enormous variations, instability, unpredictable legislative and administrative acts, and "alternating fits of tolerance and intolerance."

The weakening of central authority in Poland had a similar effect on Polish Jews. They could not enlist the support of the monarchy against intermittent and alternating attacks of the clergy, magnates, gentry, burghers, and peasants as effectively as earlier. But the feudal anarchy may not have been "devoid of a silver

1. The Muscovite kingdom to Poland's east had few Jews until 1772, when it annexed areas of Poland. I will consider Russian absolutism and Russian policies toward Jews in chapters 4 and 5.
2. Israel, *European Jewry in the Age of Mercantilism;* see my review, Levine, "Judaism and Mercantilism."
3. Baron, *A Social and Religious History of the Jews,* 9:135–47, 190–92. His structural analysis of that transition and the great significance he assigns to it suggest that we pause to consider this comparison, insofar as it may elucidate the political context of Polish Jewry in the early modern period. Within the perennial contest between emperor and pope for hegemony, papal claims of exclusive authority over Jews had been an integral part of the strategy by which certain popes sought to establish and demonstrate the supreme authority of the church over the Western world, the "plenitude of Apostolic power." With the political fragmentation of the Holy Roman Empire, the Jews became subject to the inconsistent and spasmodic policies of the medieval states.

lining," as Baron suggests for earlier periods of decentralized authority (and hints at in comparison with some of the negative consequences for Jews of nineteenth- and twentieth-century European nationalism). The decline in Poland's central authority protected Jews from the large-scale decrees, such as the expulsions that befell their coreligionists during the Middle Ages in Western European countries possessing stronger central institutions. It may also have increased the "psychological alertness, the pioneering spirit, and the communal cohesiveness" of Polish Jewry.

But this broad shift of Jews, from the domain of the weakening royal chamber to the realm of the factitious chambers, which was of singular importance to the history of Polish Jewry in the early modern period, also may have had unanticipated consequences in the West for the new connections that were being forged between princes and individual Jewish entrepreneurs, beginning in the mid-seventeenth century. Studies of these court Jews underscore their influence on the rise of absolutism and finance capitalism as well as their impact on the entry of their coreligionists into the mainstream of European society, the attainment of Jewish economic and political rights, and the development of ambivalence at the core of modern Jewish identity. These studies, however, pay insufficient attention to the actual political and economic transactions and to the reciprocal attitudes, the complex social reference, between court Jews and their Polish-Jewish trading partners.[4] What were the relations of these two social types and entrepreneurial personalities, the court Jew and the arendar, both of whom appear as the rates and patterns of development in Western and Eastern Europe begin to diverge, with consequences evident in this day?

The Gentry, the Burghers, and the Jews

Jewish alliances with the gentry were first prompted by considerations other than the weakening of centralized authority. In an earlier period, Jews sought protection from the efforts of the burghers to curtail Jewish business rights and even residential privileges. In the late fifteenth century, Jews in many Polish towns had been forced by the burghers to sign agreements limiting their rights to engage in trade.[5] But the Jews could circumvent these restrictions by teaming up with the gentry, who were pleased by the opportunity to use the Jews to break the financial power of the burghers and to lower prices. Under these arrangements, Jews could even benefit indirectly from gentry privileges. For example, imported merchandise procured through gentry channels was often free from duties and taxes. Insofar as the gentry passed on any of their savings to their Jewish agents, these Jewish merchants had a competitive advantage over burgher merchants. This only added to burgher resentment toward the Jews.

4. Stern, *The Court Jew;* Schnee, *Die Hoffinanz und der moderne Staat;* For a critical review of these works, see Francis Carsten, "The Court Jews," 140–56; and Katz, *Tradition and Crisis,* 56ff., and *Out of the Ghetto,* 28–31, 47.
5. Schipper, "Economic History of the Jews in Poland-Lithuania," 1:165.

In many towns, even where Jews met the strongest opposition from the burghers, the Jewish population increased dramatically. By the eighteenth century Jews comprised at least half of the population of towns. The gentry, in this effort to break the economic strength of the burghers, rented facilities to Jews in their town houses and urban courts. A good example of this can be seen in Cracow, from where Jews were largely excluded, even though in 1576 the Polish king issued an edict protecting Jewish trade from the attacks of the guilds and petty burghers. A noble landlord encouraged them to settle across the Vistula in Kazimierz.[6] This noble "hospitality" removed many Jews and Jewish communities from the domain of centralized authority.[7] At the same time, the efforts of Jews to protect themselves from the burghers and to compensate for the declining powers of royal patrons were not without their costs. Jews became increasingly subject to the whims of local rulers, many of whom were small-scale and capricious tyrants. This vulnerability in turn made the coordinating function of centralized and federated Jewish institutions all the more significant.

The unreliability of this protection afforded by the alliance with the gentry became obvious at an early point. By the mid-sixteenth century there is evidence of nobles murmuring against Jewish control of trade.[8] Thus these new economic roles for Jews further alienated the burghers without necessarily enlisting strong and dependable support from nobles. The benefit to individual lords from Jewish economic activities varied in accordance with their own resources and the specific trade, financial, and managerial services offered by Jews. But even those members of the aristocracy who benefited the most from Jewish trade would not necessarily refrain from expressing moral indignation and a principled rejection of the propriety and even the economic benefits of commerce. These expressions, as spontaneous and original as they sounded, could draw form and substance from venerable traditions of economic thinking, bolstered by theological discourses. What Louis Dumont calls the "primitive idea," that in trade the gain of one person is made at the expense of another, had a long and influential career in Poland, particularly regarding Poland's Jews.[9] These self-serving attitudes toward trade were mediated by clerics and publicists, whose own resentment, like that of the feudal lords, did not inhibit them from being the beneficiaries of Jewish enterprise. Both the institutional arrangement and the attitude it evoked are confirmed by the sixteenth-century Dutch traveler (cited in chapter 1), who observed in regard to Polish Jews that "allmost all trade is in theire handes, the Poles esteeming it sordide."

As Everett Hughes reminds us, members of the majority (the "good people") relegate certain indispensable tasks (the "dirty work") to members of a minority group while at the same time denigrating the value of those economic and social

6. Ibid.; Bałaban, *Historja żydów w Krakowie i na Kazimierzu.*
7. Murray Rosman assesses these economic and social relations. "The Polish Magnates and the Jews."
8. Schipper, "Economic History," 166.
9. Dumont, *From Mandeville to Marx,* 33ff. This theme will be developed in chapter 3.

functions.[10] The intensity with which the Polish gentry condemned Jewish roles and functions within the unacknowledged social order that the gentry constructed may be related to the Jews' ultimate utility to Polish feudalism. The Jews were needed not only to manage but also to maintain the gentry's presumption, as Kula pithily and paradoxically summarized it, that by intensifying the profitability of the natural economy, the gentry would enjoy more benefits from the commercial economy. It is within this context of the gentry's efforts to naturalize the Jews, to move an increasing number from the "chamber" to the "chambers," from towns to gentry villages, from free trade and crafts to trade and management related to the gentry's "natural" or agriculturally based and controlled economy, that we must examine new developments in the early modern period. By making Jewish peddlers into managers and even subcontractors, nobles seemingly solved some problems while creating others. In this position of Polish Jews, between serf, burgher, and gentry, we begin to sense the different fate of Jews in Poland and Jews in Western Europe, from the conclusion of a hundred years of religious wars in the mid-seventeenth century through the French Revolution.

The Economics of the Arenda

At the end of the sixteenth century, Jews became more prominent as leaseholders, or arendars, particularly on the estates of the nobility. The nobility was becoming more oligarchical; magnates were distinguishable by their wealth and landholdings, which were increasing, particularly in the newly annexed and newly settled areas of southeastern Poland and the Ukraine. Jews not only took up administrative positions on these larger estates but also serviced the lower nobility and competed with Christian administrators of the crown lands. The proportion of adult male Jews becoming arendars is not clear. Many Jews continued as artisans and merchants, on the smaller estates and in the villages. But professions were not always so well differentiated. What is clear, however, is the significance of Jews in this type of estate management. It is estimated that by 1616 well over half the crown estates in the Ukraine were managed by Jewish arendars. One magnate, Prince Konstanty Ostrorog, allegedly employed more than four thousand agents.[11] I shall return to the contradiction posed by the presence of this

10. Hughes, "Good People and Dirty Work," 3–11.
11. The terms of these agreements between gentry and Jews are illustrated in the following contract of 1594: "Prince Piotr Zabrzeski hereby leases all his possessions . . . in the district of Krzemieniec, including the old and new city of Krzemieniec, New Zbaraz and Kolsec with all the settlements appertaining to these estates, together with the noble boyars, the burghers, and the serfs of those cities and villages . . . all their debts, obligations and privileges, with the arendas, taverns, tolls, ponds, the mills and their revenues, the manors, the various tithes paid by the boyars, burghers and serfs of those districts, together with all the other revenues, to Mr. Mikolaj Wransowicz and to Efraim the Jew of Miedzyboz, for the amount of 9,000 zlotys of the Polish currency, for three years." Davies, *God's Playground,* 1:444. See also the many examples supplied by Goldberg, *Jewish Privileges in the Polish Commonwealth.*

quintessential outsider in a social order predicated, as Polish feudalism was, upon *philia,* reciprocity, and personal relations between lord and serf.

The Jewish arendars managed the gentry's estates (including serfs) in exchange for a fixed payment made to the landlord. Jews took all kinds of concessions in this manner; sometimes they even managed whole villages and oversaw the economic development and exploitation of forests, mines, mints, custom houses, toll roads, and breweries on the gentry's estates, using serf labor. Often a leaseholder brought in other Jews to help him manage an estate; concessions would be distributed to sublessees. Entire new Jewish communities were established in this manner. The economic power of the earliest lessee would often result in oligarchical forms of *kehilla* (Jewish communal structures) and their attendant strains. Although these communities functioned to some extent like the magnates' courts with their dependent gentry, they tried to take measures to limit the arbitrary power of the Jewish leaseholder over his sublessees. At the same time, involvement in the arenda contributed to the geographic spread and ruralization of many Jews. This added to problems of communal cohesiveness and collective protection of Jewish interests. Indeed, it may not be a historical accident that the federated structures of the Council of Four Lands developed simultaneously with the accelerated entrance of Jews into the arenda. The council was particularly well suited to respond to this new geographical and administrative position of Polish Jews, both in relation to the monarchy and in relation to the gentry.

Historians have often explained the arenda by noting that the magnates overextended themselves in cultivating new territories, or that members of the aristocracy were lazy and preferred to sit in their townhouses in Warsaw, Cracow, or provincial capitals and collect their rents—all of which might be true. But this system of leases was in fact integral to the feudal economy and to the gentry's economic thinking. It displays the complexity of economic and political ties between the gentry and the Jews. By leasing estates or directing concessions such as toll roads, bridges, mines, small manufactures, or stores to Jews for a fixed fee, the nobleman owner could reduce his short-term financial risk, ensuring for himself (if his Jewish agents were competent) a fixed income. Insofar as he may have underestimated the financial potential of assets or under circumstances where a particularly diligent and entrepreneurial arendar extracted unanticipated revenues, the lord could still increase his benefit. He could exploit short-term leases or threaten to accuse his Jewish agent of sabotage in order to extort more favorable terms or, if necessary, to recruit a new arendar. A steady stream of arendars-in-waiting was always prepared to undercut the position of their coreligionists by accepting the lord's demands. Jewish communal and supercommunal agencies tried doggedly, but on the whole without success to control the allocation of these arendar contracts so that Jews would not undermine each other or accept financial terms that they could not uphold, since the community was held responsible for the bankruptcy and debts of individuals.

In short, the Jews served as a primitive form of insurance for the risk-averse gentry; nobles demonstrated their disregard for all except immediate gain. The Jews' responsibility under these circumstances was to extract revenue and raise profits rather than increase productivity from the gentry's assets. The economics of this managerial arrangement did not provide for long-term benefits. Jews, who were pressed to make such enterprises profitable, often against the influence of pervasive market and social forces, were motivated to develop technical and managerial innovations to squeeze profits out of the margins. These included more rigorous supervision of the serfs and more efficient collection of rents and taxes, adding to the harshness of the serfs' lives and by no means making the Jewish arendar beloved. Neither did these pressures for immediate profitability increase the sense of *philia* within the natural economy or strengthen the loyalty of the serfs to their masters. In view of the short time frame within which the gentry held their Jewish arendars accountable for generating profits, and the dire circumstances to which their failure would lead, the arendars were not likely to make capital improvements that might lighten the burden of the serf or husband resources that ultimately might increase productivity. There were few incentives to repair the broken bridges.

The gentry mandated their rate of return from Jews through other financial arrangements as well. It has often been noted that Jews in the seventeenth and eighteenth centuries altered their role from that of moneylender to that of borrower. This alleged need to borrow has been taken as a measure of the declining economic position of Jews. In the first decades of the seventeenth century the kehillot had tried, again unsuccessfully, to regulate these arrangements. Increasingly there were Jewish bankruptcies and occurrences of the *boreiaḥ* (escaper) or *baal peleita* (Jewish defaulter), who evaded his creditors and sought to start anew in the unsettled and semi-incorporated borderlands between Poland, Russia, and the Ottoman Empire. These incidents, reports of which are by no means uncommon in extant communal records, jeopardized Jewish security.[12] Because of the interconnections between Jewish enterprises and the collective responsibility enforced against Jews, the financial reversals of an overextended individual could spell financial ruin for many. But this Jewish borrowing activity may have been more the cause than the consequence of incipient Jewish poverty. Money loans were often forced upon Jews by the nobility and clergy, who were looking for a fixed rate of return at a time when Europe was being flooded by waves of gold and silver from the Americas. Money was not holding its value, and prices were fluctuating, particularly for the luxury items that the gentry sought on international markets.

The success of Polish Jews in this period in squeezing profits from unprofitable enterprises and in returning unrealistically high yields from mandatory loans had something to do with their capacity to take advantage of their international connections. Indeed, the rise of the arendars must be compared with, and even

12. Halpern, ed., *Pinkas Vaad Arba Araẓot,* 557; Dubnow, ed., *Pinkas Hammedina,* 343.

linked to, the rise of the better-known court Jews in Central and Western Europe. Ascertaining the economic advantages provided by these international connections requires further research. What is clear is that reliable sources of capital and matériel available in Poland, including grain, hide, and potash, were of great importance to absolutist princes in pursuing their policies of centralization and expansion through military efforts. The princes' depleted war chests were filled with gold coins that their Jewish financiers obtained from their Polish co-religionists, who scoured the countryside for undervalued florins. The court Jews rose to power and wealth in the mid-seventeenth century by making loans and purveying matériel. They were more successful in this venture than their non Jewish competitors because of their connections with Polish Jewish arendars. The argument could be made that the Polish magnates, in fostering decentralization in Poland through the trade and moneylending taking place between Polish arendars and Western court Jews, contributed to the financing of political absolutism and early industrial enterprise elsewhere in Europe. However causal this connection may be between centralization in one region and decentralization in another, and at a subsequent stage between development and backwardness, cannot be determined at the present time. That there was some connection, however, is difficult to deny.[13]

For the Polish magnates, promoting the Jews rather than déclassé aristocrats, many of whom were retainers of the magnates and a tremendous drain on the resources of the court, reduced the political risks of the magnates. Members of the lower nobility, placed in similar enterprises and afforded the opportunity to attain a measure of financial independence, were more likely than Jews to use their economic positions to plot antimagnate intrigues. Although this unlanded nobility might have been organized into a civil service of the magnates, much as their counterparts in other parts of Central and Eastern Europe had been organized in the service of the rising absolutist princes, for the Polish magnates this may have been more difficult and more risky to attempt. The Polish aristocracy, unlike other European aristocracies, had remained without formal ranks despite the great differences that developed in the power and wealth of individuals. With the availability of Jewish managerial services there was less incentive for the magnates to subordinate unwieldy lords who zealously preserved their formal egalitarianism by recruiting them into the operations of the estate. The magnates may have thought that in the long run, it would be less expensive to support their fellow nobles' frivolousness than to pay for their rebelliousness. And in regard to the Jewish managers of their estates, the Polish feudal lords may have intuitively felt what the mid-seventeenth century Venetian rabbi Simeon Luzzatto (whose claims about Jewish profitability we already have had reason to consider) expressed categorically: "how faithful the Jews are." Moreover, Jewish dependency made Jewish managers more dependable. Debts to Jews could be reimbursed and

13. Israel, *European Jewry,* 123–33, 140–41, 256. Israel's assessment points to the need for a systematic analysis of the court Jew rather than the presentation of anecdotes.

payments for services could be made by means of concessions that were of negligible cost to the gentry; the privilege not to be expelled is a good example.[14] Particularly in the late eighteenth century, the gentry allowed themselves to act with a degree of capriciousness and violence toward their Jewish arendars that would have provoked sanctions from fellow nobles.

In those countries of Western Europe where the seeds of the modern nation-state were being planted and where it was becoming increasingly important to gauge the inner nature and outer standing of the Jew in relation to national interests rather than to feudal contracts, this claim about Jewish faithfulness provided an argument for the enfranchisement of Jews. The kind of violence against Jews that was commonplace in early modern Poland was less in evidence in Central and Western Europe, where Jewish usefulness was more readily acknowledged and where economic thinking included longer-range perspectives.

Thus Jews who retained their formal status as "serfs of the chamber" but in reality were becoming "serfs of many chambers" were caught in the struggle between the monarchy and the magnates as well as in that between the magnates and the lower nobility. At the same time, they were placed in positions of rivalry with the interests of every other segment of Polish society: the burghers, the peasants, and the clergy. The burghers, who were being undermined by the gentry and by their own inadaptability in the face of new competition against which their guilds could not protect them, blamed their decline on the Jews. The peasants were becoming more rebellious as the terms of their enserfment became less beneficial, a function of the declining Polish economy. Peasant discontent had harmful consequences for the Jews, who were becoming the most visible agents of the peasants' enserfment. The clergy's interests were most often aligned with those of the landed aristocracy. But its members generously provided religious zeal to fan the antagonism of members of all of Poland's classes toward the Jews. In the fragmented society that Poland was quickly becoming, one of the few rallying points was that antagonism. Shared passions could be readily used to obfuscate and conceal divergent interests.

Jewish Responses to the Arenda

The general hostility and sporadic attacks against the Jews notwithstanding, there is little evidence that Jews responded apprehensively to the major economic and political shifts taking place in Poland from the end of the sixteenth century. Quite the contrary. The descendants of Ashkenazic Jewry, whose forefathers had been confined to moneylending and a few other occupations, now demonstrated alacrity in facing the new opportunities, even if they sensed that other Poles deemed certain of these vocations "sordide." Some Jewish religious and lay leaders, however, did have misgivings. First, new economic opportunities and the temptations that accompanied them, particularly as they resulted in

14. Ibid., 88.

increased contact between Jews and Gentiles, might overwhelm the provisions of *halakha* (Jewish law) and the legacy of Ashkenazic Jewry.[15] Second, there were specific problems and risks resulting from the increasing Jewish stake in, and involvement with, the rising power of the magnates and the contractual arrangement by which more and more Jews developed strong ties to the aristocracy rather than to the monarchy. This contract, the arenda, was not always entered into voluntarily by the Jewish arendar; neither was its profitability to both parties assured.

At an early point in the institutionalization of the arenda system, rabbis and communal leaders, sensing the dangers that it posed for individual Jews and for Jewish communities, made some effort, albeit unsuccessful, to prohibit it. Often, it was the founders and local leaders of small communities who were most heavily involved in the arenda. They recruited other Jews to take up residence on a gentry estate or village. There the new Jewish residents serviced the arendars as sub-lessees and religious functionaries. This genesis of many Polish Jewish communities strengthened oligarchical tendencies. Well into the eighteenth century, as Jewish involvement in the different types of arenda proved to be more intractable, the communities tried to regulate that involvement; as it proved to be more profitable, the leaders of the kehillot attempted to tax the profits of individual Jews. Payments to the gentry and the king, together with large-scale Jewish poverty, led to the accumulation of enormous communal debts.

In one of the first edicts of the Council of Four Lands, promulgated in 1581, the arenda is discussed:

> May it be known to all the people of the land, the holy people of the covenant, that the heads and leaders of the Four Lands, when they observed the status and the situation of the lands at this time, which require strengthening, particularly in regard to those who are gluttonously drawn to bribes and money with which to enrich themselves by means of the great and mighty arendas, [declare:] It is necessary to be concerned lest they lead to great danger for the majority, heaven forbid. Therefore, we have made a unanimous agreement: all those who would be called by name of Israel should not have any involvement with the *czopowe* [a royal tax on drink], not in Poland Major nor in Poland Minor, nor in Mazovia, not that instituted by the King, may he be exalted, nor that by the rulers, nor by any subterfuge in the world. Neither should they lease any mint, nor a *zupa* [salt mine] in these lands, nor [collect] any custom duties, that is the duty at Cracow, Poznań, and their regions. None of these should any Jew lease in any of these manners nor should he be involved in any of these enterprises in any fashion. And any person who deigns to lease or to be involved in these matters in any conceivable way, an inevitable edict will be his to be excommunicated from the two worlds.[16]

15. See Katz, *Goy Shel Shabbat,* 70–83.
16. Halpern, *Pinkas,* 1.

The edict continues with a vivid portrayal of the social ostracism threatened in the harshest terms against the flouters of such communal regulations. It was ratified in Cracow in 1595 and in several communal registries in subsequent years, fortified by "the curse with the seven Tora scrolls . . . and strengthened with the above-mentioned punishments." Solomon Luria (1510–1574) noted that the activities of Jews in regard to this occupation were under the jurisdiction of the law of the king and local custom.[17] Rabbi Joel Sirkes (d. 1640), one of the outstanding rabbinic scholars of the period, commented but a few years later: The danger was vast from the shouting of the Gentiles in the majority of places, [who complain] that the Jews reign and rule over them and hold them as do kings and princes."[18] The condemnation of the arenda on moral grounds in the communal edicts is secondary to its rejection on political grounds, hinted at in those edicts but made explicit by Rabbi Sirkes.[19]

Other dangerous consequences of the arenda were cited in the communal registries. An edict of 1590 described the dilemma in regard to Sabbath observances of the arendar who leased a tavern or had concessions to sell the peasants alcoholic beverages, often in a corner of his house. The edict warned against some of the devices employed by Jewish arendars to circumvent Sabbath prohibitions against touching coins or using a Gentile worker to handle payments.[20] An edict of 1627 expressed concern for the security of the wives of arendars residing in small and isolated villages who may be left alone because of their husbands' travels.[21] A 1628 edict issued in Lithuania forbade the employment of non-Jewish female servants but made allowances to arendars who had special need of assistance.[22] Similarly, concern was expressed for the spiritual and intellectual development of yeshiva students who became arendars in areas where there were no scholars.[23] But efforts to limit Jewish involvement in the arenda, in the face of both the dire economic situation of Jews and the opportunities for profitability that these concessions represented, seem to have been futile.

17. See chapter 3. Luria, *Sheelot Uteshuvot Maharshal,* 36. Shemuel Shilo contends that the principled argument of *dina demalekhuta dina* (the law of the state is law) is not made in this connection for another two hundred and fifty years. Shilo, *Dina Demalekhuta Dina,* 418.

18. Sirkes, *Sheelot Uteshuvot Bayit Ḥadash,* no. 61; Halpern, *Pinkas,* 45.

19. Katz, *Goy Shel Shabbat,* 82, does not refer to this source in asserting that the discussion of serf labor takes place only within the context of Sabbath laws. Similarly, in assessing the responses to the Chmielnicki massacres, he does not emphasize the occasional political meaning assigned to those events within the elegiac literature and theodicies. These interpretations of cataclysms, in reference to the worldly relations of serfs and Jews, hardly constitute evidence of full-blown consciousness of "natural causation," a consciousness that Katz asserts does not exist. But they point to some efforts to provide a naturalistic explanation.

20. Halpern, *Pinkas,* 483ff.; Katz, *Goy Shel Shabbat,* 70ff.

21. Dubnow, *Pinkas Hammedina,* 28.

22. Ibid., 35.

23. Ibid., 10.

In 1676 the ban on the arenda was repeated, but the emphasis was now placed on communal regulation:

> Anything in the world, whatever it may be, anything that the mouth can express and the heart can think about, no person in the world is permitted to lease without the permission of the *kahal*. He must go before the *kahal* and make a proposal for what he seeks, and the leaders must assess this matter quite thoroughly, not in his presence. When there is an agreement among the majority to approve it, it must be inscribed in the *pinkas* [communal record book] of the *kahal* and then he is permitted to lease. He is not allowed to use any form of subterfuge using a Gentile partner and the like.[24]

This edict was registered in the communal registry of Tykocin (Tiktin) with a note appended that "apparently this matter has been forgotten. Therefore, in accordance with the needs of the hour, it must be announced again." Among their regulatory efforts, local communities began to control the arenda, because of both the danger of internal friction and its potential to undermine placid and predictable relations with the gentry. Control over the arenda became a source of discord between communities. The arenda was numbered among the personal assets of an individual that a just community had to protect. It fell within the domain of such halakhic considerations as *ḥazaka* (rights of possession) and inheritance law.[25] Nevertheless, several edicts, particularly in the pinkas of Lithuania, asserted the prerogative of the communal leaders—who might take a more pragmatic view—rather than that of the judges or rabbis to oversee its regulation.[26] Though religious-legal issues might have been raised by these transactions requiring the clarification of rabbis and judges (who might be assumed to be more impartial adjudicators because of less personal involvement), communal leaders were favored. There was particular concern not to allow noble landlords to gain the upper hand in negotiations by pitting one Jew against another and bidding up the price for concessions. At the same time, this concern and the claims of ḥazaka could not be allowed to stifle what was deemed to be reasonable and healthy competition.[27] Old privileges and acknowledged entitlements could not be permitted completely to curtail the economic opportunities of the young and of newcomers.[28] The principle "he who comes first, benefits" had to

24. Halpern, *Pinkas,* 148ff.
25. See Liebermann, *Taḥarut Iskit Bahalakha,* for a survey of the economic and non-economic arguments in regard to trespass.
26. Dubnow, *Pinkas Hammedina,* 18.
27. Luria, *Sheelot Uteshuvot Maharshal,* 35–36; Meir of Lublin, *Sheelot Uteshuvot Maharam Lublin.* Sirkes, *Sheelot Uteshuvot Bayit Ḥadash Hayeshanot,* 60–61.
28. Sirkes, *Sheelot Uteshuvot,* 59. The Lithuanian Council in 1634 complained that the arenda was creating a situation where "there is no sustenance" in some communities. It concluded, "We do not know what to do about this; we will bring up this issue at the next meeting."

be balanced against situations where it should be forbidden for "anyone who would be called by the name of Israel to stick his head into any matter of the *arenda.*"[29]

This assessment of the deleterious effects of the arenda was not shared by all Jews at the time. In 1624 the Lithuanian kehilla openly approved at least one branch of the arenda—the leasing of tolls—assisting a group of lessees in this endeavor and arguing that Jews should retain control "for it is a foundation upon which everything is dependent . . . for by this Jews will maintain the upper hand." Notwithstanding the dangers of Gentile resentment, the leaders of the community who endorsed the edict saw in this arrangement considerable benefit for Jews, commenting wishfully, "Would that it would be in all the lands of the Jewish diaspora that Jews would control the tolls in that their hand would be on top."[30]

With the development and internal differentiation of the arenda, special situations arose. Increasing opportunities for contracts on brewing, distilling, and purveying alcoholic drink—the *szynk* (in Yiddish *shenk*) or *propinacja*—were recorded beginning in the 1630s, particularly in Lithuania. These opportunities were viewed as a possible remedy to the poverty and decline in population that seemed to afflict this region. Communal leaders appeared eager to expand this enterprise:

"He who holds an arenda in any city in which fifteen or more households reside, or one in which there was, from olden times, a community of fifteen households, an established synagogue, and a cantor, even if at this time there is no such community because people have uprooted themselves, because of their tribulations having lost their property—therefore if the residents of this city want to protest against the ḥazaka of the arendar, claiming that as a result of this they have no sustenance in the city, the matter is given over into the hands of the leader of the court to judge and to adjudicate to grant or to make loss for the arendar against the residents of this city, the ḥazaka of the szynk, and alcoholic drinks, according to what they see fit, in order to give sustenance to others. And even if he got this ḥazaka through abundant money, the people of the court can determine how much to give him because of this. And because he had dealt with this arenda for many years, they do not have the power to trespass until the end of the period. And under any circumstance, the decrees of the ḥazaka of the arenda for many years stand, that no Israelite has the right to stick in his head without the leader of the court, to trespass over his boundaries in the hands of the arendar and his friends, except as is explained in the pinkas.[31]

29. Dubnow, *Pinkas Hammedina,* 14.
30. Ḥayim Hillel Ben-Sasson, *Hagut Vehanhaga* (Jerusalem, 1959), 138.
31. Dubnow, *Pinkas Hammedina,* 67. This special provision for the szynk is repeated some years later, in 1687. Ibid., 211.

Similarly, in regard to the arenda on the mint, special conditions and dangers required special provisions. Because of all the turbulence about coinage, the Lithuanian council warned that there was no way to know the main outcome of coins until the king and gentry convened in council there in Warsaw.

It was decided that no person who calls himself by the name of Israel should stick his head in matters of the work of the coinage, nor in rental or in any service or in any partnership until the time of the council in Warsaw that should happen in good time, and the land will be quiet and satisfied in the matter of coinage, in order that there not be additional danger. Only then will all people have permission to trade, but only with our knowledge and permission. If it should be an important matter to trade there in Warsaw, he should receive permission from the emissaries of the state of Lithuania, from the intercessors who will be there, and if he should be on the borders of any country to trade, he should receive permission from the head of the local court.[32]

The Arenda as Institutional Solution and Conceptual Problem

The perception of danger was realistic, even if the precise sources of this danger were not completely understood. As we have seen, accumulated animosity toward the rulers of the land was deflected toward the Jews, who were becoming the most visible representations of the second serfdom. The serfs blamed the Jews for the unfavorable turn that the single-crop economy had taken, and for the oppressive brutality by which polish feudalism was sustained; the burghers blamed them for the decline of town life in Poland, for the curtailment of some of the burghers' traditional freedom, and for purported losses resulting from the new sources of trade and crafts that the Jews generated and with which burgher guilds could not compete; the lower and déclassé aristocracy blamed them for the growing economic gap between themselves and the magnates, in an aristocracy, unlike others in Europe, where, there was no formalization of rank to explain disparities in wealth. The Jews were indeed most visible where these changes occurred and could conveniently be blamed for a system that was bringing various miseries to different sectors of Polish society.

But one source of strong serf resentment toward the Jews had to do not only with envy or perceived injury, and it points to a deep contradiction in Polish feudalism. I have examined the idealized image of the feudal estate as it derived from the medieval theory of feudalism and as it served to promote and legitimate Poland's second serfdom. The system of exchange on the feudal estate was completely embedded within and controlled by the estate's social relations. Those social relations were modeled after the image of the family or household (*oikos*). The lord saw himself as the patriarch. The images that integrated the feudal estate

32. Ibid., 15–16.

were organic. Its social relations were based on nonmonetary exchange; its conceptions of supply, demand, and need were governed by reciprocity. Money was thought to lead to an unwarranted abstraction of those social relations, as exchange with the outside could lead to the disintegration of the household and its domestic authority.[33]

The landlord, the noble patriarch, in developing the internal organization of the household, might have established a staff without violating the demands of *philia*. This unexceptional transition—as Max Weber describes it, moving from patriarchalism to patrimonialism—seems to have taken place in Poland, with the expansion of Poland's area of settlement and the consolidation of its feudal estates.[34] Why, then, was the institutionalization of the arenda disruptive, and how did this Jewish involvement in the arenda affect the way in which Jews were perceived, even long after the demise of that institution?

The incorporation of an increasing number of Jews into the feudal estate beginning at the end of the sixteenth century was perhaps a more visible dimension of fundamental changes taking place in Polish society. This incorporation of Jews was inconsistent with the idealized image of that feudal estate, but the terms of this idealization were now in flux. What came to be called Sarmatianism, as we have seen, was the most influential Polish codification and record of that idealized and sentimentalized image of feudal society. In its earlier versions Sarmatianism had identified all Poles as the descendants of the nation of Sarmatia, who they considered to be the progenitors of the Slavic peoples and who were alleged to have been the only successful resisters to the domination of the Roman Empire. This was a useful political myth when the Polish monarchs were trying to Polonize geographically peripheral groups and consolidate the internal organization of the country. But the new terms of Sarmatianism, developing in Poland at the same time that the gentry magnates were growing in political power and the Jews were being recruited into the feudal estates, ascribed descent from the Sarmatians only to the gentry. Moreover, in what may well have been a result of residual Renaissance influences, the Polish gentry in this period began to identify more with the Roman elite than with those who resisted Rome. Sprinkling one's discourse with Latin catchphrases became a fashionable Sarmatian affectation among the nobles. This shift in the focus of Sarmatianism, from the Polish people as God's proud, free, chosen nation to the Polish aristocracy reflected and perhaps contributed to the changes in the structure of Polish serfdom and the development of the arenda.[35] The recruitment of a patrimonial staff from an alien and despised population and the effort to transfer patrimonial authority by means of contractual arrangement differed from the "ideal-typical" transition from pa-

33. See Ferdinand Tönnies's well-known but somewhat dated study, *Community and Society*. For a suggestive analysis of money and forms of social relations, see Simmel, *Philosophy of Money*.
34. Weber, *Economy and Society*, 1:231ff.; Polanyi, Arensberg, and Pearson, eds., *Trade and Markets in the Early Empires*, 77.
35. Cynarski, "Shape of Sarmatian Ideology," 9ff.

triarchalism to patrimonialism. The Polish lords, in establishing the arenda, were introducing a population that for religious reasons could not partake in the Christian household and share in the reciprocity of *philia*. The hiring of Jewish managers, the arendars, with their leasing system and franchising of assets, violated the very core of the feudal contract.[36]

Violation of that contract led to peasant violence. The deepest humiliation for those placed under Jewish domination stemmed from religious emotions, which Rabbi Sirkes correctly sensed. Jews in positions of authority, in which they could dominate Christians, challenged deeply felt religious beliefs shared by serf and lord alike regarding the lowliness of Jews and the exaltation of the Christian pious. Although the increase of Jewish involvement may have strengthened the administration of the feudal estate's natural economy institutionally, the presence of Jews and the authority that they were delegated undermined the foundations of Polish feudalism conceptually.

Likewise, there were fundamental contradictions between the important organizational function of Jewish arendars and the conceptual implications of this function in relation to another premise of Polish feudalism: autarky. The Jews were working both for and against perceived gentry interests in connecting the economy of the feudal estates to other economies, including domestic and international markets. Jews were essential in organizing the transport and marketing of the gentry's grain to distant markets, since they were involved in importing luxury items.[37] Thus, they helped the gentry overcome the contradiction between an idealized economy of reciprocity and self-sufficiency and the satisfaction of their wants, which could be achieved only through participation in market economies. At the same time Jewish peddlers, on a lower scale, enabled the serfs, in the demonetized economy of the Polish feudal estate, to transform surplus grain into cash and thereby to participate in markets. The effect of this semicommercialized and monetized serf economy on markets, when compared with the influence of the magnates, whose resources were much greater, was probably minimal. That is, the amount of grain that the serfs, via Jewish peddlers, could sell, even on local markets, would not have radically depressed the prices that the gentry could obtain. Nor could serfs bid up the prices on merchandise that the gentry would seek. Nevertheless, the way in which Jewish peddlers enabled serfs to participate in money markets weakened the idealized autarky of the estate. And if indeed, as Kula asserts, the gentry persisted in seeing their ability to participate in commercial markets as contingent upon their success in naturalizing production, the Jews were playing at best an ambiguous role: by making the feudal estate work economically, they were weakening its idealized image. Members of the Polish gentry, part of whose power included the ability to influence attitudes and define realities, could focus selectively and at their convenience on one function or the other of Jews, on what they deemed profitable or destructive, in assessing

36. Topolski, "Causes of Dualism."
37. Rosman, "Polish Magnates," 231ff.

the utility of Jews to the feudal estate. Is it any wonder, then, that the gentry, in their personal contact with Jews, seemed to be capricious?

This equivocal position of the Jews in the arenda in relation to different segments of Polish society took on demonic overtones, leading at times to murderous and violent enactments. This was the case particularly after 1625, with the elapse of the rather short period during which the Polish grain trade was relatively profitable in international markets. An economic and social order, whose development was stimulated by one set of economic circumstances, endured long after the decline of favorable conditions. Some Jews, witnessing the Chmielnicki massacres, explained these as a reprisal for the Jews' role in the arenda, echoing the warnings of the Council of Four Lands. But neither moral exhortation nor the occasional reality-oriented social analysis of the Jews' position, adumbrated by elegists, would change anything. In most places after the Deluge, Jews picked up where they had left off, returning to their managerial positions and rebuilding their communities. The frequency with which the prohibition against Jewish involvement in managing feudal estates was reiterated, particularly in communal edicts incorporated in the records of the Council of Four Lands, is but a reflection of the magnitude and intractability of that involvement.[38]

The "Serfs of the Many Chambers" and the "Serfs of the Princely Chamber"

There are other attitudes and modes of thinking to whose development and social diffusion we must pay attention if we are to understand how Polish landlords and Jewish lessees calculated opportunity and risk, profit and loss, short-term gains and long-range goals, and how they related to developments far beyond the borders of early modern Poland. We have examined the transformation of the Polish Jewish "serfs of the royal chamber" into the "serfs of the many chambers." If we are to gain a better understanding of the different opportunities available to and the relationship developing between these Polish Jewish "serfs of many chambers" and their lords, on the one hand, and the "serfs of the princely-chamber" (the court Jews) and their princes, on the other, we must consider the history of economic thinking as transmitted by Polish Judaism, the Protestant Reformation—both in its limited career in Poland and in its more enduring influence in the West—and the Polish Counter-Reformation.

Here we must again refer to the religious and ideological beliefs—the political faith—of Poland's nobles and the images of society that they promulgated. We must consider the sources of authoritative meanings attributed by the gentry to order or lack of order. In accordance with their power and their illusions about "golden freedom," the lords shaped the main lines of feudal society. Other seg-

38. The geographic distribution of these prohibitions requires further study. It could be that the council was more free to express this opposition than were local communities, in which arendars were more influential.

ments of Polish society, including the Jews, carriers of their own meanings, accommodated themselves. Gentry religion is not just Catholicism but, more specifically, Counter-Reformation Catholicism, which battled Protestantism and sectarianism and, strengthened by the ideology of Sarmatianism, seemed to have won the first round.[39] This success notwithstanding, insofar as Poland responded to social forces and ideas developing beyond its borders, older modes of thinking had to respond to new challenges and were themselves transformed.[40] And as the international marketplaces of commodities and ideas to which Poland had some relationship changed, and as the institutions that this economic thinking sought to shape and explain began to falter, Polish economic thinking, derived in part from religious sources generated more popular concepts. These concepts were expressed in ideologies that were generally defensive and accusatory and in lurid images of the anti-order of which Jews became the paramount representatives.

39. Lüthy, *From Calvin to Rousseau,* 98.
40. Levenson, *Confucian China and Its Modern Fate,* pt. 1, xxxii–xxxiii, presents a useful dichotomy between tradition and traditionalism. The latter involves a somewhat conscious and often defensive effort to uphold meaning—usually in the form of religious beliefs or ideologies—that was faltering, being discredited by changing realities or for some other reason losing plausibility. The defensiveness at times results in violence, in the effort to obliterate that which is assumed to undermine the belief or weaken the tradition. Noble attachments to Counter-Reformation Catholicism and Sarmatianism may be located on Levenson's dichotomy closer to traditionalism than to tradition. The perceived challenges to these religious and national beliefs, as we shall see, evoked some of these predicted responses.

Chapter 3

Commerce and Currency: Cultural
Sources of Entrepreneurialism

By the latter part of the seventeenth century, as I have noted, "small changes" were beginning to appear.[1] In the Protestant countries of the north and west, a century of strife had unleashed forces of reconstruction and renewal, a commercial revolution to be followed by its industrial counterpart. In Poland, a prosperous economy was beginning to stagger.[2] A shift in the relative wealth and power between Eastern and Western Europe was taking place. By the second half of the eighteenth century the "small changes" occurring in some regions of Europe would no longer be small. In this chapter I shall consider the cultural roots of this shift and their relationship to Polish Jews.

Questions about the scope and the significance of the shift and about patterns of Jewish involvement are all the more pressing, when we take a longer look

1. See chapter 1. Glamann, "European Trade, 1500–1750," 430, 464.
2. Lipiński, *Historia polskiej myśli*, 225–28. Lipiński attributes this decline to the cumulative effect of the growing social antagonism between sectors of Polish society, the feudal state's weakening of urban and industrial development and its shrinking tax base that could not maintain adequate armies, the political crisis of the Sejm, the monarchy's minting of coins of low quality, the increasing circulation of counterfeit coins, and the fall in prices of agrarian products. Stanisław Hoszowski, "Revolution of Prices," 13, underscores how "the parallelism of the movements of prices in Poland and in Western Europe, so harmonious in the sixteenth century, began to disappear in the seventeenth century." Contrary to the image presented by some Jewish historians of steady economic decline in the last century and a half of the commonwealth, there were fluctuations. The Jews in Poland, as elsewhere in Europe, benefited to some extent from the disruptiveness of the mid-seventeenth-century upheavals; for example, the Christian guilds weakened, enabling Jews to play a more significant role in the crafts. Nevertheless, the general economic situation for Poland and Polish Jews was one of decline.

back at Europe on the eve of the Reformation. We note the geographic distribution of human initiatives and material resources between southern and eastern Europe, and the areas of northern Europe where Protestantism was about to take root:

> In the age of the Reformation, all the bases of the modern world—the capital, the riches, the highest degree of development in the arts and trades, navigation and trade to distant parts of the earth, intelligence and power—were almost entirely in the hands of that part of Europe which was Catholic and was to remain so. Italy was the prestigious center of the material and spiritual culture of the West. Spain and Portugal held the monopoly of possessions overseas acquired through conquest and the exploitation of the trade of the two Indies, the widest field of undertakings, and the greatest source of riches in the nascent modern world. Flanders was the industrial, commercial and artistic center of northern Europe. It was here that the intellectual, material, and technical preconditions for what we call the rise of the capitalist economy were gathered; not in the peripheral and semi-barbarian countries on the border of northern Europe and the Northeast conquered by the Reformation.[3]

The countries that were best endowed in pre-Reformation Europe, and that continued to be so even as late as the end of the sixteenth century, were Spain, Portugal, and Poland. But these countries, in which the Counter-Reformation became strong, were not able to increase or even maintain their wealth in the seventeenth and eighteenth centuries. In each of these countries the response to economic reverses was to intensify territorial expansion and colonization—Spain and Portugal in the New World, Poland in the Ukraine—rather than to make more intensive use of domestic resources. The results included inflation, vagrancy, depopulation, and accelerated economic decline.

This situation of the Counter-Reformation countries contrasts with that of Holland and England, where the Protestant Reformation sunk deep roots and was successfully institutionalized. By establishing favorable terms of trade, these Protestant countries siphoned off wealth from the Counter-Reformation countries. It was in England and Holland that market capitalism (and then industrial capitalism) began to develop. Different rates of economic development seemed to correspond to this larger pattern of differences between Reformation and Counter-Reformation countries, but there were exceptions. In Italy, although the Counter-Reformation was institutionally strong, it had a limited effect on the economic thinking of the city-states and the new merchant princes whose commercial strength derived from institutional arrangements going back to the Middle Ages and the Renaissance.[4] In France, a Catholic country where the Counter-

3. Lüthy, *From Calvin to Rousseau*, 36–37.
4. Their economic decline was more protracted than that of Catholic Poland. But even in the seventeenth century they did not demonstrate the same resourcefulness as the Refor-

Reformation was not particularly strong, legal and social inhibitions on gentry enterprise, *dérogeance,* survived well into the eighteenth century. Its important Protestant and Jewish minorities contributed to the development of commerce and industry. Although the Huguenots were often persecuted and French Marranos and Jews restricted, they were central and integral to France's economy, which took on some of the characteristics of the economies of Protestant countries.[5] Financial magnates of Germany, such as Anton Fugger, the sources of whose wealth and enterprises predated the Reformation, did not survive the shift because they did not have the communications, the commercial practices, or the fiscal guarantees that the new conditions in Europe and the money economy required. The seventeenth- and eighteenth-century descendants of the entrepreneurial gentry of sixteenth-century Catholic Hungary prided themselves on their paucity of commercial skills.[6]

This shift would change the contours of Europe and, ultimately, of the entire world. What we might call modernization (for lack of a better term) began with a shift from Catholic to Protestant Europe in the frequency and success with which new economic initiatives were taken and new resources became available.[7] The patterns and rates of economic development began to diverge, resulting in the West in higher levels of trade, technology, and industry; in the growth of a middle class with access to markets in which methodical acquisition could take place, supported by increasingly popular attitudes that allowed more individuals to be at ease with their desire to make money; in greater political centralization and bureaucratization based on legal-rational rather than traditional authority;[8] in economies more differentiated from political and religious control, with monetization replacing barter; and in the implementation of production based on cash

---

mation countries in confronting the economic crises of the early modern period. See Trevor-Roper, *European Witch-Craze,* 1–45; Pribram, *History of Economic Reasoning,* 86–88; de Roover, *Money, Banking and Credit,* 182; Miskimin, *Economy of Later Renaissance Europe, 1460–1600,* 165–66, 171. For a fascinating analysis of *The Merchant of Venice* and Jewish-Christian relations against the background of economic developments in Counter-Reformation Italy, see Shell, *Money,* 47–83. According to Shell's interpretation, Shylock's defense of his and other Jews' usefulness is based more on the Western argument for Jewish tolerance (that they were productive) than on the argument made in the East (that they generated revenue).

5. Lüthy, *Banque Protestante en France.*
6. Pach, "Business Mentality," 131–59.
7. See Introduction. Much criticism has been leveled against the use of this term as imprecise and not "value-free." Modernization is here used as a shorthand to designate processes that lead to economic and technological changes, among others, in a specific historical period. See Landes, *Unbound Prometheus,* 6. Also Berger, Berger, and Kellner, *Homeless Mind,* 3.
8. This distinction is central to the work of Max Weber on the rise of capitalism. The implications of the typology for Poland, where Jews rationalize systems of backwardness, will be explored later. See Weber, *Economy and Society,* vol. I. For an analysis of the development of public administration, see Raeff, *Well-Ordered Police State.*

labor rather than coerced, feudal contracts and service in kind, which continued to exist in the East. This shift corresponded to new patterns of thinking in the West that were more hypothetical and empirical than the old and that manifested greater autonomy from the authority of institutionalized religion, if not from the influence of traditional attitudes mediated by religion. It was a thinking that was oriented to practical solutions of worldly problems.[9] "Becoming modern," the "recovery of nerve," or the "struggle for the real," as twentieth-century historians and social scientists have observed, were accompanied by the belief in progress and an optimistic sense of the efficacy of human effort.[10]

But these geographic correspondences between Protestantism and modernization, and between the Counter-Reformation and what in Poland came to be called backwardness, do not establish causal links; neither do they provide interpretations of this shift. A large but uneven literature points to the connections between religions and economies, among clusters of beliefs packaged and repackaged in different ways at different times and mediated by different kinds of social structures. Yet it remains difficult to establish the active components of the Reformation and Counter-Reformation with roots in earlier modes of thinking. Which theologies and theodicies, eschatologies and epistemologies, high traditions and popular beliefs, spiritual orientations and worldly manipulations, spurred productivity in Protestant countries or inhibited the ability of Catholic countries to maximize their "small changes" and early advantages? We must search for deeper conceptual roots of this shift, roots that connect to developments in Poland and among Poland's Jews.

The commercial revolution, for example, was indeed revolutionary, not only because of the volume of trade or the velocities of currency, but because of the diffusion of patterns of economic ideas. This related to the developing ability in certain sectors methodically to exchange surplus and acquire goods and conceptually to represent and transfer value through various forms of currency. Changes in the modes of thinking accompanied, perhaps even precipitated, these commercial and fiscal changes, the "currents of psychological or even metaphysical preconditions" that, as Georg Simmel notes, "develop in infinite reciprocity" with economic forms.[11] Those modes of thinking may have emerged within a particular historical or polemical context, removed from the practical affairs of everyday life, with no visible association to commerce and currency. But they often took on a life of their own, with unanticipated consequences. We must analyze the sources of different modes of economic thinking and rationality in the West and in

9. This modern consciousness, however, unleashes its own forms of witchcraft and irrationality, particularly when its expectations of solving worldly problems are disappointed. This leads to the search for more adequate explanations but also, as often, to frustration and the search for a target of blame. Thomas, *Religion and the Decline of Magic.*

10. See Introduction. Inkeles and Smith, *Becoming Modern,* 15–35; Gay, *The Enlightenment,* 2:3–55; Geertz, *Islam Observed,* 90–117.

11. Simmel, *Philosophy of Money,* 56.

Poland, the social and legal sanctions that "restrict and mould economic enterprise to conform with accepted behavior"; and we must consider both the regulatory agencies and the regulative ideas. Examining the history of those ideas,
the "social philosophies" and the "ideological frameworks of enterprise," shall
give us a glimpse into the motives, thinking, mentality, and ideology of the entrepreneur; we shall discover where they seem to develop and, as was the case in
eighteenth-century Poland and among Polish Jews such as Solomon Maimon's
grandfather, where they do not.[12]

How did Counter-Reformation Catholicism as it was promulgated in Poland
influence the economic calculations and assumptions as well as the images and
sets of social relations by which the Polish gentry ordered their natural autarkic
economy and tried to link it both to the domestic and to the international commercial economies? As these links of feudalism became increasingly strained by
the growing disparity between productivity and profitability, investment and
return, supply and demand, intention and result, how did Counter-Reformation
Catholicism, contributing added fervor and levels of meaning to ideologies such
as Sarmatianism, accommodate gentry efforts to preserve the second serfdom
against countervailing forces? What made the Jews, more than any other minority
group within Polish society (including the Armenians, the Italians, and the Scots),
particularly suitable to be recruited for the economic roles that they played in
early modern Poland?[13] Beyond the structural conditions outlined, is there anything about the religion of Polish Jews and its legal, spiritual, or intellectual
legacies that spurred or denigrated entrepreneurship and might account for the
scope and intensity of Jewish participation in the Polish economy? Did the Judaism of the rabbinic leadership and the piety and practices of common Jews
prompt or inhibit the different types of worldly action of sixteenth-century aren-

12. Supple, "Nature of Enterprise," 402–3; Eisenstadt, "Protestant Ethic Thesis." Weber on
early modern Jewry is fragmentary and hopelessly bogged down in polemics such as to
render most of his comments of little use in understanding Jewish history. My model of
reasoning in this chapter points to affinities and even historical accidents, the greater
availability of certain ideas that, when combined with economic and political factors, led to
particular developments. My assessment moves dangerously close to the style of argument
of Werner Sombart and must be roundly dissociated from his work. I do not claim any
special Jewish origins of, or propensity for, capitalism based on genetic theory, nor do I find
Jews to be its mediators under all circumstances. Simmel, a contemporary of Weber and
Sombart, distances himself from the type of argument that Sombart makes by emphasizing
the reciprocity with economic conditions. But in at least one reference to the "Jewish
mentality," where he asserts that it is "more interested in logical formal combinations than
in substantive creative production," he goes against his own methodology. Simmel,
Philosophy of Money, 225.
13. Gershon Hundert, "Advantage to Peculiarity?" 21–38. The distinction of the Jews that
Hundert emphasizes is that unlike other minority groups in Poland, the Jews may not have
viewed themselves as sojourners. But we must consider additional cultural factors and
possible advantages.

dars and merchants, who managed large feudal estates and organized domestic and international trade? Is there a cultural context in which we can attempt to explain the decision making of the eighteenth-century Jews like Solomon Maimon's grandfather, who invested their efforts in evading gentry capriciousness rather than making the capital investment to repair bridges?

These questions have rarely been asked in reference to Polish Judaism. Indeed, there is insufficient evidence to substantiate fully the argument that I shall make. Though the Ashkenazic Jewry of Poland emerged in the sixteenth century as the "dominant center of Jewish life," a position that it was to maintain until the Holocaust, as Isadore Twersky observes, the study of its intellectual history is currently at an early stage.[14] It is my hope, nevertheless, that this speculation will be useful as a guide to future research. Examining the at times opaque polemics about commerce and currency in Counter-Reformation Poland, comparing them with discussions taking place in the Protestant countries of the West, and relating this comparison to what we do know of the actual economic position of Jews in the East and the West may bring to our attention influential but overlooked attitudes toward Jews in early modern Europe. These attitudes are sometimes positive but more often negative; they draw their animus from sources less known than the oft-cited theological and political discourses.[15] In speculating about the influence of different "ideological frameworks of enterprise" among Polish Christians and Polish Jews during the period of this shift, I shall try to identify an unrecognized and unacknowledged competitive advantage that these Jews may have had over their Christian neighbors.[16] It will be the work of later chapters to

14. Cooperman, ed., *Jewish Thought in the Seventeenth Century*, x, 146.
15. In the effort to elaborate constructs more useful for the analysis of Judaism than Weber's notions of rationalism or worldly asceticism, I develop a conceptual framework influenced by the following: Simmel, *Philosophy of Money*; Taylor, *Classical Heritage of the Middle Ages, Medieval Mind,* and *Thought and Expression*; Pribram, *Conflicting Patterns of Thought* and *History of Economic Reasoning*; Schumpeter, *History of Economic Analysis*; Kantrowicz, *The King's Two Bodies*; Courtenay, *Covenant and Causality.*
16. Many difficulties confront us in making assumptions not only about the history of ideas but also about the history of thinking, as well as in understanding the cognitive base of economic attitudes and institutions. It is no simple matter to extrapolate modes of reflectiveness from the private lives of people about whom we know so little and to make reliable generalizations. The historical impressions conveyed in sources formulated for such various purposes as theological polemics, publicistic tracts, spiritual manuals, sermons, commentaries, and the like is sparse and often contradictory. To trace the modes of thinking that are of interest to us, we must establish indicators based on judgments among alternative interpretations of abstract philosophical terms, such as realism and nominalism, whose meanings were frequently revised in different periods. The history of thinking is full of surprises and is renowned for its nonlinear development. These problems are compounded among the Polish Jews. Their religious and lay leaders left a scant record of their economic thinking; we can only infer the links between their intellectual history and their social history. With all these methodological and interpretive problems, as Benjamin Nelson urges, "we cannot neglect comparative historical perspectives." *On the Roads to Modernity,* 11.

explain why this advantage ultimately made little difference in the ability of Jews to transform the Polish economy.

Scholasticism, Realism, and Nominalism

The economic ideas, including those influencing attitudes toward commerce and the modes for representing value in currency, that became potent social forces by the mid-seventeenth century had their roots in an earlier period. Western Protestant entrepreneurs, Polish Catholic nobles, and Polish Jews were the heirs to a universe of discourse influencing their economic thinking and their economic opportunities: the great corpus of scholasticism, with its theories of knowledge and its notions of causality, influenced Reformation and Counter-Reformation Christianity as well as early modern Judaism. In its diverse conceptual strands scholasticism was refracted into the ideas and ideologies that inspire movements and schisms. Some became more influential in the East, others in the West; some had a direct influence, others an indirect one; and still others strengthened indigenous propensities or precipitated strongly negative reactions. We must examine how these contributed to the early modern shift and to the new orders that would emerge.

The schoolmen addressed economic issues directly in their debates on just price and usury, just wages, coin debasement, taxation, public debts, monopolies, foreign exchange, partnership, and contracts.[17] But a broader range of their philosophical and theological concerns may have had an indirect influence on economic thinking, calculation, motivation, and behavior: these include concepts of divine providence and human choice, of God's occasional intervention in the human sphere and natural causation, of determinism and free will, of predestination and the hope of salvation through acts of faith; the verity of human knowledge about the cosmos or human affairs and the inscrutability of God's ways; the very real existence of universal ideas that express the essence of things and the existence of ideas as mere noumena, inadequate human constructions of ultimate realities that can be posited temporarily and then dispensed with as necessary. These concepts, couched in casuistry or in metaphysical language, did not readily reveal their worldly implications. And yet they strongly influenced economically relevant attitudes—the propensity of individuals to plan and to take risks; the status of the merchant and the criteria by which trade was evaluated; and the thinking by which value, as represented in currency and capital, was believed to be generative. Without making presumptuous claims about how the early modern shift in the seventeenth and eighteenth centuries was precipitated by mere differences in interpretation of the fine points of scholasticism, or by learned debates on theories of knowledge and causality, it may be fruitful to search for intellectual and spiritual roots of that shift between East and West in the scholastic workshops that crafted the medieval synthesis of classical knowledge.

17. De Roover, "Scholastic Economics, 163.

How was that synthesis, mediated by Jewish and Moslem savants to influential Christian schoolmen, refracted into attitudes that promoted or inhibited entrepreneurialism, and how was it spread by historical developments in different directions across Europe?

Thomas Aquinas and other Aristotelians begrudgingly justified trade and saw its positive function in narrow terms,[18] as the strengthening of the community by the restoration of self-sufficiency. They paid little attention to such timeless social realities as desire and scarcity.[19] Like Aristotle, Aquinas idealized a simpler society, a glorified village, preferring it to the more complex urban and commercial society of which he had primary experience.[20] He saw the merchant as a likely perpetrator of evil, a source of corruption. In his ideal city, commercial activity would be reduced to a minimum. On the generativity of money, critical to a justification of credit, Aquinas was inconsistent.[21]

Many of Aquinas's ideological heirs, including members of the Polish gentry during the Counter-Reformation, similarly idealized lost worlds and paid insufficient attention to new social realities. Where they had the power to shape institutions, the negative consequences of these attitudes for the commerce that thrived in so many areas of medieval Europe, including Poland, would soon be apparent.[22] Elaborated in tomes calling for religious regulation of economic activity, these attitudes legitimated exchange based on booty and coerced labor rather than providing the rationale for methodical accumulation and cash labor.

But it is likely that the indirect influence of the thirteenth-century schoolmen on economic thinking, during a period of more than four centuries, was greater than their success in establishing specific laws and doctrines for regulating economic practices. For it is in the broader synthesis of Aquinas and his fellow schoolmen that we find other seeds of anticommercialism, leading to the firm

18. Aquinas's attitudes toward trade have a continuous tradition among earlier Christian thinkers. A frequently cited dictum ascribed to John Chrysostom was that merchants would be expelled from God's temple; Augustine declared that it was a vice to buy low and sell high. See Pribram, *History of Economic Reasoning*, 16. But Aquinas drew heavily, if selectively, from Aristotle's *Nicomachean Ethics* and his *Politics.* For comparably negative attitudes toward the merchant and the innkeeper, see Plato, *Laws*, bk. 8, arts. 846d–920e.
19. Calhoun, *Evolution of Standards in Business*, 69–70, and *Business Life of Ancient Athens*; de Roover, "Scholastic Economics," 163. Karl Polanyi, "Aristotle Discovers the Economy," 78–115, defends Aristotle by asserting that he was misinterpreted by those making anachronistic use of marketlike modes of exchange. Aristotle's economics focused on the household rather than the marketplace. The late date that Polanyi assigns to the development of market capitalism, and the evolutionary typology and sharp dichotomy that he proposes between "embedded" and "disembedded" (differentiated) economies, have come under criticism. Nevertheless, this argument provides useful distinctions.
20. For a brilliant description of the historical forms on which these idealizations were based, see Fustel de Coulanges, *Ancient City*.
21. Courtenay, "The King and the Leaden Coin," 206–9.
22. Tawney, *Religion and the Rise of Capitalism*, 54–60.

belief that there was "something base" about trade.[23] What Louis Dumont calls the "primitive idea," that in trade one person's gain is another's loss, was nurtured by an implicit notion of real value. This realism, which developed in relation to epistemological and metaphysical questions, had a bearing on the protracted discussions of such commercial questions as just price. Laws prohibiting usury were now promulgated and enforced with a new literalness.[24] Similarly, in regard to currency in thirteenth-century Europe, tokens, leather money, scrip, promissory notes, and bills of exchange were well established. But the theoretical discussions about coinage, like seemingly unrelated theological and philosophical controversies, began to emphasize real value.[25]

This realism, the belief that objective concepts existed outside of the human mind, had roots in the schoolmen's efforts to reconcile their conception of the Christian God with the recovered wisdom of the classical world, most important, Aristotle's idea of a prime mover and Greco-Arabian necessitarianism.[26] Realism also influenced the promulgation of sacramental causality (in William Courtenay's apt phrase), conceptions of causality that were mechanistic and magical, closer to Aristotelian concepts of natural causation than to biblical notions of an active God who intervenes in history and reaffirms the pattern of nature.[27] These concepts considerably strengthened older forms of magic, including those de-

23. Aquinas, *Summa Theologica*, 2.2 q. 87, art. 4; q. 77, art. 4. For Aquinas and other schoolmen, "the gain of a merchant or a moneychanger . . . always implied another's loss, and was, therefore, incompatible with the principle of commutative justice." See Pribram, *History of Economic Reasoning,* 16. See also Taylor, *Medieval Mind,* 1:335–45. Taylor concludes that "the most precious, the most typical and original elements of medieval life drew little inspiration from the towns" (345). But he says little about the influence of medieval thinking on the town and on its economy, particularly in mediating classical ideas.
24. Simmel's conception of the absolutist view of the world contributes to our understanding of this new literalness with which the Catholic church applied the Deuteronomic prohibitions. Nelson, *Idea of Usury,* 3–28; Pribram, *History of Economic Reasoning,* 17–20; Soloveitchik, *Halakha, Kalkala, Vedimmuy Azmi,* 23.
25. Simmel, *Philosophy of Money,* 142ff.; 512ff. This change was in accord with what can be gleaned from the historical studies of bullion flow, gold and silver prices, and coinage. See works by Attman, Bloch, Cipolla, de Roover, Miskimin, and Usher listed in the Bibliography.
26. Pierre Duhem, *To Save the Phenomena,* emphasizes the long history of these ideas. Schumpeter, *History of Economic Analysis,* 82–90, stresses that these modes of thinking are "revolutionary" and new. Pribram, *History of Economic Reasoning,* 4–7, makes a similar argument, basing it on the contrast of "the principles of Aristotelian logic with those of Neoplatonic methodology." Simmel, *Philosophy of Money,* 99, 164, 200–203, 498, 512, contrasts an epistemology based on real and universal concepts that emphasize substance with the relativistic worldview that emphasizes function. Although he suggests a dialectic between the emergence of money and the shift in these worldviews, his analysis, in contrast with that of Courtenay, seems to consider money more as a cause than as an effect.
27. For insightful analyses of the history and historiography of nominalism, realism, and causality, see the studies by Courtenay collected in *Covenant and Causality.* See also

rived from non-Christian sources, and provided them with a new vigor and a new rationale. They were useful to the Catholic church as it tried to centralize its authority in the spiritual and temporal domains by claiming to be the final arbiter of the real. They also influenced practical problems within the realm of everyday life such as the valuation of currency. Like relics thought to contain immanent powers, the value of currency was thought to be based on the real value of the contained metal, its "substance" rather than its "function."[28]

As so often occurs in history, the elaboration of one set of ideas and their political appropriation drew out opposing ideas. A new nominalism developed in reaction to this new realism. This antithesis to realism, challenging the objectivity of human concepts and the certainty of human reason, emanated from venerable Neoplatonic sources, making new and nuanced use of old ideas, as well as from more recent challenges presented by Peter Abelard and Roger Bacon.[29] Moreover, literacy, which may have become more prevalent after the advent of printing, may have strengthened nominalist connections between symbols and meaning.

The conflict between realism and nominalism was not contained for long within the intellectual domain. As early as the twelfth century it flared up in the controversy over investiture; at a later date it arose in relation to the efficacy of the sacraments and indulgences. These challenged the power of the church to dispense redemption through the administration of sacraments and were ultimately important to the rise of Protestantism. Nominalism had affinities with the concept of ascribed virtue and sine qua non causality, or what Courtenay calls "covenantal causality." Nominalists believed that the sacraments and holy objects were efficacious as occasions for reward, not because of any inherent mechanical powers, but because God made an agreement with the church vesting the power of the sacraments within that institution as an act of free will. They placed the emphasis on the artificiality of value and on the consensus that upholds it. This shift in emphasis from sacramental to covenantal causality, from inherent to ascribed virtue, was not so much initiated as it was utilized by nominalist thinkers such as William of Ockham and his followers to solve many other theological

---

Schumpeter, *History of Economic Analysis*; Pribram, *History of Economic Reasoning* and *Conflicting Patterns of Thought*; Kantorowicz, *The King's Two Bodies*.

28. Simmel, *Philosophy of Money*, 142–52, 168–70; Courtenay, *Covenant and Causality*, 203–8.

29. Simmel, *Philosophy of Money*, 512, refers to this in terms of relativism. Pribram, *History of Economic Reasoning*, 20; Lovejoy, *Great Chain of Being*. Criticisms of specific thirteenth-century scholastic ideas became the basis of sectarian outbreaks, which church authorities suppressed with firmness and brutality, when they had the power. But these opposition ideas, related to nominalism, did not provide the basis for sustained intellectual and social movements until the later Middle Ages. Duhem, *To Save the Phenomena*, 36–45, describes the modes of thinking and the attitude toward hypotheses by which appearances could be saved and such conflicts averted.

problems.[30] Even before Luther proclaimed God's inscrutability against the determinism of the Catholic church, this covenanted approach to causality weakened the well-ordered medieval scholastic cosmology, with its understanding of a distant and mechanistic deity as espoused in Aristotle's notion of the Prime Mover and brought to scholasticism through Latin Averroism.[31]

Nominalism challenged the certainty, reality, and degree of systematization of realistic theories of knowledge underscoring God's freedom and omnipotence and the limits of human knowledge. In place of deterministic and necessitarian cosmologies the nominalists suggested more contingent and occasionalistic models, alternately nurtured by either rationalism or skepticism.[32] Moreover, the nonrealistic, fictional approach to hypotheses—the argument that there was a double truth, one for the supernatural and one for the natural sphere—was useful for those who wanted to shield religious verities from scientific challenges; at a later date this same argument was used by nominalists, among others, who wanted to protect themselves and their scientific speculations from inquisitorial pressures.

Nominalist reasoning influenced economic thinking particularly in relation to the criteria by which value could be established. Whereas Thomist notions of value focused on objective criteria, such as the labor of the artisan, nominalist reasoning considered the value of goods relative to and resulting from individual needs. Commercial exchange was perceived to benefit both buyers and sellers as long as they conducted themselves without duplicity. Nominalists thus were more amenable than realists to notions of supply and demand and consequently to markets.[33] Nominalism also provided new means for calculating net lossess and gains and new methods of bookkeeping in which entries were grouped by rules divorced from the immediate objectives that exchanges were intended to serve. It favored the use of bills of exchange over the direct exchange of money and encouraged the development of new contracts of partnership. Hypothetical thinking and empirical investigation supported the development of insurance as a regular provision in business, as well as more precise calculation of risk and hence greater risk taking. It is in scholastic workshops that we find these nominalist seeds of a successful challenge to the "primitive idea." These new concepts became admissible within the theological ruminations over just price.

Nominalism began to influence fiscal matters as well. The political fragmentation of the late Middle Ages, accompanied by the decentralization of the minting processes, contributed to the monetary problems. But the conceptual foundations of minting were as important as the issues of political control. The commodity approach to currency, generally held by those under the influence of

30. Courtenay, "King and the Leaden Coin," 186.
31. Courtenay, "Nominalism and Late Medieval Religion," 57–58.
32. Courtenay, "Critique of Natural Causality," 79ff.
33. Pribram, *History of Economic Reasoning,* 25ff.; De Roover, "Scholastic Economics," 163–67.

realism, valued money according to the intrinsic value or inner goodness and purity of the precious metals they contained.[34] These realists did not ascribe sufficient importance to the fluctuations in the value of money that were a result of changes in supply and demand for bullion or for minted coins in different places and at different times. Fluctuations in the value of coins were blamed on counterfeiters and coin clippers, who were often the princes or the nobles of contiguous areas (or their agents). Jews, in Poland in particular, were often alleged to be among these "debasers."[35] "Monetary" approaches to money, under the influence of nominalism, viewed currency as simply a convenient medium of exchange, as a function rather than a commodity or substance that possesses inherent value. Monetary approaches did not emphasize the accumulation of bullion. Political legitimations of the ruler's entitlement to profit from the difference between the face values of coins and the value of their metallic content were superseded by economic arguments pointing to the benefits of upholding face value.

Nominalism also spurred the casuistic distinctions that some schoolmen started to make between prohibited usury and condonable interest. John Calvin has been praised for removing medieval restrictions on moneylending. He gave his tacit approval to the fiscal practices of refugees in Geneva who were without agriculture and industry; only their money could be deemed generative. Even before Calvin, however, theories of the generativity and the nonreality of money, nurtured by debates taking place among the schoolmen, provided more positive attitudes toward capital investment.[36] But where realism and sacramental causality remained strong, notions of economic value that were intrinsic to them continued to be fostered.[37]

The dangers of simplification are great in overstating the historical "reality" and causal impact of our own "ideal types" such as realism, autarky, and embed-

34. Between 1200 and 1700, monetary policies of Europe vacillated between the "high idealism of naive commodity theory and crude practical expedience," arbitrarily assigning nominal values and rates of exchange between different metals or attempting to "fill empty treasuries with the proceeds of unblushing monetary depreciation." Usher, *Deposit Banking,* 196.

35. Szelągowski, *Pieniądz i przewrót cen,* 34, contends that Jews were often responsible for circulating counterfeit coins. In view of Jewish management of local mints and their disproportionate involvement in trade, this is not implausible. Such accusations must be seen within the context of the diffuse and oft-contested authority for minting.

36. Lüthy, *From Calvin to Rousseau,* 71–101.

37. Schumpeter, *History of Economic Analysis,* 78–99, provides a more sociological analysis, attributing changes in attitudes toward commerce and currency to the emergence of the "laical intellectual." The learned layman not only was in a better position to assert his interests but also was more likely to impart to society "an increasing dose of his mind." "Those laical intellectuals, in or close to others in business, could never look at its problems with the aloofness of the schoolman." This may describe the situation of Polish Jews in the early modern period, among whom many of those involved in trade and finance could qualify as "laical intellectuals."

ded economies versus nominalism, commerce, and exchange economies. There is also risk in exaggerating the connection between the spread of nominalism and the growth of market capitalism in one area, and the reinforcement of realism and such economic developments as the bifurcated economy of Poland's second serfdom in another. Nevertheless, where nominalist modes of thinking and hypothetical reasoning influenced public policy, as they did in much of Western Europe and Renaissance Italy even before the Protestant Reformation, they loosened the fetters of church control and traditional authority over economic and social relations. The new churches, whatever other intolerances they might have spread, posed "the least formidable obstacle for emancipation and the rise of innovating capitalism."[38] These modes of nominalism provided the moorings of contract and consensus for new financial institutions and for intensive use of credit and fully transferable instruments of exchange; they made plausible the new ideological legitimations, expressed in the various schools of thought positively assessing trade, that we now label mercantilism. I shall examine carefully some of the "uncoordinated prescriptions by which the authors of mercantilistic tracts sought to influence economic policy, usually in a sense favorable to their private interests."[39]

But where realistic modes of thinking retained a firm hold, as they did on the Iberian Peninsula, or where modes of neoscholasticism, spread by zealous and influential clergy, strengthened the grip of such thinking, these changes did not take place. There economic relations often became a matter of custom and were codified in law. Trade, however useful or necessary, was continually linked by latterday schoolmen to those activities that endangered the salvation of the soul. It thus required careful and constant regulation; those who putatively succumbed to the temptations of usury, cheating, and unlawful gain aroused indignation.[40] The denial of the significance of commerce often led to patterns of evasion. In Poland, the renewed religious forms, including shrines and cults, reflect the strengthening of sacramental causality. We should not be surprised to discover a corresponding intensification of realism underlying Polish attitudes toward trade and monetary policy.

These scholastic concepts, whatever their social origins, were by no means confined to the intellectual speculation taking place behind monastic walls or in scholars' studies. They were explored on different levels of society, using different modes of expression ranging from the discursive, logical, and systematic to the dramatic and expressive. Political and economic as well as religious institutions embodied these concepts; they were available to the masses through prayer, ritual, magic, alchemy, theater, carnivals, poetry, and folk song. Scholastic tracts are merely the written record of a discourse that continued to engage what

38. Lüthy, *From Calvin to Rousseau,* 38. Foucault, *Order of Things,* 170, attributes the sixteenth-century reforms and controversies to these epistemological changes.
39. De Roover, "Scholastic Economics," 177.
40. Ibid., 179.

Alexander Koyré calls the "European mind" in the early modern period, even as it became more secularized.[41]

It is difficult for us to appreciate how theological distinctions and epistemological shifts may have precipitated important institutional changes. Yet rivers of blood, as well as of ink, were spilled in clarifying these positions. If for no other reason, we should be impressed by the earnestness with which these theories were argued.

Reformation, Nominalism, and Entrepreneurialism

If this analysis of modes of economic thinking that foster entrepreneurialism is correct, it should assist us in better interpreting the history of the early modern shift from East to West. That shift, as we have seen, coincided with the inflow of precious metals from the New World during the second half of the sixteenth century, disrupting the medieval system of fixed economic relations. Price fluctuations and high inflation were the result of several waves of gold and silver importation. But only in certain countries did increases in monetary supply influence the beginning of the transition from medieval organization of trade and industry to capitalistic forms in the seventeenth century.[42]

The countries that were the immediate beneficiaries of the new international market forces, including the torrent of precious metals and spasmodic increases in the monetary supply, experienced sharp economic declines, particularly in the second part of the seventeenth century. It may be coincidental that those countries in which the Counter-Reformation was strongest—Portugal, Spain, and Poland—could not sustain their wealth and power, and that the countries where the Reformation was strongest—England and Holland—now expanded their international trade and showed early signs of industrial development.[43] But in examining the way in which that medieval synthesis was refracted through the Reformation and Counter-Reformation, we find some evidence that it was more than coincidence. I shall argue that philosophical nominalism, fostered by the Reformation and mercantilism, contributed to fiscal nominalism as well as to these social structural and economic changes.

41. The secularization of consciousness does not necessarily proceed in the same direction and at the same pace as the differentiation of economic, political, and social institutions from church control. Scholastic conceptions continued to influence economic decisions, even where the state began successfully to resist the institutional influence of religion. Negative attitudes toward trade, for example, persisted long after they lost the support of official church doctrine. Both the evasion of such attitudes and their perpetuation lead to bad consciences and dissonance, at times expressed destructively. Moreover, this perpetuation made anti-commercial attitudes available to romantic philosophies and nationalistic ideologies in the nineteenth and twentieth centuries, when they were often expressed with greater destructiveness.

42. Marc Bloch, "Problem of Gold," 186–229.

43. Schumpeter, *History of Economic Analysis,* 144.

That which, rather imprecisely and anachronistically, has come to be called mercantilism was a conglomerate of "uncoordinated prescriptions" spreading in some coteries in the West at the time of the shift. It included policies that emphasized the aggrandizement of bullion, the political economics of Jean-Baptiste Colbert, and to a more limited extent the effort to formulate the canons of administration, similar to those of the Cameralists. The common denominator of these heterogeneous economic ideas and policies was a positive evaluation of trade and a strong challenge to existing restraints placed on the economy by the state and, even more, by the church.[44] Mercantilism fostered new ideas, an experimental approach to knowledge, and a qualified regard for traditional authority. Where it was sufficiently influential, it may even have spurred entrepreneurialism and have intensified economic development. As David Landes suggests:

> Mercantilism was pragmatism gilded by principle . . . the rationality principle and the Faustian spirit of mastery. This is why it could generate a continuing flow of knowledge and outgrow the political circumstances that gave it birth. Because it was built on the same cognitive basis as natural science, because it accepted the criterion of performance, it was the initial stimulus to the collection of economic and social statistics and the forerunner of the whole range of economic theory, from *laissez-faire* to socialism.[45]

44. Mercantilists, and the entrepreneurs for whom they advocated policies supportive of commerce, were not necessarily devout free traders. Often, the same mercantilist thinkers who wrote against regulation of the economy actively sought government charters of trade companies and other special monopolies. Pribram, *History of Economic Reasoning,* 36ff., points to the distinction that early mercantilist thinkers tried to make between government-granted monopolistic privileges, similar to privileges of the guild system, and those monopolies which are beneficial, not so much as a source of fixed income for the grantor of the monopoly, but because they encouraged investment, risk taking, and entrepreneurship by offering a degree of protection. The Long Parliament of 1640–1660, responding to the changing intellectual and economic climate, limited royal power to grant monopolies and supported a greater degree of economic freedom.
45. Landes, *Unbound Prometheus,* 32. See the assessment of Schumpeter, *History of Economic Analysis,* 90, on the epistemological roots of early modern science. The pragmatism and rationality that Landes underscores in mercantilism as well as in science had roots in nominalism. The application of principle may have drawn from a renewed realism, which in both scientific and economic thinking attributed a greater significance to new insight over inherited wisdom. See also de Roover, "Scholastic Economics," 183, for a balanced comparison of mercantilism and scholasticism. The term *mercantilism* was not used until the ebb of the movement itself in the eighteenth century; it was introduced into the economic lexicon by Adam Smith upon a suggestion of the French physiocrat Marquis de Mirabeau. Pribram, *The History of Economic Reasoning,* 37–38, presents various analyses of mercantilism that differ in the extent to which they emphasize the political dimensions, such as the need for strong centralized governments, or the economic dimensions, such as the need for commercial capital. These different emphases can probably be accounted for by regional differences in that which only in retrospect was seen as a coherent

Nominalism may have been the active component of the new entrepreneurialism, as well as of the new natural science. Aside from the history of nominalist ideas as manifest in Machiavelli, Hobbes, Locke, and Leibniz, Hume, and Adam Smith, there is a history of nominalist thinking whose affinities with what spurred entrepreneurial activity we want to understand.

From 1550 to 1750 the carriers of nominalism into different regions of Europe, particularly England, Holland, France, and Italy, varied. Rarely did they succeed in totally and irreversibly uprooting realistic modes of thinking, often supported by residual Catholicism or legitimated by the institutions of Counter-Reformation Catholicism.[46] Slow to disappear were old economic arguments questioning the morality of credit, the reality of currency, and the utility of trade, especially where there was well-focused resentment against tradesmen. Even in England, where the influence of nominalist ideas was the most penetrating, nominalism as a cognitive basis for political and economic thinking did not enjoy unqualified triumph. Well into the eighteenth century, the "court" theory, espousing attitudes toward commerce, credit, and currency that may be identified with nominalism, continued to encounter serious challenges from the "country" theory of economics, with its manifest realism.[47] In that most successful center of commerce, the first industrial country, strong pockets of anticommercialism endured. Colbert in seventeenth-century France was able to establish economic policy on the basis of power politics rather than of nominalist thinking mediated by church doctrine. In addition, it may be argued against this correspondence between nominalism, Protestantism, and entrepreneurialism that ideas later to be associated with mercantilism, "political arguments for capitalism before its triumph," had their advocates in different parts of Europe, including areas under the influence of the Counter-Reformation.[48]

------

movement. Historian Eli F. Heckscher, in *Mercantilism,* concedes that mercantilism is "a phase in the history of economic policy" (19). As an ideology, mercantilism was confined to small coteries whose influence was greatest by far in England. All over Western Europe mercantilism evoked a reaction, not without benefits for its opponents, who opportunely achieved a higher degree of coherence in their own economic thinking because of their eagerness to oppose mercantilism.

46. The sixteenth-century Dutch theoretician of natural law Hugo Grotius used Aristotelian logic to combat the influence of Aristotle. The economic thinking of the seventeenth-century English Puritan Richard Baxter (1615–1691) is often cited as an example of conservative positions that accompanied the rise of capitalism. Baxter, against Calvin, revived the attacks on usury. See Lüthy's important clarification of Calvin's position on usury, *From Calvin to Rousseau,* 77ff. Whether or not Baxter manifests nominalistic modes of thinking, he does share with his contemporaries in the West a concern to subject traditional economic ideas to careful scrutiny. Schumpeter, *History of Economic Analysis,* 106; Walzer, *Revolution of the Saints,* 226; Pribram, *History of Economic Reasoning,* 37–40.

47. Pocock, *Machiavellian Moment,* 427. For a critical historiography of these concepts, see Stone, *Causes of the English Revolution,* 26–41.

48. Schumpeter, *History of Economic Analysis,* 317–18, suggests that "the late scholas-

Nevertheless, it does appear that economic ideas of the mercantilists fostering the growth of market capitalism moved from publicistic tracts to public policy
and became institutionalized in new economic arrangements only in those regions where nominalistic epistemologies took root and weakened the constraints
of scholasticism. Where mercantilists' nominalist thinking supported the relaxation of regulations, the increases in monetary supply influenced the transition
from medieval organization of finance, industry, and trade to capitalistic forms.
Mercantilists sought to affect public policy without explicit recourse to arguments derived logically from bodies of doctrine. They attempted to describe how
economic relations should be ordered without applying abstract rules of distributive and commutative justice that were thought, by theologians at least, to be
infused with real significance for the cosmos and the individual's economy of
salvation.[49] The sharp line that scholastic thinkers inclined to realism drew between licit and illicit behavior was blurred by the introduction among mercantilists inclined toward nominalism of an intermediate group of morally neutral
actions, including the pursuance of self-interest in the economic sphere.[50] Self-
interest, perceived by the scholastics in religious and classical ethical terms of
avarice and greed, was transvalued by the mercantilists into a cause of civil
happiness. Avarice became a "privileged passion."[51] The pursuer of self-interest
in trade, "the noblest profession," was seen as a "pillar of society."[52] And "Private
Vices" could result in "Publick Benefits."[53]

These changes in popular thinking led to the decline of the "primitive idea"
that in trade the gain of one party is the loss of the other. The consequences of this
shift in attitude should not be underestimated. Viewing exchange as advantageous to buyer and seller led to an improved image of trade and its practitioners.
It also signaled the beginning of modern economic thinking. Even before Bernard

tics were familiar with practically all the essential features of capitalism"; in spite of the
divergence of the cognitive basis of their economic thinking from the one taking root in the
West, more conducive to capitalism, they had no "difficulty in interpreting the nascent
institutions of capitalism."

49. De Roover, "Scholastic Economics," 177. Weber's emphasis on the centrality of predestination in Protestantism is a conceptual and historical oversimplification in his ideal
type of the Protestant ethic. In displaying wealth, capitalists demonstrated that they were
graced by God but also that personal action could affect one's destiny. The history of
Protestant chiliasm suggests a psychologically and theologically more complex theory of
salvation as integral to this Protestant ethic: a belief in divine providence rather than
predestination, one that is more in accord with nominalist thinking. See Pocock,
Machiavellian Moment, 337–38, for his analysis of English chiliasm and civic
consciousness.

50. See Hirschman, *Passions and the Interests,* 17ff.

51. Ibid., 41.

52. Simon Schama, *Embarrassment of Riches,* has demonstrated that in Dutch culture a
higher degree of ambivalence toward wealth prevails. Nevertheless, this "Batavian tem-
perament" still provided the motives that I am considering.

53. Dumont, *From Mandeville to Marx,* 61–81.

Mandeville's *Fable of the Bees* and Adam Smith's *Wealth of Nations,* new conceptions of trade led to assumptions regarding the congruency of individual interests with those of the collectivity, and to notions of the "natural harmony of interests" or the "invisible hand." Here we see the beginnings of that process by which the economic point of view was freed not only from religion and abstract conceptions of morality but from political constraint as well. Although indignation against the violation of rules, punitiveness, bad consciousness, and the need for cures of the soul were not wholly alien to the Protestant orbit, the mercantilists' more nominalist approach to rules fostered greater tolerance.[54] These were some of the new principles and new attitudes toward principles with which the mercantilists "gilded" their pragmatic approach; these were bolstered by nominalist thinking.

The mercantilists gave self-interest a collective dimension as well as justifying trade as beneficial to the needs of a particular nation-state, even if that trade entailed claims that rival those of the international community. Their mechanistic model of the balance of trade, as an equilibrium, contrasted with the scholastic organic model of the equivalence in imports and exports that restores the integration of nations. The schoolmen thought that any gain in trade could be made only by a corresponding loss to a partner and the violation of concepts of commutative justice and just price. Particularly where there was the need to support mercenary armies, national trade was recognized by philosophers and merchants in Western Europe as a kind of hidden warfare, fostering the early growth of capitalism.[55] Moreover, the personal consumption of goods provided a motive for trade deemed ever more legitimate with the rise of capitalism and the new economic thinking.

But even in the West, attitudes toward currency did not change as rapidly as attitudes toward trade, as illustrated by abiding support for bullionism, with its notions of real value. Isaac Newton, certainly prone to nominalist thinking, did not find it inconsistent, as "keeper of the mint," to base his fiscal calculations on alchemy.[56] His younger contemporary, John Locke, was well known for his philosophical nominalism, as illustrated by his famous comparison of the mind to a tabula rasa and by his theory of indifference, disregarding rigid scholastic notions of lawful and unlawful actions and viewing many actions as morally neutral. He was equally well known for his fiscal nominalism, referring to money as that which "fancy or agreement have put the value on, more than real use."[57] Yet in

54. McNeill, *Cure of Souls.*
55. Pribram, *History of Economic Reasoning,* 46, 47, 49; Schumpeter, *History of Economic Analysis,* 365.
56. Dobbs, *Foundation of Newton's Alchemy.* This "lapse" of the prominent scientist may not be that astounding in view of Mircea Eliade's claim that alchemists, in "their desire to supersede time anticipated what is in fact the essence of the ideology of the modern world." Economic thinking is similar. Eliade, *Forge and the Crucible,* 173; Manuel, *Religion of Isaac Newton,* 46–49, 74–79.
57. Locke, *Works,* 46.

1698 he supported a bill to restore silver coins to their former weight and fineness, suggesting that an ounce of silver could never be worth more than an ounce of silver.[58]

Nevertheless, covenantal models drawing from ancient and medieval nominalism supported capital venturesomeness and increased entrepreneurial activity. With the passing of the seventeenth century, this contrasted more and more with the climate of opinion in the Catholic countries, where the Counter-Reformation was strong and scholastic economic thinking continued to be influential.[59] In those areas more negative attitudes to credit and banking endured, often placing upon moneylending internal inhibitions, rather than actual restraints.[60] Nominalistic thinking, as mediated by the mercantilists, shaped the entrepreneurial mentality and strengthened new procedures for the organization of commercial and financial activities. Innovations were both technical and organizational, such as the granting of charters to companies. Limited companies, such as the West Indies and East Indies companies in England and Holland, facilitated the distribution of commercial or industrial risk among owners of capital, involving neither their active participation in the management of the enterprise nor personal responsibility for anything beyond the capital invested.[61] Banking practices in post-Elizabethan England, the encouragement of citizens to lend money to the state that incurs a national debt, increased commercial relations with other countries, and the appearance of merchant adventurers who combined calculated risk taking with business acumen all manifest the influence of nominalism and led to the gradual transformation of the economic order.

58. Pribram, *History of Economic Reasoning,* 63; Schumpeter, *History of Economic Analysis,* 291, 298–99; Letwin, *Origins of Scientific Economics,* 182; Richard Ashcroft, *Locke's Two Treatises of Government,* 137–39.

59. Trevor-Roper, "Religion, the Reformation, and Social Change," in *The European Witch-Craze,* 1–45.

60. As de Roover, "Scholastic Economics," 187, indicates, "bankers cleverly shifted to exchange dealings as the basis of their operations." It was precisely among those involved with fiscal transactions—Huguenots in France, Jews in Poland—that we must search for the carriers of nominalism. See Lüthy, *Banque Protestante en France.* Insofar as the inhibitions on finance derived from the influence of neo-Aristotelian and Thomist conceptions of the nongenerativity of money, in addition to Christian restraints on usury, the Protestant countries, where nominalist theories of knowledge were pervasive, were able to break these inhibitions by posing evidence of the generativity of money or at least of the importance of capital as a component of productivity. And even at the center of Counter-Reformation Europe, instruments circumventing traditional prohibitions against usury developed in Italy and Germany, perhaps as a consequence of residual Renaissance nominalism. The *monti di pietà,* a Franciscan-run loan society for the poor in Italy, and the "German contract" in Germany made credit more readily available. Tawney, *Rise of Capitalism,* 44; Pribram, *History of Economic Reasoning,* 19–22; 25; 73.

61. The idea that commerce had providential functions entered the optimistic strains of Christian theology. See Viner, *Role of Providence.*

Counter-Reformation, Realism, and Anticommercialism

The strongest influence of realism on economic thinking in the early modern period can be seen in the countries where the Counter-Reformation was most firmly institutionalized: Spain, Portugal, and Poland. What came to be called the Salamanca school expanded the purviews of scholastic thinking in the face of changing historical circumstances. But this economic thinking, likely mediated to the Polish gentry through their Jesuit schoolmasters, who were themselves trained in those centers of the Counter-Reformation abroad, did little to stimulate the growth of capitalism as well as its entrepreneurialism and its organization of commercial and financial activities.

The early modern discussion of just price provides a useful illustration. Whereas Aquinas recognized the subjective value of the object to the seller but not to the buyer, by the sixteenth century Leonardus Lessius, Luis de Molina, and Juan de Lugo, three Jesuit theologians of the Salamanca school who had treated economic issues in their work, posited a more subjective theory of exchange value or price, listing price-determining factors such as utility.[62] The improved business analysis of these late scholastics was based not only on speculation but also on observation of the capitalism that was developing around them. But their quotidian reflections were not necessarily translated into what they advocated.[63] They fell short of integrating their analysis into the type of full theory of supply and demand that was developing in the Western mercantilist countries.[64] That just price should equal the cost of production plus a reasonable profit, a formulation made centuries before by John Duns Scotus and ultimately supportive of trade, was rejected by Domingo de Soto and Luis de Molina, representatives of neoscholasticism. Negative attitudes and legalistic qualifications could be resorted to; where there was prior antagonism toward those involved in trade, that trade could be derrogated as something base. Ultimately, these neoscholastics were more concerned with maintaining religious proprieties than with encouraging economic profitability.[65]

To whatever degree the late scholastic thinkers may have distinguished between that sinful usury and permissible moneylending; to whatever extent religious inhibitions on usury were in practice rendered moot by the economic realities of profitable moneylending in the Catholic orbit; and conversely, to whatever extent Protestant theologians and lawyers denounced usury, it is clear that where scholasticism was still influential, the theoretical and moral bases of trade, finance, and banking were shakier, and the incentives and cognitive tools for entrepreneurial activities fewer, than where nominalism influenced modes of

62. Schumpeter, *History of Economic Analysis,* 93; de Roover, "Scholastic Economics," 95–98; Dempsey, *Interest and Usury.*
63. De Roover, "Scholastic Economics," 168.
64. "The casuists of the seventeenth century" were either unwilling or unable to rejuvenate their methods of thinking. Ibid., 168, 178–79.
65. Ibid., 185.

economic thinking.[66] In the schoolmen's attitude toward the valuation of currency we find the same residual influence of realism. Where their doctrines shaped economic policy, the results were inhibiting to economic development. These schoolmen remained closer to the commodity theory of money and bullionism, with their affinities to realism, than to the monetary theory of money, with its closer ties to nominalism. For them, depreciation of coinage as an organized monetary policy from above and debasement of coins as an uncoordinated activity from below were functionally similar.[67] Although it was a prerogative of the princes to determine the precise value of currency, the use of money that lacked precious substance with intrinsic value would make commercial transactions fraudulent and unjust. Representatives of the Salamanca school, living at the time of the influx of gold and silver from the New World, became mindful of the price-raising effects of an increased supply of bullion years before Jean Bodin, to whom this insight is generally attributed.[68] Nevertheless, these schoolmen's retrenchment and their strengthened defense of sacramental causality may have forced them into a more rigid position in their realistic theories of money and their modes of economic analysis as well as in their theory of knowledge.[69]

The realism of neoscholasticism predominated, influencing the conceptualization of the political boundaries, the balance of trade, and the medium of exchange. Neoscholastic social philosophers saw the basis of mutual exchange of goods between nations in the inequality by which nature had distributed the bounty of the earth among the nations. Each national economy was viewed as a constituent part of a universal economy. In accordance with such interpretations of natural law, this raised the question as to whether a country could isolate its economy from international commerce. The goal of trade, under the influence of neoscholastic thinking, was to restore self-sufficiency or autarky, which was deemed natural and intrinsically right.[70]

It is within the context of realistic modes of thinking, and their application to economic problems by those thinkers identified with the various schools of neoscholasticism, that we must try to understand the economic thinking of the Polish gentry and of the publicists who lent coherence to that thinking. It is of particular concern to locate the sources of anticommercial sentiments by which many members of the gentry considered trade and its practitioners "sordide," as well as the sources of monetary instruments for the convenient and reliable transfer of commercial profit. There are difficulties in gauging precisely which of these epistemologies and theories of causality was mediated to the Polish lords by their Jesuit schoolmasters and other apostles of the Polish Counter-Reformation, and which of those teachings influenced economic theory and thinking. But we

66. De Roover, *Money, Banking and Credit*, 101–7.
67. Schumpeter, *History of Economic Analysis*, 99–100.
68. De Roover, "Scholastic Economics," 169–170; Miskimin, *Economy of Later Renaissance Europe*, 152.
69. See Courtenay, "King and the Leaden Coin," 202–9.
70. Pribram, *History of Economic Thought*, 42–44.

must consider the refraction of medieval scholasticism into spheres of influence, with the strength of realism and of nominalism, as one possible determinant of where market capitalism did develop, and where it did not.

Polish Attitudes toward Commerce and Currency

The second serfdom in Poland, similar to the commercial revolution in the West, was accompanied by a spirited publicistic debate. But the efforts of Polish publicists to rationalize their country's economy, to increase its efficiency as well as its legitimacy, diverged from those efforts made in the West. How did their thinking about commerce and currency differ from that of Western mercantilists, and what policies did it support?

The social position, education, and cultural background of the Polish publicists may account in part for these differences. Advocates of the main tenets of mercantilism were generally autodidacts with some literary ability, from or closely allied with the merchant class, whose economic thinking was based on empirical observation of commerce and who, "for better or for worse, were not encumbered by scholastic tradition."[71] Most of the Polish publicists were members of the aristocracy and attended seminaries and universities where they studied theology, canon law, and civil law. Some were also clerics, often belonging to transnational religious orders, who read the same religious tracts and brought similar spiritual perspectives to bear on economic issues as did their brothers elsewhere in Counter-Reformation Europe. But even noncleric Polish publicists came under Jesuit influence, unwittingly internalizing much of realist scholastic thinking. There is little evidence for any school of Polish Jesuit thinking as distinct as the Salamanca school.[72] But the Polish Counter-Reformation church tolerated beliefs in magic, bolstering already influential realist patterns of thought and sacramental causality. This realism was likely to have been a part of the educational background of our Polish pamphleteers.[73]

To be sure, the conceptual roots of Poland's economic development had a complex impact on that development. Negative assessments of trade, for example, as expressed in pamphlets or tracts or as implicit in the gentry effort to tax commerce rather than to intensify the growth of markets, did not inhibit the Polish nobility from trying to cut a good deal or from evading restrictions on trade. Even those most identified with the Counter-Reformation, Polish Jesuits, like Jesuits from Spain to China, were heavily involved in trade. They raised cattle for meat and hides, brewed beer, and imported Hungarian wines. They sold potions to which they ascribed medicinal and spiritual properties to protect

71. De Roover, "Scholastic Economics," 177.

72. Pyszka, *Professori di Vilna;* I wish to thank Professor Pyszka for clarifying this point in a letter of February 20, 1987.

73. Tazbir, *Piotr Skarga,* 46–56. For important reflections on Counter-Reformation use of the occult, see Evans, *Making of the Habsburg Monarchy.*

against the plague.[74] Moreover, they were active in various forms of pawnbroking and finance.[75] But these commercial and fiscal activities of Polish Jesuits and other Poles did not preclude strident, principled condemnations of trade and moneylending that could be evoked in attacking Jews, foreigners, and other vulnerable segments of the Polish society.[76] The Jesuits were equally resourceful in providing religious rationalizations and casuistic devices that preserved good consciences and allayed deep anxieties about salvation. These negative attitudes and restrictions actually bolstered the power of the Jesuits, who posted themselves in the marketplace, regulating this conflict between faith and entrepreneurialism. We begin to see the importance of the conceptual roots as we try to understand how Poland's economic development diverged from the "unfettered" economic development of the West.

As speculative as this analysis might be, it points to the context of Polish Jewish enterprise. Conceptions of trade, credit, and monetary policy, motives for entrepreneurship, and the image of the merchant influenced the standards by which Jewish activities and roles were assessed and, ultimately, popular attitudes toward the Jews as well. To assess those assessments and understand those popular attitudes, particularly insofar as they affected the Jews' daily social relations with their Gentile neighbors, we must attend to that debate.[77]

The economic writings of Nicholas Copernicus provide a special opportunity to examine these issues as they were debated on the eve of the Reformation.[78] This native of Poland was better known elsewhere, and is surely better remembered for his revolutionary ideas about the circulation of heavenly bodies

74. Tazbir, *Piotr Skarga,* 97.
75. Ibid., 87–88.
76. There is a considerable discussion of Jesuit moral casuistry and capitalism. See Robertson, *Rise of Economic Individualism;* Nelson, *Idea of Usury;* Tazbir, *Literatura antyjezuicka w Polsce,* 15. Because of the clandestine manner in which the Jesuits operated and the suspicion that they aroused, it is difficult to establish which side they took in important conflicts. Within the context of Polish politics, it is all the more difficult to determine whether they were liberal or conservative, monarchists or supporters of gentry prerogatives. Tazbir asserts that Jesuits were monarchists, in favor of absolutism and against the reformists among the gentry. Although they stoked Polish antiforeignism, they were an important conduit for foreign influences.
77. In this chapter, I evaluate the writings of the hundred years or so that follow the Counter-Reformation. In chapter 4, I consider eighteenth-century trends. See also Szelągowski, *Pieniądz,* chap. 3, "Poland's Share in Worldwide Trade." Whether other pamphlets and manuscripts pertinent to those questions are available in archives in Poland or the Soviet Union is not known to me at this writing.
78. Szelągowski, *Pieniądz,* 9, notes that in Copernicus's time "patriotism was purely local." Copernicus's loyalties were first and foremost to Prussia, and he considered himself a Prussian patriot. Szelągowski thinks that the genius of Copernicus was that he foresaw the uniting into an economic unit of the lands that were later to become Poland. This would overcome the particularist, separatist tendencies in the various localities.

than for his ideas about monetary circulation. But it is reasonable to assume that Copernicus's economic thinking, addressed to the court (in contrast with his private cosmological musings), expresses ideas that were admissible in early sixteenth-century Poland.[79]

What attitudes toward trade and currency are implied in the economic writings of Copernicus? As an administrator of Warmia in the border areas between Poland and Prussia, Copernicus had political purposes in writing his economic tracts. In his "Essays on the Coinage of Money," which evolved from several proposals that he wrote between 1517 and 1528, he supported the centralizing tendencies of the Polish monarchy in securing Poland's borders and in seeking control over its currency. "Experience is the mistress of life . . . [it] teaches us [that] the countries with good coinage flourish while countries that use base coins fall and die." Copernicus, seeing how Italy enjoyed an "abundance of goods," its towns and industries flourishing at the very moment when the second serfdom in Poland was beginning to consolidate, registered concern for the fate of his own country.[80]

But it is precisely in his argument for the commercial and fiscal conditions generating abundance of goods that we see the disparity between the savant's thinking and that economic thinking in the West legitimating trade and spurring the growth of modern capitalism. Society, according to Copernicus, should own everything in its territory that is required to satisfy the needs of its inhabitants. Those inhabitants should not depend on merchants to import goods. Trade, insofar as it does take place, should be conducted on a limited scale, local and direct between producer and consumer; external trade is harmful. Copernicus did not emphasize the role of the state in regulating production or fostering employment. He perceived no incompatibility between a decentralized economy made up of small autarkic units and a centralized and controlled commercial economy and system of monetary circulation. His muted enthusiasm for trade corresponds to scholastic conceptions. He did stress the state's role in restoring currency, in accordance with realist theory, under which the value of coins was determined primarily by their metal content with a slight supplement for minting

79. Lipiński, "Copernicus as Economist," 21–36. Canon Copernicus, in the second and third decades of the sixteenth century, was in Ermland, an area partly under the control of the king of Poland, partly under the Teutonic Order. Major towns such as Torun, Elbing, and Danzig had a fair amount of political autonomy and reserved the right to coin their own money. The church maintained still other administrative divisions. It is against this background that Copernicus wrote and revised his various memoranda on money.
80. Bogucka, *Copernicus,* 164. Copernicus's argument has antecedents going back to the Wiślica statute issued during the reign of Casimir the Great (1333–1370), when Poland's German neighbors called for "one even coinage in the entire state just as the law is one and the same for all and there is one prince . . . so that the commonwealth does not look like a monster with many heads . . . constant and good in value as well as in weight so that others would more willingly and more easily accept it." Szelagowski, *Pieniądz,* 33. And although this ideal was never fully achieved, Poland on the eve of the Reformation enjoyed the use of a relatively stable and transferable currency.

costs, but no more. He rejected those theories influenced by nominalism that regarded currency as a means of circulation without any substantial value and that granted the sovereign arbitrary powers to fix the rate of exchange. Keeping face value and intrinsic value close, Copernicus believed, would remove the incentive for melting down coins for their value as metal.[81]

Copernicus, unlike most of the scholastics and more like later Western publicists, expressed his critique of fiscal practices in economic rather than moral terms. But to the extent that this economic thinking influenced or reflected trends in Polish economic thinking, it does not indicate the prevalence of strong entrepreneurial motives that in Central and Eastern Europe could in the short run foster the growth of those commercial and financial institutions integral to the modern world.[82]

Colonial expansion, initiated by Copernicus's older contemporary Christopher Columbus, had an impact on Poland that Copernicus's economic thinking did not have. Throughout the sixteenth century Poland expanded in the direction of Russia and the Ukraine, drawn by fertile grain lands. The most remote feudal estates could not fully insulate themselves from economic fluctuations resulting from the swelling of silver reserves in the West. Moreover, neither the amalgamation of a variety of medieval heresies under the banner of the Reformation, nor the Catholic church's dynamic response mediated by the legions of the Counter-Reformation, left Poland untouched. These economic, political, and religious changes contributed to the power and wealth, if not the security, of the Polish lords at the expense of the centralized authority of the monarchy. Some Polish economic thinkers expressed ideas about expanding borders or amassing bullion similar to, perhaps even influenced by, contemporary mercantilist thinkers in the West. In sampling their writings on commerce and currency and underscoring differences in their thinking from that taking place in the West, I seek a clearer focus on ideas and policies that fostered and inhibited entrepreneurialism.

If in the time of Copernicus expanding and securing Poland's northern and western boundaries were of utmost concern, Polish publicists of the late sixteenth and the seventeenth centuries, such as Paweł Palczowski and Piotr Grabowski, expressed great enthusiasm for Poland's southern and eastern colonization. They saw Poland's penetration deep into the Muscovite kingdom, even as far east as India, as providing area for landless gentry, "riffraff, beggars, and criminals," as well as for defensive outposts against Tartar attacks.[83] (In the eighteenth century, such colonization would be seen as an additional opportunity for dis-

81. Szelagowski, *Piedniądz,* 12–13, 15–16; Lipiński, "Copernicus as Economist," 29–31; Bogucka, *Nicholas Copernicus,* 168. Copernicus well may have adumbrated Gresham's law, about how bad money causes good money to be removed from circulation, earlier than the Elizabethan English economist for whom the principle is named.

82. Kesten, *Copernicus and His World,* 218–24; Bieńkowska, "Heliocentric Controversy."

83. Lipiński, *Historia polskiej myśli,* 218, 222.

patching Poland's Jews.) But there was little discussion even among those Polish publicists deemed to be mercantilist thinkers as to how the expansion of territory would lead to an abundance of goods or the opportunity for intensified trade, as there was among their contemporaries in the West. Grabowski was aware of the importance of capital and advised strengthening the treasury, a central institution of Polish society. For the areas of new colonization unencumbered by old traditions, Grabowski advocated radical approaches: the nobles would pay a tax from the spoils of conquest, and the peasants would pay a tithe to the treasury. But he uncompromisingly opposed trade, even in gentry luxury items such as "carpets, leather, silk, wines, and assorted perfume." He sanctioned exports provided that a tax of a third of the price of goods could be imposed to generate income, but he had little to say about investments that a frugal gentry would make with its accumulated capital. For him, agriculture based on serf labor remained the leading branch of the economy. One type of gentry trade that Grabowski did not oppose, however, was the sale of prisoners of war in domestic as well as international markets.[84]

A clear voice of Polish Counter-Reformation anticommercialism, and with it echoes of scholastic economics, can be heard in the cleric and petty noble Andrzej Frycz-Modrzewski (c. 1503–1572). Both Poland's trade problems and its weakening currency, he contended, were a result of the greed of the merchants: "They buy things and sell them at a higher cost without improving them or adding any labor to them."[85] He spoke of money as "the nerve of war." But this analysis did not lead Modrzewski, as it did Western mercantilists, to a positive reassessment of the contribution of trade, nor to advocacy for the strengthening of central government.

Toward the middle of the seventeenth century, support for commerce as a goal of colonizing efforts appears in the work of some of Polish economic writers, such as Szymon Starowolski (1588–1656), a Dominican of middle-class origin. He called for the state to reserve funds for the development of sailing and trade with the East. With peasant rebellions becoming more frequent, he issued early warnings against the exploitation of the serfs, urging that their relations with their master be governed by explicit agreements.[86]

At first glance, we might think of Starowolski and other Polish publicists as harbingers of mercantilism. But upon further consideration of the outer limits of their proposals and the way in which these writers legitimate the social and economic relations integral to the second serfdom, we gain insight into what thwarted entrepreneurialism in Poland. For at the same time that they were calling for the expansion of Poland's borders, they were endorsing a policy with antecedents going back at least to the fourteenth century, based on modes of economic thinking quite different from those leading to the commercial revolu-

84. Ibid., 170, 219.
85. Szelągowski, *Pieniądz,* 17.
86. Lipiński, *Historia polskiej myśli,* 220.

tion in the west: The policy of containing the borders.[87] This policy restricted the exporting of goods by Polish merchants. The nobles sought to manage the foreign grain exports and to limit trade across Poland's borders in all other commodities to avoid a rise in domestic prices; no such restrictions were placed on the export of money to procure luxury items. Only gradually did the awareness grow how this effort to contain the borders contrasted with trade policy in the West, where the bullionists tried to dam the flow of precious metals, but all other resources were exported enthusiastically. Neither the nobles nor many of the publicists directly confronted the contradiction between limiting exports and generating new sources of capital for imports without depleting Poland's reserves. They simply assumed that they could control international supply and grain prices and that it would continue to be profitable for the gentry.[88] Unenforceable as it was, the policy of containing the borders merely provided opportunities for extortion. By making trade more difficult for "foreign" traders such as Poland's Jews, it had the opposite effect to what its advocates claimed: it contributed to the rise in domestic prices. If it ever had been effectively implemented, it would likely have had a crippling impact on Polish commerce.

Stanisław Zaremba, in his writings of 1623, suggested that Poland's Jews could be most useful in containing the borders. By preventing Jews and foreign merchants from leaving Poland and exporting currency, the gentry would continue to improve luxury items but seemingly without any loss of bullion; how the merchants would pay for these imports Zaremba did not spell out clearly, though he implied that frugal Jewish merchants would export Polish produce and undersell their Christian counterparts in the West. If Polish Christian merchants were to try to sell Polish exports abroad, they would surely be cheated and would not be able to bring back profits.[89] Andrzej Ciesielski, in his 1572 pamphlet, warned that Polish merchants were generally susceptible to numerous dangers. Because of

87. Górski, *Poglądy merkantylistyczne,* 89–92, traces the idea of containing the borders back to fourteenth-century England under Edward III (1327–1377), where it was soon abandoned. In Poland, King Władysław Jagiełło (1351–1434) tried to implement such a measure at the end of the fourteenth century. It appeared in the anonymous *Votum on the Establishment of the Treasury* in 1596. Starowolski and others included it in the constitutions of 1621 and 1629, when the main goal was to keep bad money out of the country. Ibid., 92–94. It was not until the sixteenth century, however, that this provision was linked to the prohibition on the export of money. The frequency with which it is mentioned points to the difficulties of enforcement.

88. Ibid., 88. The nobles and burghers in the old towns, with their royal privileges to maintain facilities and fairs, profited from containing the borders and lent their support. In new towns, such as Warsaw and Lublin, there was more opposition.

89. Lipiński, *Historia polskiej myśli,* 180. Zaremba suggested that in order to slow the outflow of money, stop the trickery of merchants, and reduce the appetites of the merchants, Jews should be allowed to sell cloth and silk to create competition. Another means would be to encourage foreign merchants to settle in Poland, acquire belongings there, and hence stop merchants from taking their money abroad. Górski, *Poglądy merkantylistyczne,* 156–65.

the collusion of local merchants in foreign markets visited by Poles, Polish merchants were forced to sell Polish exports at a price lower than what they could get at home. Therefore, it was better that only foreign merchants engaged in international trade. This restriction, he argued, would ultimately be of advantage to towns and create larger outlets for the artisans' goods. Wealthy merchants settling in Poland would pay taxes in good coins. In this way currency would flow into the country and "increase its wealth" rather than be taken abroad.[90]

The Polish concept of containing the borders departs from scholastic economic thinking, but it does not move closer to the political economies of mercantilism. Bullionism, as it developed in the West, supported the policies of the advocates of national power politics, who viewed the interests of the monarchy and the nation as congruent. National wealth was seen as a function of the state's capacity to maximize that aggregate of goods available for the pursuit of power politics.[91] This idea, developing in the West in the late sixteenth century, did not emphasize personal consumption goods as did Aquinas's concept of the abundance of goods. Bullionism was also bolstered by notions of a balance of trade, which went against the thinking of contemporary neoscholastics, who on the basis of natural law rigorously opposed the insularity of national economies. But the concept of containing the border seemed to be more in accordance with medieval theories of feudalism and to be "rooted in the privileged position occupied by the aristocratic owners of large landed properties."[92]

Even Starowolski, with his notion of the state's role in economic development, was concerned to contain the borders, to increase the buying power of the nobles and provide them with a means of exchange, rather than to strengthen the Polish state. Most of his proposals avoided the major issues: the low level of productivity in Polish agriculture, the need to reverse the decline of Poland's urban life, and the conditions under which the Polish money economy could be linked with world markets to the benefit of Poland. In his bullionist concerns, as they were translated into strong support for containing the borders, he was ready to sacrifice favorable opportunities that Poland had in his time to increase trade. Starowolski's critique of the growth of the money economy and of trade, even more than the critiques of Polish publicists of more secular proclivities than the Dominican, had strong moralistic and religious overtones uncharacteristic of contemporaries in the West, who legitimated their economic ideas by recourse to the natural sphere.[93] The nobles' lust for excess was blamed on their travels

90. Lipiński, *Historia polskiej myśli,* 157–58. Górski, *Poglądy merkantylistyczne,* 156, 164.

91. Górski, *Poglądy merkantylistyczne,* 91, speaks of this policy as a "primitive level of mercantilist views," but this is hardly the case. Protectionism under mercantilism was prompted by other considerations.

92. Schumpeter, *History of Economic Analysis,* 335–62; Pribram, *History of Economic Reasoning,* 43–45; Chafuen, *Christians for Freedom,* 37–39.

93. Lipiński, *Historia polskiej myśli,* 212–13; Gieysztor et al., *History of Poland,* 198–231.

abroad. But the Polish publicists' condemnation of luxury was not adumbrated in the absolutist terms of the Puritan preachers in the West. Neither was it accompanied by a call for greater enterprise or by changes in patterns of consumption. In their rhetoric and modes of economic reasoning, these publicists were far closer to the scholastics than to the Western mercantilists.[94]

In Poland attitudes toward credit constituted another area of monetary policy in which scholasticism influenced the rate and scope of economic development. The condemnation of usury aroused much indignation from scholastic interpreters of biblical injunctions and of Aristotle's position on the nongenerativity of money. But as in the earlier period throughout Europe, never did this condemnation wholly shape economic realities. Moneylending was fundamental to the Polish economy; the roles of merchants, artisans, and financiers were not completely differentiated. But despite the widespread, if short-lived, incursion of Protestantism into Poland, there is little evidence of the proliferation of positive attitudes toward moneylending, as did develop in other areas, particularly where Calvinism had some influence.[95] On the other hand, Counter-Reformation moneylending institutions emerging elsewhere in Europe began to have influence in Poland. We see this in the activities of Piotr Skarga, a Jesuit of gentry background who was active in combating the various sects unleashed by the Reformation. In 1588 he established the *komora potrzebnych* (chamber of the needy), a combined bank and pawnshop that provided what were supposed to be interest-free loans, along the lines of the Italian monti di Pietà established earlier in the century in Italy. For Skarga, church-sponsored free loans were a part of his broader efforts to bring back needy Protestants to the Catholic fold. In a short time, comparable institutions were established in Cracow, Warsaw, and Vilna. The Counter-Reformation Italian prototype was intended to undermine the involvement of Jews in moneylending and to siphon off the profits as much as it was implemented for social welfare and philanthropic purposes.[96] Regardless of whether the komora potrzebnych was calculated to compete with Jewish pawnbroking and banking, it did not impede the Jesuits from borrowing money from individual Jews and from Jewish collectivities.[97] As the currencies of Poland

94. Letwin, *Origin of Scientific Economics.*
95. In Chapter 1 I noted the institutional affinities between Polish feudalism and the Catholic church. The gentry, however drawn to certain Protestant beliefs and institutions, saw greater support to their claims to peasant labor deriving from a strengthened church than from radicalized Protestant sectarians, who were solicitous of peasant believers. Indeed, the gentry might have perceived deeper support within the Counter-Reformation church, which, even more than its medieval predecessor, sought to uphold faith and subordinate human reasoning in all spheres. This theological posture protected rigid institutions such as feudalism against the influence of heretical ideas and tendencies. Pribram, *History of Economic Thought,* 20.
96. Tazbir, *Literatura antyjezuicka,* 87–88.
97. There is evidence that the *monti di pietà* in Italy were likewise capitalized by loans from Jews. Szelągowski, *Pieniądz,* 26, expresses undue concern for the harm that such moneylending did to the influence of the church. In Poland as well as in Italy, the Counter-

began to lose value against other currencies, and as Jews were increasingly extorted by kings and local gentry, it became common for the Jesuits to conserve the value of their money through forced loans to Jews at fixed rates. The condemnation by Polish Counter-Reformation writers of the evils of usury and unrestrained trade are prime examples of their preference for moralism over economic analysis.

But in some of the writings of publicists of the time, we do begin to find a measure of theoretical understanding and appreciation of the value that merchants add to a commodity and the need for central control of coinage. Marcin Śmiglecki (1572–1619), a Jesuit pharmacist, in his reflections on just price, expanded the usual criteria allowed by scholastic writers. He defined it as the cost of an item plus a supplement to support the artisan in accordance with the mores of his social class.[98] Time, place, the dangers involved in bringing a commodity to market, the abundance of money, and supply and demand also must be calculated in establishing the just price of goods.[99] Such calculations of just price, however, never led Śmiglecki or any of his contemporaries to put forward spirited argument for trade and a defense of its practitioners, the merchants.

In the writings of Wojciech Gostowski (first half of the seventeenth century) we find some concern for centralization of authority and fiscal reform. In his time, complaints abounded regarding the quality of the coins being issued at the royal mint. Coins of smaller value had more silver and hence were prey for the coin clippers.[100] Gostowski joined those members of the nobility who demanded a "reduction" of money, lowering the exchange rate between the taler and the ducat.[101] He did not believe that this could be achieved simply by decree, but

Reformation church could utilize this pattern of evasion without altering its condemnation of usury. Another Polish Jesuit in this period, Marcin Śmiglecki (1572–1619), denounced usury as forbidden by "the law of God, nature, and the church" while at the same time making concessions. *Encyklopedja powszechna*, 23:712–13; Szelągowski, *Pieniądz*, 27. Śmiglecki's seeming equivocations illustrate the problems that historians have had in interpreting the role of the Jesuits in the growth of market capitalism and economic development.

98. *Encyklopedja powszechna*, 712–13.

99. Szelagowski, *Pieniądz*, 25–28, asserts that Śmiglecki was against lending money for interest but did not regard the turnover of money in trade as harmful.

100. Lipiński, *Historia polskiej myśli*, 183–184.

101. For a summary of denominations of Polish coins and of exchange rates between the Polish groszy and the ducat through the early seventeenth century, see Szelągowski, *Pieniądz*, 31–34. During the sixteenth century, the period of the price revolution, during which Polish and Peruvian mines increased the quantity of European silver, the value of the Polish groszy relative to the ducat decreased from almost thirty to sixty-one; the Polish groszy declined in value relative to the ducat at the same rate, from sixteen to thirty-one over the fifteenth century. By contrast, fourteenth-century Polish currency remained more stable, decreasing only by one-third. It is not clear whether these exchange rates reflect the lower credibility ascribed to small coins.

advocated the lowering of the real silver content of the smaller coins to reduce the incentives to export them. He recognized the need to improve the balance of trade and appreciated the benefits of exports. Against whatever evidence there was of declining demand for Polish grain on international markets, Gostowski suggested that Poland had products that were vital to other countries. But because of its high rate of exchange for hard currency, Poland was making countries like the Netherlands wealthy, while Poland itself, was becoming increasingly impoverished.[102]

By the mid-seventeenth century, the time of the Deluge, some of the proposals expressed an appreciation for commerce still greater than that found in the earlier publicistic literature. But these proposals were still clearly stamped by scholastic thinking. Trade and industry continued to be viewed as subordinate to agriculture. Moreover, little direct and positive mention is made of the role of Jews in Poland's economy. Andrzej Maksymilian Fredro (1620–1679) noted the problems of Sejm rule and of increasing political decentralization, as well as the difficulties that Poland was having in defending itself despite plentiful resources to support an army. He pointed out that Poland produced enough basic commodities to thrive without the assistance of other countries, and that other countries could not endure without Poland's unmatched plenitude and surpluses.[103] "Not he who mines gold but he who harvests the fruits of the land can be considered rich."[104] The decreasing demand and the declining prices offered for Poland's agricultural produce on international markets, did not, however, seem to influence Fredro.

But even insofar as he realized the importance of trade, he had no sense of the importance of the individual entrepreneur or of the chartered trade company (in its monopolistic and nonmonopolistic forms), as did Western mercantilist thinkers. Following Aquinas and Copernicus, he proposed, rather, that the state conduct trade as a means of eliminating the deleterious effects of the merchants and the undesirable effects of generating income for the state through taxes. This "royal trade" would be administered by a special advisory governing body, the Consultatorium, which would establish prices and fight against monopoly and usury. It would govern foreign affairs in relation to treaties and trade with other states, as well as establish domestic policy in relation to agriculture. It would impose monetary reforms, including the closing of local mints and the curtailing of the influence of the managers of the mint, who were corrupt and bribed Sejm delegates to oppose reforms necessary to strengthen Poland's economy. It is not clear whether his many proposals for training artisans, developing industries, improving conditions in the towns, establishing efficient communication and transportation by way of rivers, canals, and roadways, and controlling coinage and monetary circulation were influenced by the Western mercantilistic literature, or

102. Lipiński, *Historia polskiej myśli,* 185–86.
103. Ibid., 230–31.
104. Ibid., 232.

whether he arrived at them independently. In comparison with that of his compatriots, however, his economic vision was comprehensive. Moreover, he did try to transcend the interests of the Polish gentry in advocating some notion of the commonweal.[105]

Krzysztof Opaliński (1610–1656) came closest to his Western mercantilist contemporaries in understanding the conditions necessary for economic development.[106] He demonstrated an appreciation of the conditions that lead to the flourishing of towns, calling upon the king and nobility to care for their welfare. These conditions, he suggested, include industry and some allowance for trade, at least until indigenous sources of handicrafts are developed. But to get to that stage, merchants require special privileges, among them the state's guarantee of their freedom. In contrast to other publicists, however, he seemed to be less sanguine about the possibilities of regulating the trade of foreign merchants so that they would not export their profits. He considered the development and maintenance of river navigation to be a vital element in strengthening trade. Flourishing towns would be of benefit to the entire country in that they would increase the tax base and make possible the enlistment of soldiers and an improved defense. At the same time he called for austerity so that people could save. Thrift should be praised, and drunkenness, which leads to laziness, lack of care, and ultimately poverty, should be condemned. He called for expansion of territory as well as for an increase in the population of towns as a way for Poland to achieve greatness.[107] Some of his recommendations seem strikingly new: to transform the corvée into rent; to cultivate the culture, religion, and science of the colonies, if only to ensure their obedience; to give towns freedom; to colonize the town with professional administrators from abroad; to lend support and give discounts to craftsmen; and to build a canal linking the Baltic and Black seas.[108]

But Fredro and Opaliński's allowances for trade were not characteristic of Polish economic thinking at mid-century. There were still Polish writers, such as Aleksander Olizarowski (c. 1618–1659), who, though well read in Western literature and well informed about economic developments in the West, were prepared to dismiss trade as "filthy and despicable."[109] Olizarowski did not refer to Jews specifically, but he surely had them in mind in condemning merchants, particularly foreign merchants, and their agents as harmful to the state. He insinuated that they were spies and that they betrayed Poland and supplied Poland's enemies with needed commodities during wars, exporting good money and flooding the country with bad money. Olizarowski expressed commonly held views.[110]

105. Ibid., 235–48.
106. Davies, *God's Playground,* 1:7. Lipiński, *Historia polskiej myśli,* 221, suggests (1609–1655).
107. Lipiński, *Historia polskiej myśli,* 200–203.
108. Ibid., 210.
109. Ibid., 255–56.
110. Ibid., 259.

The economic thinking prevalent in Poland in the early modern period, supportive of feudalism and its bifurcated economies as well as of anticommercial attitudes, had its roots in elements of scholasticism that were promulgated by the Counter-Reformation and that continued to exert influence through the end of the eighteenth century. The Counter Reformation, as Lüthy observes, "wherever it triumphed . . . for a long time blocked the development of a material, technical, and intellectual civilization. Capitalistic enterprises in these countries developed at a slower pace."[111] The extent to which it is the residual realism of the Counter-Reformation that blocked this development requires further investigation. The Polish commonwealth never did establish the "good coinage" that Copernicus, during the last years of the centralized Jagiellonian monarchy, called for. His prediction that countries that use base coins fall and die, as one explanation for Poland's ultimate fate, proved to be prophetic.

I have analyzed the order of Poland's lack of order in relation to the two components to be found in any order: structure and meaning. The social relations institutionalized between gentry and serfs carried with them not only modes of production and distribution; they had affinities with modes of thinking that defined economic rationality and value as well. Labor could not be unrelentingly coerced. Polish feudalism sought legitimation from a system of meaning that could alternately conceal its inner contradictions or expose, display, and resolve them, however imperfectly; it sought to "save the phenomena." I have considered how the Jews of Poland could not only accommodate the organizational incommensurabilities of Polish feudalism but could also assist the gentry in sustaining the cherished meanings and illusions by which they made sense of their situation. Poland's Jews made the second serfdom both operable and plausible. It is within this matrix of social forces and intellectual contradictions that we must now begin to locate Poland's Jews and what element of their own meanings suited them to this situation.

Attitudes toward Commerce and Currency in Judaism

In examining factors that promote or inhibit entrepreneurialism, I have focused on two components of that entrepreneurialism: first, involvement in commerce, the methodical acquisition and exchange of goods, as well as other uses of surplus not confined to immediate forms of consumption; and second, the ability to conceptualize, represent, and transfer value through various forms of currency. What affinities might there be between philosophical and fiscal nominalism, between modes of knowing and methods of exchanging? And how might these affinities help us understand the entrepreneurial potential and monetizing roles of Polish Jews in the early modern period?

In previous chapters my explanation of institutions and markets, the social structural forces, provided a context within which to understand the commercial

111. Lüthy, *From Calvin to Rousseau*, 35.

and monetizing roles of Solomon Maimon's grandfather and many thousands of his faceless contemporary Polish Jews in the society of early modern Poland and the economy of its second serfdom. But that context has not enabled us to answer the most fundamental question: Why could Polish Jews not maintain the dilapidated connections between Poland's natural and commercial economies? Notwithstanding what we do know about Jewish managerial skills and artisanship in the sixteenth and seventeenth centuries, we might reluctantly nod in agreement with Max Weber as he accuses more than he questions: Why was the Polish Jew, particularly in the eighteenth century, not likely to develop and manage a factory and thereby employ fellow Jews?[112] My analysis of Jewish involvement in Poland's economy might even add to Weber's unfounded indignation. What prevented a Jewish arendar, who may have demonstrated advanced entrepreneurial motives and skills in organizing the employment of scores of Jewish sublessees, from establishing cottage industries and rationalizing the operations of large-scale workshops? Would he not better have served his interests, as well as those of other Polish Jews, and particularly the cash-seeking serfs, by providing them with opportunities for salaried labor rather than locations at which to procure ample supplies of drink? Why would an eighteenth-century Polish Jew not be likely to establish a Manchester on the Neman or a Łodz, which in the nineteenth century developed into a Polish textile center, with Jewish workers, managers, and investors? To infer from our observations of an eighteenth-century Polish Jew's economic behavior any understanding of his economic decision making requires that we identify still other forces to which he was subject and deeper contexts for what he did and what he did not do.

In this chapter, I have begun to elaborate on other causal factors, aside from social structural forces, that motivate productivity and entrepreneurialism. Comparative intellectual history can provide a lens through which to filter and regulate the abundant background light supplied by a continuous history of legends, beliefs, and legal norms of Judaism preserved in biblical and rabbinic sources and recapitulated in every generation. While avoiding assumptions about ahistorical *mentalités,* I shall consider the internal history of Judaism salient to commercial and financial development. It is difficult to establish the precise influence of that continuous intellectual and spiritual history on the actual economic thinking and motives of Jews in any era, and of Polish Jews in the early modern period in particular. The lens of comparative intellectual history will focus this available background light into the long shadows, shadows resulting from the paucity of sources that could give more direct insight into the world of Polish Jews. It bears repeating that the primary purpose of this speculative approach is to encourage further research rather than to presume definitive explanations.

In that history of Judaism, is there any predominance of realistic or nominalistic epistemology, determined or contingent cosmology, sacramental or covenantal causality, systematic or ad hoc thinking, empirical or intuitive modes

112. Weber, *Sociology of Religion,* 249.

of knowing? Is there any predominance of efforts to subject mundane human activities to, or free them from, normative restraint? Where were Jews in relation to the modes of thinking that spurred or inhibited entrepreneurialism through the synthesis of the High Middle Ages, modes of thinking that were refracted anew through the Reformation and Counter-Reformation, diffused in the West or East, and institutionalized in the early beginnings of market capitalism or the second serfdom? More specifically, to what extent did the religion of Polish Jews influence their economic thinking and make them more suitable than other groups in early modern Poland for particular economic activities, including the profitable management of the feudal estate and the monetization of profits? Would the religion and education of *dvorf yidn,* the provincial Jew from whose ranks Solomon Maimon's grandfather and most other arendars were recruited, or for that matter the Judaism of the more urbane merchants and artisans inspire them to posit the world of everyday life as an arena for systematic and purposeful activity? Did that Judaism provide the cognitive tools, the regulative ideas—in Simmel's words, the "currents of psychological or even metaphysical pre-conditions"—for such economically relevant behavior as financial planning or risk taking?[113] In this history of Judaism, I shall continue to focus on two aspects of entrepreneurialism: commerce and currency.[114]

113. Here is not the place to present critical assessments of the work of historians of Judaism such as Finkelstein, *Pharisees,* or Rivkin, *Shaping of Jewish History,* who have focused on economic factors, any more than it is a primary goal to present systematic arguments against the claims of Werner Sombart or the passing comments of Marx and Weber. My effort here is more specific: to identify motives and meanings in Judaism that were available to Jews at particular historical moments and that may have become salient and significant to their economic activities.

114. Baron, *Social and Religious History of the Jews.* Jewish propensities for commerce may be related to the geographic and social location of Jews in Palestine, in Babylon, and throughout the diaspora. Wherever they resided, Jews acted as "ports of trade." In fact, they often settled near "coastal or riverine sites on the border of two ecological regions such as the highland . . . and the plain." They visited fairs and "market-type institutions." Polanyi, *Primitive, Archaic and Modern Economies,* 239–43; North, "Markets and Other Allocation Systems in History," 714. These same conditions that made Jews prone to commercial involvements placed them in need of the rules and instruments of commerce, including property and contract law, risk evaluation, and maritime insurance. This need was furthered by their interaction with others possessing different modes, motives, and expectations for exchange. These conditions of standing at the margins while interacting with the center perhaps inclined Jews to universalistic and abstract modes of knowing, and to nominalism. Simmel, *Philosophy of Money,* 142, 221. These rules and instruments were fully and consistently extended to the *ger* (resident sojourners). Trade with those outside the sacred community received less-principled regulation. This double ethic had nothing to do with the paucity of Jewish rationality, as Weber suggests. It did relate to a somewhat accurate assessment of what Jews might expect from non-Jews in markets that were still embedded in social systems and where prices were never wholly established by universalistic standards of supply and demand. Nevertheless, practical, if not principled, restraints were placed on such dual standards throughout Jewish history, particularly when they

Biblical and rabbinic commercial law developed in the ancient Near East, with its agricultural based economies prone to unpreservable surpluses and uncontrollable shortages. The occasional caravan passed along the horizon. The ancient Israelites, as recorded in the narrative parts of the Bible, though involved in agriculture and grazing, had need for trade.[115] Whatever were the prevailing allocative systems and modes of exchange, the patriarchs demonstrably used some form of coinage, perhaps as a way of averting unwanted social reciprocity with would-be neighbors.[116] Biblical laws of the seventh year and of the jubilee, by curtailing property transfer rights, placed some limits on trade and capital accumulation.[117] But these laws had no anticommercial overtones per se.[118] The biblical end-of-days vision of "Everyman 'neath his vineyard and fig tree" conveys an image of societal harmony and tranquility, though not necessarily glorification of the pastoral economy or idealization of autarky. In the Jews' encounter with the classical world during the late biblical and early rabbinic periods, there is little evidence that Jews absorbed any emphasis on self-sufficiency and any of the anticommercialism implicit to the *oikos,* the household, as expressed particularly in Aristotle.[119] To judge by these early Jewish sources, if there was ever any

---

could jeopardize Jewish security or lead to the desecration of God's name. See Katz, *Exclusiveness and Tolerance,* 50–63.

115. The circumstances that led to the exodus and the birth of the Israelites as a people were, after all, precipitated by a commercial transaction: the sale of Joseph by his brothers. Joseph rationalized Pharaoh's economy and strengthened his polity. Joseph saved his family from famine but at the same time created conditions that were to lead to the Israelites' enslavement. Such economic homilies may be complicated by an abundance of textual and exegetical problems, but they identify within biblical narratives a mythic background to early biblical attitudes toward trade.

116. This is illustrated in Gen. 23 in the description of Abraham's protracted financial negotiations with the Hittites for a burial ground. See Daniel Sperber's effort to calculate the value of that transaction in relation to the claims of a fourth-century rabbi, "Sale of Makhpela Cave," 55–59. Jacob's pay-as-you-go policy, his use of money to avoid incurring any social indebtedness, is contrasted with the allocative ethos of the Shekhemites, who want to keep accounts open and continuous, based on personal exchange, and thereby to absorb or at least neutralize the stranger. This economic substratum perhaps adds violence and poignancy to the ensuing story surrounding the ravishing of Dina, Gen. 33:18–19. On his death bed Jacob reserved a special blessing for Zebulun, the scion of the merchant marine tribe. Gen. 49:13.

117. *Shemitat kesafim* limited the period for which loans could be made. Without abrogating the law, the rabbis developed techniques by which loans could be sustained.

118. Indeed, the most pastoral of biblical books, Ruth, where romance and genealogy influenced land transactions, provided rabbinic exegetes with paradigms for procurement procedure. *Babylonian Talmud* (henceforth *BT*), Bava Meẓia, 47a.

119. Polanyi, *Primitive, Archaic and Modern Economies,* 16–18, 78–115. This is all the more striking in view of the controversial claims of Polanyi and other economic historians. Citing brief but influential remarks in Aristotle's *Politics,* they present the non-entrepreneurial household as the modal economy of premodern society characterized by an emphasis on the taxing powers of church, state, and guilds, by reciprocity rather than

resonance among Jews for the "primitive idea" that in trade one's gain is another's loss, that idea must have been superseded at an early point.[120]

To be sure, the corpus of rabbinic literature is not bereft of nonentrepreneurial, even antientrepreneurial, attitudes. Rabbinic aphorisms advocate faith and laud the ascetic and the scholar who free themselves of worldly concerns. They ascribe economic achievement to methodic and unrelenting effort as well as to the punctilious fulfillment of the precepts. The fortune of having meritorious forefathers, even blind good fortune, may contribute to profits. God's providence, as we shall see, was also deemed an important factor in the economic attainments of the individual. Nonentrepreneurial attitudes often appeared, particularly in the pietistic literature. But they could not totally neutralize the sentiments, the cognitive and legal instruments provided by other Jewish sources supportive of enterprise among Jews, including early modern Polish Jewry. Whereas some Jews sighed over God's curse of Adam that begins "in the sweat of thy face," others saw opportunity in the result, "shalt thou eat bread" (Genesis 3:19).

Spurs to commerce may be found in the complex and subtle rabbinic sources that elaborated at great length on price-setting markets and monetary exchange without eliminating nonmonetary modes of allocation.[121] These sources reflected an economy in which production was not limited to immediate use; upon

---

exchange, and by price controls rather than price-making markets. Jewish law dating back to the rabbinic period, while preserving many of these nonmarket modes of exchange, reflects at this early date models of price-making markets that would qualify as such by Polanyi's most restrictive definition. North, "Markets and Other Allocation Systems in History," 709–10. According to George Dalton, Polanyi concedes that price-making markets and exchange based on money, though somewhat uncommon, are to be found in the premodern world as well. An examination of biblical and rabbinic Judaism makes this concession all the more necessary.

120. A homily illustrating the significance of division of labor and, willy-nilly, of trade is ascribed to the second-century Rabbi Zoma: "How much did Adam have to toil so that he might be able to eat a crust of bread. . . . And how much did Adam have to toil to be able to wear a garment. . . . And I merely awake and find all of these prepared for me." BT, Berakhot, 58a. The high priest, on Yom Kippur in his prayers for rain, tried to mediate between the conflicting interests of rich and poor, farmers and merchants. See BT, Bava Batra, 147a–b.

121. For an analysis of rabbinic laws of procurement, see Herzog, Main Institutions of Jewish Law, 1:137–200; Albeck, Dinei Hammamonot Battalmud, 153–68; Alon, Hamishpat Haivri, 1:476–80. The nonmonetary modes include kinyan ḥalifin, procurement through barter; the tithes, taxes, and special gifts due to the priests, Levites, scholars, and rulers; the various entitlements of the poor; and the donations to support special institutions from the Temple to the house of prayer or study. The tithes and the like are what Polanyi calls transactional modes of exchange and redistribution, exchanges based on kinship, hierarchy, political, and religious affiliations in contrast with market modes of exchange, which in accordance with his evolutionary and typological explanation of economic development emerge in the early modern period.

fulfilling one's primary obligations to family, workers, creditors, and the needy, an individual could preserve or dispose of reasonable surpluses under proper conditions. Markets and the management of surplus were not viewed as religiously or ethically tainted. They were deemed necessary and useful. Rabbinic law sought to order and regulate them in accordance with its recognition of the human condition of inequality.[122] The just price of an object to be exchanged could be based on the balance of subjective criteria established through supply and demand as well as the more particular and less consensual subjective attachments of buyer or seller, as long as there was full disclosure of information, complete agreement between the partners, and no deception.[123] Profits, at least in theory, were restricted, as expressed in the concept of *onaa*;[124] but the actual domain of marketable objects whose prices were to be regulated was gradually curtailed.[125] The extent to which the regulation of prices and restrictions on competition were actually enforceable is unclear. Even with the intensification of rabbinic studies and the prevalence of Jewish governance among Polish Jews, regulations did not impede commercial activities.

In the rabbinic attitudes toward the instruments of exchange as well, we find remarkable efforts to synthesize principle and practicality, to establish equity and distributive justice without stifling enterprise, and to establish the domain of Jewish law and self-governance without being impervious to local, regional, and transnational economic realities. The most important instrument for exchange was currency, representing value and providing the basis of credit. The Bible describes the use of this instrument at a relatively early historical moment, as we have seen in regard to commerce. Biblical law establishes distinct payments in coin, though the value may well have been associated with the actual metal content.[126] But by the conclusion of the period of the Mishna, at the end of the second century C.E., the Jews had a well-developed monetary approach to currency.[127] That coins should have recognized currency is ascribed by a Mishnaic

122. *BT, Bava Batra* 90b; Maimonides, *Mishne Tora* (henceforth *MT*), *Sefer Kinyan*, Hilkhot Mekhira, 14:2–11.

123. See, for example, the special category of *kinyan sudar. BT, Bava Mezia,* 47a; Joseph Karo, *Shulḥan Arukh* (henceforth *SA*); *Ḥoshen Mishpat,* 227:20.

124. This restriction was based on Lev. 25:14–17, which was used as a scriptural support to limiting profit to one-sixth. The concept of *onaat devarim,* overreaching with words or providing a false impression, drew from the same authority. *BT, Bava Mezia,* 49b; 61a; *MT, Sefer Kinyan,* Hilkhot Mekhira, 14:15–18; *SA, Ḥoshen Mishpat,* 227–40.

125. The applicability of these market restrictions was limited geographically to the land of Israel, or demographically to areas where there was a Jewish majority. Limits on markets that artificially limit supply and restrict prices were also in keeping with the specific item. Foodstuffs considered integral to *ḥayyei nefesh,* minimum sustenance, were to be more stringently regulated. See *MT, Sefer Kinyan,* Hilkhot Mekhira, 2, for a discussion of criteria of ḥayyei nefesh.

126. For example, the shekel corresponded to a weight. The word *matbeia* is to be found only in later rabbinic sources. Eilat, *Kishrei Kalkala,* 29–42.

127. *Mishna, Bava Mezia,* 4:1; *BT, Bava Mezia,* 47a; *Palestinian Talmud, Bava Mezia,*

source to those very features of creation that emphatically "came up in [God's] intention to be created."[128] Likewise, the rabbis were fully aware that the value of a coin could be more than the value of its bullion content and that bills of contract were transferable precisely because their value was in something other than the paper that they were written on. In these legal discussions we find the rabbis expressing a kind of fiscal nominalism;[129] and this fiscal nominalism was of influence more than a millennium later upon the economic thinking of the Polish Jewish descendants whose Gentile contemporaries came under the influence of fiscal realism and commodity theories of money.

Different transactions prompted different evaluations of coins. The monetary concept of real value, *shave,* and nominal value, *yafe,* already existed in the Talmud.[130] A coin's minting by some recognized authority, in contrast with *asimon,* a blank or a disk of bullion, began to take on legal importance.[131] The fourth-century savant Rabbi Papa, following the provision of an earlier Mishna, angrily dismissed as "a malevolent soul" one who refuses to accept coins, even those but slightly worn, at their nominal value.[132] In regard to redeeming of

---

4:1. What is recorded as a change in the position of the Mishna's editor, Judah the Prince, from a definition of money in terms of the relative value of its metallic content to one in terms of the degree to which money circulates as currency signals an important stage in rabbinic economic thinking. See Sperber, *Roman Palestine,* 69–83. Disagreements between the Babylonian and Palestinian Talmuds as to whether gold or silver "buys" the other, which is the commodity and which is the money, probably assume a common concept of money but reflect divergent economic realities. There are traces in this early Mishnaic source of what came to be called Gresham's law about bad coins driving good coins out of circulation.

128. *BT, Pesahim,* 54b. This source outlines several other aspects of creation that are of divine intention: the offensive odor given off by a corpse, making it necessary for the bereaved to separate; the manner in which people forget those that are deceased, making possible an emotional separation; and the tendency of produce to rot. One medieval commentator, Rashi, suggests that rotting impedes those who would hoard and thereby cause food shortages, starvation, and profiteering. According to these commentaries, God both makes possible and restrains capital accumulation. Against this background of hidden blessings in God's cosmos, the sixteenth-century Polish rabbi Solomon Luria presents a gloss: "Were it not for this [coinage], how would the poor support themselves, for they have no labor of the field or the vineyard?" He seems to emphasize the significance of currency not only as the basis of fiscal institutions but itself as a source of sustenance. Luria, *Hokhmat Shelomo* (on *Pesahim*), 54b, p. 287.

129. On coins, see the discussion below of ẓura, the impression on coins used for the second tithe. The Talmud emphasizes the nonintrinsic value of contracts by pointing to the absurd case of whether there is any consideration of *onaa* where someone sells a contract to a perfumer to use, say, for wrapping. *BT, Pesahim,* 56a–b.

130. *BT, Bava Meẓia,* 52b.

131. See *Tosafot* on *asimon, BT, Bava Meẓia,* 44a; Sperber, *Roman Palestine,* 47–52.

132. *Mishna, Bava Meẓia,* 4:6–7; *BT, Bava Meẓia,* 44a. Maimonides, *MT, Sefer Kinyan,* Hilkhot Mekhira, 12:12, seems to accept the exchange of coins based on the nominal value, as long as the coin still circulates even at a deflated value and the purchaser can still

maaser sheini, the biblically decreed tithe that was to be consumed only in Jerusalem, the opinion of one rabbinic authority was that it could be made portable only by means of a fully minted coin. Rabbi Akiva went so far as to adduce scriptural support for this special provision against the literal meaning of the verse.[133]

Despite this appreciation for the social significance of coinage and the associated nominalist approach to value, the rabbis had great difficulties in providing the thinking and the norms by which good currency could be upheld and, when necessary, regulated. Rabbinic notions of the representation of value in coinage were undermined by other legal requirements as well as by practical factors such as atrophied coins and fluctuating markets. The Mishna already questions the purchasing power of coins, in the barter exchange of *ḥalifin.* The emphasis placed by the rabbis on the *zura,* the mintage of the coin as that which adds symbolic value to the bullion, underscores their monetary rather than commodity approach to money at this early point in its history. But the technical requirements of purchasing objects rather than merely establishing personal obligation, as well as monetary fluctuations and economic instability that added to the complexities of rabbinic law, led the rabbis to emphasize nonmonetary modes of exchange. Soon contractual agreement, an even more abstract mode of actual purchase than currency but one allowing for greater detail in the terms, became a favored mode of procurement.[134]

---

exchange it. For the one who gave the coin to value it against his interests at the original rate of exchange would be to act by the standard of *midat hassidut* (special piety).

133. *BT, Bava Mezia,* 47b, 54a. Rabbi Akiva interprets the command, *vezarta,* (and you shall bind up the money in your hand), as referring to *zura* (image). See *MT, Sefer Zeraim,* Hilkhot Maaser Sheini, 4:9–10. Maimonides seemed to establish the law in agreement with Rabbi Akiva, insisting on minted coins but also deeming it particularly meritorious to redeem this tithe at its full value. Ibid., 2:2. Rabbi David ben Zimri in his commentary emphasizes the connection between monetary exchange and one of the two modes of treating this tithe: *pidyon* (redemption), rather than *ḥilul* (symbolic desecration), in order to make it consumable outside the walls of Jerusalem. The reason for Rabbi Akiva's ruling is not clear. It could be that since the money used to redeem *maaser sheini* was to be a symbolic amount, Rabbi Akiva was concerned to establish its approximate value and make the object used for redemption portable and exchangeable for consumables in Jerusalem. For this, coins with their nominal value were more useful than other media of exchange.

134. *Mishna, Bava Mezia,* 4:1; *BT, Bava Mezia,* 45b. See the dispute of Rav and Levi as to whether a coin can be used to barter for, rather than to purchase, the item. The position of the rabbis seems to be that coins, which merely symbolize value, cannot fulfill the requirement of a barter transaction. The purchaser must enact the transaction through the transfer of an object, of symbolic value relative to the total transaction, but the object itself must be of intrinsic value. A coin in this regard might be considered a symbol of a symbol. The third-century rabbi Joḥanan further narrowed the power of money. He ruled that although in accordance with biblical authority money does purchase, movables cannot be exchanged for money but require one of the other modes of possession, such as transport or elevation, that constitute the consummation of a purchasing agreement, lest the seller subsequently

In contrast at least with Rabbi Akiva's opinion on maaser sheini, which supports a more nominalistic approach, in matters of ritual law the rabbis advocated a realistic stance toward the valuation of coinage, as if to fulfill some absolute standard decreed from above.[135] A long and complicated halakhic literature, with entries all through the Middle Ages and the early modern period, and with the participation of leading Polish rabbis in the sixteenth and seventeenth centuries, evidences the efforts to establish the real equivalent weight of coins in gold or silver, based in some cases on the actual weighing of kernels of grain. Though mindful that kernels vary in size and weight in different places at different times, these savants sought to establish real value relative to some age-old standard in coinage. Here greater significance seemed to be attributed to the real rather than the nominal value of coins.[136]

Prohibitions on the taking of interest, *ribit* or *neshekh,* might have imposed serious limitations not only on monetary exchange but on commerce as well: the lines between finance, crafts, and commerce were fluid, even in the premodern organization of production. Here we discover cultural preconditions of enterprise among Polish Jews, in contrast to their non-Jewish contemporaries. It is significant to note the differing approaches of the rabbis and the schoolmen to the same biblically ordained prohibitions. Among Jews modes for circumventing the prohibition on interest were practiced from an early time, often positing that the leader is, even to a symbolic extent, a partner, as in the *hetter iska* agreement. Alternatively, Jews would resort to a Gentile intermediary, though there was a minority rabbinic opinion restricting the biblical allowance of interest that could be taken from a Gentile.[137] The rabbis in the talmudic period and afterward,

---

assert, "Your [undelivered] grain has been burnt." The commentaries suggest, however, that this precaution should not prompt a general ruling. The majority of rabbis believed that according to biblical law money indeed purchases. But for the actual purchase of a specific object through ḥalifin the rabbis required a different mode of purchase such as transfer. Albeck, *Dinei Hammamonot,* 155–57, 368–76; Sperber, *Roman Palestine,* 126–53. The talmudic rabbis tended to curtail the scope of monetary purchase, particularly in the late tanaitic period. This was even the case for land purchases. As Samuel, in the third century, stated, "Israel procures only by contract." *BT, Bava Batra,* 54b.

135. Where payment in specific coins is biblically decreed, such as five silver shekels for the redemption of the firstborn, or compensation for damages in the case of seduction of a virgin (Exod. 22:16), slander (Deut. 22:19), or the fatal goring of a slave by one's ox (Exod. 21:32), there was great concern to ascertain the equivalent value in precise contemporary terms.

136. For somewhat unsystematic surveys of the fascinating history of these efforts to establish real value of currencies outside the domain of commercial law, see Weiss, *Middot Umishkalot Shel Tora;* Benish, *Middot Veshiurei Tora.*

137. *BT, Bava Mezia,* 70b–72a, 104b; *Bava Batra,* 70b; Schipper, *Toledot Hakalkala Hayyehudit,* 1:143–60, 2:413–46. Baron, *Social and Religious History of the Jews,* 4:339–40; Stein, "Jewish Law on Interest," 3–40. For a summary of the halakhic issues of banking and moneylending, with reflections on the realia of sixteenth-century Italy, see the essay of Yeḥiel of Pisa, *Ḥayyei Olam,* in *Minḥat Kenaot,* ed. D. Kaufman (Berlin, 1898).

despite their concern to ensure the availability of capital without transgressing the halakha, did not directly abrogate the theoretical prohibitions. They even expanded them conceptually to include *avak ribit,* practices suggestive of but not involving actual interest taking. Yet these strictures, even as they expanded and became conceptually more elaborate, had no practical consequences in the daily lives of Jews.[138] The schoolmen, concluding on the basis of their selective reading of Aristotle that money was not generative, challenged the very concept of credit. This did not prevent clerics, as we have observed, from getting involved in moneylending. But to the rabbis, the generativity of money, a needed component of enterprise, was self-evident. This rabbinic attitude protected the livelihood of more than an occasional pawnbroker.

The rabbis' recognition, in theory, of the generativity of money did not make them inclined to allow those profits derived primarily from fluctuations in the purchasing power, value, or purity of coins. Already in the period of the Talmud the rabbis were concerned to formulate rules for loans and transactions where, as often occurred, profit and losses were largely a result of monetary changes.[139] Rabbinic stringency was matched by the popular imagination for circumventing these rules, which in turn dampened rabbinic enthusiasm for the "circulating coin."[140] At times the rabbis used the prohibition on *gezel* (theft) to bolster what were otherwise complicated grounds for prohibiting the taking of profit from the fluctuating value of coins.[141] The imposition of such standards of piety and scrupulousness was countered by the talmudic concern, no less pious and altogether practical, "that the doors not be locked to those in debt." For the rabbis, the need to ensure stable conditions for commerce militated against the close restriction of moneylending; for the church fathers, the context in which they forbade usury was the preference for philanthropy as a means of preserving their concept of community.

The rabbis might have tried to adjudicate in the most complex commercial or fiscal transactions with the considerable accumulation of legal precedent and principle available to them. In view of the significant involvement of Jews in minting during the Middle Ages, for example, a halakhic literature on the economic issues of relating nominal value to bullion content, denominating coins, establishing exchange rates with other currencies might have developed.[142] Yet

138. *SA, Yore Deia,* 177:5; Katz, "Base of Interest," 236–37.

139. *BT, Bava Kama,* 97a–98a; *Bava Mezia,* 46b.

140. Kahanah, *Mehkarim Besifrut Hatteshuvot,* 330–48; Shilo, *Dina,* 401–8.

140. The eleventh-century North African rabbi Isaac Alfasi expanded this concern for illicit gain through currency fluctuations to include business, marriage dowries, and the like. Kahanah, *Mehkarim,* 332; Shilo, *Dina,* 403. This reinforcement of ribit as an illicit gain may have had the opposite effect, as some commentaries indicate: the problem of gezel, or illicit gain, could be eliminated through contractual agreement, whereas there could be no such agreement to transgress a religious prohibition on ribit.

142. Managing the mint required not only technical skills. I have not discovered any sources on the considerations of Jewish minters when approaching these problems. Per-

by the twelfth century some French-German rabbis, and subsequently some Sefardic rabbis, urged acceding to the kings' rules for calculating rates of repayment of loans when the value of coins had fluctuated and there was concern to avoid usury or theft. They did so despite the fact that these calculations related to religious as well as monetary concerns and that the Talmud and later rabbinic literature had developed their own legal principles for adjudicating in these cases. The reasons for this ruling, and what it might reflect of the rabbis' fear of the rulers or even their respect for the rulers' fiscal and administrative policies, are not clear. The rabbis based their ruling on the selective application of the doctrine *dina demalekhuta dina* (the law of the kingdom is the law).[143] The actual terms of the ruling imply a principled recognition of seigneurage, rulers' prerogative to regulate the currency.[144] One thirteenth-century rabbi, Solomon Ben Aderet, even reports his consultation with Gentile savants on the rights of the sovereign in fiscal matters: "And in the past, I asked Gentile scholars and they told me that these are of the decrees of the sovereign for which it can be said, "This coin will be exchanged in this manner or that. And since it is so, we establish that the law of the kingdom is the law."[145]

Subsequently the rabbis—in particular the Sefardic rabbis, who issued most of the rulings on monetary fluctuations—encouraged compromise or enforced the local custom of merchants.[146] The rabbis gave their tacit approval to local customs in Germany, where an increasing number of Jews was being pushed out of trade and was resorting to lending money not only to Gentiles but to Jews as well. A broad retreat among the rabbis from applying rabbinic law and precedent to questions of coin fluctuations prevailed at least until the sixteenth century. At that time Solomon Luria, followed by other but by no means all rabbis, challenged the application of dina demalekhuta dina that had supported this abdication of rabbinic authority to the sovereign. He asserted that the rabbis' yielding to the sovereign was merely "an established custom in their days."[147] While this Polish rabbi was quite specific in the legal and literary grounds on which he rejected this

---

haps Jewish agents merely minted the coins in accordance with specifications provided by their masters, in which case there would be little discussion of the modes of calculation by which coin values should be established. Although consistency in this division of labor appears to be unlikely, it is not clear what can be argued from this silence. The responsa literature pertaining to money deals primarily with issues of coin clipping. In the responsa of Maimonides questions about the activities of Jewish minters are raised, but these pertain to the commercial transactions regarding bullion. Polak, "Jews and the Mint in Egypt," 24–36; Assaf, "On Jews and the Mint," 256–57. For comments critical of Jewish involvement in money changing in early modern Poland, see Sirkes, *Sheelot . . . Hayyeshanot*, 16; *Sheelot . . . Haḥadashot*, 43.

143. See Shilo, *Dina*, 403–8; Katz, *Exclusiveness and Tolerance*, 48–63.
144. Schumpeter, *History of Economic Analysis*, 289; Usher, 221–26.
145. *Sheelot Uteshuvot Harashba* (Leghorn, 1788), 3:34, quoted in Shilo, *Dina*, 405.
146. Kehanah, *Meḥkarim*, 337–38.
147. Luria, *Yam Shel Shelomo on Bava Kama*, 97a.

abdication of rabbinic authority, can we infer from his ruling any renewed commitment to the regulation of monetary issues by the criteria of halakha? Luria lived in a period when communal structures were becoming elaborate, autonomy was strong, and rabbinic rulings in fiscal matters had some influence. Yet there is no clear evidence for a dramatic growth in monetary law as would have been recorded in the responsa, the commentaries on the appropriate sections or rabbinic codes, and the pinkas of the Council of Four Lands and local communities in the seventeenth and eighteenth centuries. In fact Solomon Luria's contemporary Moses Isserles ruled that the principle of dina demalekhuta dina prevailed in all matters.[148]

What prompted concessions among rabbis under certain circumstances and retrenchment behind rabbinic law under others, requires additional attention.[149] Certainly, changing economic factors discouraged some of these rabbis from any effort to establish real value based on the criteria that Jewish law brought to bear in specific commercial transactions or loans.[150] The inclination of the rabbis to allow Jews, not only in practice but in principle, to accept local governmental valuations of the currency (where in fact there was a government with sufficient authority to regulate the valuation of currency) enabled Jews to establish a more flexible money supply, to assume lower borrowing costs, and to have a better capacity to invest. Within those segments of the economy over which they had some control, the harmonization of their fiscal calculations with those of their neighbors improved prospects for greater employment and production of goods and services. This nominalist stance that the medieval rabbis took toward currency fluctuation, allowing Jews to set value in relation to the external system rather than inner criteria, thus may have stimulated economic growth among Jews.[151] Moreover, the rabbis might have understood that the Jews had a special

148. *SA, Ḥoshen Mishpat,* 369:8.

149. See Shilo, *Dina,* 433–41, and Katz, *Goy Shel Shabbat,* for summary statements on this difficult issue. Because of the internal mechanisms of halakha and the deference of the rabbis to their predecessors, their response to their contemporary situation, and what we may learn about that situation, is often limited.

150. These economic factors, including patterns of bullion flow and balances of trade between East and West, are surveyed in chapter 1. See references to the studies of Attman, Bloch, and Usher as well as to those of Bogucka, Hundert, and Mączak, which focus more on Poland.

151. Miskimin, *Economy of Later Renaissance Europe,* 162. Miskimin emphasizes that the acceptance of government valuation had positive effects only when it was "immune from irresponsible expansionary acts of ambitious princes" who would establish the nominal value of coins with insufficient attention to any real calculation of bullion values, leading to rapid inflation and low economic growth. This may be expressed in the rabbis' insistence that dina demalekhuta dina applies where the sovereign has established rules governing fluctuations in coin values, thereby justifying Jews' faith in the monetary system and credit of the government. The alternate approach of favoring local custom and contractual agreement shows the confidence of the rabbis in the practical solutions arrived at by Jewish merchants to these vexing problems, at least where there is a modicum of economic stability.

advantage in recognizing the nominal value of coins insofar as Jews had a heavier tax burden than others and often had more fiscal relations with the sovereign, particularly in Poland. At least for that part of his income that would go to pay the heaviest taxes, a Jew had no incentive to exchange those coins for less than face value.[152]

But it may be more than coincidental that these concessions were made by the rabbis precisely at the same time that scholastic economic thinking crystallized, mediating strands of philosophical and fiscal nominalism. Again this invites a speculative argument, the details of which may require refinement. As in the early rabbinic period, Jews in this period were experiencing still another encounter with the classical world, this time a literary one. We have considered the influence of scholasticism, particularly the conflict between different theories of knowledge and their impact on medieval economic thinking. What influence, however indirect, might this conflict have had on medieval Jewish economic thinking? Might traces of philosophical nominalism in medieval Judaism have reinforced any tendency to fiscal nominalism among Jews? And what of this nominalism might have been mediated to early modern Polish Jews, more than to Polish Christians, providing the metaphysical and psychological preconditions of entrepreneurialism and placing the Jews at an advantage in their commercial and financial transactions?

The impact of scholasticism on Judaism and on Jewish economic thinking is largely indirect and difficult to gauge. Jews during the High Middle Ages were involved in the translation and mediation of "recovered" wisdom of Greece (*ḥokhmat Yavan*). Aquinas, according to some reports, was influenced by the writings of Maimonides.[153] Nevertheless, the scope and intensity of these trans-cultural influences, of the admixture of Aristotelianism and Neoplatonism, upon medieval Judaism were rather limited.[154] "Philosopher-scientists," writes Isadore Twersky, "sought to maintain 'peaceful coexistence' between Greek science and rabbinic lore."[155] Their concepts of cosmology, epistemology, and causality, to whatever extent they were influenced by *ḥokhma*, simply did not attain the level of systematization that these concepts reached in medieval Christianity.

---

152. Ibid., 159.

153. Haberman, *Maimonides and Aquinas;* Dienstag, *Studies in Maimonides and Aquinas;* Pines and Yovel, eds., *Maimonides and Philosophy.*

154. See Maimonides, in an oft-cited passage from the *Guide of the Perplexed,* 2:25. For a summary statement of these influences in the sixteenth century, see Herbert Davidson, "Medieval Jewish Philosophy, 106–45, as well as other articles in Cooperman, ed., *Jewish Thought.* For an assessment of this influence in regard to Jewish law, see Urbach, *Baalei Hattosafot,* 76; Falk, "Jewish Law and Medieval Canon Law," 78–96. Falk argues that canon law has a more narrow focus than Jewish law in that the former "is only interested in the proper organization and government of the Church." He does not discuss scholastic concepts behind that law, whose influence on economic thinking might be deemed far more pervasive.

155. Twersky, *Introduction to the Code of Maimonides.*

Their discussions of biblical interpretation, metaphysics, and faith and law were generally confined to the realm of the speculative.

On Jewish law in particular scholasticism had little direct and consciously acknowledgeable influence.[156] The comprehensive domain of halakha, in fact, was shaped rather by legal precedents, internal processes, and actual economic exigencies and historical conditions. Concepts of natural law, integral to scholasticism, were virtually without influence.[157] Similarly, the idealization of communities based on self-sufficiency and autarky, with its anticommercial and antimonetary implications, these thoughts of Aristotle now spread by the writings of Aquinas, were wholly lacking as a foundation of economic thinking in medieval Judaism, much as they were inconsequential to rabbinic economic thinking.[158] But I am not so much interested in the history of ideas as in interpretation of the thinking and motives from the diverse patterns by which ideas spread. The limited and indirect influence of such scholastic conceptions as realism, determinism, and economic control upon Judaism, and upon the different legal and social contexts within which Jewish and Christian attitudes toward commerce and currency were established, suggest differences in thinking and motives with economic implications.

Maimonides was the prism through which various insights on medieval Jewish philosophy were refracted. But even in the prolific writings of a rationalist of his caliber, systematic economic thought was less developed than it was among Christian scholastics, who like Aquinas may have demonstrated some interest in economics, if only for the sake of comprehensiveness. Maimonides, though enumerating economics as one of the sciences, was reluctant to postulate an independent, deterministic economic science that would formulate the rules of economic activity and predict comprehensible results; rather, he underscored God's providence as the source of nurturance and was willing to leave his study of economics at that. But this concept of providence, with its cosmological and epistemological underpinnings different from Christian determinism, had implications for Jewish economic thinking.[159]

Maimonides' cosmology was both in harmony and in conflict with the

156. Falk, "Jewish Law and Medieval Canon Law," 91, gives a singular example, ascribed to Rabbi Gershom of Mayence (960–1028), of a provision clearly identified with canon law that influenced the enactment of excommunication. Baron, "Economic Views of Maimonides," 170. Albeck, *Dinei,* 13–31; Twersky, *Introduction,* 356–514.

157. Fox, "Maimonides and Aquinas on Natural Law," 75–106.

158. Pribram, *History of Economic Reasoning,* 12.

159. As Baron notes, "It is truly remarkable that the Jewish people, whose transformation into a predominantly mercantile group had made rapid progress during those very centuries in which Jewish scholasticism and jurisprudence reached their highest degree of fruition, never produced an economic thinking to lend theoretical formulation to the existing reality. . . . It was not a lack of recognition of the economic springs of human conduct but the conscious attempt to prevent the Graeco-Arabian social philosophy from modeling the economic relations among Jews which determined the relative aloofness of medieval Jewish thinkers." Baron, "Economic Views of Maimonides," 121–28.

Greco-Arabic model. It posited a natural order ruled by the principles of natural causation. But also, like the biblical cosmology, it posited a social sphere of special providence, ruled by covenantal causality and allowing for miracles.[160] In regard to human beings and the children of Israel, Maimonides believed God's vigilance to be direct. But the conditions under which God rewarded bounty, though far from capricious, were more indeterminate than God's direction of the natural order. This contingency had affinities with covenantal causality and nominalism and might have supported a less interventionist posture toward economic affairs. In all this, Maimonides' conception differed from the mainstream of scholastic economic thinking, particularly that which dominated the Counter-Reformation.[161]

In several other aspects of his thinking Maimonides manifests and perhaps strengthens Jewish propensities for nominalism. Best known is his discussion of *taamei hamizvot*, or the explanation of the precepts, for which he provided historical and functional interpretations in his more philosophical writings, particularly in the *Guide of the Perplexed*. But even in the *Mishne Tora* he did not imply sacramental causality or underscore the ontological moorings of the precepts. Fulfilling the precepts has "teleological-spiritual" but not magical ends.[162] Maimonides' use of the rabbinic aphorism *dibra Tora kileshon benei adam* ("the Tora communicates in the language of mortals"), an accommodation of meaning to reality, is nominalistic. Similarly, his attitudes toward astrology and the ontological status with which he posited the attributes could have lent support to early nominalism in Jewish life.[163] His nominalist propensities are again illustrated in his astronomy and in his formalistic approach to hypotheses. Here he departed sharply from other savants in the Aristotelian and Arabic traditions, including Aquinas, who took a more realistic approach.[164]

Both the influence of Maimonides' ideas and the reaction that he precipitated among subsequent generations of rationalists as well as mystics were

160. Maimonides' position on providence is subject to different interpretations. See *Guide*, 1:73, 2:38; Twersky, *Introduction*, 397; Funkenstein, *Theology and the Scientific Imagination*, 221. Courtenay, "Critique of Natural Causality," makes an important distinction between al-Ghazali and Ockham on the question of natural causality. And though Christian scholastics also had to allow for God's intervention and explain miracles, they asserted this deterministic cosmology with great enthusiasm, in no small measure because of its affinities with the interests, as they perceived them to be, of a powerful and centralized religious institution. It also lent them legitimacy as the interpreters of the church's authority and its comprehensive efforts to regulate the different spheres of activities of its believers. This propensity to establish determinism influenced their tendency to systematize knowledge and regulate other spheres of human activity, such as economics.
161. See below for a comparison with Max Weber's *Protestant Ethic and the Spirit of Capitalism*.
162. Twersky, *Introduction*, 356, 418–40.
163. Barkai, *Madda, Magya*, 7–35.
164. See Maimonides, *Guide*, pt. 2, chaps. 11, 23, 24; Duhem, *To Save the Phenomena*, 33; Twersky, *Introduction*, 367–68; 481–82.

strong.[165] What effect, however indirect, these philosophical ideas may have had upon the economic thinking and attitudes toward money among Jews is far more difficult to ascertain and requires further investigation.

Before focusing on the economic thinking of Polish Jews, I should restate my main hypothesis. What little we may glean of the manner, however unsystematic, in which Polish Jews thought about their economic opportunities and problems, it was not especially susceptible to the notions of determinism and realism that scholasticism might have mediated. The direct influences of rationalism, particularly of Maimonides' philosophical writings, among most Polish Jews in the sixteenth to eighteenth century were likely in decline.[166] But their economic activity may have been supported by a less deterministic cosmology according some significance to worldly activity and characterized by a more nominalistic approach than that of their gentile neighbors. If there is validity to this analysis of the legacy of medieval Judaism available to Polish Jews, in contrast with the modes of thinking available to Polish Christians through Counter-Reformation Catholicism, might not those Jews have had sets of motives and orientations similar to those developing in the entrepreneurial sectors of the West?[167]

The assessment that this study requires of the relative strength of nominalism and realism in different circles of Jewish life and in different geographic regions is difficult to make at this time. Current research on the intellectual and spiritual life of early modern Polish Jewry leaves these questions very much in flux. Nevertheless, a few trends may tentatively be identified. There is no evidence of any direct influence of Polish scholasticism on Jewish economic thinking. The points of social and intellectual contact between Jewish and Polish scholars were few. And whereas to a very limited extent both were drawing knowledge and inspiration from centers of learning in Prague and in Italy, they were doing so independently of one another.[168] Nevertheless, among some Polish rabbis in the fourteenth and fifteenth centuries there was interest in speculative philosophy in general and Maimonides' version in particular.[169] By the late sixteenth and the seventeenth centuries the image of philosophy among Jews in Poland had become more negative, further limiting any influence of scholasticism and any conscious effort to absorb currents of thought in the proximate gentile society of Poland or the

165. There is a considerable literature on the diverse influences of Maimonides and the anti-Maimonidean controversies. Of the more recent writings, see, for example, Idel, "Sitre Arayot," 79–91; *Kabbalah: New Perspectives*; and "'Deus Sive Natura'"; Tirosh-Rothchild, "Concept of Tora," 1:104ff.

166. One indicator can be seen in the infrequency with which Maimonides' *Guide* is republished in this period in contrast with the publication record of the *Mishne Tora.* See Friedberg, *Bet Eked Sepharim*, vol. 2. Elbaum, "Hebrew Ethical Literature," 146–66, and others now assert that this decline has been overstated.

167. What Weber identifies as a more deterministic outlook was necessary in the Christian orbit to spur entrepreneurialism because of theurgic and world-rejecting tendencies not as pronounced in Judaism at the time.

168. Shmeruk, "Yiddish Literature in Poland," 258–314.

169. Kupfer, "Cultural Image of Ashkenaz Jewry," 113–47.

more remote society of Western Europe. Even those few students and teachers interested in dabbling in "Gentile wisdom" confined the uses to which Aristotelianism could be put to the explanation of "the logics of the Talmud and the homilies in a manner that they should be found to be worthy among the Gentiles." Those who retained some interest in rationalism were becoming less concerned to appear "wise in the eyes of the nations."[170]

The study of astronomy among Polish Jews exemplifies these tendencies. It was approached with an enthusiasm comparable to that which was applied to metaphysics, and it was as insular. There are virtually no traces of the revolution brought about by Copernicus, even in the musings of another Cracowite, Moses Isserles.[171] This same period witnessed a significant growth of *yeshivot* (talmudic academies) in Poland. There was an intensification of pedagogic debates, begun in Germany two centuries earlier, challenging the acceptability of philosophic constructs in the house of study and the validity of *pilpul* (casuistry) in its different forms as a method of interpretation and establishment of the law. Pilpul, in its nonrealist approach to hypotheses, may have had affinities with nominalism.[172] It is against this background that Solomon Luria, who himself had an equivocal relationship to rationalism, took his position against the application of dina demalekhuta dina to the laws regarding a coin whose value has changed.

The intellectual development that may have had the most important impact on the balance of realistic and nominalistic trends among Polish Jews came from abroad. In the late sixteenth and the seventeenth centuries the two primary schools of Kabbala in Sefad began to spread by way of Italy through Europe and to take root in Poland. Moses Cordovero seems to have invested his kabbalistic symbols and interpretations with greater nominalism. Significantly, it now appears that his approach was more influential than scholars initially had believed. It also had a more enduring influence, corresponding perhaps to the period through the end of the seventeenth century in which there were signs of Jewish en-

170. On the discussion of alien or gentile wisdom in sixteenth-century Poland, see Assaf, *Mekorot Letoledot Hahinnukh*, 1:40–41; H. Ben-Sasson, *Hagut Vehanhaga*, 11–17; Elbaum, "Hebrew Ethical Literature"; Kaplan, "Rabbi Mordekhai Jaffe," 262–82; Y. Ben-Sasson, *Mishnato*, 2–5. Jacob Katz and Hayyim Hillel Ben-Sasson discuss the degree to which Polish Jews were insulated from Polish society in the early modern period. Katz notes that the intellectual and spiritual insulation of the heirs of Ashkenazi Jewry from the larger society resulted in the relaxation of religious tensions, particularly when compared with the religious challenges to Ashkenazi Jewry in an earlier period. Ben Sasson argues against the depiction of a Polish Jewish community sealed off from and oblivious to what was transpiring in Christian Europe. He points to actual contact and social reference. A synthesis of these two contrary positions is possible: Polish Jews were not involved in any religious discourse with their neighbors but had some interest in what was going on in the world around them as well as some concern for how those neighbors would think of them—for reasons of security as well as to sanctify God's name.

171. Levine, "Paradise Not Surrendered," 203–25; Fishman, "Rabbi Moshe Isserlis."

172. See the work of Mordekhai Breuer on the history of pilpul, particularly "Rise of 'Pilpul' and 'Hillukim.'"

trepreneurialism. Isaac Luria's approach to mysticism, which ultimately proved to be more influential than Cordovero's, seemed to purvey a realistic approach to symbols. Among its other influences, it invested ritual activity with new sacramental powers.[173] The *sefirot* (the mystical conception of the ten stages of emanation) were seen to have extended their control to the terrestrial world.[174] They were ascribed a stronger reality. The popular religion of Polish Jews in the early modern period undoubtedly absorbed conceptions of magic, even providing magical rationales and incentives for the performance of the precepts.[175]

It may prove to be all but impossible to trace the relative degrees of direct influence of either Cordoveran or Lurianic thinking. Suffice it to say that these trends were in the air. But to whatever extent Lurianic Kabbala might have been a source of realism to Polish Jews, it did not foster the degree of sacramental causality that we find in the Polish Christianity of the same period, with its popular religion, magic, witchcraft, Mary cults, shrines, and the like.[176]

The biblical conception of a free and omnipotent God may have become attenuated at times but was never completely abandoned, even in the most deterministic of Jewish rationalisms or mysticisms or the most magical of Polish Jewish folk beliefs and practices.[177] To whatever extent the promulgation of Cordoveran or Lurianic Kabbala may have fostered nominalism or realism among Jews, a thesis requiring substantiation, the conflict was less extreme than it was in many Christian circles.[178] Although there may not have been Jewish Ockhams or

173. See Ben Shlomo, *Torat Haelohut,* and the controversial study by Rivka Schatz-Uffenheimer, "Cordovero and the Ari," 122–36, in which Cordoveran metaphysics is seen as nominalistic. The triumph of Isaac Luria's system carried with it, according to this argument, a new realism.

174. Tishbi, *Mishnat Hazzohar,* 1:390.

175. The legal valence of *kavvana* (contemplative intention) in the performance of the precepts presents an interesting problem. It might be assumed that where the principle *mizvot einan zerikhot kavvana,* (the performance of the precept is not contingent on intention) prevails, a more sacramental approach to the precepts is manifested, emphasizing the action rather than the state of mind. Yet it is precisely as a concomitant of the popularization of Lurianic Kabbala, from the end of the sixteenth century, that we find a greater emphasis on contemplative intention. This is formulated in great detail in new incantations attached as prolegomena to the recitation of specific prayers and the performance of specific rituals.

176. Dan, "'No Evil Descends from Heaven,'" illustrates this in the monistic theodicy of the sixteenth century. Notwithstanding the religious tensions of the period and the efforts to explain recent catastrophes, mythological symbolism of the Zohar was muted, and the nonreality and contingency of evil were emphasized. This approach, at least among rabbis, can be seen in their theoretical treatment of witchcraft and demonology, in a sense real personifications of evil. While the veracity of such phenomena was beyond doubt, they reverted to pre-Zoharic explanations of the one and good God and the nonreality of any supreme principle of evil.

177. For an analysis of intriguing combinations of mysticism and rationalism in early modern Europe, see Yates, *Rosicrucian Enlightenment,* 206–33.

178. Courtenay, "Nominalism and Late Medieval Religion," 57. Perry Miller, *New England*

Erasmuses, accompanied by the secondary intellectuals who popularize their masters' insights, nominalistic thinking continued to be less dangerously available to Jews. In the history of Jewish mysticism in particular, an inner dialectic balances between abstraction and concretization, between the efforts to comprehend metaphysical mysteries in human terms and the reticence in regard to anthropomorphism which to some extent renders the extremes in nominalism and realism moot.[179] A symbol suspected of being tinged with excessive realism could be summarily dissolved with a pious pronouncement: *kivayakhol* (as if). The availability of this moderate nominalism may have influenced the economic thinking of Polish Jews.

The problems of providence, determinism, and free choice are likewise expressed in a considerable homiletical literature that probably is a sparse written record of popular preaching. Both rational-philosophical and mythological-mystical influences are manifest, though these problems do not receive systematic treatment. A fuller treatment of the spiritual world of Polish Jewry is necessary before we can comprehend the intellectual and emotional tensions that were aroused by these problems in their reciprocity with economic forces, and the motives for economic activity that they generated. To what extent do we find the combination of predestination and worldly asceticism that has been identified, at least by Weber, as a spur to enterprise? A few sixteenth- and early seventeenth-century comments on providence illustrate the concern with the issues of the world of everyday life, such as distributive justice and the efficacy of human action, as much as with issues of a more otherworldly significance, such as theodicy. Rabbi Moses Isserlis (1523–1572), the most prominent sixteenth-century Polish rabbi to harbor an interest in Aristotelianism, suggested that two determining variables intervene between God's providence and a person's economic fate: person's character and the constellations at the moment of birth. Those astrological forces, the rabbi goes on to explain, have a continuing influence on that character. God distributes wealth in accordance with the individual's innate ability to withstand temptations of sin. "For it is impossible to make him wealthy based on his merit if God does not grant to him . . . a different *teva* [character] and change his constellation. And this is virtually impossible. For free will is granted to the individual in accordance with his constellation."[180] But even in positing this strong predestination (Ben-Sasson even compares him with Calvin), Isserlis does not exclude religious merit or diligent and virtuous activity from his considerations of what makes people wealthy. Solomon Luria likewise grants a small but significant role to human action in assessing the religious

Mind, emphasized the importance of the contract and the image of commercial transactions in the theology of New England Puritans. In a more recent study, David Zaret, *Heavenly Contract,* makes a similar point.

179. Tishbi, *Netivei Emuna Uminut,* 25–29.

180. Isserles, *Torat Haola,* pt. 3, chap. 53, 117a–b, cited in H. Ben-Sasson, *Hagut Vehanhaga,* 78.

meaning of worldly success. "Reaching the level and wealth and the like for Israel is impossible without merit, and this is in addition to his actions." It is only for the Jews that there is any efficacy in one's actions or the merit of one's forefathers; the economic success of Gentiles is completely determined.[181] The popular Polish homileticist, Ephraim of Luntchiz (1550–1619), presents more extreme positions on this question of the efficacy of human action, suggesting that human sustenance is providentially determined. He appropriates the biblical proof text of autonomous economic endeavor, "in the sweat of thy face shalt thou eat bread," for other purposes.[182]

Success in worldly activities and wealth must at times have evoked religious responses. Good fate might be interpreted as a sign of merit, and people of wealth might try to convince themselves and others that their good fortune was a sign of religious virtue.[183] But there was a limit to which wealth could be taken as a sign of virtue, let alone as a reflection of salvation. For example, Rabbi Yedidya Gotlieb (d. 1645), a seventeenth-century Polish homileticist, declared that "in every generation our eyes see that God has given all good things . . . to those who do not deserve them." The rabbi comes to terms with the reality of undeservingly rewarded Jews and Gentiles by dismissing those rewards as ultimately bad for the soul.[184]

This observation of Yedidya Gotlieb points to a serious problem that Jews had in attaching religious significance to worldly achievement and therefore of deriving entrepreneurial motives from religious reflection and spiritual tensions. Why the wicked flourish and the righteous suffer—the classic problem of theodicty—was not experienced merely as an individual problem demanding resolution: The painful observation "all good things . . . to those who do not deserve them" touched on the collective existence of the Jewish people and its relationship to God.[185] The wealth and power of Christians made all appearances suspect. To whatever extent Jews might want to value and venerate the appearances of worldly success, they could not attribute to those appearances an unequivocal indication of inner virtue and ultimate redemption. Jews, in their primary responses to these appearances, had to obliterate the ties between the inner world of Jewish meaning and the larger world of everyday life. For that quotidian world, at any given moment in its pre-Messianic state, might pose an

181. Luria, *Yam Shel Shelomo,* chap. 5, no. 23, 41, cited in H. Ben-Sasson, *Hagut Vehanhaga,* 81.

182. H. Ben-Sasson, *Hagut Vehanhaga,* 90–110.

183. Ibid., 98. Within this upper class there were signs of increasing rivalry between the "man who rose by his own strength" and those who inherited old wealth. This conflict illuminates the entrepreneurial opportunities as well as the relative economic stability of this period, which allowed for the transfer of wealth and status from generation to generation.

184. Ibid., 104.

185. Ibid. To be sure, Weber exaggerates the degree to which Jews experience fate in national rather than individual terms. See *Sociology of Religion,* 112ff.

overwhelming contradiction to the most cherished Jewish beliefs. But Jews firmly believed that ultimately in the world of redemption the inner world of Jewish meaning surely would be vindicated. The claims of Christians in this period that their outer successes constituted proof of the truth of Christianity made it all the more necessary for Jews to devalue power and wealth in the outer world as signs of redemption.[186] Jewish enterprise, particularly as the existence of Polish Jews became more precarious, required other motives.

Though Polish Judaism may not have generated theological or eschatological incentives that directly spurred entrepreneurial activities, neither did it create strong inhibitions. This deregulation of commerce has its antecedents in rabbinic Judaism formulated before the early modern period, but it was quite pronounced in sixteenth-century Poland.[187] It is in this deregulation that we find among Polish Jews greater latitude to exploit new economic opportunities.

Among early modern Polish Jews, and characteristically for Judaism in general, there was no important legacy of negative attitudes toward trade per se, in contrast with anti-commercial attitudes fostered by Christianity and some traditions of Islam.[188] Someone who made an honest living in trade would be religiously beyond reproach in regard to trade itself.[189] What would be questionable, however, particularly among the pietists and the homileticists, would be the deflection of the merchant's and the tradesman's attention from the study of Tora and excessive concern with material matters.[190] In sixteenth- and seventeenth-century Poland, negative attitudes toward trade derived primarily from concern about how trade might interfere with the fulfillment of the commandments. Asceticism was not idealized to the same degree as it was among *hasidei Ashkenaz,* the German-Jewish pietists, several centuries earlier. It was deemed best for Jews to earn a minimal living with minimal effort. Insofar as moneylending and even trade could provide sustenance with dignity and with limited effort, they were looked upon positively. The study of Tora could be put to the service of a remunerative vocation, and the professional scholar could make claims on the community for support. Other professions, including crafts and labor, were seemingly a matter of religious indifference. The guilds, among both Polish Jews and Polish Gentiles, took on ancillary religious and social functions and accorded their members a measure of dignity.[191] But they were not seen in the religious terms of vocation or calling, as the Puritans viewed such involvements.

At the same time, whatever principled religious indifference there was toward economic activity had to be sharply curtailed, not so much by the theologi-

186. This cognitive dualism is quite different from, though related to, the dualism discussed by Max Weber as the "double ethic" of a "pariah people."
187. Baron, *Maimonides,* 183.
188. Ibid., 170.
189. H. Ben-Sasson, *Hagut Vehanhaga,* 56.
190. Ibid., 65.
191. Kremer, "Labor and the Workers Guilds," 294–325.

cal resistance to world rejection as much as by considerations of the security of Jews. Collective responsibility, often foisted on Jews by king, gentry, and other officials, prompted religious and communal leaders to be mindful of Jewish vocations and to use religious institutions to attempt to regulate business activities. And though new enterprises and business arrangements undertaken by Polish Jews in this period strained halakhic principle and precedent, many of these activities could not be a matter of religious indifference.[192] Bridging concerns for the physical and spiritual security of Jews was the rabbis' concern to avoid *ḥilul hashem* (desecration of God's name) or that type of behavior by Jews that would lead to disgrace and to the disapproval of Gentiles.[193]

In monetary matters Polish Jews were less limited by clerical restrictions than their Catholic neighbors. At the same time, they benefited from modes of cognition supportive of different modes of financial analysis. Long after models for credit institutions had developed in such Catholic bastions as Medici Italy and in the house of Fugger, restrictions on credit abided among most Catholics.[194] Even when ignored and circumvented, as they often were, they placed inhibitions on finance. Particularly in the orbit of the Counter-Reformation, they drew conceptual strength and justification from Aristotelian and Christian notions of the nongenerativity of money.[195] There were scholastic thinkers who began to sanction instruments for moneylending. The patterns of evasion became important to the history of banking. But even in most Protestant regions, where the ban was effectively removed by the mid-seventeenth century, *usurer* continued to be a title of contempt and opprobrium. Bad consciences had economic consequences: moneylenders passed on the social cost of their stigma. Jews, by contrast, operating free of such inhibitions, could charge a more favorable rate for their services and their risk.

Credit, a prerequisite for enterprise, was relatively unfettered among early modern Polish Jews from both scholastic and halakhic restrictions. As we have seen, the devices by which "brothers" could be treated as "others," were well developed from an early date.[196] Moneylending may have been less central to the

192. Katz, *Goy Shel Shabbat,* 82.

193. See Jacob Katz's discussion of the changing concept of *ḥilul hashem* in *Exclusiveness and Tolerance,* 158–62. Whatever the source of concern, it is not clear to what degree Polish Jews conformed to the religious demands of the supervisory institutions. The conflict between scholars and leaders intensified in this period, in part having to do with different perceptions of the commonweal or general welfare. In comparison with the position and influence of scholars in medieval Germany, scholars in Poland up through the middle of the seventeenth century seem to have been less powerful.

194. Braudel, *Wheels of Commerce,* 2:150, 394, 479–81, 575.

195. Oresme states, "It is monstrous and unnatural that an unfruitful thing, a thing specifically sterile such as money should bear fruit and multiply of itself." Thinkers as diverse as Francis Bacon and Martin Luther concurred that "it is against nature for money to beget money." Shell, *Money, Language and Thought,* 51.

196. Nelson, *Idea of Usury.*

Fig. 5. *Polish Jew Returning from Synagogue*. Aquatint, 1819 by P. Debucourt (1755–1832) based on an eighteenth-century sketch by J. P. Norblin de La Gourdine (1745–1830). A wooden synagogue is in background.

economics of Polish Jews than it had been to that of their German Jewish ancestors. But even trade, peddling, and participation in the crafts involved various
instruments of credit that touched upon the laws of usury.[197] Although these laws
were far from settled, generating lively discussions among Polish rabbis, the
mechanisms for circumventing interdictions on moneylending by the end of the
sixteenth century were sufficiently well developed that religious law posed no
insurmountable obstacle to the development of Jewish credit markets. As Joshua
Falk (1555–1614), one of the leaders of the Council of Four Lands and an important rabbinic commentator, summarized regarding the laws of usury:

> Since we found that they were lenient and they made it public, decreeing the
> precise formula, we derive from this that it is permissible. And it is proper to
> reveal to individuals that they are in accord with the law and the trustees of
> the community and they will teach the way, each one as he sees fit. And
> similarly they should write on the contract that it was done in this manner
> and with the above licence . . . though all of these are *temuhim* [confusing]
> and appear to be a *hearama* [evasion]; nevertheless, to meet the needs of the
> hour, they should not be forbidden in order to provide sustenance for the
> children of the covenant.[198]

The council occasionally discussed limits on the actual rate of interest.[199] Not
burdened by these Aristotelian qualms as to the generativity of money, Jews were
eminently suited to develop commercial exchange. Finance was less controversial among Jews than among Christians well into the early modern period. Thus, in
Jewish attitudes toward moneylending, we see another area where internal Jewish developments may have placed Polish Jews in an advantageous position in the
Polish economy and enabled them to be more entrepreneurial than Polish
Christians.

But more significant than the prevalence of uninhibited moneylending
among Jews were the instruments and institutions of credit, developing among
Polish Jews and sanctioned by their religious leaders. The abstracting concepts
allowing for greater transferability and interchangeability may have provided
them with a competitive edge over their Christian neighbors. These concepts,
insofar as they were more slow to develop and take hold in Christian Europe,

197. De Roover, *Money, Banking and Credit,* 345. Whereas different legal statuses were
assigned to merchant bankers, money changers, and pawnbrokers, differences in their
actual economic activities were not always so clear. In regard to Polish Jewry in the early
modern period, there is insufficient material to differentiate sharply between their economic roles.
198. Joshua Falk formulated rulings on usury in connection with the council's meeting at
Gramnitz in 1607. These were republished in a folio in 1692 and cited in a work by a
disciple, *Lehem Panim,* which is reprinted in the *SA, Yore Deia,* 2:114a–b, as the
conclusion.
199. Halpern, ed., *Pinkas Vaad Arba Arazot,* art. 343, p. 146 (1674); art. 890, p. 468
(before 1684).

especially in Christian Poland, made Jews better prepared to participate in commercial and financial markets.

An example of this advantage may be seen in the utility of the *mamran,* a fully negotiable instrument of exchange introduced by Polish Jews by the end of the sixteenth century.[200] The advantage that it afforded is evident from the effect that fully negotiable instruments had elsewhere in Europe. Historians point to the statutory recognition given to unlimited endorsement in the Low Countries earlier than in France, Germany, Italy, or even England as a major factor contributing to seventeenth-century Dutch commercial success. Although models for these instruments had appeared among European merchants hundreds of years earlier, they were less negotiable. The doctrine of negotiability was not "finally matured" until the seventeenth century.[201] The availability at a somewhat earlier date of such instruments as the mamran among Polish Jews further illustrates economic advantages enjoyed by those Jews over their gentile neighbors.[202]

This history of commercial paper indicates additional advantages of Jews in conducting international commerce in the Jewish courts and juridical apparatuses that made agreements enforceable or led to a greater sense of trust between Jews in far-flung communities. Contrary to the practice through the early modern period, as Usher describes it, of "transacting all important business in person if possible," Jews could conduct among themselves a wide range of banking activities without the informal sanctions of a geographically based commercial community. The absence of this trust is particularly apparent among the Polish gentry. With whatever commercial instruments at their disposal, the renown of the nobles for litigiousness added to the cost and detracted from the effectiveness of their commercial endeavors. As Jews became more attached to the estates of the aristocracy, and with the increasing decentralization of Jewish communal life, the economic behavior of Jewish tradesmen may have become more like that of the Polish lords, and they may have lost a valuable competitive edge. The Council of Four Lands and its federated structures were at best only partially successful in regulating against Jewish "escapers."

200. Fuss, "Mamran Contract," 51–67.
201. As Usher observes, "The evolution of the seemingly simple concepts involved a singularly long and complex process." *Deposit Banking,* 74.
202. Here we are not concerned with the legal innovations of this note, whether, as Sombart suggests, we can "deduce modern credit instruments from rabbinic law" or whether the Jews were the first to introduce this depersonalized economic transaction and influence its spread throughout Europe. Sombart, *Jews and Modern Capitalism,* 83. I am concerned simply to infer the thinking that accompanies the use of such bills of exchange and the convenience resulting in commercial advantages, which Jews, as the first to introduce these instruments into Poland, may have enjoyed. Involvement in these modes of economic thinking may foster nominalistic thinking, which in turn strengthens entrepreneurial capacities. Shell, *Money, Language and Thought,* 3. The prevalence of the use of these instruments cannot be ascertained. A search of the sample of rabbinic responsa computerized at the Bar Ilan University Responsa Project, Ramat Gan, Israel, pointed to one source: Rabbi Meir Eisenstadt, *Shut Panim Meirot,* no. 5.

The vast network of community-supported Jewish schools, from the *ḥeder* (children's school) to the yeshiva, ensured a high degree of popular access to law and doctrine. Neither the differences in the intellectual attainments nor the social distance between "professional" rabbis, teachers, and judges, on the one hand, and merchants, artisans, and arendars, on the other, were insuperable. The dvorf yid, to be sure, may not have possessed deep learnedness. Lithuania in the eighteenth century was not the home of great Talmudic academies, as it became in the nineteenth and twentieth centuries. Literacy, a primary source of the modes of thinking that I have identified with nominalism, was widespread, at least among males.[203]

Inferring popular practices and modes of consciousness or mentalities, particularly as they may have motivated economic activity, from the normative—the "law on the book," the Tora studied in the academies—is risky.[204] Nevertheless, the intensity of Tora study among so many Polish Jews in this period and the concentration on the theoretical study of halakha, independently of the applications to day-to-day life, served to sustain a vision of order and concern in human relations, even if that vision was honored only in the breach or if its details were rendered irrelevant by circumstances. Moreover, this effort to maintain at least the spirit of the law, rather than consistently and doggedly attempting to fetter life to abstract principle, generated as an unanticipated consequence modes of rationality. With the expansion of communal authority in Poland, the registries of those kahal structures, the *pinkasim,* took on the authority of precedent, drawing from more ancient rabbinic sources—at times genuine points of law, at times legal embellishments and legitimation. To whatever extent this corpus and its interpretive institutions were authoritative to individual Polish Jews at particular times, it is clear that they were there and available.

Here I must underscore a very different context in which Jewish jurists influenced worldly activities of Jews, in comparison with the restrictions placed by Catholic clerics and philosophers upon Christian merchants in the Middle Ages, lasting in some areas through the early modern period. Catholic religious regulation of economic activity had an immediacy for the achievement of salvation. Communal and rabbinic regulation of the economic activities of Jews was prompted mainly by the concern to preserve social order.

These differences between Christian and Jewish approaches to economic affairs were reflected, for example, in the different involvements of Jesuits and rabbis, who often took up their respective stations at the very same Polish trade fairs.[205] At the fairs many dubious commercial practices developed in relation to traditional religious rules. Theologians were frequently obliged to make hairsplit-

203. Stampfer, "Reading and Writing," 459–83.
204. This is a pitfall of Weber and Sombart, on the one side, and even some Jewish historians, on the other. Jacob Katz, in several of his works, presents enlightening methodological statements on distinguishing the descriptive from the normative in different literary genres. See *Halakha Vekabbala,* esp. 311–39.
205. Usher, *Deposit Banking,* 110–34.

ting distinctions between the licit and illicit, and to reinterpret traditional rules under pressures from changing economic conditions and from merchants concerned for the salvation of their souls. The Jesuits, whose liberal position on dealing in foreign exchange spurred the growth of fairs, wrote their pamphlets to enable merchants to carry out their business without jeopardizing their salvation.[206] In contrast to other religious orders, such as the Dominicans, the Jesuits demonstrated remarkable leniency in regard to usury. Despite their condemnations of discounting credit instruments, they provided the casuistry by which this was accomplished under the concealment of fictitious forms of exchange transactions. Whatever the results of this "leniency," as has been suggested by some historians, for the growth of institutions of early capitalism, the theological and legal scrupulousness demanded to sustain these fictions called for the services of clerical consultants.[207]

The rabbis, by contrast, were overseeing social order and tending to ancillary social and religious functions. In regard to that social order, their concern in enterprise among Jews had to do with supporting contractual agreements and preserving the mutuality of expectations; in transactions conducted between Jews and non-Jews the concern was to avoid any practices that would jeopardize the collective welfare of Jews or lead to *ḥilul hashem,* the desecration of God's name. The rabbis did not offer comparable guidance in regard to personal redemption nor pen such handbooks; business for Jews had become irrelevant to their economy of salvation.

But the context in which Judaism influenced economic thinking and activity also was different from the Protestant context. Protestant predestination, with its orientation toward result rather than process, spurred believers to greater exertion, assiduousness, and concern to apply systematic reasoning instead of sacramental actions to worldly problems. At the same time, the belief in the inscrutability of God's ways could weaken the religiously motivated adherence to residual regulations of economic behavior. They simply were not deemed relevant to the saving of one's soul. Jewish attitudes salient to economic thinking were not as extreme as those of medieval Catholicism, which made rewards contingent on sacramental acts; neither were they as radical as those of early modern Protestantism, which suggested that human efforts are irrelevant and

206. De Roover, *Scholastic Economics,* 171; Pribram, *Conflicting Patterns,* 28.
207. See Robertson, *Rise of Economic Individualism.* Robertson argues that Calvinism "acted as a notable check on economic progress and on the rise of a rational and practical in place of a theologically determined philosophy of business" (103). The Jesuits, on the other hand, had a maxim: "There is nothing like business." For a spirited argument against this Jesuit thesis of the origins of capitalism, see Brodrick, *Economic Morals of the Jesuits.* To whatever extent the Jesuits may have been positively inclined toward business and tolerant of moneylending, their criteria in ruling on the propriety of transactions were not primarily economic. Their influence on economic thinking and activity diminished throughout the seventeenth century in the centers of economic development. De Roover, *Scholastic Economics,* 172.

God's ways ultimately inscrutable. "Rain in due season" depended on observing God's commandments. Worldly successes, the attainment of wealth and power, may not have been deemed by Jews as wholly predestined, as a necessary sign of religious virtue and a reassuring reflection of one's salvation. But for the Polish Jewish entrepreneur in this period, as for the Puritan, achievement and worldly success provided evidence of still greater rewards in the world beyond.

This leads us to a summary of the religious dimension of Judaism, which may have influenced the economic thinking and activities of Polish Jews. We have already had recourse to a special feature of the sociology of Judaism, analytically inseparable from the sociology of Jews in their historical conditions: whereas God was experienced as vigilant and involved in the world of everyday life, that order over which God presided was considered an inversion of the ideal cosmic order. The Jewish God was perceived as neither fleeing the world, as was the Protestant God, nor finding a comfortable abode, as was the God of medieval Catholicism. The Jew was both world-rejecting, experiencing the manifest as an illusion, and yet worldly, insofar as the world of everyday life was the arena in which God could be encountered. Insofar as appearances were suspect, Jews, unlike Protestants, could not interpret wealth, accomplishment, and merit to be an outer display and ultimate validation of inner virtue and salvation. Although weakening the links between wealth and salvation dampened an important incentive for achievement, this freeing of the outer world of religious meaning also freed it of religious regulation. Insofar as appearances were not bearers of religiously valid truths, work (and thinking about work) would exist in a seemingly secular domain. This may have fostered an ad hoc, experimental approach to economic behavior, an empirical approach to economic thinking and to its systematization, and a consensual approach to economic regulation. The scope of this particular domain was affected by a variety of factors. The anticommercialism and monetary theories inimical to enterprise that scholasticism mediated had no direct influence on sixteenth-century Polish Jews.

At the roots of Jewish commercial law, division of labor and social interdependence, rather than autonomy and autarky, were deemed natural and desirable. The rabbis posited a strong concept of currency as an institution and as an instrument of commerce, and yet they equivocated in regard to the actual power of specific currencies, as commodities or as moneys, to exchange or to purchase. This equivocation provides a conceptual background to the intricate and complex discussions in commercial and ritual law, in constant counterpoint with economic realities of Jews living under diverse circumstances.

At the same time, in regard to Polish Jewry in particular, because of the increased economic differentiation, geographic dispersion, and decentralization of authority that accompanied the new arrangements with the gentry, the rabbis and communal leaders had increasing difficulty legislating and regulating Jewish economic behavior. Especially in new areas of enterprise where Jewish law was ambiguous or not fully spelled out, Jews were influenced more by their "ritual instinct"—customs and patterns of evasion often legitimated by precedent or the opinions of secondary intellectuals—than by the learned responsa of the rabbinic elite.[208] Whole areas of economic activity, hitherto regulated by Jewish law, now became unfettered. The halakhic considerations were rendered moot. This is reflected in the responsa literature, the commentaries, and the new genre of legal and homiletical digests, the *hanhagot,* that became increasingly popular in this period. While rabbinic scholars were not necessarily disinclined to comment on areas of Jewish law (such as Temple worship) that were no longer applicable, in this period Jewish commercial law received relatively little attention. The sections on business law, in what becomes in this period the most authoritative code of law, the *Shulḥan Arukh,* evoke less commentary.

Although it would appear that the domain of rabbinic law was contracting and that religious considerations were eliminated from important types of activity, one can hardly see in this the early signs of secularization. The Jewish cosmology remained essentially Jewish, alive with religious meaning. That meaning becomes amplified in those areas to which it continued to be attached. For at the very moment that the purview of halakha began to shrink, another development in Jewish religious history began to have the opposite effect. The popularization of Kabbala and its attachment to common ritual and faith bolstered the religious cosmology in which Polish Jews acted and thought, and in which they attached new religious meanings to expanded domains of activity.

For more than a century following the period known as the Deluge, the more Sarmatian-oriented gentry, comporting themselves with smugness, continued to compare developments in Poland favorably to what they presumed to be taking place in the West. The gentry's inclination to blame others for the failure of Polish serfdom—and, with increasing frequency and viciousness, Polish Jews—did not encourage a more positive identification of Jews with the culture of Polish Christians. Neither did it support entrepreneurial motives over otherworldly orientations among the Jews. The intensity of Polish Jewish culture through the twentieth century relates to that alienation from Polish culture and society. Attributing faults and responsibility to others did not enhance Poland's situation; gentry optimism and myopia proved to be costly.[209]

208. Katz, *Goy Shel Shabbat,* 176.
209. The significance of the mid-century Deluge should not be overemphasized at the expense of earlier, more enduring and elusive factors. Others, as Hoszowski, "Revolution of Prices," 15, notes, were searching for the "real causes" of Poland's problems. In this chapter I have examined some of their findings. In chapters 4 and 5 I shall assess the adequacy of the proposals of Polish commentators who did confront a broader range of problems.

Chapter 4

"How Far Behind Have We Remained:"
Libations, Libels, and the Rhetoric
of Reform

In analyzing the position of Jews in the Polish economy of the sixteenth and the first half of the seventeenth centuries, I have focused on the management of feudal estates by Jewish arendars. Relative to Polish Catholics under the influence of the Counter-Reformation and Sarmatianism, Polish Jews, whose economic thinking became more unfettered from religious inhibitions and whose economic activities were less effectively proscribed by a religious elite, might have had a slight advantage in exploiting the "small changes" crucial to economic development and successful modernization. Moreover, some dimensions of the Judaism of Polish Jews may have generated among them entrepreneurial motives. If this analysis is correct, we might anticipate that the economic activities of at least a small segment of Polish Jewry in the late seventeenth and the eighteenth centuries would compare favorably with other entrepreneurs in the West—the court Jews in Central Europe, the Huguenots in France, or the Calvinists in Holland—resourceful and industrious members of small coteries who played roles in the economic development of their respective countries disproportionate to their numerical size.

The court Jews, for example, were pioneers in a dual sense: they contributed to the rise of centralized courts and to the capital accumulation necessary to fund and establish new enterprises in economies devastated by a century of religious wars, amassing for themselves legendary fortunes. At the same time, these few Jewish entrepreneurs, by demonstrating how "useful" the Jews were and how acculturated they might become, displayed to both Gentiles and Jews a deeper involvement of Jews in European society. Were the arendars the court Jews of Poland?[1]

The comparison soon falters. The Polish republic during this same period experienced uneven but precipitous economic decline. At a different rate, perhaps, and to a different extent than in the larger population, many Jews became pauperized, regardless of their entrepreneurial potential.[2] Few of the arendars became renowned for the vastness of their wealth and enterprise, and whatever contribution they did make to the Polish economy was obscured by that economy's general downward drift. And the eighteenth century in Poland was not a period of increasing tolerance toward Jews, as it was, however haltingly, in centers of Jewish population in the West; it was a period of increasing capriciousness and religious persecution.[3]

With Western Europe at the threshold of the modern period, Poland experienced a tragic resurgence of the infamous blood libel leveled against Jews.[4] As the

1. The fate of individual court Jews varied considerably. See chapter 3; Israel, *European Jewry*, 123–44; Shohet, *Im Ḥilufei Tekufot*, 31–34, 49ff. Amazingly, some court Jews succeeded in transmitting this accumulated capital for several generations, despite the currency fluctuations and financial instabilities of early modern Europe. Grunwalde, "German Jewish Banking History," 191–99. Unfortunately, there is little by which we can compare income distribution among Jews in the East or West, other than in a general sense. The stellar rise of the court Jews in the West should not conceal the existence of a sizable underclass of disenfranchised and mendicant Jews known as *Betteljuden,* who rarely lived above subsistence level. Their economic position was similar to that of indigent and déclassé Jews in the East. These included the *boreiaḥ* or *baal peleita,* the "escapers" to the south and east who left behind unfulfilled contracts and unpaid debts, for which the local Jewish communities had to cover, and who are mentioned with increasing frequency in the communal registries. These bankrupt Polish Jews often demonstrated economic resilience in developing new enterprises in the newly settled regions. But to whatever extent the impoverished and the entrepreneurial were represented within the Jewish communities of the East and West, of growing significance in the West was a Jewish middle class of tradesmen and artisans, who also contributed to the economic development in their region. In Poland this class was considerably weakened, particularly because of the antagonism of gentile burghers.
2. An earlier generation of Jewish historians emphasized large-scale poverty among Polish Jews, particularly in the eighteenth century, and used it to explain a variety of internal developments, including the rise of Hasidism. A far more complex picture is now emerging.
3. Perhaps in this regard the situation of Polish Jews was closer to that of the French Huguenots after the 1685 revocation of the Edict of Nantes. The Huguenots were humiliated and persecuted, but they continued to be vital to the French economy throughout the eighteenth century.
4. Weinryb, *Jews of Poland,* 150–55, underscores the difficulty in deriving from the archives a clear assessment of the scope and frequency of persecutions and the degree to which they caused Jews to feel insecure, much as it would be difficult to assess the safety and security of contemporary Jewry by examining current newspaper accounts of street crime. Undoubtedly, Polish serfs, burghers, and even nobles in early modern Poland were also subject to attacks and were caught in the crossfire. It is also clear that Polish officials

noted Polish Jewish historian Meyer Bałaban observed, "no city was free of it."[5] The accusation had roots in pre-Christian beliefs and received its familiar form in medieval Western Europe. It not only was conveyed through folklore and popular religion but received the sanction of no less a luminary of Western culture than Geoffrey Chaucer, in the *Canterbury Tales*. In the seventeenth and eighteenth centuries, allegations that Jews made ritual use of Christian blood or desecrated the Communion wafer were pressed with tragic persistence in towns and small villages of Poland, particularly around the time of the spring festival of Passover.[6] The recorded number of these incidents is high enough to confirm the impression of eighteenth-century Polish Jews—that the blood libel, rather than religious tolerance and economic enterprise, was on the rise. In early modern Poland, as

---

often pursued and prosecuted those who attacked Jews. The lords, in particular, defended "their" Jews when this persecution could result in financial loss. Jewish communities defended themselves, employed militia, and were not reluctant to use extrajuridical means when Polish courts could not pursue murderers. Nevertheless, attacks upon Jews were not random. Weinryb concludes that "one can thus see a connection between false accusations plus pogroms and the competitive struggle for livelihood between the burghers and the Jews" (153). Although it is difficult to make valid generalizations from incomplete data, there are other patterns, such as the frequency of the blood libel and similar accusations in the eighteenth century and in the eastern area that call for some explanation.

5. Bałaban, *Letoledot Hattenua Hafrankit*, pt. 1, 100–101.

6. Following its renewal in Poland, this libel had a career in Europe and the Middle East in the nineteenth and even the twentieth centuries. For a chilling modern-day legitimation of this fantastic tale, see Charles Lamb's infamous essay "Imperfect Sympathies," 126–27, in which he complains, "I cannot shake off the story of Hugh of Lincoln." The history of this libel has been recorded in several studies. Strack, *The Jew and Human Sacrifice*, 276–77, 280, claims that the first case of the blood libel was in Fulda in 1235. He attributes it to the confusion of the Hebrew words for blood and money, *dam* and *dammim*. Hay, *Europe and the Jews*, asserts that the first blood accusation was made by a converted Jewish monk named Theobald in the middle of the twelfth century. The alleged victim, William of Norwich, became the first child martyr. In 1255 the Jews of Lincoln were accused of killing Hugh, a small child. This accusation formed the basis of Chaucer's report. Trachtenberg, *The Devil and the Jews*, underscores the use of a child's blood by quoting from Johann Eck: "They desire innocent Christian blood, not that of an old Christian whose innocence, acquired through baptism, has been forfeited by his subsequent sins." The *Jewish Encyclopedia*, S.V. "blood accusation," 3:260–67, pointed out that the earliest accusations mention no ritualistic purpose, neither for Easter nor for Passover. The clergy, in codifying popular beliefs about Jewish use of blood or other body parts, by the thirteenth century presented these alleged acts as an imitation of the crucifixion before Easter, using a Christian child. The Jews, it was said, celebrated Easter by performing a burlesque of the sacraments. Hsia, *Myth of Ritual Murder*, 229, concludes that "although still occasionally haunted by the specter of blood libel charges, not one Jew within the German-speaking lands of the empire was executed for ritual murder after the sixteenth century." If this was the case, it sharpens the question as to the factors that contribute to the increased frequency of the blood libel in Poland in the seventeenth and eighteenth centuries.

we shall see, the blood libel, which seemed religious in its expressive form, may have carried hidden economic motifs.

Polish Jews, in fact, did not successfully prime the pumps of their country's economy in the early modern period. Although it may be that there were Jews poised for and well equipped to undertake large-scale trade and even some industry, there is no avoiding what is abundantly clear: the actual conditions of Poland and its Jews, from the second part of the seventeenth century, provide little evidence of Jews fostering anything similar in scope and pace to the economic development in the early industrial and capitalist economies of Western Europe.

Being productive involves not only motives; it is contingent on factors beyond the control of any would-be entrepreneur, however skilled, resourceful, prepared to take risks, and attentive to opportune "small changes." There are political and administrative forces that countervail the entrepreneurial spirit. And the social consensus recognizing which economic activities are in fact productive is not necessarily based on rational criteria, as expressed in accounting flowcharts or cost-benefit analyses. Ideologies often influence the opportunities for entrepreneurialism by defining the very terms of productivity. Those ideologies, as they affected expectations of Polish Jews to save the system of feudal agriculture during the last years of the Polish state, require attention.

Although what was developing in the West was not being replicated by Jews in Poland, awareness among Polish Christians of those developments began to influence their attitudes toward Polish Jews. Throughout the eighteenth century the Polish aristocracy was anxiously following the development of the West's booming economy. The Polish lords, like the Melanesians observing the arrival of cargo ships laden with the products of early modern West European technology—and often with as little understanding of the scientific and economic thinking, the technological processes, and the social and political organization behind the advent of the cargo—gazed wantonly at the accomplishments of the West as they responded defensively. What they now perceived in the new scientific advances and dramatic economic progress in the West contrasted starkly with more than a century of economic decline, peasant rebellions, internal strife, and foreign domination in Poland. Some of these Polish observers tried to convince themselves and others that Poland's economy continued to complement that of the West; some salved their wounded pride by focusing on the increasing political ferment in Western Europe that threatened the very structures of early modern Europe in the second half of the eighteenth century. For most Poles, it would become increasingly difficult, but not impossible, to deny Western successes and to overlook Poland's failures. The traditionalist, conservative, Eastern-oriented Sarmatian gentry, with their mythological and romanticized notions of Poland's role between East and West, persisted in glorifying Poland's "lack of order." Yet an increasing number of Poles, like Stanisław Staszic (1755–1828), a leading ideologist of the short-lived Polish Enlightenment, was prepared to acknowledge, "How far behind we have remained. . . . Poland is still in the fifteenth century; for the rest of Europe, it is the end of the eighteenth century!"[7]

The despair and self-flagellation connected with this awareness of backwardness became powerful in its ability to mobilize and incite. As Poland's troubled eighteenth century wore on, bringing with it three partitions, greater efforts were made to attribute blame, if not to establish the cause, of the country's declining productivity and increasingly severe agricultural and trade problems. The peasants grumbling in the tavern, the burghers rioting in the streets, and the clergy in the church and in the marketplace sanctimoniously inciting them; the publicists in the coffee houses, the orators in the Sejm, and, with a somewhat different set of concerns, the Russian bureaucrats in the chancery, trying to consolidate tsarist rule in newly annexed Polish territories, all began to focus on the same explanation for Poland's malaise: the Jews.

How do we understand the limited economic effectiveness of Poland's Jews and their confinement within specific enterprises such as the arenda in the second half of the seventeenth and in the eighteenth centuries? What light does that understanding shed on the failures of Polish feudalism and on the persistent efforts of the nobility to preserve serfdom, despite incentives to transform coerced into free labor? What initiatives were fostered in eighteenth-century Poland by diverse intellectual currents originating in and associated with the West, such as physiocracy and the Enlightenment, and how did these Western ideologies, as absorbed by members of Poland's aristocracy, stimulate defensive complexes rather than activate incentives to emulate Western successes? And how do we decode and interpret the new allegations, including charges of unproductiveness and subversiveness expressed discursively and dramatically, against the very group that profitably managed Polish feudalism?

The Propinacja

A seemingly minor enterprise, but by no means marginal to the Polish economy or to the Jewish role within it, illuminates these larger issues: the propinacja, a specialized form of the arenda, the manufacturing, wholesaling, and retailing of grain-based intoxicants.[8] In Poland, from the middle of the seventeenth century to the end of the eighteenth century, there was a dramatic increase in the man-

7. Cited in Jedlicki, "Social Ideas," 94.
8. An important literature has developed on the social, political, and economic implications of drink. In addition to Kula's excellent analysis of the propinacja, see LeDonne, "Indirect Taxes in Catherine's Russia"; Smith and Christian, *Bread and Salt.* Regrettably, none of these fine studies of grain-based intoxicants in Poland and Russia treats this question of Jews and the propinacja. The insufficient attention paid by these detailed studies to this particular detail is rather puzzling. The line between legitimate divisions of labor in research and the narrowing of perspectives that weakens the power of explanation and even distorts is rather thin. See Levine, "Gentry, Jews and Serfs," 223–50.

ufacture and sale of grain alcohol.[9] As well as can be ascertained from the limited data, in the heyday of Polish grain production, in 1564, income from the manufacture of alcohol accounted for 0.3 percent of the overall income of royal properties. Although this proportion of revenues increased by a large factor in the ensuing years, a century later it was still no more than 6.4 percent. Yet by 1764 it accounted for fully 37.6 percent of the overall income. By 1789 the proportion of revenues from the sale of alcohol reached 40.1 percent.[10] In view of the growth in total income for the Polish economy during this period, this increase in the proportion of income derived from alcohol sales indicated an even larger growth in the quantity of alcohol manufactured.[11] Although precise figures are unavailable for noble estates and private towns, there is little reason to assume that the pattern varied considerably.[12]

That the primary customers for this drink were the enserfed peasants is corroborated by frequent reports of peasant intoxication.[13] But the extent to which the consumption of alcohol among the serfs increased in this period cannot be demonstrated. They may have used part of their own grain to produce home brews, at least before the seventeenth century.[14] The increased revenue

9. Rutkowski, *Badania nad podziałem dochodów,* 1:66–68; Leskiewicz, "Le montant et les composants." Cited in Kula, *Economic Theory of the Feudal System,* 134. This assessment of transformations in the structure of the feudal estates' revenues is based on the important research of the "Lwów school" of economic history, unfortunately interrupted by World War II. More recent studies lend support for Kula's model of the second serfdom and the integral role of the propinacja in those areas east of the Vistula River where the majority of Poland's Jews resided. These studies likewise often fail to explain Jewish involvement in the propinacja. Geographic variances include such facts as that in Great Poland and Silesia at an early point in the consolidation of Serfdom, peasants were able to make partial payments of rent. But because of the unreliability of coinage and the low levels of monetization of those areas, it is unlikely that these differences considerably alter the pertinence of Kula's model. Although much of the analysis that follows is based on that school's incomplete history of prices, the importance of the propinacja to the Polish economy is corroborated by nonquantitative sources as well.

10. Kula, *Economic Theory of the Feudal System,* 139. Russia, to which many of Poland's grain-growing districts were annexed, had at this time a slightly lower percentage of its budget revenue coming from the tax it collected on alcohol production.

11. Ibid. In this same period (1564–1789) on the same estates the proportion of the total income derived from the combined sale of raw materials and semifinished products decreased from 61.6 percent to 39.4 percent.

12. Although there were important differences between the various types of estates, including the average size of landholdings and the number of days a month that the serfs were obligated to work on the landlord's land, the structure of revenues was consistent.

13. Braudel, *Capitalism and Material Life,* 168.

14. Kula speaks of vodka and alcohol interchangeably, as do I. In fact, vodka was more expensive than most peasant drink (which resembled beer) because of the intensive distillation it required. For references on the technical issues of liquor production, see LeDonne, "Indirect Taxes in Catherine's Russia," 176ff., and Smith and Christian, *Bread and Salt.*

Fig. 6. *Cracow Inn and Peasant.* Wood engraving by Gorazdowski in *Kłosy,* 1885–1890, based on a painting by Walery Eliasz (1840–1905).

from alcohol does indicate greater success in institutionalizing the monopoly on its manufacture and distribution within the economy of feudal estates, as well as the increased quantities of grain that the gentry deployed particularly for this purpose.[15] These trends direct our attention to the organization of supply rather than to possible psychological motives and needs reflected by any increased demand. The supply became increasingly managed by Jewish arendars and their sublessees on behalf of the Polish noble landlords.[16]

The Jewish inn, or kretchme, was a part of everyday life in the Polish towns and countryside of this period and continued to be one through the twentieth century.[17] Particularly in the lands of partitioned Poland annexed by the Russians and in that border region which became the pale of settlement, Jewish involvement in the production and distribution of alcohol became significant even though economic forces and administrative structures that promoted this involvement were very much different from what they had been in prepartition Poland. A traveler's account of the 1830s gives us a sense of how these taverns, which had hardly changed over the centuries, appeared:

> It was principally in his capacity as innkeeper that I became acquainted with the Polish Jew. The inn is generally a miserable hovel . . . partitioned off in one corner of a large shed, serving as a stable and yard for vehicles; the entrance is under a low porch or timber; the floor is dirt; the furniture consists of a long table or two or three small ones in one corner, a bunch of straw, or sometimes a few raised boards forming a platform with straw spread over it for beds; at one end a narrow door leads into a sort of hall filled with dirty beds, old women, half-grown boys and girls not overburdened with garments, and so filthy that however fatigued, I never felt disposed to venture among them for rest. Here the Jew, assisted by a dirty-faced Rachel, with a keen and anxious look, passes the full day in serving out to the meanest ‘ customer beer and hay and corn; wrangling with and extorting money from intoxicated peasants.[18]

15. Serfs on many estates were obligated to purchase a minimum quantity of drink, particularly for holiday or personal celebrations. At times, serfs were threatened with physical punishment if they did not meet their quota, or the drink would be poured out and they would have to pay for it nonetheless. See Gierowski, *Rzeczpospolita,* xii–xiii.

16. Mahler, *Yidn in amolikn poiln,* 108–13, examines the different specializations including the management of a single subcontracting of several hostels, inns, beer breweries, and distilleries.

17. Opalski, *Jewish Tavern-Keeper,* a study of the propinacja as it is reflected in Polish literature of the nineteenth century, lends support to this assessment of social and economic relations.

18. Stephens, *Incidents of Travel,* 2:189. The character of the Jewish innkeeper has been immortalized in Ḥayyim Naḥman Bialik's famous poem "Avi," in *Kol Shirei Bialik,* 347. A vivid description of relations between Polish peasants and Polish Jews in the territory annexed to the Austrian Empire can be found in Demian, *Darstellung der Oesterreichischen Monarchie,* cited in Macartney, ed., *Habsburg and Hohenzollern Dynasties,*

The importance of the propinacja in the economics of Polish Jewry and the ambiance of the inns are captured in Jewish legal and homiletical sources, as well as in Polish administrative documents going back to the seventeenth century.[19] Folklore is replete with stories set in provincial taverns. The purveyor of drink is a prominent type. The social relations between the Jewish proprietor-lessee and the peasant clients range from fraternal to businesslike to violent.

Some rabbis and moralists, while underscoring the limited economic and vocational opportunities available to Jews, nevertheless, expressed some reservations about this source of revenue. Jewish modernizers were quick to point out the indignities and discrimination from which Jews suffered that forced them to participate in such unproductive enterprises as the propinacja rather than fulfill their entrepreneurial potential. These modernizers echoed the condemnatory tones of Polish publicist literature. Even contemporary Jewish historians have

---

195–97: "When the peasant drives to market, he calls in on the way there at several Jewish taverns, leaves the payment till the return journey, then on that repeats all his visits and drinks away half, sometimes all, the money he has made at the market. He swills down twenty to thirty glasses at a sitting. His wife is not a hair's breadth behind him. On Sundays and holidays they walk to the church in their best clothes, but barefoot, carrying their boots under their arms. At the entrance to the village in which the parish church stands they put on their boots; after Divine Service they take them off again in the same place and then go into the taverns with their husbands or kinsfolk. There they drink brandy till sundown, without eating so much as a morsel of bread; then they start off, singing, for their villages, which are often a couple of leagues away, and often spend the whole night lying in heaps on the road. At their frequent meetings the Jew enters into intimate conversation with him, listens to his complaints and often gives him sound advice. In these frequent conversations he learns what each peasant possesses, what he has to sell, what he is short of and what he can do without. Now the Jew is already master of the poor helot's property. Very soon the peasant drinks himself into indebtedness to the Jew, and this does not worry the creditor. . . . The peasant feels only his immediate need, and immediate relief of it is all he wants. So his household remains eternally in the same state of wretchedness, and the peasant's continued habit of regarding the Jews as his friend gradually engenders an unlimited confidence in the Jew which is infinitely advantageous to the latter. To remedy this evil the Austrian Government has prohibited Jews from leasing the taverns in the country and the towns, and in 1780 ordered that Jews might reside in villages only as agriculturalists or craftsmen, because they had so corrupted the peasants as tavern-keepers. But this wise measure was relaxed. A decree of 1792 permitting Jewish distillers of brandy and all persons gaining their livelihoods from permitted trades, whether Jews or Christians, to continue to reside in the villages. The Jews have therefore gone on living in the villages, calling themselves distillers, while putting in a Christian as nominal licensee of the inn, but in reality continuing to practice the forbidden trade and continuing to constitute a great danger for the population." Although political and economic conditions in Austria were different from those in Poland, the realia of the two areas, and the social relations between Jews and peasants there, were similar.

19. In chapter 2, I examined several communal edicts of the Lithuanian Council and edicts compiled in the registry of the Council of Four Lands which refer to the propinacja. These give the sense of a newer enterprise. See also Horn, *Regesty dokumentów;* Katz, *Goy Shel Shabbat.*

been delicately apologetic for Jewish involvement in the propinacja, presuming that the Jews were not being productive.[20]

The scant demographic and economic data that we have, albeit of questionable reliability, at least for the eighteenth century provide further evidence of Jewish involvement in different facets of the propinacja. In the middle of the eighteenth century it was reported that 20 to 30 percent of Polish Jews were engaged in some aspect of alcohol production. According to the census of 1764–1765, a sizable majority of the Jewish population in villages, as well as 15 percent of the Jews living in towns, was involved in alcohol-related enterprises.[21]

Repairing the Perpetuum Mobile

What explains the development of the propinacja, particularly after the middle of the seventeenth century? How do we account for the high incidence of Jews in this branch of the Polish economy? To account for the increasing importance of the propinacja in the landlord's total revenues as primarily a function of the organization of supply rather than as an expression of demand for alcohol, we must examine the propinacja relative to changing economic forces and unchanging gentry thinking about those forces, thinking that became resistant even to acknowledging change. We must take another look at the market, the macroeconomic forces that influenced international and domestic fluctuations in grain profits, and the wheat field, the microeconomic forces ordering production within the natural economy of Polish feudalism. In the wheat field the ongoing conflict between the landlords and serfs for a more favorable distribution of profits became particularly intense as the natural economy became less profit-

20. Simon Dubnow, for example, emphasizes the impoverishment of Polish Jewry; lacking other vocational opportunities, they took over this demeaning task from the corrupt and indolent gentry. See Dubnow, *History of the Jews,* 4:83. Even the economic historian Ignacy Schipper fails to point to the economic functions of the propinacja. He calls it "an old sickness which became more serious in the days of Stanisław Augustus." He explains that the "enlightened" people of the generation—those who could transcend their own interests—condemned it as part of the exploitation of the peasantry. The riots of 1768 in the Ukraine moved the gentry to give up the part of their income that was derived from this source. Jews were therefore eliminated from these occupations, and the Jewish population of the small towns in the East dwindled. Schipper praises "Polish statesmanship" in discussing the efforts to promote reform among the Jews. See Schipper, "An Economic History of Polish and Lithuanian Jewry," 1:197.
21. Mahler, *Yidn in amolikn Poiln,* 94–95, based on the 1764 census, claims that 28 percent of the Jews in the Ukraine were involved in the arenda, and a considerable proportion of them were involved in some facet of the propinacja. By 1783 an increasing number of Ukrainian villages was without arendars, probably because they were expelled. There are even higher estimates for the involvement of rural Jewry throughout Poland in the propinacja. For an assessment of the census data on which this estimate is based, see Tartakower, "Polish Jewry in the Eighteenth Century," 2:110–14; Gross, ed., *Economic History of the Jews,* 132–40.

able. How did the propinacja straddle the ever-widening gap between the idealizations of Polish serfdom and its realities?

Heretofore I have emphasized the increasing profitability of grain revenues from 1500 to 1625, corresponding to the consolidation of Polish feudalism. As I now extend the time frame to include a period of unmarketable surpluses, we need a clearer sense of the differential impact that these fluctuations had on different classes of Polish society. What power and resources did some have, and not others, to turn this situation to advantage?

A measure of this class difference is suggested by Witold Kula's calculations of the relative terms of trade of the upper nobility, lower nobility, and peasants between 1550 and 1750.[22] Grain profits in the period 1550–1600 indicate an improvement in the economic position of both the magnate and the serf. However unevenly the windfall profits of the second part of the sixteenth century were distributed, this short-lived and relatively modest improvement in the peasant's standard of living might have provided incentives for voluntary enserfment; it at least might have weakened the resistance to gentry efforts at this time to translate into social realities what members of the gentry considered to be their legal entitlement to free labor. The temporary reversal in the economic fate of the lower gentry, followed by a period of undramatic growth in their terms of trade, may account for the rising frequency of bankruptcy among the lower gentry and the opportunities the magnates took to increase their landholdings. What is most striking, however, is the steady decline in the terms of trade of the now-enserfed peasantry. The deteriorating economic situation of the serf, particularly after 1625, when the demand for Polish grain on international markets sharply declined, may provide the background for the escape, rebelliousness, low productivity, and even malicious destructiveness—*dezolacja*—of the dispirited and the undernourished. It might even outline the psychological climate for the increase in drunkenness among the serfs and the political environment in which the lord made greater quantities of intoxicants available. Drunken peasants are more easily beaten into sullen obedience.

But there are additional socioeconomic and sociocultural factors in the feudal system of seventeenth- and eighteenth-century Poland that suggest the economic utility of the propinacja and point to the suitability of the population from which its manufacturers and managers were recruited. The noneconomic incentives for the preservation of feudalism must be emphasized. For feudalism in

22. See Kula, *Economic Theory of the Feudal System,* 123–24. The calculation of terms of trade is based on the selling price of the agricultural produce that someone is likely to bring to market and the purchase price of the commodities that the seller then procures. Terms of trade can give some indication of how the standard of living of a particular social group changes over time. Accordingly, with 1550 as the base year (100), the index for terms of trade for the Polish upper nobility in 1600 is 276; in 1650, 385; in 1700, 333; in 1750, 855; for the lower nobility in 1600, 80; in 1650, 144; in 1700, 152; and in 1750, 145; by contrast, the peasants' index for terms of trade increased to 205 in 1600 but declined to 169 in 1650, to 118 in 1700, and was as low as 51 in 1750.

Poland, as we have seen, was not only an economic relationship; it also described a set of patriarchal social relations, canonized in Sarmatian culture, that the lord tried to preserve even when there might have been economic incentives for its transformation.[23] When it could, the gentry opposed the development of a labor market and agriculture based on rent payments rather than on feudal service. As late as the second part of the eighteenth century, the limited efforts at industrialization that were undertaken within the feudal organization of labor and markets further illustrate the concern of the gentry to preserve these patriarchal social relations, which were not merely deemed instrumental but were perceived by the gentry as ends in and of themselves.[24] The availability of free-floating currency that could loosen the social structure was consequently seen as harmful to the idealized structuring of the relations between lord and serf. Moreover, according to gentry economic theories that supported maximum autarky and self-sufficiency of productive units, any cash expenditure was frowned upon. In the words of Gostomski, a late sixteenth-century writer on economic organization and bookkeeping for feudal estates, "It is not only harmful but shameful to buy with money, as a result of neglectfulness, what could be had without expense."[25] This evocation of honor is an excellent illustration of how the courtly ethos and patriarchalism of Polish feudalism attributed significance far greater than economic rationality to the well-run estate. The ability of peasants to generate surplus cash for use in purchasing goods produced outside the estate was frowned on by the landlord as depleting his own wealth. That the landlord himself, when he could afford to, removed exorbitant sums from this economy for luxury items was in no way seen as contradictory to the policy toward the serfs.

It was with tenacity and ingenuity that the peasants generated the surplus necessary to maintain a market relationship regardless of prevailing agricultural and economic conditions. They raised this surplus by working their own plots more efficiently than those they managed for the landlord, by moving landmarks and by selling the grain designated for feeding draft animals or for the next year's seeding. Their perseverance and inventiveness were matched by the gentry landlords in one specific area: siphoning off peasant surplus. The rise of the landlords' overall income at the end of the seventeenth century and during the eighteenth century in fact was not a consequence of improved efficiency of demesne production or of rising prices on local or distant markets. It must be attributed to their increasingly intensive management of estate resources, including the great exploitation of serf labor and the more reliable and efficient, if often harsh, methods of siphoning off peasant surplus.

The propinacja, as it initially developed, was but one of the landlords' mechanisms for this intensive management. It was derivative of the gentry economic thinking and theory of feudalism, which sought to circumscribe monetary exchange among the serfs and to establish, within the natural economy and pa-

23. See chapter 2; Jedlicki, "Social Ideas and Economic Attitudes," 92ff.
24. Jedlicki, "State Industrial Economy," 221.
25. Cited in Kula, *Economic Theory of the Feudal System,* 141.

triarchal society, distribution based on personal relations. In the sixteenth century and the first decades of the seventeenth century, when grain prices were highest, the serfs were able to produce a surplus of grain for which there were cash markets. The landlords mandated some cash payment for rent and tithe and tried to tax and control trade as a means of limiting peasant cash holdings. Although this further reduced the peasant standards of living, it at the same time forced peasants to generate still larger surpluses, compelling the landlords to implement even harsher measures with which to control that surplus revenue. And even after the decline in grain prices in the seventeenth century, and with the coinage problem becoming more severe, the serfs nevertheless succeeded in generating cash surpluses. The serfs, marketing their surplus grain on the side and wielding the degree of freedom achieved by having a few coins jingle in their pockets, now could cut directly into gentry profits and gentry control. That freedom was constructed to weaken patriarchalism. Still more efficient mechanisms for drawing off surplus profits of serfs had to be developed.

It is in this regard that the manufacture of alcohol operated as a siphoning-off mechanism. Cash that the peasant would somehow succeed in accumulating, that could be spent outside the feudal estate, and that could solidify and even strengthen his position in relation to local markets had to be drawn off. These mechanisms preserved both the economic and the patriarchal social relations of the estate as idealized by the gentry. The usefulness of the propinacja is illustrated by those records of estates in the eighteenth century actually requiring serfs to purchase a minimum amount of alcohol as a part of their obligation to the landlord. Thus, what the gentry tried to create within the autarky of the feudal economy with its idealization of patriarchal relations was a mechanism of closed monetary circulation, a perpetuum mobile.[26]

This perpetuum mobile might have worked, at least for a while longer, had the nobles not based their social order on two assumptions that proved to be false: that the supply of cheap labor was unlimited, and that the demand for Polish grain, at increasingly higher prices, was unchanging. With the decline of dependable labor supplies and stable market outlets for grain, the fiscal incentives for the gentry to siphon off serf monetary profits became as pressing as the desire to preserve the natural economy of nonmonetary exchange.

The declining prices of grain on the world market after 1625, the increasing frequency and severity of peasant rebellions and foreign invasions from the mid-1600s on, and the political vicissitudes of eighteenth-century Poland all reduced the profitability of grain and made the shipment of grain to international markets more difficult.[27] And though these events might have increased the demand for grain on local markets, the prices that the landlords, particularly the large magnates, did get could not provide them adequate and reliable cash sup-

26. Ibid., 134–44.
27. While the bottom was falling out of the international grain market, the Swedes were interfering with Baltic shipping, making it doubly difficult for the Polish nobility to profit. At the same time Russian grain became competitive on Dutch markets.

plies to suit their appetite for imported items. Despite their usual market strategies and their normal legal and administrative controls over their serfs, they were unable to consolidate their economic position under these turbulent circumstances.

The propinacja provided an important solution to these crop, shipping, labor, and marketing problems by producing a profitable end product for Polish grain. The profits realized from grain-based intoxicants far exceeded those derived from selling that same quantity of grain on the open market. The propinacja created an expanding and stable local market that did not involve problems of transportation, although it occasionally needed some priming through such devices as mandatory purchases by serfs. The transportation costs per unit of grain were less in vodka than in unprocessed grain.[28] Moreover, controlling the nourishment of serfs—whether the same measure of grain might be ingested as bread or as alcohol—increased gentry control over the bodies and spirits of their serfs. That the propinacja contributed to the ruination of the peasants was not a cost that had to be considered by the gentry as long as the source of labor was viewed as infinite. But the contradiction within gentry economic thinking between concern for immediate profit and disregard for long-range losses eventually did confront the gentry.

One eighteenth-century member of the upper nobility, Prince Joseph Czartoryski, in his essay "My Opinion on the Principles of Economics," observed the significance of this arrangement: "Without the sales of the propinacja, we would not be able to assure ourselves of a regular income in currency. In our country the vodka distilleries could be called mints because it is only thanks to them that we can hope to sell off our grain in years when there is no famine."[29] Czartoryski's comparison of vodka distilleries to mints reflects gentry notions of how economic profits are generated and how the effects of natural disasters like famines can be simulated and exploited. It also reveals what the serfs attribute to, and the gentry expected of, the most visible managers of the feudal economy: Poland's Jews. The benefits of that Jewish involvement in enterprises such as the propinacja and the mint exceeded economic utility and administrative exigencies.

The Jews and the Propinacja

Having examined the social, economic, and cultural forces that contributed to the increased manufacture and marketing of grain-based intoxicants, the ques-

28. In the United States this difference in cost was a major incentive for farmers west of the Appalachian Mountains in the late eighteenth century to manufacture whiskey rather than to transport grain. The construction of the Erie Canal, making that grain again competitive in the east, resolved the conflict expressed in the Whiskey Rebellion. See Rorabaugh, *Alcoholic Republic.*

29. W. Kula and J. Leskiewiczowa, "Ks. Józef Czartoryski: 'Myśli moje o zasadach gospodarskich,'" *Przegląd Historyczny* 46 (1955): 445–52, cited in Kula, *Economic Theory of the Feudal System,* 137.

tion remains: why the Jews? Other than historical accident and economic opportunity, what are the causes, latent motives, or manifest meanings behind this prominence and visibility of Jews within the propinacja?

It may have been merely as a result of their prior involvement in the arenda that Jews were initially recruited to organize the different facets of this increasingly important enterprise. Jewish sources show that the propinacja became one of the concessions that could be given over directly to Jewish lessees or subcontracted by Jews who managed entire estates. The wealthier arendars had the requisite capital to establish breweries and distilleries. They might have been associated with a network of Jewish taverners in the countryside and even traveling salesmen, who moved from plot to plot selling drinks to thirsty peasants. On the small estates contact between the landlord and the taverner was more direct.[30] Viewed from this perspective, the propinacja, although it generated an increasing proportion of gentry profits in the last years of the seventeenth and in the eighteenth centuries, does not seem to call for special attention. It was part of a larger set of exchanges between gentry and Jews well institutionalized by the end of the sixteenth century.

There were specific advantages to Jewish involvement in the propinacja, however, that cannot be overlooked. Gentry economic thinking, particularly under the conditions of declining profitability of grain production and the deteriorating stability of the feudal estate, placed landlords in a dilemma. It had become all the more important for the serfs to produce surpluses and for the nobles to control those surpluses. The peasants were forced to maintain a market relationship that the nobles otherwise considered undesirable in order to monetize their surplus crops, providing payment for rent. This market relationship, often expanded to enable serfs to pay their tithes to the landlords' kin among the clergy, and to purchase simple manufactured goods like nails, cloth, and salt, was facilitated by Jewish merchants in the towns and Jewish peddlers in the countryside. Though the nobles needed the additional cash revenue, this market relationship undermined the autarky of the feudal estate and, according to the economic calculations of the nobles, removed wealth from the estate.

Here we see the important role played by Jews in linking the wheat field and the market, the natural and commercial sectors of the economy, as the gap between the two was expanding. Jewish arendars and managers supplied the mechanisms by which the economic contradictions inherent in feudalism could be transcended and the fictions of Sarmatian autarky sustained. The problem for the nobility came down to how to accentuate the advantages and reduce the disadvantages of this economic relationship between serfs and Jews. It was the propinacja that provided the perfect solution. The peasants would be induced to raise a surplus, still of benefit to the feudal lord even if it had to pass through the hands of the Jewish innkeeper. Incentives for increased serf production to be

30. The question of how the institutionalization of the propinacja affected income distribution and capital accumulation within different levels of the gentry and, parallel to this, within the Jewish community awaits further documentation.

spent on drink would keep money within the natural sector of the feudal economy; siphoning off their surplus would preserve feudal autarky. At the same time, the propinacja would absorb Jews into an enterprise that would limit their development of those local markets that the gentry could not wholly control. The propinacja was thus a remedy for the inefficiencies and failures of the devices of coercive surplus extraction. It was a feeble effort of the gentry to maintain profits despite uncertain returns on grain. That it also kept the Jews and the serfs from gaining the modicum of freedom that participation in exchange markets allows (whether consciously intended or yielding a secondary benefit) was no less desirable a consequence of the propinacja for the nobility.

Toward this end the propinacja served two purposes. It successfully drew off monetary profits that could be brought into what was to be a closed and personal system of exchange, and it engaged a growing proportion of that segment of the Polish population—the Jews—most prone to monetize exchange relations, provide liquidity for the peasants' grain surpluses, and peddle goods to serfs on the most remote estates. And as the marketing problems of Poland's grain became increasingly severe as a result of inefficient estate management, domestic strife, and uncoordinated noble imposition of tolls and duties, or because of grain surpluses, declining grain prices, and inflated currency on international markets, members of the nobility were able to maintain and even increase their profits from grain. These profits, necessary to enable the nobles to have access to international markets, procure luxury items, and preserve their standard of living and their authority, were generated by the transformation of larger quantities of grain into intoxicants purveyed through the large chain of taverns franchised and managed by Jews. The nobles enlisting their Jewish agents into this enterprise were able to profit from declining profitability and increasing backwardness.

If the propinacja was a siphoning-off mechanism that compensated the nobles for the shortcomings of feudal measures of surplus extraction, and that insured that the adaptive modes of the other economic actors would ultimately work in the nobility's interests, the prominent position of Jews within this enterprise served an additional function, as a masking device by which some of the internal contradictions of the system were concealed. Removed from their position in the interstices of local and international markets that they had maintained as tradesmen in the Middle Ages, they now were promoted to a position at the intersection of the commercial and noncommercial sectors, where the personalized system of production met the impersonal system of exchange. In this position Jewish economic activities masked gentry efforts—from others but even, and perhaps with the most unfortunate consequences, from the gentry itself—to dominate the serfs personally and to exploit them economically. The gentry sought compensation for the negative results of their own persistent efforts to sustain demesne agriculture, that is, the feudal social and economic systems, which were accompanied by peasant rebellion and sabotage.

Jewish management of the propinacja enabled the gentry to enact their theoretical notions of domination and autarky in spite of the pressures of other realities. The intoxication and impoverishment of the serfs made them more docile and controllable, contributing to their exploitation. Inducing the peasants to drink made them more indebted and drew off any surplus capital that they might have spent outside of the feudal economy. That the peasants were encouraged to drink away, in the Jewish-managed taverns, money that they might have used to purchase manufactured goods or to pay their church tithes did not endear the Jews to other groups within the Polish population such as the town merchants and clergy who sustained the loss. Nor were déclassé members of the lower gentry particularly enamored with Jewish involvement in the propinacja, except when the Jews were in their employ; they themselves probably wanted to run this concession, when they could afford the required outlay of capital. They would run the propinacja on behalf of their cousins, or even brothers, to whom they often had been forced to sell their own estates. The marginal average rise in the standard of living of the lower gentry in this period may indeed reflect that certain members had their own alcohol-related businesses, with or without Jewish managers. But this small improvement demonstrates that they could not achieve economies of scale similar to those of the magnates or the large Jewish arendars. The relative deprivation of the lower gentry was expressed on occasion in bellicosity, litigiousness, and the fostering of intrigues. Ultimately, however, the propinacja had a unfavorable effect on the economic interests of the upper and lower nobility because it reduced the productivity and the reliability of the serfs as a labor force. The outbreaks of peasant violence, increasing in frequency from the middle of the seventeenth century, were often (but not exclusively) aimed at Jewish vendors of vodka and their coreligionists. Gentry landlords at times had to share refuge and plan common strategies with their Jewish leaseholders against murderous peasant mobs.

As the failures of feudalism as a socioeconomic system became more evident through the course of the eighteenth century, even to the most fatuous of the Polish gentry, the role of the propinacja as a device to save the failing system came under new scrutiny. Questions of Jewish productivity were linked to these failures, even by those who profited or would have liked to profit from Jewish involvement. What was most frequently and judiciously avoided was a comprehensive analysis of the problems of Polish feudalism and its autarky, for which the propinacja and the Jews connected with it provided a stopgap. That the propinacja actually could have been deemed a productive enterprise, under the prevailing economic conditions, could not be acknowledged. The old indignation in regard to the deleteriousness of Jews was now given expression in a new key: the rhetoric of reform, to the accompaniment of accusations of nonproductivity, was staged and choreographed in a renewed communal drama.

From Economic Decline to Partition

The propinacja, as we are beginning to discover, is not just a specialized institution significant for its organization of production, trade, labor, and finance, though arrived at through trial and error by members of a declining elite unable to comprehend the forces that were weakening them and desperate to save the system of Polish agriculture. It is a manifestation of important patterns of gentry economic thinking and gentry culture, canonized in Sarmatianism and institutionalized in Polish feudalism. The propinacja illustrates how the gentry passed on to others much of the cost of blame for the "serious regression and decline in the second half of the seventeenth and the first half of the eighteenth centuries," relative to the "golden" sixteenth century. It also shows how the nobles shirked financial and moral responsibility for the consequences of the peasant rebellion and foreign invasions of the middle seventeenth century, as well as for the failures of the feudal estate and its natural economy.[31] Thus, the propinacja represents a more general mode of problem solving.

Nevertheless, this broad significance accorded to the propinacja beyond its usefulness in the gentry's achieved short-term goals evokes skepticism. However integral this pattern of response may have been to gentry culture, was it indeed a singular and inevitable response to Poland's "serious regression"? The effects of those economic trends that I have been examining were often cumulative, and awareness of them was attained only gradually. That awareness, however, was heightened by decisive political events occurring in this period. Poland's loss of sovereignty, its denationalization, was formalized in the partition of 1772 and completed in the partitions of 1793 and 1795, but in fact the regression began considerably earlier, during this same period in which the propinacja was deployed and implemented to save the economy. Were there no individuals, groups, or coalitions that could successfully intervene to alter the course of this political decline?

This question prompts us to reconsider the political history of the period, in search of neglected "small changes," unexploited opportunities, and adequate measures that the gentry might have taken to save Poland, politically and economically in the eleventh hour.[32] Were there no compelling modes of thought

31. Wójcik, "Poland and Russia in the Seventeenth Century," 114–15. Wójcik divides historians between those "obsessed" with the devastations and those obsessed with the agricultural failures. Contributing to those failures were the decline of both external and internal markets for grain; the competition from Russian grain, which had become cheaper on Dutch markets despite higher transportation costs; the decreasing marketability of Polish foodstuffs on Western markets and the increasing demand for flax and hemp, neither of which the commonwealth possessed in exportable quantities; the increase in the amount of land lying uncultivated; the fall of the level of agricultural technology; the decline of the towns; and the circulation of bad coinage. He emphasizes the fact that more research is needed to understand the causes of the crisis and the process of decline.

32. By way of comparison, Russia had had its "time of trouble" at the beginning of the seventeenth century, during which its internal chaos and decline were as bad or worse than what Poland was to sustain by the mid-seventeenth century. By the end of that century the Muscovite state showed signs of overcoming its economic stagnation. For example, there is evidence that the Russian serfs made intense demands for industrial goods. These demands were met by legislation to protect fledgling industries from foreign competition and to

developing in Poland or appropriated from the West that could have provided new solutions to the internal crises and threats from abroad and, at the same time, could have suggested more effective ways of exploiting the entrepreneurial skills of other groups within Polish society? Why did the urban middle class not provide the seeds of revitalization as it did in the fifteenth and much of the sixteenth centuries, when the burghers of towns like Cracow and Zamość mediated influences of Renaissance Europe?[33] Within the degrees of freedom that a minority group such as the Jews could have established for autonomous action, were there no initiatives that they themselves might have taken, similar to those taken by court Jews and Huguenots in the West, that would have contributed to the centralization of political authority and would have transformed the Polish economy and society rather than preserved a failing system of labor organization and surplus extraction?

A few examples of unexploited "small changes" and lost opportunities in this period illustrate this general failure to respond to decline that we have identified with the *Propinacja*. The military victory of Jan Sobieski (1629–1696) over the leader of the Turkish forces, Kara Mustapha, at the gates of Vienna in 1683 was a much-acclaimed instance of consolidated Polish action and a modicum of gentry cooperation overcoming serious dangers.[34] The Polish king's triumph contributed to freeing Christian Europe of several centuries of vulnerability to Islamic

---

foster domestic trade rather than by efforts to siphon off serfs' surplus income, as the Polish gentry attempted to do.

33. Bogucka, "L'attrait de la culture nobiliaire," 23–41. Bogucka sees "Sarmatization and all it carried with it in the way of ideology and manners," in sharp contrast to the entrepreneurialism of the bourgeoisie (28–29). She speaks of the Sarmatization of the bourgeoisie not so much as a result of the "attractiveness" of the noble model as of the "anemic" quality of the bourgeoisie's own model and the weight of the ruinous wars of the seventeenth century, which had particularly severe effects on the towns (40–41). Only where ethnic and religious attachments remained strong—for example, among non-Catholics such as the Jews and among the bourgeoisie of Pomerania whose Polonization was weak, who were Lutheran or Calvinists, and who maintained contact with the bourgeoisie of Holland and Germany—was there resistance to Sarmatization and the growth of "indigenous culture marked by particular, original traits." Nevertheless, it would be interesting to explore the degree of Sarmatization among those Jews who had the most contact with gentry landlords, such as the arendars had with the magnates. The organization of the court and the appropriation of some gentry mannerisms among the Frankists as well as the Hasidim raise some questions about the degree to which Jews were "hermetically sealed," as Bogucka contends, from Polish influences. Another explanation is provided by Jedlicki, "Social Ideas," 90ff. He argues that the burghers had been immobilized too long by impoverishment, which stemmed from the gentry's attempt to control and ultimately to destroy the economic position of the towns by "feudalizing" the activities of the artisans. Although artisans and tradesmen, through their guilds, were partially able to resist these pressures of the gentry, the exemption from competition that these same guilds provided limited their capabilities of being commercially or technically innovative.

34. Davies, *God's Playground*, 1:473–89.

penetration and to freeing resources, heretofore committed to this line of defense, for the accelerated development that would take place in the West. It was the source of Polish pride, even of messianic speculation in subsequent years. In commemorating this legendary event, Poles paid considerably less attention to the fact that at this fortuitous moment a Central European court Jew, Samuel Oppenheimer (1630–1703), had provided vital war supplies to the Polish forces.[35] But even this military victory, of great importance in European history and in the annals of military history, did not prompt the Polish gentry to establish a standing professional army. Nor did it lead Poland to explore new legitimations for trade and for a strong central state that could tax trade and float bonds through a national bank, devices that were necessary to fill national war chests and that had been developing in the West.[36] Moreover, this victory at the gates of Vienna did not bring about any new recognition of the potential usefulness of Jews. Accounts of the booty taken from the grand vizier's camp made at least as much of an impression as the political ramifications of the battle. The leopard skins, bedecked horses, and ruby- and sapphire-studded quivers of the Turkish soldiers more than their valor, inspired the Sarmatian gentleman and influenced fashion all through the eighteenth century. These Eastern styles, as we shall see, were particularly in vogue in the 1780s. During the Polish constitutional crisis, members of the conservative gentry preferred to evoke Poland's seventeenth-century triumph, selectively remembering and symbolically enacting the grandeur of the East, even as their own country was being vanquished; the Sarmatian lords conjured up those images of Poland's military leadership in its fleeting alliance with the West, rather than focusing on the West's philosophical, constitutional, and commercial successes that now challenged Poland as it confronted disaster.[37]

Poland's economic decline only exacerbated its domestic political situation, making it less able to withstand the scheming of its neighbors. Royal succession in countries all across Europe precipitated foreign intrigues. The election of kings in Poland at the end of the seventeenth century and throughout the eighteenth century presented irresistible conditions to Poland's neighbors for blatant intervention.[38] The Saxon monarchs in turn stoked Sarmatian "animosity and suspicion towards foreigners and things foreign," particularly those associated with the West. Resistance to their rule was expressed by many members of the gentry in smugness and in the conviction that Poland was altogether different from the

35. Stern, *Court Jews*, 21ff.

36. Pocock, *Machiavellian Moment*. Whig economic doctrine and criticism of these policies was quite different from that of the conservative Polish gentry. Members of the Polish gentry did not take a principled stance on the citizen-soldier. They seemed to be perfectly content with hiring mercenaries, when they could afford them, or with conscripting their serfs. Their own bellicosity seems to have been fulfilled through a fondness for military trappings and juridical contentiousness.

37. Jedlicki, "Native Culture and Western Civilization," 65.

38. See chapter 1. For a description of the influence of a German court Jew, Bend Lehmann, in the election of Frederick Augustus, the Saxon monarch, see Stern, *Court Jew*, 77–82.

West. This lent support to the Sarmatian gentry's romanticization of the native past and the rejection of changes associated with modernization.[39]

Poland's political weakness is further illustrated by its inability to benefit from the mid-eighteenth-century wars fought on Polish soil. The War of the Austrian Succession (1740–1748), followed by the Seven Years War (1756–1763), could have worked to Poland's advantage. The country's dwindling earnings from agricultural exports as a result of the agrarian revolution in the West might have been offset by the desperate economic conditions of Central Europe plagued by wars for fifteen out of twenty-three years. The magnates did benefit from occasional short-lived upswings in the economy. But they were not prone to making large capital investments.[40] Other Poles likewise might have benefited from new, if only temporary, markets. But as with Poland's situation at the conclusion of the Thirty Years Wars in the West in 1648, its weakness did not enable the country to profit from the upheaval beyond its own borders.

The limits of this pattern of response and problem-solving capability in the Propinacja are illustrated in the mid-eighteenth century in the approach of a few members of the gentry, mostly magnates, who did try to take advantage of some "small changes" and special opportunities. Even before the dissemination of Enlightenment ideology made the West into a mecca, reform-minded landlords turned westward, particularly toward England, to emulate what they perceived to be its successes. Some became proponents of Europeanization and attached to Sarmatianism and its influences a pejorative sense.[41] In 1744 the young Stanisław Poniatowski, who would become Poland's last king, in his "Letter of a Landlord to a Certain Friend from Another Province," proposed emulating England. He presumed that in its laws and domestic constitution, that country was quite similar to Poland.[42]

But during the last decades of Poland's Saxon era it was the fashions, manners, and new technical methods of England rather than its new modes of social organization, management, and economic thinking that evoked some interest within Poland.[43] Reform-minded gentry looked to new plows, fertilization, and crop rotation, which they introduced on their feudal estates, in the hope of raising agricultural yield. On some latifundia small-scale industry and the exploitation of natural resources, such as minerals and timber, were organized. As in Peter the Great's Russia a half-century earlier, experts were brought from abroad to teach the technological discoveries and insights of the West and to attempt to replicate its successes.[44] But the unreliability of the enserfed peasants who provided the

39. Michalski, "Sarmatyzm," 113–68.
40. Gieysztor et al., *History of Poland,* 262.
41. Michalski, "Sarmatyzm," 119–38.
42. Ibid., 135.
43. Ibid., 138.
44. An area in which early reforms and imitation of Western Europe were envisioned was education. In 1740 piarist priest Stanisław Konarski established the Collegium Nobilium in Warsaw. This encouraged the Jesuits, who heretofore had had large influence over the

labor force, and the inefficiency of these enterprises, limited the successes of the innovations.

It is reported, for example, that the Radziwiłłs, a Lithuanian magnate family that maintained Protestant connections throughout the eighteenth century, were among the first to diversify their activities into sheep herding. Such enterprises seemed comparable to those which developed two hundred years earlier in England. Sheep herding in England was accompanied by the expulsion of peasants from the land and the development of cash labor markets. In Poland, however, these shifts in agriculture often were prompted by such concerns as making better use of peasant women and children, along with peasant men, during the rainy season. In the organization of small-scale industries along the lines of feudal agriculture, the autarky of the lord's estates, his access to free labor, and his control over monetary circulation were emphasized rather than efficiency and profit. Thus, if Prince Radziwiłł owned large flocks of sheep in the Ukraine, he would have his serfs transport the wool by wagon to his textile factory in Lithuania instead of selling it to a local wool factory; he could supply his factory with wool from local sources that was even less costly than the total expenditures for raising and transporting his Ukrainian wool. But since he did not consider labor as an expense, the only investment that he had to account for was the dyes he purchased in Königsberg.[45] Despite savings for labor, under these inefficient modes of manufacture the textiles produced could not compete in price or in quality with imports from Prussia.

A number of Jewish leaseholders were active in managing the estates of reform-minded nobles. There are reports, for example, of two brothers, Samuel and Gedalia, from Galicia, who became the arendars for the Radziwiłł estates. Through stern management, including harsh treatment of their Jewish sub-arendars, they considerably increased the revenues from these estates. At the same time, the conditions of the peasants on the Radziwiłł estates contributed to the spread of peasant rebellions. The most serious incident, from 1739 to 1744, was set in Jewish memory as the "decrees of Voskchilo," named for the peasant

---

education of young aristocrats, to make changes in instruction and in the expansion of secondary education. The University of Cracow was also improved in this period. Konarski, writing between 1760 and 1763, urged his compatriots to follow the example of England and other Western countries in improving public administration, expanding the economy, strengthening Poland's defenses, and improving education. Jedlicki, "Native Culture and Western Civilization," 69; Michalski, "Sarmatyzm," 136–38. The Commission of National Education, established in 1773 in the wake of the expulsion of the Jesuits, began to secularize and modernize the curriculum presented to young lords—the only recipients of formal schooling. This generation of the nobility, including some persons more open to "progressive ideas," would come of age in the 1780s. As impressed as Konarski and other Polish reformers were by what was going on in England and other Western countries at that time, they made no mention of the parliamentary debates relating to the granting of civic and economic rights to Jews.

45. Kula, *An Economic Theory of the Feudal System,* 36.

leader Bunty Woszczyłowskie. The brother arendars, though wealthy and power-ful, could not contain these riots, which led to massacres of Jews and to forced conversions.[46] Problems of restraining the serfs added to gentry losses. But even without such losses it is unlikely that estates such as the Radziwiłłs' could have achieved any economy of scale. Vast and far-flung magnate estates, farmed out to Jewish managers, were further divided into the smaller productive units of the sub-arendars. As efficient or entrepreneurial as these Jewish managers or lessees might have been, there were virtually no incentives for them to coordinate among themselves and the landlords the different stages of economic production with any measure of economic rationality.

The results of such efforts to innovate and to introduce small-scale industry were similar to those of feudal agriculture. Even reformist nobles solved their marketing problems and losses by the usual technique: they imposed upon peas-ant families requirements for a minimum purchase of manufactured and traded goods. It was forbidden to import goods such as cloth, glass, and earthenware, and particularly alcoholic drink, to estates where these items were manufactured. The lords' efforts to keep all money spent by peasants in the coffers of their estates never proved to be effective, however, for there were formidable economic stimuli for peasants, Jews, and others to trade in contraband. Moreover, the imposition of monopolies upon the social and economic structures of feudalism did not provide firm moorings for industrial and commercial development. Thus we see how the reform-minded gentry, as well as the more conservative members of the gentry, preserved feudal modes of economic organization; those modes are most clearly manifested in the propinacja, the thinking upon which it was based, and the social and economic arrangements that it necessitated to compensate for its own inefficiencies. Reformers now tried to transfer arrangements to forbid competitive imports and compel serf purchases to the new areas of economic enterprise.

This selective attention paid by Polish reformers to what was transpiring in the West limited the possibilities of replicating in Poland the economic develop-ment that they looked upon with such admiration. Among other things, they paid scant attention to the position of the coreligionists of their arendars in the West and drew no lessons for making better use of Jews in Poland. Moreover, even if in glancing westward they had perceived "how profitable are the Jews," this feudal

46. There is some evidence that the Polish Catholic gentry incited the Russian Orthodox peasants against the Jews to divert attention from their own exploitation of the serfs. Although the Jews indeed seemed to be the special target of the murderous rioters, the serfs turned against the landlords as well. I. Halpern, "Gezeirot Voskchilo," in Halpern, *Yehudim Veyahadut,* 277–78. Halpern asserts that the estates managed by these two arendars had belonged to a Hieronim Radziwiłł and associates him with Solomon Maimon's grandfather (277–78). The only Hieronim Radziwiłł of whom I have found record lived between 1622 and 1677, considerably earlier than Maimon's grandfather or these events. The Radziwiłł grandfather with whom Maimon's grandfather was associated, I believe, was Karol Radziwiłł (1734–1790). See Introduction.

organization limited innovation and initiative. Jews and other entrepreneurially inclined Poles would have had few opportunities to develop enterprises rather than manage the stopgap measures implicit in the propinacja. And as the social and political cleavages within Polish society became sharpest, Polish Jews were increasingly caught between the forces of decentralization and centralization. Ultimately, they were blamed for ruining the natural economy of the feudal estates and the commercial economy of the state. Under these conditions, for the Jews to develop trade and manufacturing on any scale competitive with the West would have been impossible.

It is in this period of political disintegration and economic decline that we hear reports of increasing gentry capriciousness in their treatment of Jews. Members of the gentry, under attack by violent serfs or by burghers demanding political concessions, often tried to redirect these assaults onto the Jews. In this coalition strategy, nobles tended to be more successful in enlisting burgher loyalties. They could compensate the burghers for their curtailed municipal autonomy by joining them in their attacks on Jewish trade and artisanship, their confiscation of Jewish merchandise, and their expulsion of Jewish residents. The extortion of Jews by gentry confederacies increased during the last years of the Polish republic as centralized administrations became less effective. This rising gentry capriciousness, whatever its cause, left a mark on Jewish literature and folklore and cast the image of the *poriz* (gentry landlord) as whimsical, wanton, and harsh.[47] These were the circumstances under which Solomon Maimon's grandfather, an arendar, could not enforce his contract mandating landlord responsibility for the maintenance of fixed assets; he could not get his *poriz* to repair the broken bridge.

In 1764 the szlachta abolished the Council of Four Lands, which had provided a degree of protection from this capriciousness to Jews in remote areas. A fiscal and administrative explanation for this *gezeira* (decree), is provided by Dov Ber of Bolechow, a wealthy merchant from eastern Poland with strong ties to the Berlin Jewish Enlightenment, the Haskala. In his memoirs he asserts that the

47. This image of the gentry is particularly developed in the autobiographical musings as well as the aphorisms of Jacob Frank. In Frank's appetites and the capriciousness and occasional brutality with which he behaves toward his disciples, one can observe his fascination with Polish gentry, as well as his gentry affectations. See Levine, *Ha'khronika*. The legends surrounding the life and activities of the reputed founder of Hasidism, Israel Bal Shem Tov, describe the assistance that he is able to extend to Jews, often in isolated villages controlled by tyrannical and capricious landlords. The mendicant Hasidic leader and the court, spanning various geographic regions provided better protection to the dvorf yid than the kehillot could afford. In regard to the Bal Shem Tov's attitude toward what I call capriciousness, see Avraham Rubinstein's interesting reading of his ascension dream in "The Epistle of the Besht to Reb Gershon of Kitov," 137–38. The Bal Shem Tov petitions the Messiah on the cruel treatment of Jews who accepted apostasy during the blood libels to spare themselves torture before death but who nevertheless were brutally murdered. Here too, as with Maimon's grandfather, we observe a broken agreement between gentry and Jews and the resulting indignation.

poriẓim, perhaps most particularly the reform-minded gentry, expressed unusually keen interest in administrative efficiency. They saw the expenditures of Jewish self-government—in Dov Ber's characterization "a bit of honor that by the heavenly compassion upon us, God in his mercy did not abandon us"—as wasteful. In keeping with that same economic thinking, inherent and well institutionalized in the propinacja, these members of the gentry believed themselves better able, by their own devices, to siphon off the profits and to tax a disunited Jewish community.[48]

The First Partition and the Rhetoric of Reform

Whether it was the result of gentry capriciousness, the inadequacy of reforms, the growing social and political divisions of Poland, or, as Dov Ber of Bolechow and other Jews may have believed, divine retribution for the gentry's dissolution of the Council of Four Lands, Poland was weakened and torn asunder by the increasing machinations and interventions of its neighbors during its last three decades as a sovereign state. Both liberal and conservative factions of the gentry, by trying to bypass the unwieldy instruments of collective decision making available in the Parliament, fostered intrigue and invited this foreign intervention. Unlikely alliances were forged: The reform-minded, Western-oriented gentry turned eastward to feudal Russia, which was losing its own early initiatives in emulating the West; members of the conservative, Eastern-oriented gentry, seeking to preserve Sarmatian culture, were forced to turn to the turbulent West. The results of these alliances were equivocal and frustrating to those lords hoping to save their country. And they provide a background necessary for an understanding of the declining position of Polish Jews, caught between policies developing in the East and West and the Polish gentry, who would identify with those policies.

The standard-bearers of reform, now led by the Czartoryski family, began as early as 1762 to look toward Russia for support. Hoping that the next king would come from their family, they did all that they could to undermine the weak and ailing Saxon king of Poland, Augustus III. The Czartoryskis promoted administrative reforms such as the abolition of the liberum veto and the establishment of a hereditary monarchy. The conservative gentry fought energetically to preserve their political prerogatives through the elected king and the szlachta veto, citing both Rousseau and the French physiocrats in support of their "golden freedom." The two factions had an intense confrontation in 1764 when a new king had to be chosen. Catherine the Great interceded on behalf of her former favorite Stanisław Poniatowski, a nephew of the Czartoryskis. The Western-oriented, "enlightened" king who had the backing of his magnate family, showed

---

48. Dov Ber of Bolechow, *Memoirs*. These devices included the use of arendars as tax farmers, a regression to the very conditions in Poland that spurred the growth of Jewish self-government in the fifteenth century.

some eagerness and talent for implementing administrative reforms. A representative of another important magnate family, Andrzej Zamoyski (1716–1792), became chancellor under the new king, and by the time of the Sejm of 1766 was already designated "chief proposer of legislative reform."[49] The royal court in Warsaw, against dominant Sarmatian trends among the nobility, came under the influence of Western European visitors. Western European clothing and manners, more than social and political ideas, became fashionable among its wealthier members. Courtiers began to complain that the king seemed to prefer dining with artists and physicians to dining with senators and dignitaries.[50]

These complex relationships and social references, ranging in effect from the highly personal to the most blatantly utilitarian, which developed between the reform-minded and conservative factions of the gentry and neighbors to the east and west, are illustrated in the events leading to the first partition of Poland. The reformers, continuing to find little political support for their proposals among those who might have been their natural allies in the "enlightened" West, were all the more dependent on Catherine. Catherine might have lent support to the reformers; she was no great enthusiast of the conservative Polish gentry's myth of everlasting rebellion, on which the liberum veto was based, and she no longer needed the liberum veto as a cover for foreign intervention. Catherine could be an enthusiast of Parisian Enlightenment without weakening the influence of Saint Petersburg in Warsaw. But in this Polish conflict, whatever ideological proclivities or residual personal loyalties Catherine might have harbored, her policy vis-à-vis the contentious Polish lords soon emerged: to play off one against the other. Moreover, her agenda for consolidating power in Russia guided her administrative actions in Poland as well. The same woman who was Diderot's avid royal correspondent was also a neophyte member of the Russian Orthodox church. The empress, born a German Princess, flaunted attachment to her new religion as a means of gaining the support of the Russian people. She demanded of the Polish reformers guarantees of the rights of the Russian Orthodox minority in Poland as a quid pro quo for these changes.[51]

The issue of religious tolerance weakened the position of reformers and widened the division between them and the conservative gentry. The conservatives were willing to incur any cost to preserve their concept of golden freedom as expressed in, and made possible by, the absolute veto power of individual members of the gentry. The linkage that Catherine imposed between the administrative reform abolishing the liberum veto and the religious reform granting ecclesiastical rights to the Russian Orthodox peasants led the conservative gentry staunchly to uphold the central position of the Catholic church. Two centuries of Jesuit education had inculcated among many members of the gentry the notion that heresy led to calamity and that all non-Catholics were ultimately aliens, no

49. Gieysztor et al., *History of Poland,* 274.
50. Michalski, "Sarmatyzm," 139–46.
51. Gieysztor et al., *History of Poland,* 275–77; Troyat, *Catherine the Great.*

matter how Polish they may be in any other respect. Conceding religious rights to these peasants who in recurrent riots and estate burnings had already demonstrated their capacity for destructiveness would only increase the harm that would befall Poland.

The Russian Orthodox serfs fulfilled their expectations in 1768 during peasant rebellions and estate devastations. These were particularly destructive along the Russian Ukrainian borderlands, also an area containing nomadic Tatars, who often incited rebelliousness. These were the territories that had been most intensely colonized by Polish gentry accompanied by their Roman Catholic missionaries and their Jewish arendars. As in past peasant rebellions, the greatest fury befell the Jews. The slaughter of tens of thousands of Jews in some areas of the Ukraine in 1768 was subsequently recorded in Jewish sources with a poignancy second only to the descriptions of what took place during the peasant rebellious of 1648.[52] Tensions mounted. As in 1648, foreign intervention and gentry devisiveness followed. Reacting to Russian pressure for Poland to grant religious rights to Russian Orthodox serfs, a gentry confederation meeting in Bar in 1768 made threatening gestures and fomented small-scale local rebellions. The Russians responded with troops, and many Jews were caught in the cross fire.

It was now the conservatives who in 1769 sought assistance from the West. Ideas circulating in bastions of the Enlightenment in France and in the Germanic countries had more of an influence on the rhetoric with which Polish Jews would be assessed, if not an ameliorative influence on their actual fate. Count Michał Wielhorski, the Paris representative of gentry confederates now meeting in the southeastern Polish town of Balia, turned to Jean-Jacques Rousseau for consultation on the Polish situation.[53] Rousseau responded in his *Considérations sur le gouvernement de la Pologne* (1772).[54] In this work, the author of the *Social Contract* mentions nothing about either the "general will" or equality. He advises the serfs and the burghers that their involvement in government and legislation in the foreseeable future is "neither possible nor prudent." In no way does he temper his regard for a Poland in which an aristocracy holds so much of the power

52. Dubnow, *Toledot Haḥasidut,* 12ff.
53. Michalski, *Rousseau i sarmacki republikanizm,* 3–8. Wielhorski supplied Rousseau with material about contemporary Poland upon which to base his reflections. What other sources of information on Poland Rousseau had at his disposal and the extent to which he was influenced by this Polish informant are not clear.
54. Rousseau, *Government of Poland.* Willmoore Kendall, in his Leo Straussian introduction to this work, points to "secret writing." He asserts that Rousseau was pretending, and perhaps using this work to address an audience beyond Poland in regard to his qualms about modern, expansive, territorially based political regimes. Alternately, Kendall suggests that Rousseau may have turned conservative in his old age, or that "an old Rousseau was prepared to play games" (xv). Judith Shklar, *Men and Citizens,* dismisses this work of Rousseau as "pseudo-realism," claiming that Rousseau himself knew that it was a "superficial fantasy" (95, 176). Michalski, *Rousseau,* 34–35, suggests that Rousseau used this work as an opportunity to criticize the English parliamentary system, mindful of the positive reference to England of some Polish reformers such as Stanisław Konarski.

in its own hands and is responsible for the situation of millions "born free but everywhere in chains."[55] Though recognizing the liberum as a source of anarchy and recommending modifications, he related to it rather positively.[56] Neither does he try to assess the strong influence of the Catholic church in Poland and its political and theological opposition to his concept of civil religion.[57] On the eve of Poland's first partition Rousseau glorifies Moses and the ancient Israelites as founding a political community worthy of Poland's emulation. Those Israelites sustained their identity and freedom, even when scattered around the world and lacking a state and government of their own.[58] This glorification of antiquity was rather common among Enlightenment writers. But Rousseau felt no obligation to advise his Polish clients about how to incorporate the Israelites' contemporary descendants, who constituted 10 percent of the population of Poland.

The long-term influence of Rousseau's silence and evasiveness in regard to the obvious problems of Poland and Polish Jews is difficult to assess. But Rousseau's contemporary, another French Enlightenment adviser to the Polish gentry, the Abbé de Mably (1709–1785), in a proposal that drew considerably more attention from Polish publicists than Rousseau's was far more explicit and perhaps more influential: Jews should be removed from the economic arena and be resettled on uncultivated lands.[59] Their significant roles in Poland, the French priest recommended, should be filled by Poles.[60]

Rousseau's vision of Poland was far from reality, but it was close to that vision cherished by his clients, the conservative, Sarmatian, Eastern-oriented gentry. His attention, and that of fellow enlighteners in the West, was no less selective and self-serving to what was going on in Poland than was the attention of the Polish nobility, both proponents and opponents of reform, as regards developments in the West.

It is a matter of abiding debate among scholars exactly what Rousseau intended to express in this tract. *Considérations* could surely be interpreted by Rousseau's gentry clients as an expression of approval for their aristocracy, elected monarchy, and weak and decentralized rule. Whatever peculiar set of circumstances prompted these conservative lords to turn westward to the bastion of Enlightenment at this particular moment, the encouragement, legitimation, and limited practical guidance for extricating their country out of the social, political, and economic quagmire that they did receive from Rousseau and Mably must have been gratifying, if not useful. It was certainly useful in lending support

55. Rousseau, *Government of Poland,* 94.
56. Ibid., 35–42.
57. Ibid., 20, 62.
58. Ibid., 5–6.
59. Gieysztor et al., *History of Poland,* 279; Hertzberg, *French Enlightenment and the Jews,* 77; Gay, *The Enlightenment,* 1.18.
60. Kendall, Introduction to Rousseau, *Government of Poland,* xi; Gabriel Bonnot de Mably, *Du gouvernement et des lois de la Pologne,* (1795), cited in Hertzberg, *French Enlightenment and the Jews,* 77.

to the Sarmatian party against the Western-oriented reformers of the Polish gentry. And it was useful in lending support to all parties in Poland to evade any discussion (as did Rousseau) or to propose measures of questionable implementability and unquestionable harshness (as did Mably) in regard to the future of Poland's Jews.

Some members of the Polish gentry at this time began to fall under the sway of still another Western thinker, French economist François Quesnay. A surgeon by trade, Quesnay founded the cultlike school of economics known as physiocracy. Although its influence in France soon waned, in Poland it enjoyed a brief but vigorous revival. The traces that physiocracy left in Polish thinking were no more salutary to the situation of Polish Jews than was the influence of Rousseau and Mably. Quesnay, who was deemed the last great Aristotelian of economic science, had led an intense battle in France against both mercantilism and republicanism. Quesnay and the elder comte de Mirabeau, in their major works *Théorie de l'impôt* and *Philosophie rurale,* published around 1760, did not attack Jewish economic enterprise directly. Their notions of productivity, however, which challenged the economic utility of finance and trade, could be used to call into question the "usefulness" of the Jews;[61] Linking productivity, as they did, to agriculture and large-scale manufacturing was a way of undermining the already precarious situation of Jews, who in France and Poland had been and were to remain landless. In the physiocratic conceptions of agricultural monarchies as the only truly constituted societies, and in the French publicists' arguments for the most efficient mode of production, Polish gentry landlords could find support for the familiar institutions of Polish feudalism and for systematization of their own economic thinking, translated into economic realities by devices such as the propinacja. For Quesnay, the commercial economy of the Polish gentry was an alien entity, distinct from the nation, comprising elements parasitical to the body of the natural society.[62] Moreover, Polish physiocracy provided "scientific" support for the gentry's dual standards toward trade, condemning its benefits and economically benefiting from that condemnation.[63] Hence physiocracy bol-

61. For an assessment of Quesnay's and the elder Mirabeau's influence on the perception of Jews in France, Hertzberg, *French Enlightenment and the Jews,* 72–77. The famous Dutch economist Isaac de Pinto, of Marrano descent, published *Traité de la circulation et du crédit* in 1771. In his efforts to refute the physiocrats and Mably, he was concerned with the Jewish implications of their arguments, though he seldom refers directly to Jews. He defends credit and monetary circulation as adding economic value against what he called "the frenzy of the soil." The failures of the Polish economy, based as it is upon agriculture, calls into question the argument of the physiocrats. He likewise legitimated the activities of bankers, brokers, speculators, and traders, economic roles in which Jews were heavily represented. This defense of finance had no recorded influence in Poland.

62. Lüthy, *From Calvin to Rousseau,* 92ff.

63. Louis Dumont reminds us of the enduring plausibility of that "primitive idea" that the gain of one party in trade results in the necessary loss of the other. This contrasted with Hume's conception, increasingly popular in England, that the increase of riches and com-

stered anti-Jewish sentiments. In physiocracy, a stepchild of the French Enlightenment, the Polish gentry could even discover emotionally satisfying links with deep-seated religious feelings installed, in the name of Christianity, by their Jesuit teachers. It provided them with a combination of "essentialism and nominalism, of liberalism and authoritarianism."[64] Catherine II likewise had a flirtation with physiocratic ideas.[65] The influence of physiocracy in small but powerful circles in Poland served as a bridge between the Enlightenment and Sarmatianism. Even beyond those circles, its assumptions went unchallenged, permeating the rhetoric of reform in the pamphlets and parliamentary debates of the Polish commonwealth's twilight years.[66] As with Rousseau and Mably's assessment of Poland's problems, the physiocrats' thinking about Poland most readily served their own purposes. And no thinking was generated that was of benefit to Polish Jews.

Cameralism was another fashionable school of thought that had some influence in mid-eighteenth-century Europe and echoed within the Polish rhetoric of reform.[67] Most influential in the Germanic countries, cameralism provided a theoretical foundation and elaboration to the well-ordered police state. Cameralism posited questions of the economy as wholly derivative of politics and the problem of the state: the interests of the individual were held to be subordinate to the interests of the community. In the Hapsburg Empire, where a chair of police and cameral sciences was established at the University of Vienna in 1763 to train civil servants, the cameralists made strong claims about the scientific base of *Kameralwissenschaft*.[68] One of the first professors of cameralism at that university was Joseph von Sonnenfels (1732–1817), an apostate Jew who dabbled in Kabbala and alchemy with the same empirical conviction with which he lectured about the *Nationalökonomie*, morals, education, religion, politics, diplomacy, war, and finance. It is particularly the harsh voice of the cameralists and the certitude with which they advocated policies—amplifying the tone of Joseph II's Edicts of Tolerance of 1782 and 1789—that we hear in some of the Polish proposals to reform policy toward Jews. Those proposals were made with little concern for Jewish sensibilities or for human costs. But for cameralism, as for physiocracy and for the Western Enlightenment, to be translated from rhetoric

---

merce in any one nation, rather than causing harm, actually promotes the riches and commerce of its neighbors. Jedlicki, "Social Ideas," 89.

64. Lüthy, *From Calvin to Rousseau,* 92ff.

65. Higgs, *The Physiocrats,* 88.

66. Gieysztor et al., *History of Poland,* 262, discusses Polish affinities to physiocracy in terms of Poland's "peculiar liberalism." But liberalism is hardly synonymous with weak structure and lack of regulation. For a description of Dupont de Nemours' brief visit to Poland, see ibid., 298; James McClain, *Economic Writings of Dupont de Nemours,* 41; Lipiński, "Fezjokraci w Polsce," and *Historia polskiej myśli,* 332–57.

67. See Schumpeter, *History of Economic Analysis,* 159–61; Pribram, *History of Economic Reasoning,* 89–96.

68. Small, *Cameralism,* 16ff.

into public policy required the support of a strong centralized state, which in Poland did not exist. Hence ideas could be appropriated but not implemented; at times, this failing was distinctly advantageous to Jews. Nevertheless, as we shall have occasion to observe, ideas can be influential even when they prove to be unimplementable.

The rhetoric of reform, independently of any specific efforts to alter the situation of Jews, established unrealistic standards by which to assess the role of Jews in Polish society. At the same time, that rhetoric of reform evoked a strong ideological reaction against which Polish Jews were even less able to defend themselves. But it was the military force and diplomatic machinations of the East, rather than ideologies of the West, that had the most immediate influence on Poland. Catherine II had plans for Poland and its unruly gentry. Seeking pretexts for more massive interventions in Poland's internal affairs, she exploited the inability of the king and gentry to deal with the peasant rebellions and the intransigence of some of those Polish lords. That the Russians, as a provocation, might have actually incited the Tartars in these border regions, as some Polish nationalists charged, seems unlikely. The Russians likewise had problems with peasant rebels. Moreover, Catherine had other reasons to covet Polish territory at this particular moment. Having lost Austria as a reliable ally, she needed Polish territory as a launching ground for attacks on Turkey, should war between Russia and that country ensue. She encouraged Poland's neighbors to join her. The intentions of those neighbors, succinctly summed up by Frederick II, to "keep Poland in lethargy," began to take on new possibilities. Frederick's efforts to weaken Poland, which had been confined in the past to tricks like using captured mints in Saxony to issue debased Polish coins and to make claims on small but significant territories, were now intensified. Frederick had only to draw Maria Theresa into his scheme to make the interests of different segments of Europe coincide.

On August 5, 1772, Prussia, Russia, and Austria signed treaties in which Poland lost about 30 percent of its territory and 35 percent of its population.[69] Estimates of the number of Jews residing in the partitioned areas diverge considerably. It would seem, however, that only two-thirds of Poland's nine hundred thousand to one million Jews remained under Polish sovereignty after 1772.[70] Austria received the largest number of Jews, living on the fertile lands of Galicia. Prussia and Russia incorporated fewer.[71] The consequences of this event for the

69. Gieysztor et al., *History of Poland*, 281–82.

70. Smoleński, *Stan i sprawa*, 37–38, citing the eighteenth-century Polish publicist Tadeusz Czacki, estimates that on the eve of the first partition Polish Jewry numbered nine hundred thousand. By the opening of the Four-Year Sejm in 1788 that number had reached one million, a rather large increase over a sixteen-year period. He does not make clear whether the latter number includes the lands of prepartition Poland.

71. Greenberg, *Jews in Russia*, 1:8, citing Dubnow, contends that Russia inherited two hundred thousand Jews. Pipes, "Catherine II and the Jews," 3–20. Klier, *Russia Gathers Her Jews*, 19, presents estimates that the Hapsburgs received between 172,000 and 225,000 Jews, Prussia 65,000, and Russia only 45,000.

Jews of Poland were considerable. What was heretofore a fairly homogeneous population with strong ties between different communities was now divided among four states. And although the new political boundaries, to be altered through two more partitions, were far from impermeable to the actual movement of Jews and their merchandise and to the circulation of their ideas, those Polish Jews living under the sovereignty of Prussia, the Hapsburg Empire, Russia, or the failing Polish commonwealth came under the influence of different political and economic forces.

Indeed, the leaders of the annexing powers did use Jews to further their own political goals. As happened with the arendars, who stood between the conflicting interests of the gentry and the serfs and often aroused the ire of both, the Jews, encouraged to undertake certain economic functions by the annexing powers, incurred resentment and hostility. In those regions annexed by Prussia, the Jews were agents of economic development that did not favor the Poles. Prussian officials merely dumped the most indigent Jews over the border back into Poland. The Russians manipulated Jewish rights with effects that were predictably destabilizing to the areas of Poland that they controlled. Since Jews as lessees provided a source of income for the nobles, the Russians attempted to weaken the arenda system so as to undermine the Polish gentry. The Austrians did what they could to pauperize the Jews of Galicia, an area designated to be a backwoods of the Austrian Empire suitable for economic exploitation, and fostered stagnation.[72]

Within Poland, an increasing number of Jews were expelled from villages and towns, where burghers were no longer forced by gentry or officials of the king to allow Jews to live.[73] Moreover, for the Jews observing the dismemberment of their country, the partition must have encouraged some reflection in regard to the plight of their fellow Poles, with whom they had sustained such an ambivalent relationship. This reflection must have affected the attitude of Polish Jews to the symbols of authority inhabiting their everyday life much as German Jews during the Reformation perceived in their own religious terms the significance of rioting peasants pulling down the steeples of Catholic churches.[74] The Polish gentry were now losing their own political autonomy, a mere eight years after they eliminated Polish Jewry's "bit of salvation," the Council of Four Lands.[75]

72. See Hagen, *Germans, Poles and Jews;* Wandycz, *Lands of Partitioned Poland.*
73. Mahler, *History of Modern Jewry,* 300–301. Mahler asserts that "as a rule, Jews were expelled by those wealthy estate owners who had reorganized their holdings on a rental basis to replace serf labor." But he brings no evidence for this interesting observation. Citing Czacki, he declares that a new class of seventy-two thousand unemployed Jews and nine thousand absolute paupers develops in this period.
74. See H. H. Ben-Sasson, "The Reformation in Contemporary Jewish Eyes."
75. There is some evidence that Jacob Frank saw in the partition an event heralding still greater cosmological events. And whereas this is hardly evidence of the reaction of Jews closer to the mainstream, it might be presumed that Frank, in his less self-centered rantings,

Among reflective Poles as well, what was to be only the first partition of Poland called for some explanation. More was lost than territory, population and national pride. This supreme tragedy, as Polish patriots viewed it, created a new set of economic problems that required a response. The economic measures imposed within the lost territories served the partitioning parties well but were at variance with the local economies of the annexed territories and the now-reduced Poland. One of the most significant economic consequences of the partition for the Polish gentry was that the key port of Danzig was lost for grain trade.[76]

The earliest reactions of educated Poles to their national tragedy, though not lacking in insight, did not lead the majority to any specific and unified action. Modernizers and traditionalists, occidentalists and Slavophiles, liberals and conservatives all sought consolation for their losses and vindication of their own positions, rather than specific object lessons, in interpreting the reality of growing Western material wealth and technological advancement and in assessing the political and military successes of the Russian Empire. Gazing to the West or to the East, they now looked upon the perpetrators of their tragedy. Neither Western technological and material culture nor Slavic transnationalism had served the interests of the Polish commonwealth. The equivocal nature of the enemies from without, and the difficulties and even the dangers of blaming powerful occupiers of Polish lands, who had brought about Poland's humiliating losses, intensified the search for those who could personify the forces of disintegration from within. New and renewed ideologies, including the Enlightenment and Sarmatianism as well as ideologies that would synthesize elements of both ideologies, now emerged. These ideologies could instruct, inspire, and focus a revitalized national identity, if not provide coherent policies and point to new international alliances. But a compelling and plausible explanation for Poland's travails was still needed, an explanation with which a new consensus could bind that fragmented nation, was yet to emerge.

------

expressed sentiments held by many Jews. See Halpern, *Yehudim Veyahadut,* 405–7, in which he suggests that Naḥman Krokhmal's conception of the decline of nations was influenced by his reflection on the partitions of Poland.

76. This had less of a direct impact on Jewish merchants who were involved in overland trade with German territories and in transshipment to the East than on those who engaged in trade dependent on the Vistula. See Hundert, "Security and Dependence." Greater dependency on land routes may have been of some advantage to Jewish merchants who were already heavily represented at various trade fairs. For example, of the 242 traders who came from Poland to Leipzig in 1766, 182 were Jews from Lisa and Brody. Brody in particular became an important town of trade, to the economic advantage of its Jews and of the Potocki family, which owned it. It also became a center of the East European Haskala. See Schipper, "Economic History of the Jews in Poland-Lithuania."

The Propinacja and the Rhetoric of Reform

The new assessments of productivity raised questions about the propinacja itself. But those questions rarely went beyond the surface of this institution, nor did they relate to how the propinacja typified the gentry's approach to problem solving. In the critique of the propinacja as it developed through the eighteenth century, we see the confluence of internal political conflict, the intervention of external forces, and the encroachment of new ideas from abroad. The early influences of physiocracy and the Enlightenment did not spur high levels of productivity in Poland. But they did create new and more sharply defined standards against which the most vulnerable segments of the population could be evaluated. As the prominent role of Jews in the vodka industry came under increased attack, the contribution of Jews to the Polish economy and their responsibility for the problems of serfdom was more widely discussed. What was largely avoided, however, was a comprehensive analysis of Polish feudalism and within it the key role of the propinacja. That the propinacja was a productive enterprise under prevailing economic conditions was rarely a conclusion that Poles arrived at. Reformers were suggesting with increasing frequency that the Jews take up agricultural labor. But they did not confront the harshness with which feudal agriculture was organized. The Jews expressed little more for agricultural labor than "aversion.[77] The Western concept of productivity, which had been crafted under different socioeconomic conditions from those of Poland, was applied by the followers of the Polish Enlightenment in evaluating the propinacja. Slavophiles as well as the Russian bureaucrats of the annexed territories, in spite of their conservative inclinations, soon joined the Polish supporters of the Enlightenment in writing pamphlets and tracts condemning Jewish involvement in the propinacja. Their old indignation was expressed in a new key—the rhetoric of reform.[78]

Yet in Polish publicistic literature the earliest discussion of the propinacja had little to do with Jewish involvement. Rather, it addressed the question of distributing the benefits of the monopoly among the various sectors of Polish society. During the Sejm of 1719 one early complaint about the sale of alcohol was registered by the gentry against the clergy. The latter came under attack for not paying enough taxes, for accruing too much land through bequests, and for exporting too much Polish wealth by sending extravagant gifts to Rome. At the same time, the church was criticized for profiting greatly from alcohol sales at inns located on it lands. The gentry's self-servingly pragmatic argument was that the profits from sales of the propinacja should circulate in the feudal economy.[79]

---

77. Smoleński, *Stan i sprawa,* 11–12. Agriculture was supposedly known among Jews as the hell of the peasant. In 1775, according to this report, only fourteen Jewish families were engaged in agriculture.
78. Levine, "Between Polish Autarky and Russian Autocracy," 66–84.
79. Gieysztor et al., *History of Poland,* 300.

Competition for the profits of the propinacja can also be seen in a 1775 Sejm debate that touched on the issue of Jewish involvement in this lucrative monopoly. Because the magnates who raised the point were trying to undermine the economic position of the lower gentry, and because they no longer needed Jewish managers and capital to run the propinacja, they decided to exclude the Jews. One member of the upper gentry complained that Jewish innkeepers were competing unfairly with the nobility. He alleged that Jews undersold their competitors and attracted more customers than non-Jews by cheating the peasants to acquire grain at prices below the market level. In conclusion he argued that Jews should be barred from the propinacja. But if Jewish involvement was a liability to one class, it was an asset to another. The representatives of the lower gentry vociferously opposed this measure, calling it a violation of the laws of nature. For the poorer gentry, who could not afford the capital outlay needed to manufacture and market drink, granting concessions to Jews was a major source of income. In turn, any abridgement of this privilege conflicted with their economic interests and legal prerogatives. Thus, both opposition to and support for Jewish involvement in the propinacja were couched in economic terms.[80]

An assessment of the propinacja in terms of the dispute over the distribution of wealth was soon counterbalanced by a consideration of its injurious effect on the serfs. The Russian administrators of the newly acquired Polish territories, who were the consolidators of autocracy and enjoyed no direct economic benefit from the propinacja, tended to view the issue from that perspective.[81] Concern over the adverse effect of excessive drinking was not new. In fact, the liquor industry in Russia, second only to salt extraction as a source of revenue, came under the criticism of church officials and others as far back as the eleventh

80. Ringelblum, *Kapitelen geshikhte,* 122–24.

81. For a discussion of how historians of Russian Jewry emphasize religiously motivated or economically motivated anti-Jewish sentiments, see Klier, *Russia Gathers Her Jews,* 15ff. Shemuel Ettinger raises the question of how Russians' mythological perception of Jews, rather than familiarity with real Jews (before the first partition of Poland in 1772 there had been virtually no Jews on Russian territory), in contrast with the abundant experience of the Poles, affected the respective attitudes toward Jews in Russia and Poland. Ettinger, "Ideological Background," 193–225. Pipes, "Catherine II and the Jews," skillfully sorts out the contradictions in Catherine's policies in regard to the Jews. He quite correctly encourages an analysis of those policies in relation to Russia's "own affairs . . . a byproduct of concerns that have little if anything to do with the Jews themselves" (3). It is an important corrective to underscore the rights that Russian Jews received under Catherine, at least on paper. But the emphasis placed by Russian administrators on the harmfulness of Jewish economic activities may have had at least as much of an effect on Jews as the privileges for Jews that those administrators may have enforced. The history of Jewish entrance into European society in the early modern period must analyze sources other than privileges and decrees. It is in this regard that we must pay attention to statements of Russian bureaucrats that may be particularly insidious, even when their policies toward Jews are liberal by the standards of the time.

century.[82] Jews in Russia were at that time a very minor factor in the liquor industry. Nevertheless, from the first partition of Poland until well into the nineteenth century, any investigation of peasant unrest, often initiated after crop failures and peasant rebellions, pointed an accusing finger at Jews as producers and purveyors of peasant misery. Dark pictures were painted of evil Jews who withheld grain from starving peasants because it was more profitable to use that grain to make alcohol than bread. What more likely contributed to these grain shortages was the disorganization in markets in the annexed areas of Poland. Because of the new opportunities for grain sales in the Russian heartland, with its sizable population and its greater successes in exporting grain to foreign markets, the Polish gentry could get a better price shipping the grain to the East than in handing it over to local bakers or even to local brewers. This pushed up bread prices and resulted in famine among the serfs. Revenues from alcohol expanded from 20 percent to 30 percent of Russia's entire budget during the 1770s. There was little reason to question the profitability of the propinacja.

A year after the first partition of Poland, Michał Kachovsky, a minor tsarist official from the district contiguous with the newly annexed Polish territory, made a survey of eastern Poland. Kachovsky noted grain shortages and inflation, attributing them to Jewish profiteering and shady practices, and he outlined their supposed effect on Polish serfs:

> The privilege of selling alcoholic beverages is given to them even in places where there are no inns or they travel to the villages and pour there. In a word, all their means of supporting themselves are certain to impoverish the peasants. They sell alcoholic beverages at high prices and nowhere will one find from them drink as it should be: they mix with the alcoholic beverages the plain beverages and all sorts of grasses which quickly lead to the loss of consciousness and to drunkenness of the farmers who buy beverages from

82. Smith and Christian, *Bread and Salt,* 74ff. Church officials and tsars occasionally protested against drunkenness and ensuing moral problems. But policies about drink were more influenced by the potential for state revenue than by concern over deleterious social outcomes. Ibid., 224–26. Moreover, in the eighteenth century Russian monarchs strengthened the economic base of the service gentry by awarding concessions and contracts for the production of drink to retired army officers and those to whom they wanted to express gratitude. The increase in urbanization in Russia moved people into areas with deficient water supply—one reason for an increase in demand for kvass. Moreover, a large segment of the population was in nonagricultural production, causing supply problems for all kinds of edibles, including drink. In the period of Peter the Great, at the beginning of the eighteenth century, the average annual alcohol consumption per male was four pints; by the time of Catherine the Great it had increased to ten. Ibid., 221. The main problem for the tsars was efficient and reliable revenue collection, prompting the remark of one commentator that at the end of the eighteenth century "a considerable proportion of the population became addicted to alcohol, but the state too became increasingly dependent on it." Ibid., 218.

them; and when they bring the farmers to this position, they rob them of their money, and on top of that they write down debts at will, and after that they will collect the debts from money and from grain. . . . And to this we have to add the grain that they exploit for the production of alcohol that they then sell. And from this it is clear what is the cause for the high price and the shortage of grain in this region. And because the residents have not made any economic calculations and have not paid any attention to them, they do not feel their own and the peasants' recognizable and obvious decline.[83]

Kachovsky recognized that the Jews were acting as the gentry's agents in this enterprise. But because he presented members of the Polish gentry as innocent observers who had not fully considered the consequences of the propinacja, he accorded the Jews all of the blame. The tone of Kachovsky's memorandum had a great deal of influence on the rhetoric of reform in regard to Jews as it was expressed both in Poland and in Russia in the years that followed. And this harmfulness was emphasized at the same time that Russian officials gave Jews special concessions to operate the propinacja.[84]

Although Polish reformers could no longer ignore the precipitous decline of the Polish republic, they almost all avoided a direct and constructive confrontation with the social, political, and economic problems reflected by the propinacja. Rather, when Poland was threatened by internal dissolution and by the territorial and political avariciousness of its neighbors, Polish reformers and "men of the Enlightenment" preferred to indulge in condemning the Jews for their involvement in the propinacja and for its pernicious effects. Some members of the upper gentry apparently joined the condemnation of Jewish involvement in the propinacja, for the sake of greed rather than to express the need for reforms. They hoped to wrest a large proportion of this profitable business from the lower gentry, who continued to require the investments and managerial skills of Jewish agents. The "unproductive" economic roles that Jews chose for themselves increasingly came to be seen as the cause rather than the effect of Poland's backwardness.

The Limits of the Polish Enlightenment

The Polish borders were no more sealed to Western ideas than they were to the contraband products of Western technology. Polish reformers generally attributed the new economic vitality and productivity in the West to technical innovations. But an increasing number of reformers, in the wake of the crises of

83. Cited in Slutsky and Buba, "History of the Jews in Russia in the Eighteenth Century," 74–78. For an analysis of the factors influencing Russian policies toward the Jews in the late eighteenth century, see Ettinger, "Foundations and Purposes," 20–34. The different approaches of Russian and Polish officials to Jewish communal affairs was examined in Nadav, "Rabbi Avigdor ben Ḥayyim," 200–219.
84. Pipes, "Catherine II and the Jews," 13–17.

the first partition, began to appreciate the links of that vitality to new modes of political, social, and economic thinking and to the institutions by which they were embodied in those rapidly developing countries. Commentators on political and economic affairs, such as Piotr Switkowski and Ferdynand Nax, took a broader look at why there were not more steam engines and textile machines on the Vistula or the Neman.[85] By the 1780s the awareness of Poland's backwardness began to impinge on the consciousness of more and more Poles. A considerable number of pamphlets, many anonymous, calling for sundry reforms, circulated throughout Poland. This publicistic literature guided the legislative and constitutional debates that would take place during Poland's "bloodless revolution," the Four-Year Sejm. It was written and discussed by those younger members of the gentry who were the beneficiaries of the educational efforts of Stanisław Konarski and an older generation of Polish reformers. Some began to see themselves as the Eastern outpost of the Western European Enlightenment. Trips to the West were part of a gentleman's upbringing. French, and to a lesser extent German and English, were the languages of refined discourse, and the better educated nobles read literature written in those languages. The last Polish king, Stanisław Poniatowski, for example, in his youth traveled to the West, where he was impressed by certain of its political and cultural developments, particularly by centralized, enlightened royal absolutism. He dreamed of rousing his country from cultural and economic stagnation. In one attempt to realize this dream, he founded the *Monitor,* a journal modeled after the English *Spectator.*[86] This journal, at least in its early years, went so far as to attack Sarmatianism.[87] Priests were also important mediators of Enlightenment ideas, to which they were exposed during extended visits to Rome. But even among the clery new philosophies had little influence on religious thought, and much less on religious sensibilities.

These members of the Polish gentry now looked with approval on developments in England, France, Holland, Prussia, and even the thirteen colonies in America that had recently united and waged a successful war of independence. Among other startling changes, Western-oriented gentry could observe accomplishments of Jews in the West and their growing participation in the economic and even cultural affairs of their respective countries. How did these observations influence Polish reformers' perceptions of Jews in their own country?

The short-lived Polish Enlightenment based its efforts to reorient the terms of productivity on two assumptions: that something significant had taken place with the British industrial revolution, and that the gap between Poland and the West would be perpetuated if the Polish economy continued to depend on the exportation of grain and other agricultural produce.[88] A fundamental change of attitude among the gentry was necessary if Poland's situation was to be changed. A

85. Jedlicki, "Social Ideas," 94.
86. Bain, *Last King of Poland;* Kukiel, *Czartoryski and European Unity;* Jedlicki, "Native Culture and Western Civilization," 69.
87. Michalski, "Sarmatyzm," 144.
88. Jedlicki, "Native Culture," 95.

small coterie of Enlightenment writers stressed the importance of accumulation, the use of surplus for development, calculated investment, and the protection of fledgling industry from foreign imports. These Enlightenment writers, perhaps also influenced by the Central European cameralists, admired Frederick II's system of state economic control. Grants from the Polish treasury, they believed, would initiate new branches of industry and support programs of public works—the construction of ports, canals, a merchant fleet, roads, factories, and mines. Some of the Polish enlighteners also subscribed to the redevelopment of towns and local markets. Proposals were made for the establishment of a national bank. But few considered the degree of political and economic centralization, particularly the effective taxation of the gentry, that would make these proposals workable. An even smaller number advocated the extension of burghers' political rights, limitations on gentry rights to serf labor, the granting of the privileges of money rents and land inheritance to peasants, and the economic rehabilitation of Jews.[89]

A few publicists dealt more directly and extensively with the problems of Poland's Jews. They included some Poles who may have been encouraged by Jews to undertake this advocacy and who were attentive to the discussion of Jewish rights taking place in the West, perhaps because they had resided in Berlin or Paris. An anonymous pamphlet calling for improving the situation of Poland's Jews began to circulate in Warsaw in 1782. The "Nameless Citizen" who put forward this reform proposal manifests influences of the French Enlightenment in criticizing Jews' beliefs and behavior, in locating the source of their "evils" in the shortcomings of Polish society and the Polish government, and in placing a great deal of confidence in education as the means by which to transform Jews as individuals. This thinking is not radically different from that expressed in the influential tract issued at the time by the enlightened Prussian official Christian Wilhelm Dohm, "On the Amelioration of the Civil Status of the Jews."[90] Moreover, the particular areas of improvement of Jewish life and the degree of intervention into it that Nameless Citizen advocates reflect the influence of the *Toleranzpatent* issues in that same year by Joseph II. The author advocates respect for the general principle of "Mosaic" religion but emphasizes that "customs" impeding Jewish participation in modern life, such as food restrictions and the large number of holidays, must be changed. The education of Jews should be more under the control of the Ministry of Education. Jews should be encouraged to use Polish and to translate their books into that language. Nameless

---

89. Jedlicki, "Social Ideas," 97. These reforms were by no means perceived to be inextricably linked. Chancellor Andrzej Zamoyski, for example, commuted service into rent for some of his serfs and drafted a code (rejected by the Sejm in 1780) in which he sought to curtail the political rights of the landless gentry and expand the rights of the burghers. The king's "chief proposer of legislative reform," as he was known, responded less than positively, however, to any improvements in the situation of the Jews. A. Gieysztor et al., *History of Poland,* 284, 290.

90. Katz, *Out of the Ghetto,* 57ff.

Citizen was particularly adamant about the harmful effects of communal autonomy, which makes of the Jews a *corpus in corpore.* No less an authority than the
father of the Berlin Haskala, Moses Mendelssohn, would have concurred with the
anonymous publicist on this point. Without destroying Jewish "spiritual autonomy," the Jew should be better incorporated into Polish society. This unique and
curious tract seemed to have little influence on the general tenor of the Polish
enlighteners when it was first issued. In the parliamentary debate that developed
at the end of the decade, however, it did have influence, though not without
arousing the opposition of a wide spectrum of Poles, including some Polish
Jews.[91]

In 1783 Jacob Hirsch petitioned officials in Belorussia to establish a Jewish
school with a modernized curriculum, similar to those being established in the
West. Teachers, at least initially to be Jewish, could be obtained from Germany
with the assistance of Moses Mendelssohn. The establishment of this type of
school, Hirsch argued, need not be a burden on the government treasury but
could be supported by a more efficient use of Jewish tax money. In 1786 Elias
Ackord, a Polish Jew born in Mogilev who studied medicine in Berlin and then
returned to practice in Warsaw, wrote a pamphlet on Jewish reform. Ackord
reportedly included in his proposal a German translation of the pamphlet by
Nameless Citizen. Why, at the behest of whom, and for which audience he prepared this translation is not clear. It may have been part of the efforts of certain
circles in Warsaw to prove, contrary to popular opinion, how enlightened and
liberal Poles really were, and thereby to court favor and support in the Prussian
capital. Ackord appended to the claims that he made in this pamphlet a review of
experiences from his own life; he made his concerns known even when they were
at variance with those of the original author and even when they did not paint a
flattering image of Polish realities. While supporting the full integration of Jews
into the life of Poland and underscoring the evils of communal autonomy, he
rejected the author's proposal that Hebrew books be eliminated. He also showed
considerably less enthusiasm for universal Jewish conscription than did the anonymous author whose work he translated. Ackord expressed great optimism that
the Nameless Author's positive sentiments toward Jews would prevail and that
Jews, granted new opportunities to solve their practical problems, would take
greater interest in "worldly sciences." This phrase most likely refers to the natural
sciences, of which critics of the Jews often indicated that Jews were ignorant and
which occupied a prominent position in the educational agenda of various maskilim (enlighteners). Other publicistic efforts to improve the Jewish situation
included the distribution of two medical self-help books that were issued in 1789
and 1790 by Polish Jews who had come under the influence of the Berlin Haskala,
one by Moses Marcuse and the other by Menaḥem Mendal Lefin, which was
published with the financial support of his noble patron Adam Czartoryski.[92]

91. Smoleński, *Stan i Sprawa,* 50ff.
92. Shmeruk, "Moses Marcuse of Slonim," 361–82.

Another reform proposal on behalf of Jews circulated during this period of new enthusiasm for constitutional reform was addressed to King Stanisław Poniatowski by Abraham Hirszowicz, one of his agents. Hirszowicz saw the strong-armed and persistent intervention of the king as absolutely necessary in forcing the lords to see beyond their personal and immediate interests, on the one hand, and in making the Jews accept and implement reforms, on the other. He stressed that the Jews were valuable to the country but were in dire need of reform. He argued for Jewish access to all crafts, and for land to farm. Unemployed and poor Jews should be pressed into public projects such as road construction. He also advocated legislation concerning the personal and communal lives of Jews. This included regulating their dress and the money spent on celebrations so that it would not be wasted on ostentatiousness. Similar restrictions were frequently stated in the Jewish pietistic literature. Hirszowicz sought to restrict rabbinical activity to the synagogues, limiting the services of rabbis to larger areas and transferring powers of taxation from the offices of the kehilla to the municipal agents but not abolishing Jewish autonomy. He wanted to provide hospitals for every community and to regulate the age of marriage in order to ensure educational opportunities and vocational skills for the young.

These proposals of Jewish and non-Jewish publicists in the 1780s indicate that ideas for the improvement of Polish Jewry's situation were entertained. But they had less of an impact than they might have had, even among most of the reform-minded men of the Enlightenment, because of the insufficient attention that was paid to the need for political centralization and to the significance of commerce in expanding markets and in spurring and capitalizing rapid industrial growth. Even these gentry enlighteners expressed contempt for the tradesmen, whom they derisively called the town loafers. As Jacek Jezierski, an entrepreneur of gentry origin, put it, "There are no true burghers in Poland, only useless inhabitants of our country; there are no merchants, but plenty of hucksters."[93] The image of the Jew as huckster and purveyor of ruinous drink to the serfs was unchanged. Occasional reports in the Polish press presented a different image of Western European Jews. The reputation of Moses Mendelssohn in particular aroused the following comment: "For us, who are accustomed to our Itziks and Moskes who sit in the stores and get the masses drunk, it is a wonder to see people from that nation and that faith in other lands who are so useful and educated."[94] In the 1780s the role of French and German Jews in the cultural life of their respective countries provided the advocates of reform for Polish Jews with evidence of the feasibility of their position. On the other hand, such comparisons were readily used to castigate and blame Polish Jews for their own shortcomings rather than to argue for Jewish rights.

The burgher tradesmen, instead of ideologically and polemically defending

93. Jedlicki, "Social Ideas," 100.
94. Cited in Ringelblum, "Hasidism and Haskala."

the economic utility of their activities, did little more than demand an altered position within the legal order. Besides their demands for specific political and economic rights, such as the attainment of land and estates, they did not have a broad vision of change within Polish society. Their social reference was toward the gentry, and their aspirations were congruent with the more conservative sectors of Polish society; they could be easily co-opted. A few Jews in this period attained some prominence in the royal court as suppliers or as doctors. Some, like Elias Ackord, participated in the publicistic debate. Jewish merchants and financiers, on however large a scale, could not be admitted to the nobility, nor could they attain civic and economic rights except through conversion to Catholicism.[95] Their upward mobility, therefore, was completely thwarted. Moreover, as a result of the advantages held by the burghers, who were occasionally ennobled, the Jews in Poland had few allies in pressing for a more positive attitude toward trade.

During the last years of the Polish state, as it was about to be overwhelmed by the political and economic forces that had weakened it, the Polish Enlighteners propagated a keen awareness of Polish stagnation. The inferiority and backwardness of Poland in every respect, vis-à-vis England and Holland, were recurrent themes in the publicistic literature of the Enlighteners, including King Stanisław Poniatowski's *Monitor.*[96] The king and the men of the Enlightenment began to suggest that what were seen as essential Polish values, thinking and modes of reaction, were a manifestation of retardation and a cause of underdevelopment rather than a viable alternative to the West.[97] Their gaze at what was transpiring in the West was now unflinching, even if in their analysis of the disparities between Poland and the West they tried to preserve a modicum of national pride. The tone of this dismayed analysis is exemplified in Stanisław Staszic's 1791 statement, "How far behind we have remained." The king and other espousers of the Enlightenment insisted that under the right conditions Poland could catch up with and overtake those whom now it could only envy.[98] Backwardness thus was added to the list of Poland's ills for which Poland's leaders had to seek some cure, or at least some justification.

95. Even conversion would not have assured privileges because of the Frankists who at that time—and to this day—were on the minds of Poles. More sincere and devout apostates would have found it difficult to gain acceptance in Polish society.

96. The enlightened king Stanisław Poniatowski's personal situation well illustrated the obstacles faced by the Enlightenment in Poland. Bain, *Last King of Poland,* 138ff. To implement any change, and to maintain his minimal authority against the confederations of the gentry and the rebellious peasantry, he needed the continued support of his former paramour, Catherine II. In Russia the Enlightenment did not inspire Catherine to support Polish political reform or to feel any obligation to stabilize that country's polity or economy. She was content to see her neighbor remain hopelessly behind.

97. Jedlicki, "Social Ideas," 95.

98. Ibid., 94ff.

Sarmatianism, Nativism, and the New National Messianism

The Polish Enlightenment served not only as a new ideological prism through which the gentry could reflect Western successes. It held up an unflattering mirror as well, in which Poles who wanted to could view what was taking place in their own country. That examination of the West, used to criticize Poland, provoked a negative reaction. Defensive Poles could debunk the ideas of the Polish enlighteners by associating them with the general decadence ascribed to the West and by focusing on the reports of increasing societal conflict and the threats of revolution. Suspicions and innuendoes that the Polish enlighteners were under the influence of freemasonry lent an aura of sectarianism, even of subversiveness, to the bearers of modernizing ideas.[99] Conservative Poles popularized satires of French affectations and Western-oriented snobbery.[100]

The preservation of serf labor at any cost was an issue more urgent to the largest segment of the gentry, including some members who toyed with Enlightenment ideas, than the issue of the widening gap between Poland and the developing West.[101] Some lords began to press feudal values with renewed urgency. Sarmatianism now provided old ideas with which to confront new problems; it lent the coherence and legitimation to the Polish economy that some Polish enlighteners were beginning to question.[102] Sarmatians indignantly resisted all efforts to increase political and administrative centralization; their concept of the Sarmatian people excluded enserfed Poles and non-Catholics. They idealized Poland's position within the international orbit by maintaining, against all evidence, a positive view of Poland's economic complementarity with the West, and by attempting to explain the country's economic dependency on the West in terms other than of backwardness or modernization. In opposing the reformers among the gentry, and their assaults on Polish self-esteem and national pride, these conservative ideologues denied "how far behind we have remained"; they rejected the need for development, growth, or change.[103] Polish modernization and Polish nationalism seemed to be at odds.

These ideologues claimed that in the global division of labor Poland was different from, but ultimately as productive as the West. They described Poland's complementary relationship with the West in the terms of rural versus urban, agrarian versus industrial, or food producer versus food consumer. This argument was most appealing to the majority of the Polish gentry who did not want to

99. Polish freemasonry requires the attention that this movement in other countries has received from historians. There is no evidence at this time that the movement in eighteenth-century Poland provided anything of a meeting ground for Jews and Christians as it did elsewhere in Central and Western Europe. See Katz, *Jews and Freemasons in Europe.*
100. Jedlicki, "Native Culture," 65.
101. Michalski, "Sarmatyzm," 118–19.
102. Cynarski, "Shape of Sarmatian Ideology, 16–17.
103. Michalski, "Sarmatyzm," 115–16; Jedlicki, "Social Ideas," 92.

confront the danger of Poland slipping into irreversible backwardness and who resisted the proposals made to avert that danger and to revitalize the country.

The Sarmatian ideologues regarded Poland as entitled to enjoy the benefits of Western material development without having to become like the West, much as members of the Melanesian cargo cult waited for bounty to arrive on European ships crossing the horizon. The idealization of the Polish feudal estate as a perpetual-motion machine implied that occasional irregularities would promptly be remedied by internal measures; consequently these ideologues viewed all changes as extrinsic and ultimately undesirable. Again, a selective and distorted reading of the emphasis that French physiocracy placed upon productivity resulting from the efficient exploitation of the soil was used to legitimate and idealize Polish patriarchalism and serfdom. The Sarmatians argued that it was important for Poland to remain rural and therefore supported by agricultural production. Under these conditions, rather than if Poland were to become a country of urban, industrial food consumers, the traditional values of life would be preserved.[104] This sentimental preservation of tradition for its own sake, what I have termed traditionalism, was now flaunted as an important mode of patriotism.[105]

Sarmatianism, in its "self-complacency and megalomania," thus immunized its followers against a sense of political, social, and economic upheaval. It preached that there was nothing new under the Polish sun. Poland had already experienced incursions from the west and peasant rebellions in the east, annexations and civil wars, political upheavals and economic reverses, plagues and pestilences, religious controversies and persecutions. Sarmatianism, by blunting the significance of the present moment and its problems, provided a soothing rationalization for preserving the status quo. Sarmatian publicists grasped for hope even where the results of change were undeniable, as, for example, in the annexation of Elbing and Danzig as a consequence of the first partition and in the Prussian imposition of customs duties on Vistula trade with its palpable influence on the gentry's trading position. They tried to convince themselves and others that Prussians would make concessions on the partition treaty, that grain could be shipped through the ports of Kurland, that Black Sea trade could be better organized, and that Britain would become a more active trading partner.[106]

The introduction of new programs for economic change, comparable to those that had brought industrial and commercial success to the West, required more positive attitudes toward trade and monetary exchange. At most they received lukewarm approval through the Polish modernizers' imaginative evocation of old values.[107] The need to protect domestic industry was couched in the traditional terms of antiforeignism. Instead of talking about the economic benefit that could be derived from protecting fledgling industries at home, the modern-

---

104. Jedlicki, "Social Ideas," 93ff.
105. See the Introduction for my discussion of Joseph Levenson's use of traditionalism.
106. Jedlicki, "Social Ideas," 96.
107. Ibid., 96.

izers promoted the very terms of antiforeignism that they had eschewed, and they legitimated the exclusive use of Polish goods and the imposition of custom duties as patriotic. The purchase of imported luxury items now was frowned upon by the modernizers, who evoked traditional Sarmatian attitudes toward that which was foreign. The effectiveness of these rhetorical devices was limited. Even die-hard Sarmatians conveniently suspended their antiforeign sentiments in procuring the imported luxury items they so coveted; they would not be moved by the new standards of patriotism to protect fledgling industry if this would inconvenience them. And even gentry statists, recognizing the need for political and economic reforms, concentrated on reducing the costs of maintaining the state, and particularly the army, rather than on expensive administrative reform that would require effective taxation of the nobility. And those expenditures that proved to be absolutely unavoidable they tried to pass on to the burghers and the Jews.[108]

This new rhetoric, accommodating as it was to the culture and the political economics of Sarmatianism, likewise led to old results in regard to that segment of the population most keenly perceived to be foreign—Poland's Jews. The call for protectionism, which in Western countries might have created an economic climate suitable to small-scale Jewish enterprise, in Poland limited Jewish productivity. This revitalized Sarmatianism did not promote a more positive attitude toward Jews; the climate and policies that it supported reduced Jews who might have been tradesmen, financiers, and manufacturers to hucksters and paupers. The unqualified condemnation of imports, legitimated by an emotional appeal to patriotism rather than by more rational economic reasoning, overlooked the need for foreign materials that could expand and strengthen Poland's industrial capacity. It also tainted the involvement with international brokers of finance and raw materials, among them Jews, who were crucial to the rapid economic development of other parts of Europe. The new rhetoric postulated a new polarization that Poland's Jews were in no position to bridge. The autarky that had been imposed by Polish agrarian feudalism upon the local economy, in its relationship with international markets, was now transposed to the national economy. National autarky and self-sufficiency, however unrealistic these goals were, now stood at the heart of both the modernizers' and the nationalists' programs for revitalizing Poland.

The reluctance of most Polish modernizers to speak out on behalf of institutions such as free labor and open markets may have been a calculated stance to avoid arousing more opposition than they could handle.[109] More likely, their efforts to promote Polish Manchesters without adopting the infrastructures and political economies that had contributed to the development of that city, including changes in the terms of labor and the rationalization of markets, reflect basic

108. Ibid., 92.
109. Ibid., 94. Gay, *The Enlightenment,* 2:31, reminds us that slavery and child labor were not wholly incompatible with the worldview of the *philosophes.*

limitations in their own thinking and in their modernization program. Similar to an earlier generation of reformers, the enthusiasm that these Polish modernizers displayed for the West was ultimately superficial. Most continued to affirm the entitlements of the gentry to serf labor. Their optimism derived from a myopic perspective on what threatened their country; their acceptance of the weakness and disorder of the Polish commonwealth followed from their strong sense of fatalism.[110] All of this weakened the possibility of active and sustained efforts of reform. Although many Polish Enlightenment thinkers advocated changes in individual attitude and behavior, believing that these would lead to societal change, few paid sufficient attention to the need to strengthen a centralized state. Most were more or less at peace with feudalism and a weak central authority.[111] At the very moment when Enlightenment ideas were precipitating a revolution in France, the social visions of the Polish men of the Enlightenment were limited to respect for legal order, including the nobleman's right to serf labor.[112]

In the late 1780s, when it was most important for the king and the gentry to respond to the economic challenges of the West and to unite against the encroachment of neighbors, Sarmatian "self-complacency and megalomania" underwent a still stronger resurgence.[113] Nativism, the new idealization of the Polish way of life, in part was a reaction to the abrupt changes in the West. Those reports of growing social tensions in the West, culminating in the French Revolution, as well as the impression of the prevalence of unbridled materialism resulting from industrial development, militated against the West serving as a model for Polish change, even among many of the Western-oriented enlighteners. Whereas several decades earlier a pejorative sense had been attached to the term *Sarmatian* by Konarski and other publicists, in the 1780s, in the very circles where there had been strong identification with a universalist European culture dominated by the French Enlightenment, old Polish dress came into vogue even among the most enlightened gentry.[114] Adam Czartoryski (1734–1823) perhaps best exemplifies this combination of attachment to Enlightenment Europe with an attachment to the dress, manners, and values ascribed to an old Poland. A literary work, *Ode to the Mustache,* using the term *Sarmatian* with pride and with no negative connotation, was written by a member of his coterie.[115] At the same time, reference to Russia, even among the most ardent Polish Slavophiles, was considered negative because of that country's association with the partition and its constant and crude intervention into Polish governance. Nativism, therefore, stood above both occidentalism and Slavophilism.

As nativism became the basis of a political nationalist movement, it provided a defensive reaction to the growing awareness of backwardness in Poland's

110. Michalski, "Sarmatyzm," 139.
111. Jedlicki, "Native Culture, 70.
112. Jedlicki, "Social Ideas," 94.
113. Michalski, "Sarmatyzm," 118.
114. Ibid., 150.
115. Ibid., 149.

shrinking territory, assigning metaphysical significance to a political and economic situation that otherwise might for many Poles have been the source of
shame. With the gentry caught between conflicting forces emanating from East
and West over which they had little control, Polish nationalism became increasingly otherworldly. Failing to generate collective, concrete solutions to
Poland's problems, Polish ideologues began to speak of the country's messianic
role. Poland's worldly struggles had cosmological significance far greater than
their political and economic manifestations; those struggles were the birth pangs
of supernatural transformations. The new messianic nationalism projected the
image and elaborated a theory of the "chosen" people of Poland as a bridge; in
their unique and troubled role, they served as the link between East and West, and
between worldly and otherworldly forces. This bridge theory was to account for
Polish suffering and to compensate for the double humiliation of backwardness
and denationalization.[116]

Sarmatianism afforded protection to its adherents against the disillusion-
ment and despair that accompanied political, social, and economic failures; saving
the system of Polish feudalism became one of its paramount functions. Now
bolstered by messianism and nativism, neither crisis conditions nor the calls for
reform of the Polish Enlightenment seriously challenged the Sarmatian conception of order, or perhaps more accurately, Sarmatian justifications of disorder and
"self-satisfied stagnation."[117]

These ideologies—Sarmatianism, nativism, and messianism—conceptually
and emotionally influenced not only legislative and public debates about Poland's
future order but also what was taking place in the street. They lent themselves to
powerful dramatizations of disorder; they focused blame by deflecting attention
from unmanageable threats from without to the identification of the enemies

116. That an ideology such as Sarmatianism, under conditions of adversity, should be
bolstered and elaborated rather than disconfirmed and abandoned, is not unusual. Ideologies protect their predictive powers by providing their own theodicies which describe
the conditions under which their promise (such as for rain in the proper season or for a
heaven on earth) may not be fulfilled. In conceptualizing disparate realities, ideologies spin
for their true believers a seamless web of meaning. Even when this web becomes frayed at
the edges or torn in the middle, ideologies resist the ensuing cognitive dissonance. They
often evoke *increased* commitment from believers, with hostility, even violence, directed
at the sources of disconfirmation. A growing, timely literature has developed on millennial
beliefs and violence and on explanations of human misery that lead to social destructiveness. See Barkun, *Disaster and the Millennium.* For an analysis of the relationship
between inner group processes and the shift of ideologies, theodicies, and assorted gnostic
myths of death and rebirth from cognitive and interpretive functions to the mimetic and
motivational, leading to the disinhibition of destructive behavior, see Levine, "On the
Debanalization of Evil." Even when ideologies fail to mobilize political action, they may
continue to be politically significant as a result of social psychological functions of protecting their followers from anxiety and insecurity, as well as providing them with a sense of
destiny.
117. Jedlicki, "Social Ideas," 93.

within. They thereby achieved a degree of consensus and solidarity—fleeting, perhaps, but otherwise unattainable in early modern Poland. In envisioning that order, these ideologies established the boundaries for any realistic participation of Poland's Jews. As we try to understand the limits of that participation, we must be attentive to these ideologies in both their discursive and their dramatic forms.

Functions and Forms of Antisemitism

It is against this background that we must consider the functions and forms of expression of one additional ideology: Polish beliefs about the destructiveness of the Jews. Sporadic and localized pogroms throughout the centuries of Jewish residence in Poland were perpetrated by fanatic clergy, peasant rebels, zealous burghers, and scheming gentry, drawing from traditional, Christian-inspired anti-Jewish sentiments. In the late seventeenth and the eighteenth centuries, however, an undercurrent of anti-Jewish feeling led to renewed attacks, distinguished not so much by their increased frequency as by their specific expressive form. These attacks corresponded to problems in Poland's economy and economic thinking to which I have attributed particular significance. These include low productivity, an imbalanced agrarian economy with small and unsuccessful pockets of industry, an increasingly negative trade balance depleting the wealth of the country, a foundering system of monetary exchange that could protect neither impoverished serfs nor ostentatious magnates from waves of inflation, negative attitudes toward commerce and currency that thwarted investment, and other problems for which the propinacja could provide limited compensation. New modes of economic thinking—from selective appropriation of Enlightenment concepts of productivity, used by some members of the nobility as a self-serving critique of Poland's Jews to Sarmatianism, as it became more nativistic yet more otherworldly—did not resolve these economic problems. How did the failures of feudalism relate to the revival of the blood libel, as it recurred in Poland and as it subsequently spread to other areas of Central and Eastern Europe in the nineteenth and even the twentieth centuries?

An illustration from the mid-eighteenth century points to a general pattern of events. In 1753 a Christian child in the Ukrainian town of Zhitomir went missing under mysterious circumstances. After a period of search in which rumors and initial suspicions of Jewish involvement spread, the child's body was found. The enthusiasm of the mob, as it often happened, was incited by local priests. Chief among them was Kajetan Sołtyk, later to be imprisoned and exiled by the Russians for his Catholic zeal and his incitement of rebellion against the granting of religious rights for Russian Orthodox peasants. In a letter of May 26, 1753, he noted to the Archbishop of Lwów that when the child's body was moved past a tavern, "it began suddenly to bleed profusely from its left rib." Local Jews, including the rabbi and prominent and wealthy community leaders, were arrested. They were tortured until they expired or until, in the dreadful pain, they offered the confession that was sought. Sołtyk unwittingly offers a candid glimpse of the conflict between religious passions and pragmatic considerations in the Poland of his time:

> On that very day on which the event occurred, six miles from here, they informed me of the matter and I did not delay intervening in it with all my strength as in a matter of faith and the honor of God issuing proclamations appropriate to the religion. But when some of the agents made problems for me, fearing their masters regarding the imprisonment [of the Jews], I was forced to turn myself to those estates and rebuke the masters and also to warn them. Only then did they make haste in turning them over to my hands and now I already have thirty-one Jews and two Jewesses under my authority, bound in chains among them the most important and wealthy tax farmers in these districts.[118]

The agents of the gentry who supervised the large estates were genuinely concerned about how this unfolding "matter of faith and the honor of God" would affect gentry revenues. These guardians of their masters' Jews had to be circumvented, and the lords themselves had to be both inspired and intimidated, as Father Sołtyk was eminently capable of doing. Only then would they "make haste" in turning over their Jews. In many of the blood libels, as in this case, the local church officials, in cooperation with police authorities, were able to extract some sort of confession. At times they were even able to get Jewish prisoners to accept baptism in exchange for the opportunity to be killed outright and avoid more severe torture.[119]

What prompted this sudden rise in the blood libel? On the most fundamental level, the blood libel, like the witchcraft accusation, must be seen as a deep-rooted survival of pre-Christian attitudes that ultimately is Christianized.[120] Indeed, in this period of blood libels there were people accused of witchcraft as well.[121] Demographic pressures and the need for a guilt-free method to imple-

118. Cited in Bałaban, *Letoledot Hattenua Hafrankit,* 102.
119. See Rubinstein's interpretation of Israel Bal Shem Tov's ascension vision of 1747, in "The Besht's Epistle." Rarely did baptism itself save Jewish lives and there are even records of priests going back on their agreement with Jews, savagely torturing neophytes.
120. A large ethnographic and anthropological literature on witchcraft in the early modern West has developed. This witchcraft finds believers not only in Counter-Reformation Catholic countries but in regions under the influence of Calvinism as well, where meddling with the supernatural was generally frowned upon. Of particular interest is the ambivalence of the clergy to such magical forms. On the one hand, manifestations of magic attest to supernatural powers, and on the other, their popularization, especially in the lower reaches of society, can signal a lack of church control over those same powers. In the case of the blood libel, church-sponsored as it appears to be, the Polish clerics seemed not to have had any such ambivalence. See Evans, *Making of the Hapsburg Monarchy,* 342–57, for a fascinating treatment of these issues.
121. Evans argues that Poland was "a little tardier" in its witchcraft trials, compared with other sites of the Counter-Reformation, such as the Hapsburg Empire. Seventy percent of those publicly accused of witchcraft were condemned after 1675; in 1701–1725, 32

ment common modes of birth control may have made the blood libel particularly useful. In the eighteenth century there was a dramatic rise in the population of Europe, and Poland's peasantry suffered from the general economic decline. The exposure of newborn and unwanted children, a prevalent practice, often increased as a function of such population pressures.[122] In small towns of Poland the blood libel may have been a convenient method for a struggling serf both to free a place at the table while freeing his burdened conscience: he could transfer the blame for infanticide (often with the connivance of his priest) to his Jewish neighbors. Suspicion of a wife's infidelity, clergy lapses in chastity, and reluctance to subdivide diminishing estates or other assets may have prompted serfs, burghers, gentry, and clergy to want to be rid of bothersome children.

But conflicting Polish child care practices in this period may have found in the blood libel an actual and psychological resolution. Even the children of the nobility were not protected from harsh treatment.[123] Infant care was relegated to surrogates, and little attention was paid to the choice of suitable wet-nurses, governesses, and tutors. The magnates often put their children in the care of stewards of distant estates and did not reclaim them until they had reached the age of six or seven. Confidence in the quality of noble blood was thought to enable children to flourish despite childhood adversities; at the same time, the concern not to spoil children, particularly not to "feminize" the males, accounts for the fact that a mid-eighteenth-century reformer, Stefan Garczynski, chided parents for this "neglect" of their children.[124] Moreover, gentry parents, quite calculating as to the usefulness of children to the honor and finances of the family, kept their emotional distance from their children, who because of the high infant mortality rate might not live long enough to fulfill those expectations. The parents thereby fatalistically contributed to that weakening of their children which they most feared, unconsciously motivated perhaps by the painful memories of lovelessness and abuse endured during their own childhoods.

In the second half of the eighteenth century, under the influence of the reformers and those oriented toward the West, a new "quickening of interest in children" developed.[125] The reformers shifted the responsibility for the sur-

---

percent were condemned. Jews were not necessarily a target of these public accusations and trials, though the belief that they evoked subterranean powers, as we shall see, certainly was widespread. Ibid., 406.

122. In England, for example, as late as 1878 about 6 percent of all violent deaths were infanticides. Even in the eighteenth century it was not an uncommon sight to see the corpses of infants lying in the streets or on the dunghills of London or other large cities. Infant mortality rates in early modern society were high, but not all of these deaths were due to disease or accident. One popular method of committing infanticide was dosing the child with alcohol. See Langer, "Checks on Population Growth," 92–99; Hanson, "'Overlaying' in Nineteenth-Century England," 333–52.

123. Lorence-Kot, *Child-Rearing and Reform,* 22ff.

124. Ibid., 4.

125. Ibid., 25, 93–112.

vival of children and for their welfare "from the province of God to the province of parents."[126] The new interest in parental responsibility for their children "enabled those who spanned the two eras to construe their deprivations and to write about it for an audience which was increasingly eager to condemn the unenlightened attitudes of the past."[127] But since altered parenting practices could not keep up with the rate of change of attitudes, values, and public opinion, the gap generated guilt; and that guilt was particularly intense and difficult to relieve when parents' failed expectations of themselves resulted, as they often did, in tragedy for a child. The blood libel, under these circumstances, became even more useful. The death, even the murder, of these children could be perpetrated with greater psychological dissociation and in a more guilt-free manner if it could be blamed on Jews. The Jew was an especially credible target for this projection, bolstered as it was by cannibalistic myths often related to strangers, popular Christian attitudes blaming Jews for deicide, and suspicions that Jews continue to do violence to the sacraments.[128]

But there were other areas in Europe in which belief in witches persisted, in which Jews were believed to be harmful and perfidious outsiders, in which population increases, diminishing resources, infidelity, and child abuse corresponded to infanticide and high levels of child mortality, but without any recorded efforts to blame the Jews. Though all these factors contribute to an interpretation of the blood libel, they do not explain why this form of attack on Jews was renewed in Poland in the early modern period.

That the account of the Zhitomir incident, like those of blood libels reported by Solomon Maimon and others, mentioned a tavern or occurred within the precincts of an inn may be coincidental. If, as I have contended, those institutions were common on the Polish-Jewish landscape, the recurrence of this imagery is hardly remarkable. On the other hand, the commercial front of the propinacja may provide an interpretive entryway into the netherworld of Polish anti-semitism and blood libels.

From the beginning of the eighteenth century we have explicit expressions of the economic themes encoded and enacted in the perverse blood libel. A group of priests succeeded in getting a demented Jewish apostate by the name of Jan Sirafenovich to confess to the Jewish uses of Christian blood.[129] In the report attributed to him, Sirafenovich asserted that during the Jewish wedding ceremony, the rabbi gives the bride and groom not a sip of wine but an eggful of Christian blood extracted from murdered Christian children. Similarly, he said, such an egg brimming with Christian blood is used to anoint the eyes of dying

126. Ibid., 5.
127. Ibid., 25.
128. A sizable but uneven literature treats Christian Jewish relations from the psycho-analytic perspective. For better examples of this approach, see the work of Leon Poliakov, particularly *History of Anti-Semitism*; see also Cohn, *Warrant for Genocide.*
129. Bałaban, *Letoledot Hattenua Hafrankit,* 56–60.

Jews.[130] On the evening of the holiday of Passover, Jews eat a special wafer called afikoman, which is baked with Christian blood. For a two-week period the rabbi is authorized to sprinkle the blood of murdered Christian children on the doorposts of Christian homes. This ritual casts a spell on the Christian residents, making them more favorably inclined to do business with Jews than with their fellow Christians. At other times Jews obtain from the rabbi a special sheet inscribed in Christian blood and then bring it under the doorstep of a Christian house. Sirafenovich suggests that such talismanic uses of Christian blood account for Jewish business successes.

The tenor of these allegations may help us understand why Solomon Maimon shuddered on remembering the blood libel concocted against his grandfather, an arendar. The plausibility of the blood libel was strengthened by Polish anticommercialism and by the suspicion and envy evoked by Jews through their business and managerial successes. Those successes were still viewed, particularly by the Polish clergy and gentry, through the prism of the Counter-Reformation. Their assessment of those practices on which Jewish commercial success was based had not become "unfettered" from scholastic conceptions of just price and value. For Polish Catholics in the seventeenth and eighteenth centuries, entrepreneurial motives had not received the religious sanction that they did in countries in the Protestant orbit during the same period.[131] The intuitive sense and tenacious conviction with which the "primitive idea" that someone's profit is someone else's loss was held in Poland may have led to such primitive enactments as the blood libel.

The blood libel dramatized the discrepancy between the religiously ascribed definition of Jews as lowly and perfidious and their achieved position as privileged and powerful, between their theoretical status as "serfs of the chamber" under the sovereignty of the monarch, and their daily existence as serfs of the many chambers of an increasingly capricious gentry.[132] A discrepancy between theory and reality was especially palpable in the role that Jews played in Polish patriarchal feudalism. As the most visible wielders of authority, they functioned for the serfs as lords of the manor, and yet their presence in the feudal community violated the most basic sense of *philia.* Here we see the tension between their utilitarian and symbolic roles. Indeed, when we look at the alignment of those who were prepared to defend the Jews against the blood libel—popes, kings, and magnates—we observe that it was those who benefited most from Jewish economic activity or who needed the Jews to demonstrate their own power against

130. It was customary among Polish Jews to place a bit of yellow yolk on the eyelids of the dead as part of the *tahara,* or funeral preparation. As with the other details of this "confession," Sirafenovich distorted Jewish rituals as well as invented new ones.

131. See discussion of these relationships in chapter 3.

132. For a provocative exploration of the way in which disparities between economic and political power are experienced, see Arendt, *Origins of Totalitarianism,* 17ff.

their local representatives and the forces of decentralization who were willing to protest this absurdity.[133]

This drama of the blood libel gave expression to associations between real and symbolic elements of everyday life as they were perceived by Polish Christians in their relation with Polish Jews: grain as sustenance; blood as vitality; and wine, in Jewish ritual, as an expression of joyousness, spiritual elevation, and (particularly around the Passover season when the blood libels were popular) freedom. Grain-based intoxicants, provided by Jews, were enjoyed by peasants but reinforced the bonds of their serfdom. The alcohol made from the grain, produced by serf effort, did not contribute to serf sustenance and vitality. Jews involved in the propinacja siphoned off surplus serf profit; that profit represented the economic and metaphorical link between blood, as expended effort, and money, as reserve sustenance. The economic activities of these Jews, so productive in relation to the interests of the gentry, were perceived to be leechlike and parasitical to the Polish body politic. That body politic was experiencing circulatory problems in a double sense at this time. Blood and money are media of circulation;[134] both bodies and economies, as reflected in the function of the propinacja in eighteenth-century Poland, were in sorry condition. The growing recognition of the harmful effects of an economy that promoted alcoholism for economic and political purposes took on additional symbolic meaning. Alcohol, in accordance with Slavic folklore, was experienced as a facilitator of contact with other worlds, including the netherworld to which Jews were commonly believed to have close links.[135] An integral part of the representation of that netherworld in the world of everyday Polish life was the belief that the Jew, by providing alcohol, was eager to bring about the serfs' debasement and ruination. To unravel meaning we must mix metaphors of blood and money; to gain some insight into not only *what* but also *how* a blood libel means, we must try to understand the expressive forms for the attacks that dramatized the economic relations of gentry, Jews, and serfs.[136]

133. It is understandable that in response to this spread of the blood libel in mid-eighteenth-century Poland the Council of Four Lands sent a special emissary to the pope requesting a proclamation defending the Jews against the libel. They cited as precedents popes Innocent IV and Gregory X in the thirteenth century, among others, who vigorously defended the Jews. Those defenses against the blood libel, promulgated throughout the Holy Roman Empire, served the papacy well in its concern to uphold its supreme authority against local parishes and against the emperor and his local representatives. Rome had less influence among village Russian Orthodox priests. Baron, "Plenitude of Apostolic Power," 110.

134. For a fascinating analysis of this relationship between blood and money, captured in their Hebrew terms *dam* (blood) and *damim* (money), see Shell, *Money, Language and Thought.*

135. Opalski, *Jewish Tavern Keeper,* 12.

136. The connections between economic strains and collective violence have been pursued in several studies. There have been efforts, for example, to draw correlations between lynching mobs in the American South and economic cycles. The findings of these studies

Other classes of Polish society injured by the enserfment of the peasantry and the gentry's subsequent economic measures could find a plausible explanation for their new economic problems in the Jewish management of the propinacja, and they enthusiastically colluded in attacks on the Jews. The burghers could rage against the Jews for two reasons: they had been bypassed as agent for this profitable concession, and their economic position had further declined because they could sell fewer imported and manufactured goods to peasants who drank away their money. The clergy could blame the Jews for leaving the peasants without the resources to pay tithes. The Christian clergy were instrumental in orchestrating attacks because they controlled, and therefore could invoke, the religious symbols used to legitimate the blood libel.

The blood libel must be seen in relation to the declining effectiveness and rising criticism of the propinacja. That the propinacja was an integral part of the gentry's efforts to compensate for the declining profitability of grain sales, and to save an idealized notion of social order that included an economy based on personal obligation and the squandering of surplus, was generally overlooked. Members of the gentry, who profited the most from this arrangement, joined the other classes of Polish society, with which they were at economic odds, in harmonious denunciations of the Jewish exploiters. They passed on both the risk and the blame to their Jewish agents in exchange for having given those Jews the opportunity to sustain themselves and to pay the high taxes that even late-eighteenth-century Jews owed to the increasingly impotent monarch. The possibilities for short-term profit did not exclude the opportunity for members of the gentry to vent their moral indignation at Jewish expense; and when, as was often the case, there were other Jewish candidates waiting to take up the managerial responsibilities of an arendar under suspicion and about to fall from grace—perhaps under a new contract even more favorable to the lord—there was no need to pose even the modicum of resistance experienced and described by Father Soltyk. Even the gentry lessors of the propinacja, when they had no economic ties with the particular Jews under attack or when inspired to sacrificial piety, likewise could enjoy the spectacle.

Trials of Jews for ritual murder corresponded to other voluble and volatile manifestations. By the mid-eighteenth century the siphoning-off mechanism for saving Polish feudalism began to falter. Its harmful side effects became more

---

have been called into question. A more successful effort has been made by George Rudé, *Revolutionary Europe, 1783–1815,* who contrasts the limited scope and frequency of riots in seventeenth-century France, despite food shortages, with the behavior of the crowd during the French Revolution. These riots corresponded to economic distress suddenly surfacing in 1789 and took on increasingly greater political modes of expression and goals. In Poland the blood libels, in contrast with the peasant rebellions in 1648 and 1768, deflected the peasants from any political goals of achieving amelioration; and on a micro-social level this form of collective violence probably strengthened the integration of feudalism by choosing the wrong target and providing catharsis.

salient. The Jews' participation in the feudal system through the propinacja could no longer mask the internal contradictions and failures of that system. Attacks against Jews were expressed in still another key: administrative and constitutional reform proposals, which reached a crescendo during the Four-Year Sejm, leveled attacks against Jewish involvement in trade, in the arenda, and in the propinacja, with little attention to the forces that promoted that involvement. During Poland's "bloodless revolution," echoes of the blood libel were to be heard.

Chapter 5

The Polish Enlightenment, the Four-year Sejm, and the Limits of Reform

The three extant accounts of the meeting are vague. Written over an interval of more than a hundred years, they contradict one another on important details. But they convey a singular impression: only the most dire circumstances would have brought together the warring factions of the Jewish community represented at that meeting, which took place somewhere in Poland at the turn of the nineteenth century.[1] This chapter reconstructs those circumstances, the war of words at the Four-Year Sejm, in relation to similar debates elsewhere in Europe as well as to the war being waged by other means against Jews throughout Poland.

1. Halpern, "Rabbi Levi Yizhak of Berdichev and the Royal Decrees of His Days" (Hebrew), in Halpern, *Yehudim Veyahadut*, 340–47. The paucity of internal sources on Jewish responses to the Four-Year Sejm, in contrast to the abundant material on Jews in France during the Revolution, is reflected in the secondary literature as well. Ringelblum, Dubnow, Schipper, Gelber, Dinur, Mahler, Shatzky, and Eisenbach, among others, have written important essays on these failed efforts to implement constitutional reform. Dubnow and Schipper seem to emphasize Jewish passivity. Mahler stresses the involvement of the pioneers of the Jewish Enlightenment in Poland. Dinur assesses the historical significance beyond legislative failures. The discussion and treatment of Poland's Jews at this Sejm must be inferred from pamphlets and proposals, for there is little firsthand testimony. The scattered documentation has been collected in Woliński, Michalski, and Rostworowski, eds., *Materiały do dziejów Sejmu Czteroletniego*, esp. vol. 6, edited by Eisenbach. It is not known whether this work includes all the material on the Jewish question that was extant at the time that it was compiled after World War II, or whether editorial bias influenced the selection. Another important survey of this literature is Gutterman, "Proposals of Polish Jews." Gutterman emphasizes Jewish activism and national pride in Jewish responses to the Four-Year Sejm, but the evidence does not consistently support his view.

The only firsthand report of this special meeting, with behind-the-scenes reflections on the problems of Poland's Jews as raised during the Four-Year Sejm, is given by Menaḥem Mendel Lefin (1749–1826). Like Solomon Maimon, Lefin was a disciple of Moses Mendelssohn, hailing from the East. He became the most important mediator and popularizer of Enlightenment values among Polish Jews. Lefin remained an observant Jew all through his life, as did his Berlin teacher. Reminiscing in his later years, most likely around 1820, he recalls a meeting that took place in the winter of 1791–1792. He remembers how he tried to mobilize representatives of Polish Jewry to make a unified and effective response to the dangers at hand. He seemed to have particular difficulty in enlisting the support of those whom he summarily identified as the "deceivers of Israel": "If the Gentiles, whose hands are mighty against us, because of our many sins, arise and attack us with such sustained enthusiasm, how could it be that we should not most certainly try to defend ourselves and to respond to their libels, day and night, as far as our hand reaches?" Notwithstanding pious bows to religious sensibilities that locate the cause of all crises in "our many sins," what dangers did this man of the Jewish Enlightenment see in these protracted meetings in Warsaw? Regarding what "sustained enthusiasm" for attacks and for libels, was this Jewish reformer sounding the alarm at the time that Polish reformers were assiduously at work trying to formulate and legislate a constitution? And who were these deceivers of Israel, so unwilling to participate in the defense of Jewish honor and rights?

This call for collective action must be understood within the context of Lefin's political and literary activities. Lefin spent much of his youth in Satanow and the villages of Podolia, close to the early centers of both Frankism and Hasidism. The extreme forms of heterodoxy and antinomian behavior and the effects of communal strife that he witnessed made a lasting impression on him. It is with these experiences in mind that he formulated his theories of religious and communal reform in his later years. In 1780 he journeyed to Berlin, where he became close to Moses Mendelssohn and his disciples. More temperate and stable, though less brilliant and original than his contemporary Solomon Maimon, Lefin too was seen as a potential agent for disseminating the values and orientations of the Berlin Enlightenment, the Haskala, in Eastern Europe. Indeed, his friendship with Mendelssohn provided an important credential for his activities throughout his life: a later generation endowed him with such titles as "the father of the Galician Haskalah" or "the Mendelssohn of the East." As in the case of Maimon, however, the support of the Berlin enlighteners, the Maskilim, wavered and proved to be unreliable at the time that he needed funding for the publication of his Enlightenment tracts. David Friedlander, condescending toward his "backward" Polish Jewish brethren and impatient with their "reform," could not appreciate Lefin's educational strategy: to reform, to make productive, and to inculcate modern sensibilities among Polish Jews by the call to restore pristine but disused Jewish forms.

Upon returning to the East, Lefin was befriended by a powerful Polish gentry family, the Czartoryskis. According to a Jewish legend, albeit with no substantiation on the Polish side, Lefin was appointed tutor to one of the young Czar-toryskis. The dedication of one of Lefin's books, *Refuat Haam* (1794), reveals that Lefin received financial support from the senior Czartoryski in that important work.[2] This translation and adaptation of the 1760 medical manual of the famous Swiss doctor Simon André Tissot (1728–1797), *Avis peuple sur la sante,* was widely circulated among Polish Jews. In his concern for the public health of small Jewish communities and in his desire to arrange productive employment for the many poor Talmudic scholars, Lefin envisioned a cadre of paramedicals trained and guided by his medical manual.

Lefin also was involved in formulating proposals to improve the conditions of Jews residing on the Czartoryski estates, and he was present in Warsaw for a time during the Four-Year Sejm. Under the sponsorship of his patron he submitted proposals to the commission on education and the special commission on the Jewish problem. A decade later, he was in Saint Petersburg when a similar discussion on the political and economic status of the Jews residing in areas annexed from Poland was convened by the Russian tsar, Alexander I. These experiences provided him with ample opportunities to practice what he preached, "to defend ourselves and to respond to their libels, day and night, as far as our hand reaches."

In his later years Lefin retired to Austrian Galicia, where he eschewed political activities in favor of writing educational tracts for the hoi polloi, in the traditional genres of biblical exegesis and *musar* (ethical tracts), through which he attempted to popularize his moderate approach to Haskala. To the chagrin of his fellow travelers of the Jewish Enlightenment, in his concern to reach the Jewish masses he violated the canons of linguistic purity by writing in Yiddish. His disavowal of politics notwithstanding, he continued in a single area of publicistic activity, waging one last but already lost battle against Hasidism. By the beginning of the nineteenth century that movement had captured many of Poland's communities, particularly in the southeast. His anti-Hasidic polemics, both in form and substance, were original and subtle.[3]

In one of his more overt and strident anti-Hasidic tracts (never published, perhaps because of Hasidic control of printing presses) he recalled this same meeting and reported his failure at evoking a collective, political response, allud-

2. Lefin, *Refuat Haam.* A version published in Berlin in 1789 under the title *Moda Lebina* was perhaps a prospectus for the longer 1794 edition, but the project did not receive the immediate financial backing needed. See Shmeruk, "Moses Marcuse."

3. Unlike most of the anti-Hasidic polemics, which were critical or satirical, Lefin tried to identify what attracted Jews to this movement and then to provide an alternate set of values. His most popular work, *Heshbon Hanefesh,* an ethical guide, was a reworking of Benjamin Franklin's *Poor Richard's Almanac,* with its chart for scoring the performance of deeds. In view of Max Weber's attention to Franklin as a popularizer of the spirit of capitalism, Lefin's literary borrowings and popularization are all the more interesting. See Levine, "Between Hasidism and Haskala." *Heshbon Hanefesh* was subsequently adopted by Israel Salanter, founder of the East European *musar* movement, which promoted a contemplative and pietistic ethicism, particularly among yeshiva students and the *baalei battim* (middle class). In certain circles of pious Jews to this very day, this guide has readers.

ing to the identity of the opposition: "Everyone turns to his way and waits for the miracle. And in regard to this [the rabbis] have said in the story of Neḥunya ben Kane, 'I say appropriate matters and your response is, Heaven will show mercy!' " In contrast with the Hasidim—quiescent and quietistic, as Lefin would lead us to believe—during the hostile exchanges of the Four-Year Sejm, Lefin described the tactics that he used to defend Jewish interests:

> A dispute already commenced with these ministers in regard to our Holy Tora, whether it stood in opposition to the laws of reform of the state. My response in the aforementioned writing was to the education commission concerned with the enlightenment of the Jews, the abolition of religious quarrels, teaching them love for their fellow countrymen and ministers. I explained everything rationally and without any trickery. . . . For example, in regard to clothing and speech, they asked why it was that Jews in every land speak the language of the country—the exiles of France speak French, of Germany speak German, of Spain speak Spanish, of Arabia speak Arabic, etc.—and similarly they wear the native attire in Germany, France, Ishmael [Muslim countries], etc. And even the Jews of Poland themselves wore the customary dress of the land when they first arrived. . . . Similarly, they wanted to annul the power to excommunicate, to chase out the rabbis from the land. The sect rejoiced in this and agreed with all their heart to this idea because they are nothing but zealots and ascetics (perhaps this a remnant from the days of the polemics of the wicked Messiah, and particularly the sect of Frank in Lvov, and the dispute about Rabbi Jonathan, etc.) they oppose all wisdom and practical virtue, they shame any wise man who is not of their people.[4] I answered them in this composition that the case was quite to the contrary. The principle of the Tora of Israel is constructed upon love, wisdom, and the glory deriving from man, and its paths are paths of peace. And immediately from the beginning it is explained that the scholars of the Talmud placed the commandment of loving your neighbor as yourself as the foundation of everything.[5]

Lefin sided with his coreligionists against the Polish reformers on issues such as conformity in "clothing and speech": Most Jewish enlighteners, such as his

4. Lefin's insinuation of Sabbatian or even Frankist origins for the Hasidim was not original. See Wilenski, *Hasidim Umitnaggedim*. His casual and respectful mention of "Rabbi Jonathan" perhaps indicates that he did not accept Jacob Emden's accusation that Jonathan Eibschütz, to whom he was probably referring, was a Sabbatian.

5. Lefin, *Teshuva Beinyanei Haddat*. BT. *Avoda Zara*, 18a attributes this story to the second-century rabbi Hanina ben Teradion. In response to Hanina's affirmation of faith, "Heaven will show mercy," Jose ben Kisma impatiently underscored this warning of the dangers involved in his defiance of Rome by persisting to study Tora in public. Lefin, in reminiscing about this meeting, remembered his warnings and statements as "appropriate matters." His association of the Hasidim with Hanina ben Teradion is remarkably positive in comparison with the resentment that he expresses elsewhere.

teacher Moses Mendelssohn, expected of Jews the same conformity with the ways of the larger society that the Polish reformers were now demanding. Lefin even used Enlightenment formulations about the "principle of the Tora of Israel" to defend Jewish traditionalists and obscurantism. He contrasted his own spirited and savvy defense of Jews, even those with whom he personally might not agree, with the betrayal of "the sect," the Hasidim, whom he accuses of collaborating with the Gentile reformers to undermine rabbinic authority. Those Hasidim against whose intolerance and lack of cleverness Lefin could not miss the opportunity to take a swipe would surely not have agreed to changes of "clothing and speech." And yet because of their own conflict with communal rabbis and the manner in which they withdrew from communal efforts, they refused him support.[6]

In an earlier tract Lefin also described the harmful and inappropriate politics of the Hasidim, alluding to a specific meeting that included the participation of one of their leaders: "Not long ago one of their masters appeared here in Warsaw who after he left the region in which he had been the rabbi, following a controversy which he caused, arrived here out of the depths of the Ukraine among the other Jewish delegates. Because he did not succeed here to play his role of Saint Simon upon the column, he departed. Nevertheless, his opponents still feel the dangerous outcomes of his discontent."[7] Lefin seems to be referring to Levi Yiẓḥak, whose name was later identified with the Ukrainian town of Berdichev. He had been the rabbi in Żelechów (Zelikov), a town close to Warsaw; after his debates in 1781 with Rabbi Abraham Katzenelbogen of Brest Litovsk (Brisk, Brzerc) he left this area. Legend associated Rabbi Levi Yiẓḥak with the indented pillar of a synagogue in Praga, a Warsaw suburb, at which he allegedly prayed to avert decrees. In Lefin's pamphlet written for Gentiles he describes the Hasidic master's political style—his otherworldly orientation of awaiting miracles, and his flaunting of asceticism in order to impress the masses and evoke their support. This he compares with the pillar sitting of the third-century Christian saint Simon.

Lefin's outbursts against Hasidism did not conceal his disenchantment with the Polish Enlightenment, as well as with its spokesmen and their rhetoric of reform. Even Joseph II, the champion of Enlightenment reform, received a mixed review. In retrospect he realized that what the Polish reformers really sought was not useful suggestions by which to ameliorate Jewish conditions but plausible criticisms by which to blame the Jews for their own lowly conditions and for Poland's plight.[8] Such attacks on Jewish life and on its rabbis echoed polemics instituted in the Middle Ages by the Catholic church. The aging Lefin could recall

6. Lefin most likely had in mind his French pamphlet "Essai d'un plan réforme ayant pour objet d'éclairer la nation juive en Pologne et de redresser par la fes moers" (Warsaw, 1792). Copies are in the Czartoryski Library in Cracow and the Schocken Library in Jerusalem.
7. Lefin, *Teshuva Beinyanei Haddat.*
8. Lefin, *Likkutei Kelalim,* art. 3 (n.d.), cited in Gelber, "Mendel Lefin Satanower," 271–305.

from his childhood polemics staged in Lvov in 1759, with the Frankists as accesso-
ries and accusers. These reform commissions were seemingly inspired by new
Enlightenment ideals. But were they truly new,. would they prove to be of enduring influence, or were they continuous with those polemics, thinly veiled in
Enlightenment trappings?

Abraham Baer Gottlober, writing more than a half century after Lefin, provided the second account of the unusual multilateral meeting convened in the
late eighteenth century. The mood of this meeting conveyed by Gottlober is more
harmonious than in Lefin's description. Gottlober presented an invaluable though
occasionally confusing record of the generation that preceded his. He was born
around 1810 and raised in a Hasidic environment in the Ukraine. During the third
decade of the nineteenth century he "converted" to the Jewish Enlightenment
that was spreading among small coteries within the Galician and Russian lands of
partitioned Poland. By about 1880, when Gottlober was writing his chronicles,
Hasidism was viewed by Maskilim with less acrimony than it was in the late
eighteenth century or in Gottlober's youth.[9]

Gottlober, in reports of a high-level consultation that took place at an unspec-
ified date between the leaders of the major parties of the Polish Jewish community
to discuss pending legislation, projected onto the past the sources of reconciliation
to which he aspired. The same Levi Yiẓhak of Berdichev whom Lefin depicted as
dangerously otherworldly and as responding inappropriately to the crisis, is reported by Gottlober to be the actual organizer of this gathering. Gottlober's
arrangement of the participants according to parties exaggerated the degree to
which the factions of Jewish life, in the generation preceding his, were differentiated and internally organized. At the same time, he tried to uncover the roots of the
reconciliation he espouses by placing the origins of the leaders of the Hasidim, the
Maskilim, and the Mitnagdim (conservative opponents of the Hasidim) in one
town, Berdichev: "God had so designated it that the three heads of the sects should
be destined to come from one place to sit together in conference with still others
who were convened, most of whom were Hasidic masters."[10]

Gottlober is forced to acknowledge that not very much came of the meeting.

9. It was perhaps the early stirrings of Jewish nationalism that led even men of the Enlightenment like Gottlober to call for rapprochement between the groups that divided
Jewish life. Gottlober himself suggested the dubious hypothesis that Hasidism, in the
challenge that it posed to traditional life and conventional piety, may have prepared the soil
for the spread of the Enlightenment as its successor movement. Yet there was little evidence for this; and in the face of the abiding hostility of Hasidism toward the Haskala,
Gottlober had to qualify this hypothesis in his later years. This new tolerance, developing
among the Maskilim at the time when Gottlober was writing his memoirs, was not reciprocated by the powerful and well-institutionalized Hasidic movement. If hostility was any-
where on the decline, it was between the Hasidim and the non-Hasidic traditionalists, or
Mitnagdim, who by the middle of the nineteenth century were forming a powerful coalition to oppose the modernizers and their programs.
10. Gottlober, *Zikhronot Umassaot,* 1:175.

In spite of the bickering, emissaries were sent to Warsaw, but they failed to reach a consensus. The consultation ultimately failed because the leaders did not "understand the disease of their people and what would cure them." In concluding, Gottlober comments cryptically but with chilling foreboding, "Not everything which is not implemented is immediately void and will not be done at some later date. For there are some places where there seems to be an upper covering, but underneath there is in fact an open grave. They were joyous and jubilant regarding the situation as it appeared to them and to what they thought was reported, and yet ultimately the plague, against which they had not sought bandage and medicine, did break out."[11] Gottlober was vague in regard to the specific historical events of his account. What "upper covering" concealed which "open grave"? Why were they "joyous and jubilant," and when did that "plague," against which they took no preventive measures, "break out"?

A third account was pieced together at the beginning of the twentieth century, primarily from legends still circulating among Polish Jews at the time. Azriel Frenk, a journalist and ethnographer, reports on a meeting of rabbis and Hasidic masters held, he claims, around 1809 in response to the Napoleonic constitution, which granted equal rights to the Jews.[12] At this meeting the leaders acted with deliberateness and in consensus; they proclaimed a special fast day involving the recitation of penitential prayers and psalms; at the same time, they ordered the collection of redemption money to be transferred to the *shetadlanim* (intercessors), who were delegated to lobby "that the wicked decree involving equal rights shall be annulled." The Hasidic masters and other traditional Jews expressed particular indignation over proposals submitted by wealthy assimilated Jews in March 1809, suggesting that Jews should be forced to change their appearance and their dress in conformity with Polish styles. Under this constitution, as Frenk describes it, the position of Jews actually deteriorated.

According to Frenk, Levi Yiẓḥak was among the leaders in Warsaw present at the meeting. Frenk cites the same story as Lefin about the Hasidic master praying at the pulpit in the synagogue in Praga; only he adds that the legend of Levi Yiẓḥak and the indented pillar was still preserved in that synagogue in his day. In Frenk's version, Levi Yiẓḥak, disheartened by the reform measures, offered thanks to God that he no longer resided in Żelechów but rather had now settled far away in Berdichev. For in Warsaw, where the reform measures were being promulgated, "the impurity emerges, rises up, and radiates to its whole environment." Only the greater masters and the more righteous, commented Levi Yiẓḥak, can overcome it and remain holy. To what dangers of "impurity" was Levi Yiẓḥak responding?

It is unlikely that Frenk is correct in dating this meeting from the period of the Napoleonic constitution. Levi Yiẓḥak, advanced in years by 1809, would hardly have been able to make the arduous trip from the Ukraine. Moreover, Levi Yiẓḥak's public support for the tsar against Napoleon would have exposed him to

11. Ibid., 1:178.
12. Frenk, *Yehudei Polin,* 23, 72; Halpern, "Rabbi Levi Yiẓḥak," 340.

arrest and undermined his political effectiveness. Frenk's oral history may have elicited from those he interviewed memories of Jewish responses attributed to the wrong constitutional convention. Similarities in the details of the reports of Frenk and Gottlober, and their compatibility with the observations of Lefin, an actual participant in the Four-Year Sejm, suggest that we have before us three differing accounts of what was one and the same meeting. Indeed, Frenk himself, in a different connection, records reports of a meeting of Jewish leaders, summoned in July 1791 at the Zelwa fair, to organize a delegation to Warsaw, which proceeded to "confront the brewing evil that there should not be promulgated new reforms, heaven forbid."

These accounts of the Zelwa fair meeting have preserved a range of Jewish reactions to the Polish constitution of May 3, 1791, the Four-Year Sejm, and the deliberations that took place before and after May 3 in regard to the situation of Jews in Poland. A shared sense of foreboding in regard to the constitution prevailed, evoking a range of responses from different sectors of the Jewish community. Indeed, after the constitution was issued, the Jews had good reason to be concerned. Despite their numerical, political, and economic significance in Polish society and the attention they received in discussion of reform, the new constitution was silent about the Jews, affirming and augmenting traditional privileges only for Christians. It promised Jews no improved status. In fact, the constitution's silence on Jewish matters allowed for the abrogation of age-old Jewish rights by the promulgation of local laws and seemed to ratify old sanctions. It is no wonder that what many Poles viewed as "sagacious legislation"—what Edmund Burke in England would enthusiastically characterize as an "unheard of conjunction of wisdom and fortune" in which "all, from the King to the day labourers, were improved in their condition"—Jews dismissed, with a shudder and a sigh, as a *gezeira* (decree).[13] Reform proposals made by Maskilim thus seemed to have had the effect only of curtailing privileges while not resulting in new opportunities for Jews. The Hasidim in particular had reason to be concerned: even those Jewish reformers otherwise committed to preserving Jewish rights demonstrated little sensitivity to the needs of the Hasidim.

The Four-Year Sejm claims our attention if only in the missed opportunity to reform and transform Poland and Polish Jews. Yet emphasizing the failure of the proposed changes should by no means indicate that these proposals were merely of historical interest, without actual historical impact. In sifting through the profusion of recommendations to reform the Jews in this period, knowledge of the unsuccessful outcome of the debates over these visions of the Jewish future, many of them so grim, does not dispel our unease. Why this consternation, and with what efforts did Jews have to draw together at that moment to preserve the status quo?[14]

13. Burke's statement was reported in *Gazette of the United States,* October 29, 1791, and is cited in Haiman, *Fall of Poland,* 49–51.
14. Interpretations of the significance of the Four-Year Sejm are many and varied. Piotr Wandcyz, *Lands of Partitioned Poland,* 7, has called it Poland's "bloodless revolution" in

New Opportunities for Polish Reform

In seeking to understand the background to the treatment of the Jews of Poland toward the end of its sovereignty, I have examined the ideological and political strength of the different groups of Poland's reformers, including the proponents of Enlightenment, such as Poland's last king, Stanisław Poniatowski. Conditions outside Poland, however, made it a favorable moment for Polish reformers to focus their efforts on implementing changes that heretofore the rigid polity and economy of their country had resisted. On August 16, 1787, Russia declared war on Turkey. With Russia engaged in the south, the king and members of the Western-oriented, modernizing elite within the Polish gentry, who had been until that moment dependent on Russia to maintain their domestic political position, could now turn to Prussia for support in bringing about change. As tensions brewed between Prussia and Austria, Prussia was all the more interested in enlisting Polish support in the event of war. This combination of external forces, though tenuous, provided Poland with a degree of freedom in which to determine its internal affairs. The advocates of specific policies could take advantage of this new alignment of forces between Poland's neighbors to promote collective action without foreign meddling. Yet precisely how to use the international situation to the greatest advantage was not clear.

The Western-oriented gentry consequently came to be viewed as the Prussian party. They were particularly upset by the recurrent and humiliating interventions made at the Polish court by the proconsul Otto Magnus von Stackelberg, who represented Russian interests. They were tired of pursuing Russian support. Furthermore, they were intrigued by the big power policy of Frederick William II and his alliances with England and Holland. This party's reformist faction advocated a hereditary monarchy and a simple majority vote, which would strengthen Poland's central government and limit the influence of Poland's neighbors. This gentry faction considered granting rights to the townspeople, and was also concerned with peasant reform, though it was willing to appease the conservative gentry by making no strong motion on this issue.[15]

Some of the conservative magnates saw potential in strengthening the alliance with Russia precisely at this time, and even in lending military support in the hope of gaining influence with Catherine II and obtaining ports in the Black

---

response to that country's situation: "By the eighteenth century, the constitutional and socioeconomic system of the old commonwealth was in full decay." Robert Palmer, *Age of Democratic Revolution,* views it as another example of the revolutions that took place in the second half of the eighteenth century. There seems to be a good deal of agreement that not much was accomplished. Whether this failure can be attributed to the inadequacy of ideas or to the lack of political stability in Poland and the eventual loss of independence preventing the gentry from implementing these reforms continues to be a matter of discussion, as Jerzy Jedlicki, "Social Ideas," 101, indicates. Jewish historians are likewise in agreement about the results for Jews but disagree on the exact causes. See n. 1.

15. Gieysztor et al., *History of Poland,* 306–7.

Sea area. This could open new opportunities for Poland, they argued, in compensation for its declining influence in Baltic trade. It could also improve the profitability of the large estates in the Ukraine, which needed new markets for their grain surpluses. The conservative gentry faction was well organized and well represented. Its members were hostile to reforms in general, which they believed to be unpatriotic aping of the cultural mores of France and the West, and to scuttlebutt about constitutions. It may be expressive of this hostility that the native Polish costume and uniform of Sarmatianism, the *kontusz,* long since abandoned even by many of the conservative gentry and replaced by Western styles, again became fashionable in 1788. Although prone to Pan-Slavism, the conservative gentry could not wholeheartedly turn eastward because of conflicts with Russia along national lines. They tried to affirm native, indigenous, and traditional Polish mores.[16]

On October 20, 1788, the Sejm voted to increase the size of the army to one hundred thousand and actually began planning taxes to support this policy. By January 1789, under the protection of Prussia, the Sejm, departing from the usual practice of convening short sessions, prolonged its power for an indefinite period of time. In March of that year it passed measures by which the gentry would be taxed for the first time. The collection of this tax, however, was only partially successful.

New peasant disorders in the spring and pressures from the townspeople for extended privileges made the deliberations in Warsaw all the more urgent. The unstable international situation could rapidly turn against the possibilities of reform; the efforts to raise taxes to support the army needed to defend those reforms were faltering; and the cumulative effects of economic stagnation could no longer be avoided. But the Polish style of parliamentarianism, requiring unanimity, proved unequal to the task of taking prompt action.

It was clear that before the minimal economic program—a shift from dependence on grain exports and an increase in industrialization—to which a majority of the reformers were committed could be implemented, important political changes would have to be made. On September 7, 1789, nearly a year after the Sejm had first been convened, a deputation was appointed to draft a constitution. The "Paris plague," as it was called by its detractors, was now quite virulent in Warsaw.

At the very moment that Jewish corporate responsibility, communal autonomy, and the fundamentals of Jewish life were being examined and debated in Paris, with the full participation of official Jewish delegates, the development and the results of that "plague" in Warsaw were altogether different. By 1790 in Metz, one of France's most anti-Jewish cities, its rabbi was enthusiastically proclaiming, "From Paris comes a voice which announces redemption and salvation for our

16. Thane and Crossick, Introduction to Thane, Crossick, and Floud, eds., *Power of the Past,* 2.

brethren of Israel."[17] In Warsaw, pogroms were brewing. From what is known about the lobbying activities of Polish Jews during the parliamentary debates culminating in the proclamation of the Polish constitution on May 3, 1791, that advocacy appears to have been more sparse than it was in France. In the publicistic debate that had taken place during the 1780s over Poland's future, other than a few proposals made by Hirsch, Ackord, Lefin, and Hirschowitz concerning the large number of Jews in Poland who would be affected by any changes, there is little that attests to Jewish visions of the future.[18] We know little about the activities in this period of other Jews who might have been politically active—official representatives of the kehillot, maverick enlighteners, Maskilim (including doctors who had received training abroad),[19] Jews with magnate patrons, and the small group of Jews with connections to the royal court, among them *syndyks* (Jews appointed by the king to represent court interests within the Jewish community who played a rather equivocal role), and wealthy merchants with trade connections to the West. Although it is likely that there were behind-the-scenes efforts to create alliances—for example, with the Western-oriented gentry, whose political support might have been enlisted, if necessary, through bribes—those efforts remain as elusive now as they must have been then. The reactions on the Jewish streets of small villages all over Poland to what was going on in Warsaw

17. Gutterman, "Proposals," 2.
18. In France, the Royal Society of Arts and Sciences in Metz in 1785 sponsored an essay contest on the question "How to Make the Jews Happy and Useful." The range of responses was as varied as it might have been had the question been posed in Poland. And yet the legislative career of the "Jewish question" went in different directions in these two countries in the years that followed. One of the three winners of the essay contest was Zalkind Hurwicz, a Polish Jewish enlightener, the son of a rabbi who became a French patriot and even joined the Jacobin party during the Revolution. For a summary of his essay, see Hertzberg, *French Enlightenment and the Jews,* 298–99; 334–35. Excerpts from this essay appeared in Warsaw in 1789, anonymously translated and published. See Eisenbach, *Materiały,* 6:113. Hurwicz's harsher remarks about Polish Jews were carefully deleted. Little reference is made to this work among Polish publicists, perhaps because of the author's Jacobin connection. One publicist who does engage in a polemic with this erstwhile Polish Jew is Tadeusz Czacki (1765–1813), in his *Rozprawa o żydach i karaitach,* written around the period of the Four-Year Sejm but published only years later in Lvov, 1807. He repeats Hurwicz's contentions that Jews are ethically low, prone to cheating, usury, and superstition. But he does not bother to repeat the French Jewish enlightener's assertion that under the right circumstances these Jews could be reformed. Gutterman, "Proposals," 39–45.
19. Another winner of the prize essay who received attention in Poland was Abbé Gregoire. The Jewish "court doctor" Solomon Polonus translated his writings and along with his own comments presented them, according to Czacki, to the king himself. Polonus retained close personal and professional ties to the Jewish community of Warsaw. He hoped that events in France in regard to improving attitudes toward Jews and the Jewish struggle for equal rights would provide an example for Poland. Gutterman, "Proposals," 47–49.

are difficult to gauge. As the debates proceeded in the Sejm, some segments of Polish Jewry mobilized, either to defend existing privileges or to press for specific concessions. But there were few calls from Jews for attaining the general rights of citizenship, and little imagination among them for what that citizenship would entail.

The opening salvo of parliamentary debate on the status and situation of Poland's Jews was set off by Mateusz Topór Butrymowicz (1745–1814), deputy starosta, sword-bearer, and deputy of the Pińsk District.[20] In February 1789 he issued "The Way to Form Jews into Citizens Useful to the Country," a revised and (probably) expanded version of the pamphlet that had appeared earlier in the decade by "a nameless citizen" and that had already been brought out in a German translation by Elias Ackord.[21] Butrymowicz, though unsparing in his criticism of Polish Jews, summed up the causes of their problems and attributed blame for their lowly condition in terms uncharacteristically compassionate, even by the standards set in the discussion of Jewish rights ongoing in Western and Central Europe at the time. Poland's Jews were impoverished as a result of their ambiguous status within the existing class structure and the persistent persecution and discrimination that afflicted them.

Butrymowicz argued that it is not the religion of the Jews that is the source of their shortcomings. Though for centuries, he says, they have manifested idleness, sloth, and hypocrisy and have been a burden in many countries, no one has tried to discover what makes them bad. True to his teachers of the Enlightenment,

20. Butrymowicz was educated by the Jesuits in Pinsk. What little we know about his reformist orientation seems to be consistent with the relatively sympathetic tone and substance of policies that he espoused on behalf of Jews. His estate in Krystynow was the model of a well-ordered manor. He was concerned for the situation of serfs and artisans and built a school in which to educate children. He maintained a positive attitude toward commerce quite independently of his support of Jewish trade. He favored the removal of customs houses and other impediments to free trade between Poland and Lithuania and called for a reassessment of trade agreements signed with the Muscovite state that gave exceptional privileges to Russian merchants in transit trade. He opposed demands of the burghers, the archenemies of the Jews, at the Four-Year Sejm and argued for administrative reform, of which well-ordered Jewish communal structures were an example. *Polski słownik biograficzny,* Cracow, 1937), 3:152–54.
21. Eisenbach, *Materiały,* 78–93. Gutterman, "Proposals," 23–25, questions the assertion, repeated but unsubstantiated by historians, that this pamphlet was first issued in 1782. Similarities in tone and substance to Joseph II's Edict of Tolerance, issued in 1781, and to the patent specifically addressed to Jews in much of his empire might have prompted the publicistic activities of Nameless Citizen. That the original pamphlet was issued anonymously was not at all uncommon for this literature. On the other hand, the relatively sympathetic treatment of the Jews from the pen of this anonymous author raises the possibility, wholly unsubstantiated, of some Jewish involvement or sponsorship. Lefin reports how he was encouraged to write proposals without attaching the name or religion of the author so that this anonymous advocacy would be considered in accordance with the merits of its argument and would not be dismissed by the delegates to the Sejm as serving Jewish interests.

Butrymowicz sprinkles his tract with attestations regarding the influence of the environment on human development. "A human being is not born bad or good, intelligent or stupid." Religion, education and law "shape a human being."[22] The Jews of Holland, England, and Prussia, who are assiduous, hardworking, patriotic, and honest merchants, share the virtues of all other citizens of their respective countries, yet they observe the same traditions as Polish Jews:

> In a country that for centuries has strictly maintained tolerance, [the Jews'] religion has been cause for contempt, degradation, and different varieties of oppression. This was done intentionally so that the Jew would wear his manacles with respect and kiss the hand that beat him over the neck. [We] wanted him to be useful to the country, but did not want the country to become his homeland; [we wanted] him to be hardworking, but did not want the fruits of his labor to be handed over to him; [we wanted] him to be friendly and faithful to that which unceasingly oppresses him. Finally [we] wanted through contrary means to arrive at a favorable result. I do not need to say what came of all this, as we see well confirmed the general maxim that people are what their law makes them. The Jew in Poland has become slothful, lazy, faithless, and, in short, the way he is today.[23]

According to Butrymowicz, Jews resist farming in Poland because they observe the hardships of the serfs and because they are not permitted to inherit land. Involvement in such an occupation, under existing circumstances, would only lead them into "poverty and misery," into "perpetual bondage."[24] Consequently they live in towns, where they have limited employment opportunities, arouse conflict, and precipitate the decline of trade. Because they are excluded from the craft guilds, they become indolent and impoverished. Butrymowicz repeats the popular belief that Jews in the countryside who run inns victimize the peasants by making them drunk and impoverished. Unlike his fellow publicists, however, he was careful to point out that it was the landlords who made most of the profit.

Butrymowicz went on to note that the Jews are taught from earliest childhood that they are hated, and therefore must hate. Because they must pay for every favor, they resort to cheating; because they are barred from schools and social intercourse, they despise education and are condemned to backwardness. Ultimately they turn to their religion, which makes false promises to them that they will rule over the world.

Following this comprehensive diagnosis of the problems, in tone and in substance sympathetic when compared to the opinions held by many of his compatriots, Butrymowicz makes a series of recommendations. But these have some of the familiar harshness of medieval church decrees; they echo the certitude with which the enlightened despots and the well-ordered police state tried

22. Eisenbach, *Materiały,* 79.
23. Ibid., 80–81.
24. Ibid., 81.

to impose social change by fiat. The Jews, Butrymowicz argued, must be placed within a reconstituted Polish burgher class, where they will receive all of the privileges and freedoms granted to ordinary citizens and be forced to give up any special privileges that they enjoyed in the past. Secular matters would be entrusted to municipal judges or to the kehilla on the condition that Christian assessors be appointed to sit on the court. Most religious issues would continue to be regulated by the kehilla. There should be no interference with Jewish beliefs, which Butrymowicz generously cedes to God's jurisdiction. Yet certain Jewish rites must be adjusted to conform with contemporary Polish life. He asserts, for example, that the excessive number of Jewish feast days render Jews unproductive and idle up to a quarter of the time; religious restrictions on food and drink isolate Jews socially and encourage them to disregard their environment. He calls for a Sejm commission with Jewish representatives to consider different ways of implementing these reforms.

To further this integration of Jews into the burgher class, Butrymowicz would have Jews driven from innkeeping in the countryside to trade and crafts in the towns. If necessary, they would be allowed to maintain inns in towns, provided that competition from non-Jewish innkeepers would force them to maintain proper pricing and quality of drink and that they could be supervised against exploiting the peasants. They would use Polish as the official language for all juridical and administrative matters. Jewish printing shops would be closed, and the importation of Jewish books banned. Jewish books would be translated into Polish, which would "afford insight into what evil they may carry, and more important still, open Jews to the way to knowledge." Jews would also be forced to wear woolen clothing instead of their traditional garb. This reform would save Jews money, spur the domestic textile industry, and prevent ridicule of the Jews. It would also make it difficult for Jews to hide goods stolen from city merchants. The wearing of these clothes, Butrymowicz emphasizes, has no religious basis; Jews in other countries conform to local fashion. Jews would also be conscripted into the army for three years of military service; this would teach them good habits. At first they would serve only as carters because of their skill in handling horses. Under the right conditions, however, they would again demonstrate military valor as they had done in the past.

He concludes this detailed proposal for reform with an appeal to his countrymen to recognize the logic of his position: "Jews differ in their religion, but why should they differ in their nature?" This, it should be noted, was the closest that any of the Polish men of the Enlightenment approached to the abstract and principled arguments made by their counterparts in the West, where literary debates did yield legislation for political and economic rights, even if these reform measures often proved to be temporary and reversible. Moreover, unlike most other Polish advocates of the Enlightenment and reform, Butrymowicz saw the problem of Polish Jews within the context of the problems of Polish society.[25]

25. Although critical of Jews for not establishing factories, for example, he acknowledges

Although he placed the burden of adjustment on the Jews, Butrymowicz did not avoid the context in which the Jewish problem had to be viewed.[26] He assumed that the Jewish position in Poland could be defined by public law, national in scope but administered locally by conscientious and just officials. At the same time, he assumed that the state could encourage Jews to live their lives more in accordance with its needs by indicating to them what was essential and what was peripheral to Jewish practice. This distinction, Butrymowicz believed, would be accepted by the Jewish masses under the right circumstances.

However moderate Butrymowicz seemed to be in his criticism of Jews, and generous in what he offered, as compared with other Polish proposals for reform, his plan evoked a sharp response from a Jewish spokesman. Rabbi Joshua Herszel Jozefowicz, the rabbi of Chełm and a participant, according to Gottlober, in the meeting of Jewish leaders to respond to the May constitution, wrote a pamphlet, "Thoughts on the Way of Reforming Polish Jews," published in 1789, shortly after the appearance of Butrymowicz's tract.[27] While praising the delegate from Pińsk's good intentions and noble efforts, he pointed out that Butrymowicz's stance is warped by his status as a member of the gentry, which does not allow him to see the problems from the inside.

The Jews, Rabbi Joshua Herszel argued, render many services to the country in which they live; they deserve better treatment and improved opportunities. They want to stay in Poland, build factories, and engage in crafts and business. They are skillful in all trades. Jewish craftsmen, however, are few because of impediments placed in their way by municipal authorities. The rabbi, like the gentry publicists whom he criticizes, puts Jewish economic activities in a broader context. Jews are attacked for exporting money, he says, but this is necessitated by their commercial activities in Poland as much as by their personal needs. Insofar as Jews run country inns and sell spirits to the peasants, they serve the landlords and make very little profit. The rabbi declares that there is no basis to the accusation which Butrymowicz uncritically repeats, that Jews place noxious herbs in the drink to hasten intoxication; sleeping peasants do not make good customers for drink. Butrymowicz's insinuation that Jews are hostile to Christians is totally unfounded. The proposal to impose a ban on the import of foreign Jewish books would condemn Jews to backwardness, idleness, and uselessness. In defense of allowing Jews the right to retain their traditional garb, Jozefowicz argued that if Jews are to be suspected of wronging gentiles, it would be, after all, an

---

the social structural and economic impediments, unlike in his other criticisms of Jewish economic activities. Polish manufactured goods cannot compete in open markets with imported goods because of the small scale and inefficiencies of Polish industry. Jews, from this perspective, are making a rational economic choice in confining their professions. Nonetheless, Butrymowicz advocates measures that would encourage Jews to assume industrial roles.

26. More characteristic of Butrymowicz's contemporaries among the Polish enlighteners were evaluations of Polish Jews that overlooked this context.

27. Eisenbach, *Materiały*, 98–105.

advantage that they wear distinguishable clothing. Jewish communal autonomy must be strengthened through the appointment of regional rabbis. In summary, he says, if there is to be reform, matters of religion must be left out of any such program. To do otherwise would inevitably involve forcing Jews to violate their beliefs. The rabbi called for a delegation to be appointed by the king to consider the Jewish question. At the same time, he repeats his request for respect for Jewish customs and religion.

Rabbi Joshua Herszel Jozefowicz's response to Butrymowicz points to the limited dimensions of Jewish life, whose reform a traditional Jew would find to be acceptable, particularly when demands for reform and revision came from outside the Jewish community. Preserving the traditional prerogatives of Judaism to define the many aspects of Jews' lives directly clashed with the intents and efforts of Polish reformers, who wanted to build the state and centralize authority along the regimented lines of absolutism. The Jews were to become another segment of the population over which that state would have full control.

Burgher Responses

A powerful reaction was soon to follow such assertions of Jewish rights and the call of Butrymowicz for changes in the structure of Polish society. Warsaw was quickly becoming the staging ground for a battle between the Jews and the burghers. The battle was waged along two fronts: the rhetorical flurry from the parliamentary chambers, organized by an influential burgher lobby, was drowned out by the riotous shouts from the Warsaw streets of Christian burghers trying to eliminate the competition of Jewish merchants. These merchants were taking advantage of the protracted debates to peddle their wares. Though Jews in the late eighteenth century were normally prohibited from trading in Warsaw, in accordance with the Polish custom they were permitted to trade during the few weeks when the Sejm was in session. Both the war of pamphlets and the legislative debate now focused on the immediate crises rather than on the position of Poland's Jews within a reconstituted society.

In responses addressed to the king and the Sejm, entitled "The Exposition of the Laws of the City of Warsaw with Regard to Jewry and an Answer to Their Demand for a Settlement Area," Michał Swiniarski urged that the Jewish proposal for residential rights be rejected and that even small colonies of Jews be prohibited from forming. "Jews have ruined and undermined the ambiance of all Polish towns by their countless cunnings and they are now eager to see the collapse of Warsaw."[28] The proposal denied the legal basis upon which the Jews asserted their municipal privileges. On the contrary, Swiniarski argued, the age-old prohibitions against the Jews settling and engaging in business activities remained in force. The author also took issue with the view that Jews are useful to the country; in fact, he declared, they increase the poverty in Polish towns and among their

28. Woliński, Michalski, and Rostworowski, *Materiały,* 2:23–37.

craftsmen. The mere formality upon which the Jews were now basing their right to stay in Warsaw—the longevity of the Sejm debates—was invalid. Swiniarski contended that a special resolution would have to be passed extending the right of the Jews to stay in Warsaw for longer than the six-week period that the Sejm normally met.

Kazimierz Chromiński (1759–1816) appears now to have taken up the defense.[29] In the pamphlet ascribed to him, "The Specification of the Right to Free Living and Trade for Jews in Warsaw," he criticized Swiniarski's interpretation of the history of Jewish privileges in Poland. He reviewed the Jewish rights to reside in and trade near towns. In regard to Warsaw, the document pointed to the 1768 law on free trade in the city, which stated that in keeping with the old customs, and for the public good and the moderation of soaring prices, "trade is not to be prohibited to Jews during the Sejm debates." That the Jews had not exercised this right in recent years, the author added, is a result of their lack of political influence and resources with which to guard their freedoms, insure the enforcement of this law, and defend themselves against violence.[30]

Chromiński adopted a particularly assertive tone in countering the accusation that Jews are responsible for the decline of towns, are unproductive, and have no loyalty to their country.[31] He also expressed indignation at the disrespectful attitude of the municipalities toward Judaism. Chromiński argued that the Jews are skilled craftsmen and to expel them would do the country no good. The reform of the status of Jews, he asserted, would be absolutely necessary to assure Polish Jews of their government's concern. They must be guaranteed the right to develop trade and crafts.

Another proposal to deal with the conflict immediately at hand between the Jews and the municipality (and their respective advocates) was submitted by Stanisław Kubicki to the Sejm in January 1789: the Jews should be allowed to extend their stay in Warsaw, but they should be taxed. For this proposal he likewise found legislative precedent. The most well-to-do Jews, however, were to be exempted from the requirement; he urged that they be granted settlement rights.[32]

The municipality of Warsaw, however, was in no mood for compromise. Representatives of the burghers' interests—through their agent and chief publicist, Swiniarski—monitored the discussion of the Jewish question carefully, seeing in it a threat to their interests and trying to prevent any law that could

29. *Polski słownik biograficzny*, 3:448; Eisenbach, *Materiały*, 27–42. Eisenbach implies that Chromińsky's advocacy was sponsored by Jews, though he does not conjecture who those sponsors were. He further observes that this is a limited indication of Jewish efforts to change their legal and class status.
30. Eisenbach, *Materiały*, 31.
31. Ibid., 35.
32. Ibid., 43–46. Kublicki specifies only those engaged in artisanry and agriculture, in contrast with those who "enrich themselves in ways that are harmful to the country." He makes no specific mention of the merchant among those who do "benefit the country."

permit Jewish citizenship. Swiniarski retorted with still another pamphlet, entitled "News on the Elemental Principle of Towns in Poland," which represented the political program of all towns under royal sovereignty.[33] The pamphlet, written as a historical review, argued for putting an end to the detrimental influence of Jews, and foreigners in general, on towns and crafts. Jewish residence in towns led to those towns' impoverishment, Swiniarski averred; their kehillot eagerly sought to destroy the burghers. The author advocated segregating Jews from Christians, expelling the Jewish population from the country's major towns (including Warsaw), and granting Jews permission to deal with retail trade only in small localities. He held that Jews should be resettled in the countryside and directed to farming.[34]

In the middle of 1789 a proposal expressing a very different burgher policy was sent to the Sejm by the representatives of the Lithuanian towns, supporting Butrymowicz's stance.[35] Its authors argued that there was no reason to expel Jews from towns or to isolate them economically. They suggested, instead, that agreements be concluded between particular municipalities and their local Jewish communities so that Jews be made citizens of towns and become subject to municipal legislation. Foreign and domestic trade would thus be regulated by the wealthy merchants of the town oligarchy, both Jewish and Christian. It is not known why Lithuanian burghers appeared to be more favorably disposed toward Jewish merchants than their Polish counterparts. To be sure, trade rights to be granted at the discretion of local citizens rather than as an integral provision of the public law that Polish reformers were promoting could be of occasional short-term benefit to Jews. But as momentum gathered for a constitution, placing Jews at the mercy of town councils became precisely the strategy of those Poles most opposed to Jewish rights.

It is not clear how interested the upper stratum of Polish Jewry, living largely in Warsaw, was in representing Jews elsewhere in Poland and in sustaining political activity and advocacy on behalf of what they perceived to be the long-term welfare of their fellow Jews. Some appeared to have merely pressed their own immediate personal interests. The reformist fervor in Warsaw notwithstanding, a few wealthy Jews were willing to sidestep the abstract formulations and ideological controversies as efforts in the Sejm became less likely to produce a broad solution to Poland's "Jewish question" involving a new status for Jews in Polish society and in public law. They lobbied for ad hoc, partial, negotiated solutions to collective Jewish problems—or as was the case more frequently, special privileges for themselves. This push for private deals is reflected in a document submitted to the Sejm in late November and early December 1789, entitled "A Humble Request from the Warsaw Jews."[36] Following what must have been high-

33. Woliński, Michalski, and Rostworowski, *Materiały*, 2:32–57.
34. Ibid., 44–45.
35. Ibid., 154–58.
36. Eisenbach, *Materiały*, 129–32. Eisenbach suggests that this proposal was submitted

level wheeling and dealing, a prodigious financial offer was made to the crown on behalf of three hundred Jewish families in exchange for the right to settle and permission to trade in two hundred towns heretofore closed to Jews. In addition, the signers of the agreement would pay the regular municipal taxes owed by all town residents and would conclude separate agreements with individual towns assuring the successful and profitable marketing of that town's produce.[37] The financial inducements were backed by judicial arguments taken from charters going back to Casimir the Great and successive Polish kings who granted privileges to the Jews. The representatives of these wealthy Jewish families ascribed the abrogation of their rights to live in towns and to participate in free trade and crafts to the burghers' fear of free competition and their lack of concern with the public good. This group of Jews, about whom we know virtually nothing else, concluded its appeal by stressing the contribution of Jews to the country. The new rhetorical tender of utility now accompanied the usual medium of payment.

Although a number of deputies carefully considered this request, opposition to the municipality of Warsaw was immediate and unequivocal. In early December 1789 a response, "Remarks on the Humble Request," was issued, in which the Jews were depicted as being at odds with any country in which they chose to live.[38] Laws cannot erase biases, the author asserts, nor can there be any point in making Jews free citizens. Jews have failed to take advantage of the privileges already granted, yet they crave new ones. The author declares that given citizenship in Warsaw, Jews would leave the smaller towns, causing harm to trade and crafts in those places. At the same time, they would introduce cheap trade and poor crafts into Warsaw, thus undermining its long-settled traditions of craftsmanship.

By the end of 1789 the deputation of townspeople was well organized. Hugo Kołłątaj, a gentry priest with Enlightenment proclivities, argued for the townspeople against the Jews. He recommended that radical administrative measures be used to insure the eventual assimilation of Jews. These would include the prohibition of traditional Jewish attire and beards. Kołłątaj likewise proposed a severe limitation on Jewish communal autonomy. He proposed that Catholic priests should adjudicate in a court of appeals for Jews; their own rabbinic courts should rule solely in matters of ritual. He supported the admission of townspeople to the Sejm, their access to official posts, and their right to buy landed estates. His more conservative fellow members of the gentry were not at all agreeable, com-

---

by "enlightened" Jews of Warsaw, in consultation with kehilla representatives from around the country.

37. Eisenbach notes that Jews were not yet equipped for partnership in the general fight for national reform but could offer their assistance in the financial sphere and in the organization of the country's internal trade. This assessment of Jewish capacities seems unfounded and apologetic for those representatives of the crown, the gentry, and the burghers more interested in extortion than in constitutional reform.

38. Eisenbach, *Materiały,* 133–35.

paring the granting of burgher rights to the revolution simmering at that moment in France. Indeed, in the Parisian fashion of political processions to the court, on November 25, 1789, in Warsaw, 272 burgher delegates, representing 141 cities, were received by the king. But unlike in Paris, the Polish burgher delegates made the expulsion of the Jews from the towns one of their main demands.

On December 4 Mateusz Butrymowicz submitted to the king a new proposal, entitled "The Reform of the Jews."[39] In it he essentially repeated the main provisions of the anonymous pamphlet that he had submitted earlier that year, urging free access for Jews to all occupations except the propinacja, participation in all guilds and fraternities, state inducements for Jewish farming in the countryside, and equal rights for Jews, including citizenship, with no obligation to pay extra taxes. An immediate response to Butrymowicz's new pamphlet was forthcoming in the same month, most likely from Piotr Świtkowski.[40] The author claims to appreciate Butrymowicz's efforts to improve the situation of Poland's Jews but takes issue with him on specific points. He argues that the Jews in Europe, who no longer have any homeland, preserve their laws only as a way to remember their past homeland in Palestine.[41] If they are to assimilate into Polish society and become useful citizens, they must not be given the right to govern themselves by their own laws, which are based on ancient Oriental laws. Świtkowski is wary of leaving power in the hands of the rabbis, whom he considers to be fanatics. The rabbis, he continues, are irresponsible judges and should be subject to local law, as is the case in other countries. He concludes, therefore, that even the limited powers of excommunication and religious adjudication that Butrymowicz was willing to grant the local Jewish communities are excessive and would impede the process of reform. He agrees with Butrymowicz's plan to grant Jews rights as citizens but warns that giving Jews too much freedom would only perpetuate their cunning; with no other inducements Jews would profit only from trade and not seek more productive employment in the crafts or farming. Only Jewish proprietors and apprentices of the crafts should be allowed to settle in towns. Moreover, he asserts that Jews should be conscripted, as was beginning to happen in some countries, where Jews had even achieved the rank of officer. In regard to the ban on importing books other than religious texts, Świtkowski argues that for educational purposes it might be advantageous to allow Jews to keep Yiddish books for a limited time but subsequently to have them translated into Polish.[42]

39. Ibid., 118–28.
40. Ibid., 135–41.
41. This explanation for the role of Jewish law is close to remarks made by Baruch Spinoza in his *Tractus Theologico-Politicus* (1670), but there is no evidence of direct influence. Świtkowski makes the same argument as regards European Arabs.
42. This more pragmatic attitude toward Yiddish is the same as that of Lefin. He refers to his teacher Moses Mendelssohn's strong condemnations of the use of that language. Nevertheless, in order to inculcate the values of the Jewish Enlightenment, Lefin persists in using the language of the masses of Jews in biblical commentaries and tracts.

The alignments were further complicated. In the midst of the raging debates between representatives of burgher and Jewish interests on the question of Jewish rights and autonomy, an impassioned plea arrived from Wilno at the end of 1789 or the beginning of 1790. "The Prisoner of Nieśwież to the Sejm Estates Currently in Session in Regard to the Need for Reform of the Jews" was addressed by Szymel Wolfowicz to the Sejm; in it he complained about the abuse of the kehillots' power.[43] Wolfowicz saw himself as the advocate of the lower classes in what had been a complex but essentially local struggle between the wealthy leaders who tried to dominate the communal structures of Vilna and its middle-class artisans and tradesmen. The kehilla leaders had Wolfowicz arrested, and the conflict now pressed itself on the attention of the Sejm in Warsaw; it was accompanied by a spate of pamphlets taking diverse positions.

According to Wolfowicz, the problems of the Jews can be traced directly to the kehilla, which maintains illegal monopolies and abuses its people by levying illegal and oppressive taxation. The power of the kehilla, to govern the Jews is at the root of this problem: "So it is, most gracious Estates [of the Sejm]. The Jews of Poland are an autonomous people, or more correctly, a 'state within a state.' "[44] Wolfowicz calls for the complete elimination of Jewish civil authority: "It always appeared that religion was still tied to citizenship, such that any reform of the Jewish nation was not possible. However, in that the separation of civic matters from religion is not so difficult, the Sejm now convening will therefore attain praises by transforming the Jewish people to both a more content and a more useful people to the state."[45] Wolfowicz willingly concedes that his reflections on the harm rendered by the kehilla as an institution are based on his personal experiences in Wilno. But there is a generalized principle. He urges that his assessment not be perceived as a bitter complaint against his people, nor as an act of hateful vengeance against those kehilla leaders who had him arrested and were responsible for his suffering. Who can be sure, he cautions, that other kehillot, currently rather equitably administered and just, "will not reach the same level of ambition and violence?"

Wolfowicz's primary concern is that the Jewish people be useful to the country that tolerates them and supports them and that there be greater mutual trust and appreciation between Jews and their country. This will be accomplished "when it is seen that we obey laws in regard to the jurisdictions of the state, and when it will be found that our morality is improved by proper behavior toward Christians." Wolfowicz, in the stylized reverance and pathos of Jewish and Polish petitionary literature, underscores the auspiciousness of the moment:

> We have no freedom or security while at the same time the general Enlightenment makes claims everywhere on behalf of the rights of human-

43. Eisenbach, *Materiały* 141–53. For the background of this communal schism, see Klausner, *Toledot Hakkehila.* Mahler, *History of Modern Jewry,* 297, 307.
44. For the history of this expression, see Katz, "State within a State," 29–58.
45. Eisenbach, *Materiały,* 142.

ity. . . . I have resolved to submit to the Most Gracious Estates my remarks in regard to the Jewish governance, knowing that the state cannot during the Sejm forget the Jews. Most Gracious Estates who in your wisdom are preparing for everyone a better lot in the future will not want to leave the Jewish people in their former disarray. On the contrary, you will want to inscribe in the sacred book of laws whether or not we are to be content and useful. . . . O, Your Majesty, Our Most Gracious Lord! O, Most Gracious Confederated Estates of the Commonwealth! When you take under the protection of the law our Jewish nation, give us a specific civic standing so that you will not have to write special laws, privileges, and punishments for the Jews.

Wolfowicz makes specific recommendations for the elimination of special privileges that Jews often receive but that unnecessarily separate them from their Polish neighbors, including their rights to be judged by special laws and to use a different language and attire. Adjudication in matters strictly religious, Wolfowicz recommends, should be headed by arbiters and a rabbi. But all adjudication in civil matters must be given over to the authorities. He concludes his epistle with a plea that attention be directed toward his dire situation in prison, in which he has been starved and forced to work in a factory, and that since he is innocent of any wrongdoing, he should be immediately released.

Wolfowicz's epistle and proposals were very much in the spirit of Joseph II's patent of 1782. Only a short time before Wolfowicz addressed his epistles to the Sejm, the patent was in fact extended to the Polish Jews residing in Galicia, now annexed to Austria. The response to Wolfowicz's proposals is not known. They belie the divisions and tensions within the Jewish community that hampered the consolidation of a unified political position. This conflict must have given encouragement to burghers and others who feared any successful outcome to Jewish advocacy and any ratification in a constitution or in public law of old Jewish privileges or new reform measures. It was not long thereafter that the Sejm had to respond to violence taking place considerably closer than in Wilno.

From the Rhetoric of Reform to Political Violence

By the end of 1789 the exchange between Jews and burghers surpassed the battle of words, as provocative rhetoric lapsed into political violence. There were no inhibitions of tone and content, as illustrated in a poem written in 1789 and published in 1790: "How to correct this, here is a cure. Trees are in abundance, but gallows are sparse. So each year we must hang one hundred Jews. Crime will diminish . . . in this way turn bad into good."[46] What came to be called the Black Procession of the burghers began in Warsaw in early 1790. That city's mayor, Jan Dekert, led a protest of delegates. Dressed in black, they proceeded from the Warsaw city hall to the castle, where the Sejm was in session, and then to the

46. Ibid., 252. The poem is cited in Haber, "Jewish Innkeepers," 13.

residences of the two speakers of the Sejm. They demanded that the Jewish question be excluded from any reform measures to be implemented on behalf of the municipalities and, ultimately, that the Jews be expelled from the munici-palities.[47] The artisans who joined the procession were more blunt in expressing their demands: unless the competition from Jews were eliminated, furriers and tailors threatened bloodshed. On March 22, 1790, the Sejm issued a declaration expelling all Jews from Warsaw other than tradesmen with special permission. Although the Warsaw burghers lost the economic battle, they won the political war. Noble bargain hunters, though they may have joined the municipal officials and artisans in opposing the general political efforts to ameliorate the Jewish situation, were more willing to tolerate Jews, enjoying the reduced prices offered by persistent and agile Jewish peddlers who plied the streets with their wares and evaded thuggery and police harassment. That the "mighty" Sejm, in responding to the burghers, was in the process of excluding them from public law and its protection meant little to these Jews, who were scrambling for a meager live-lihood. Tension mounted throughout the Warsaw spring.

A contract awarded on May 15 by the army to forty Jewish suppliers seems to have precipitated the riots. The following day, violence erupted. A Polish tailor named Fox attacked a Jew carrying his wares, but the Jew succeeded in escaping. In response to Fox's screams, a large group of Christian artisans gathered. The rumor quickly circulated that the Jews had murdered a Polish tailor. The demand for revenge began to spread. The rioters attacked the Jews on Timocaka Street, but the Jews had barricaded themselves and were able to resist. Jewish artisans in other districts, however, were attacked and had their wares stolen. Only after the army intervened did the violence abate.

The angry Sejm delegates ordered an investigation. Despite calls for Jewish "improvement" and increased productivity, new regulations demanded im-proved enforcement of the restrictions on Jewish artisans. On June 22 a special committee of deputies was designated to analyze the Jewish problem, taking into consideration ordinary citizens as well as enlightened Jews, and to report back to the Sejm within a month. The war of words now was heating up.[48]

The committee included, among others, Butrymowicz, whose position on the status of Poland's Jews was by now well known, and Jacek Jezierski. Jezierski, a self-made gentry entrepreneur, had little appreciation for the economic utility of commerce, expressing contempt for what he called the "town loafers."[49] In a pamphlet issued shortly after the Black Procession, entitled "Everybody is Wrong," Jezierski asserted that Jews could become skillful craftsmen and useful citizens, though at present their deleterious behavior was undeniable. The "dis-gusting ones" were most harmful as leaseholders and in the propinacja, only

47. Frenk, *Haironim Vehayyehudim Befolin,* 96; Shatzky, *Die Geschikhte fun Yiden in Varshe,* 1:85–103.
48. Dubnow, *Diverei Yemei Am Yisrael,* 8:164.
49. Jedlicki, "Social Ideas," 98.

somewhat less so as merchants. Nevertheless, he warned, the expulsion of the Jews stood in contravention of the principle of tolerance and was likely to bear negatively on the level of services in the cities. It would be difficult to murder the Jews and completely eliminate them, he concedes somewhat ruefully. Moreover, he opposed suggestions that the Jews be pressed into labor. Yet he insisted that under the right circumstances they could bring much benefit to Poland. Were Jews eliminated from the propinacja, they would on their own accord turn to industry and agriculture. Competition from Jews would ultimately be beneficial for the burghers, though it would greatly arouse burgher resentment against them. This competition, as Jezierski's fellow nobles always recognized, would be in the financial interest of the gentry since it would bring down prices.[50] Against this position other delegates saw the elimination of Jews from cities as a crucial means of rehabilitating the third estate.

It was outside the meetings of the special committee that more new thinking about the problems of Jewish reform seemed to be taking place. A very few non-Jewish Polish writers began to place the economic situation of Polish Jews within the broader context of the decline of Poland. Unlike so many of the writers of reform literature, particularly that which touched upon Jewish involvement in the propinacja, these writers now sought remedies rather than blame. In the 1790 pamphlet "The Principles of Agriculture, Labor, and Trade," by Bartłomiej Dzieńkoński, a Białystok teacher, the author points to the increasing indebtedness of the serfs as the reason for their drunkenness and poor performance as workers.[51] The serfs themselves, according to Dzieńkoński, choose to deal with their problems by turning to drink. At the same time, however, the lords force them to buy drink only at the local inns. Because a lord does not have to concern himself with competition, the Jewish innkeeper can serve an alcoholic beverage of low quality. Dzieńkoński points to the Jewish involvement in the exploitation and ultimate ruination of the serfs but emphasizes the fact that the Jews are merely agents for others. Members of the gentry are the ones who profit in the short run, but ultimately they are responsible for undermining their own position. Rather than the usual prescriptions to remove the Jews from the propinacja and to force them into agriculture, Dzieńkoński takes a wholly new approach. He recommends that the gentry monopoly on the manufacture and purveyance of alcoholic drink be ended, allowing the serfs to open their own taverns; the competition would result in an improvement in the quality of the drink and, willy-nilly, would drive many Jews out of the propinacja into other professions, including agriculture. This call for peasant entrepreneurship and reliance on market forces to remedy Jewish situation was uncharacteristic of the thinking taking place at this troubled moment in Poland.

An anonymous pamphlet appearing at this time placed even stronger emphasis than did Dzieńkoński on the context in which Jewish economic activity must

50. Haber, "Jewish Innkeepers," 18.
51. Ibid., 15–16.

be assessed. According to this writer, the Jews make commerce possible by creating close and convenient markets for the gentry's produce and the serfs' surplus. By maintaining inns, the Jews facilitate long-distance travel. It is the lack of temperance among peasants that makes them imbibe, not the Jews' business acumen. If Christian peasants were to replace the Jews in managing estates and the propinacja, they would be no less motivated by considerations of profit but would end up being less skillful in generating it. The author requests that the Sejm promulgate reforms without interfering with the arendars.[52]

These unusual expressions of appreciation for the Jewish contribution to the Polish economy, and of concern to protect Jewish economic interests during this period of social and legislative change, raises the possibility that Jewish influence and patronage stood behind these proposals.[53] There is other evidence of Jewish initiatives, particularly in response to the riots. A letter addressed to those representatives of towns who speak for broader political rights for their citizens appeared in French.[54] Dated May 30, 1790, it appeals to the sense of justice and reason, implying that the French Revolution has conferred rights of citizens upon Jews. It is not true, the author argues, that Jewish craftsmen are cunning and dishonest. Moreover, when Jewish merchants go bankrupt from unpaid debts, their coreligionists are willing to help them, affording protection to Christians who would trade with Jews. The author concludes the letter by asking for permission for the Jews to settle in Warsaw, asserting that not much good would come of their expulsion; in any case, the Jews would be able to settle in the Warsaw suburb of Praga.

Still another response in support of Jewish interests appeared in Warsaw in May 1790, in the *Journal hebdomadaire de la Diète.*[55] Virtually nothing is known in regard to the background of the document other than that it was sent by Warsaw Jews to the burgher representatives of Warsaw who were in the Sejm for the first time. The appeal, unique in tone and approach and clearly influenced by the spirit of the French Revolution, reflects an unusual consciousness of common interests between Jews and Poles of the same class. It appeals to the Polish

52. Ibid., 11, refers to additional publicistic literature lending support to Jewish involvement in the propinacja. A pamphlet referring to the Ukraine, for example, justifies this involvement on the grounds that the Jews serve an important function in spying. Moreover, the pamphlet continues, the precarious position in which the Jews are placed vis-à-vis the Ruthenian serfs ensures their loyalty; because Jews are despised by the serfs and in constant danger, they will serve even the gentry landlords with the smallest holdings.

53. This suspicion cannot be confirmed or disconfirmed.

54. Eisenbach, *Materiały,* 188–90, 272. Eisenbach suggests that the authors come from a nascent Jewish middle class and were influenced by liberal ideas. He sees in this letter evidence that the Jews understood their significant contribution to the economy of Poland and were ready to leave the Jewish class and unite with the burghers to fend off gentry influence. Ibid., 274. We know nothing about this letter's author, nor about how representative this thinking was. The letter probably indicates the imagination for a pragmatic alliance rather than expressing class consciousness and solidarity.

55. Ringelblum, *Kapitelen Geshikhte,* 173–79.

burghers directly for understanding and a sense of common cause with Jewish tradesmen and artisans. The Jews, the author defiantly proclaims, are an integral part of the third estate. As such, they have the right to demand the advocacy of this class, first, because they are human beings, and second, because the delegates of that estate in actuality represent them as well in the Sejm. "You engage in labor," the writer declares; "we do as well. . . . You are merchants, we are merchants. You are fearful of losses, so are we. You like profits, we do as well." Despite the problems and interests that Jews and burghers share, the Polish burghers, this author complains, have pressed for policies that would impoverish their Jewish counterparts. The writer declares indignantly that the burghers hypocritically base their claims against the gentry on natural law while ignoring the provisions of that law when dealing with the Jews: "You speak of rights, yet you have expelled thousands of families."

Sejm Actions

In August 1790 the commission of deputies charged with drafting a proposal to reform the Jews completed its work. Curiously enough, the report was not submitted to the entire Sejm until late May 1791. Similar to earlier reform proposals, it echoed the critique of Jews and Judaism by now commonplace in the literature of the philosophes and the enlightened despots, without echoing the anticipation, expressed in Paris, Berlin, and Vienna, that the situation of the Jews could be ameliorated. It called for increased civil intervention into the personal and family arrangements, education, social relations, and communal life of Jews through measures that had aroused a good deal of Jewish opposition when applied elsewhere, while granting Jews few rights of any consequence.[56]

This proposal seemed to order the complete elimination of discrimination against the Jews. In the wake of the Josephine edicts, it allowed Jews to participate in trade, crafts, and public education and to celebrate their holidays and rituals, and it recommended the cancellation of the onerous head tax that singled them out from other Poles. Yet any promises contained in these proposals to include Jews in Polish society stopped short of giving Jews residential rights in towns. Only "productive" Jews would be given permanent settlement certificates. Others would have to be content with rights that were little more than theoretical and were largely unworkable.[57]

The spheres of life in which the rabbis could have any authority was to be severely limited in this effort. Teachers and scribes, more readily controllable by local bureaucrats and gentry, were to assume many of the rabbinic functions. The rabbis would lose their power to excommunicate; other rabbinic functions would be performed by the state. Jews would have to submit to civil courts in

56. O'Brien, "Ideas of Religious Toleration," 5–71; Bernard, "Joseph II and the Jews," 101–19.
57. Eisenbach, *Materiały*, 254ff.

most instances of litigation, even when it involved an internal matter. Their
educational curricula would be dictated by the special committee on Jewish
education that was to be convened by this commission. Jews would be forced to
dress the same way as Christians. In violation of Jewish custom, which insisted on
prompt burial of the dead, the Jews were ordered not to conduct burials any
sooner than twenty-four hours following death.[58]

It was this commission and the special committee on education, apparently,
that Menahem Mendel Lefin had sought to influence and some years later spoke of
so disparagingly. Although Lefin prepared his report with "cunning" tactics to
win the favor of the delegates toward Poland's Jews and their needs, his success
was limited, as he himself later admitted: "It was not fated for me to be able to
show it to the commission, and it was to no avail except for an abridgment and
selections." Here it is likely that he was referring to his French pamphlet, calculated to evoke the Enlightenment principles that he assumed inspired the work of
the delegates. Whether in fact he sincerely believed that there was goodwill and
concern for ameliorating the situation of Poland's Jews among any of the Polish
delegates during the period of the Four-Year Sejm is not clear. In retrospect,
however, he spoke with bitterness of his experience as an advocate on behalf of
the Jews at the Four-Year Sejm and railed against the motives, attitudes, and
intentions of the Polish reformers with whom he dealt. He said that the "sustained
enthusiasm" of the gentiles, "whose hands are mighty against us," press their
"libels day and night" against the Jews; the ministers vilify the Tora by arguing that
it "stood in opposition to the laws of reform of the state."[59]

Even granting to Poland's Jews the few concessions made within this reform
proposal was deemed unacceptable by important groups of their Polish compatriots. The resistance by the burghers and by other Sejm delegates was strong
enough to cripple the commission's political efforts to gain passage for its proposals. Whether because of internal conflicts caused by the death of Bishop
Garnysz, the commission chairman, because of calculated obstruction, or be-

58. Fashionable scientific theories declared that death was elusive, that ostensible signs of
death were misleading, and that often those appearing to be dead might regenerate themselves. Hence the injunction against prompt burial. This intervention into Jewish religious
and communal life had been rampant in Germany in the second half of the eighteenth
century. In 1772 the Jewish community of Mecklenburg-Schwerin appealed to the young
but already accomplished philosopher Moses Mendelssohn, as well as to the more traditional religious leader Rabbi Jacob Emden, for their intercession in averting the decree.
Mendelssohn proposed a compromise whereby the duke would rescind his order to
postpone burial for three days on condition that a doctor certify death before any burial
were conducted. Mendelssohn proceeded to urge the Jewish community to reconsider its
position in that hastening burial was merely based on the authority of recent custom and
that in ancient times Jews certainly did delay burial. Moreover, he cited the usual scientific
arguments, accompanied by horror stories, in support of delay. Emden, upon receiving
Mendelssohn's letter, respectfully chastised his younger colleague. Katz, *Out of the Ghetto,*
143–44.
59. Lefin, cited in Gelber, "Mendel Lefin Satanower."

cause of the general evasiveness of the Sejm delegates in confronting many problems on which the fate of Poland depended, parliamentary debate over the proposal was delayed long enough to allow the Sejm to pass a constitution that
wholly neglected 10 percent of the population. But there was little cause for
Jewish celebration that "the wicked decree involving equal rights shall be annulled, . . . that there should not be promulgated new reforms, heaven forbid."

During the period in which the Sejm delegates were arguing over the scope
and provisions of the new constitution, the international tensions, which had
provided a favorable climate for Polish self-assertion and reform, were gradually
abating. This easing of international tensions also undermined Poland's always-
precarious internal solidarity. The provincial gentry demonstrated their hostility
toward reform; the advocates of constitutional reform had to pay for the political
support that they sought from the conservative gentry by making broader concessions. The burghers, observing the political style of their counterparts in France
without being attentive to the democratizing goals of the third estate, became
more militant. Deliberations on reform continued. But the bombast and intrigue
demonstrated by many of the leaders of Sejm factions did little to foster the much-
needed political alliances and consensus. Time was running out.

Under considerable pressure and by circuitous measures, legislation was
passed. On March 24, 1791, electoral reform was implemented.[60] On April 18,
1791, the Law of the Towns was passed, granting significant rights to all Christian
burghers, including foreigners, and recognizing the citizens of the towns as free
people.[61] The towns were granted the right to elect to the Sejm twenty-one
representatives to participate in committee deliberations as plenipotentiaries, to
take the floor on matters concerning towns, industry, and commerce, and to vote
on the Sejm commissions for the treasury, the police, and the judiciary.[62] Burghers were given the right to purchase estates and were granted access to lower
administrative and judicial offices, including the rank of officer in the army (except in the cavalry). Two hundred burghers were admitted into the gentry. At the
same time, the peasantry was provided some protection under public law. The
exclusion of the Jews from this law and the decisive gains of their most bitter
political opponents, the burghers, set the tone for their treatment under any
constitution that would follow. With the burghers appeased, and the misgivings of

60. See Jedruch, *Constitutions, Elections and Legislatures of Poland,* 207. He contends
that the three hundred thousand members of the lower gentry out of a total electorate of
seven hundred thousand were disenfranchised so that they could not be manipulated by
the magnates. The right to vote was based on owning land or, if leasing land, paying a
minimum of one hundred zloty a year in taxes. This legislation had no positive effects on
Jews.

61. Woliński, Michalski, and Rostworowski, *Materiały,* 4:77, 92; Jedruch, *Constitutions,*
207–12.

62. They were not represented, at least initially, on the education commission, where
much of the deliberations about the Jews transpired. They were not without influence,
however, as we shall see.

the conservative gentry allayed by the moderateness and inconsequentiality of legislation regarding the peasantry, the constitution committee could now proceed without obstruction. On May 3, 1791, to the shouts of "The King with the nation, the nation with the King," the constitution was ratified in Warsaw.[63] Abroad it was greeted with enthusiasm. Edmund Burke described it in glowing terms; a special Te Deum was sung in Rome offering "thanks for the advantages which the new constitution of Poland secures to the Catholic religion";[64] in Philadelphia and Richmond it was toasted for its bold and sweeping reform.[65]

Despite all the proposals in circulation calling for reforming the situation of the Jews, it soon became clear that the omission of the Jews from the constitution would result in the deterioration of the Jewish situation.[66] Letters from burghers and craftsmen complaining about heavy taxes also called for the enforcement of the April law. With constitutional rights reserved for Christians, the April law now was construed as providing for the expulsion of Jews from all free towns, as well as for their elimination from trade and from the crafts. This exclusion of Jews from the constitution indirectly, but no less significantly, affected the many Jews living on gentry estates and in sectors of towns owned by the nobility. Moreover, the interventionist tone of the constitution, backed by the absolutist ethos of Enlightenment values, made those Jews who in theory were excluded from public law in actuality subject to the whims of local authorities. The passion of the mobs strengthened the administrative logic of parliamentarians. Citizens were transformed into outsiders.

63. Jedruch, *Constitutions*, 212, calls this ratification a coup d'état, with the king sending recall notices after the Sejm's Easter break only to representatives who were not strong opponents of the constitution. A slim majority, bolstered by the new deputies from the towns, voted in its favor.
64. *Dunlap's American Daily Advertiser*, September 26, 1791, and *Gazette of the United States*, September 28, 1791, cited in Haiman, *Fall of Poland*, 49.
65. Wandycz, *Lands of Partitioned Poland*, 8. A report from Berlin dated as early as May 17, 1791, speaks of the events of May 3 with less enthusiasm and greater perspicacity: "Our politicians do not consider the revolution in Poland as so clearly established, as it is pretended to be. They argue that the revolution was too quick in its operation, and planned with too great haste, to be so suddenly established. It will probably produce great tumults at some future period, and bring forward some very powerful confederation against it. The Russian party at Warsaw was united in opposing its progress. The Prussian interest remained neutral, and took no part in it." *Dunlap's American Daily Advertiser*, July 25, 1791, cited in Haiman, *Fall of Poland*, 40.
66. Wandycz, *Lands of Partitioned Poland*, 8, asserts that articles 4 and 11 define the nation as the entire population rather than merely the gentry, as was the case with Sarmatian concepts. Furthermore, he indicates that the right of habeas corpus was extended to the burghers and the Jews. But the constitution refers to the Law of the Towns of April, which is quite specific in granting rights to Christians only. He further declares that "the reformers had plans of a new autonomy for the latter but did not include them in the Constitution." Indeed some, but by no means all, reformers did have such intentions; yet the fact that the constitution was issued, as whatever type of political compromise, without referring to 10 percent of the population had to have consequences.

The evasiveness of the constitution on Jewish issues must be seen within the context of what was and was not accomplished in the Four-Year Sejm. Other legislation vital to the stated interests of segments of the Polish population also received scant attention.[67] But the failure of the Sejm to establish a public law that would define, centralize, and coordinate the relations of the state to all residents of Poland points to a shortcoming of the constitution—with implications that were particularly severe for Poland's Jews.[68]

With the legal status of the Jews unresolved, there was a call on May 24, 1791, to raise the taxation on Jews by 50 percent. Butrymowicz countered by arguing that proper reforms would bring in still greater revenues from the Jews. At this critical juncture the commission of deputies on Jewish reform was too divided to be effective. Butrymowicz continued to promote the submission of the draft reform, completed months earlier, to the entire Sejm; Chloniewski asserted that the proposal conflicted with the interests of the towns. He put forward a new draft that granted Jews the right to settle and practice trade and crafts, as long as this did not conflict with the provisions of the Law of the Towns of April 1791—meaning that no change whatsoever would be made in the situation of the Jews.

The climate was so hostile to the Jews of Poland that even the Frankists, who for more than three decades had been converts to Catholicism and had received privileges not accorded their former coreligionists, were spoken of disparagingly.[69] A publication of the municipality blames them for sending the country's money abroad. Further suggestions were made to isolate the Frankists by administrative measures from the rest of the Jewish population. Yet there is evidence that the Frankists had some representation, or at least supporters, in the Sejm.

Support for Jews was occasionally expressed, however. A letter from two Eastern districts, the voivodeships of Kiev and Volhynia, dealing mainly with the problems of the Russian Orthodox and the Uniates, also argued that peasants, Jews, Karaites, and Gypsies be treated in accordance with the provisions of natural law.[70] Moreover, the authors of the letter took issue with the view that the Jews bring no profit to the Polish economy. Regrettably, we know little about the circumstances of such appeals on behalf of the Jews.

67. Jedlicki, "Social Ideas."
68. Constitutions do not necessarily assure any form of equality, as the status of blacks in the American constitution well illustrates. Whatever degradation and disabilities members of a minority group endure, however, their exclusion from an assured status in public law makes them more vulnerable to the capriciousness of the majority.
69. Woliński, Michalski, and Rostworowski, *Materiały,* 2:367, 372. It was precisely at this time that their leader Jacob Frank, who had left Poland in the turmoil of 1772, died in a suburb of Frankfurt-am-Main. See Jacques Calmansohn's comments on Frank in his "Essai sur l'état actuel," 9–12.
70. Eisenbach, *Materiały,* 277.

Jewish Perceptions of Danger

Many Jews correctly perceived the new dangers inherent in their exclusion from public law. Not only were they not to receive specific rights and privileges, but traditional privileges such as juridical and communal autonomy might be revoked. Furthermore, they worried that the state would intervene on their behalf only in regard to such matters as forcing them to change their traditional clothing and to shave their beards. There is some evidence of Jewish communities across Poland mobilizing and sending petitions, proposals, and emissaries to Warsaw to put political pressure on the Sejm against the "wicked decrees" and "new reforms."

On June 4, Jewish delegates in Warsaw referred to the commission's report still tied up in committee and to a proposal made by Pejsak Chaimowicz, a longtime representative of the king to the Jewish community whose commitment to Jewish welfare rather than his own power and wealth was questionable.[71] At the same time the delegation presented a new proposal (accompanied by the usual offers of special payments), demanding residential rights in all towns, including the Warsaw suburbs; freedom in trade and crafts; and the right to build factories and houses, purchase or lease land, and maintain gardens.[72] This proposal also called for the elimination of forceful conversion of Jewish children under the age of eighteen and an end to the punishment of the wives and children of debtors. Jews should be judged and punished by established courts, it declared, not by individual members of the gentry. The rights of Jews to observe their holidays and customs should be assured. Jewish courts, kehillot, and assessors should be recognized by government officials. Old privileges that had been granted to Jews by the crown and the gentry should not be abrogated. These Jewish delegates sought a well-defined and well-coordinated position in public law and resisted the capricious governance of local officials. Unlike their counterparts in France, however, they made no principled demands for full equality or comprehensive civic rights. In Poland such expectations appear to have been unrealistic. For the largest number of Jews, the most pressing concern was that there be no deterioration in their economic, legal, and political situation.

71. Ibid., 272; Gutterman, "Proposals," 92–96. Gutterman describes Chaimowicz as a prototype of the *syndak,* or *sendyk,* a Jew appointed as the king's representative to the Jewish councils, often with broad administrative responsibilities, including informing the court of what was transpiring among Jews and extorting royal payments from co-religionists. In contrast with the court Jews of Central Europe, who were often popular among Jews, the syndaks were often viewed by Jews and Christians alike as first-rate thieves. Though deposed from his position in 1784 because of charges of corruption, Chaimowicz regained his position during the Four-Year Sejm, helping the king extort money from Jews. His reform measures reflect some concern to rationalize Jewish courts and communal structures and seem to have received a somewhat positive response from some Warsaw Jews. Gutterman sees their purpose as little more than to increase the revenue of the treasury.

72. Eisenbach, *Materiały,* 276–78.

Throughout the summer the mobilization of Jews gathered momentum, with letters sent out to the Lithuanian communities requesting that their leaders convene at the Zelwa fair in August, to insure "that there should not be promulgated new reforms, heaven forbid." The meeting lasted four weeks, and a letter, "A Voice Calls to All of the Jews of Lithuania," was circulated, describing (in the safely equivocal language of such calls for emergency action) the mood at the Sejm, where the king and nobility harbored "good intentions on behalf of Israel," requiring the intercession of "militant, God-fearing people, people of reputation, in order that they should stand before the king and ministers and appeal for the good of Israel." The letter continues:

> In connection with the fact that there have been heard terrible calls that have made the earth tremble, a voice resounding in the mountains announces and proclaims that the rulers of the people and the kingdom have gathered in the capital city of Warsaw, in which the gracious king, our lord, as well as the lords, the elect of the people, occupying the seat of justice, [have gathered together] to judge us justly and mercifully and bring peace to us, brother Jews, and this matter demands great efforts and earnest endeavors to knock on the door and beg for the good of the rest of our people. And it is strange in the eyes of the lords of the kingdom that in all of Lithuania there is not a Jew who would perform endeavors for us, like the Jews of the crown, who stand without break at their post and knock at the door of the lords of this kingdom.[73]

Money was raised for this delegation. Women were not to wear new dresses, nor dresses woven with strings of gold or silver, for three years. "This money is sacred and intended for the expenses of the delegates of the communities who will travel to Warsaw in order to redeem Israel from the evil of the new reforms, heaven forbid." The emergency session of representatives was to be held on November 29, 1791.[74]

Several months later, in honor of the king's birthday on January 17, 1792, the rabbi of Lublin, Levi Herszek Szawelowicz, of the prominent rabbinic family Margoliot, issued an enthusiastic statement:

> Your Majesty, O gracious Lord, . . . Now, when the entire land is beginning to enjoy contentment, because of the mint of Your Majesty's rule—so wise and worthy of praise—it is possible to hope that under the just and charitable rule of Your Majesty, even the children of our religion will merit equal treatment, freedom and security. With your permission, my merciful King, I shall give over together with other rabbis our notification and you shall in your compassion receive our modest request. In our cities in general and in

---

73. Ibid., 293–94; Gutterman, "Proposals," 120. The original document was apparently lost during World War II. Eisenbach (as well as Shatzky and Halpern, who refer to it) apparently has reconstructed it from Frenk.

74. Gutterman, "Proposals," 121.

the places where the members of our religion live, it is customary to pay a tax from the [ritual slaughter] of poultry.[75]

The rabbi goes on to assure the king of the reliability and profitability of this potential source of royal income, which the rabbis could collect without troubling the king's ministers and deliver to Warsaw: "I have composed this proposal in the midst of the people of my religion, and I shall try to bring it to a conclusion without bothering the King. And this on the condition that in the coming days when new laws will be established this will be done with our knowledge—the rabbis—and they will decide it in accordance with the rules of our religion." The rabbi offers the king hundreds of thousands of golden coins a year in exchange for his not issuing edicts that would contravene Jewish law, and for his recognizing the authority of the rabbis so that they may preserve the traditional way of life.[76]

Neither was there a paucity of private deals offered by a few wealthy Jews, with what seemed to be little regard to how these offers might affect the negotiations undertaken at the same time by representatives of various communities. On September 6, 1791, ten Jews from different cities, including Sandomierz, Kutno, Pińczów, and Tykocin, submitted a request to the king that 130 Jewish families be granted the right to settle in Warsaw.[77] Other private proposals were made in the coming months. One, made at the beginning of January 1792, provided generous donations to the king that would continue for twenty years after the present monarch's death, and annual payments to the treasury and the army, as well as payment for kehilla debts and an offer to pay a meat tax. The Warsaw municipality was offered a comparatively large sum for each of one hundred families granted residence and commercial, though not civic, rights.[78]

The attempts of wealthy Jews to purchase special privileges were encouraged by the king and his minister and fellow Enlightenment enthusiast Scipione Piattoli (1749–1809), as well as by Kołłątaj and Potocki. Piattoli especially encouraged these deals as a way of enriching both the king and himself. Negotiation sessions became undignified spectacles in which the king's representatives tried to extort the largest sums that they could from Jewish leaders in exchange for privileges rather than for the rights that Jews in the West were receiving as a result of the expansion of public law and the inclusiveness of citizenship. As such, they were different in degree but not in kind from the negotiations that had taken place for centuries between rulers and shetadlanim. The negotiations were comically described by the Russian ambassador to the Polish court, who noted that the Jews bargained with the king over the amount of money they would be obliged to pay, not knowing exactly for or against which reforms they were negotiating these

75. Eisenbach *Materiały,* 298.
76. Gutterman, "Proposals," 122, declares that this opposition to "any change which brings with it an injurious effect upon the traditional way of life" was characteristic of the concern of most Polish Jews at the time.
77. Eisenbach, *Materiały,* 295, docs. 37, 39.
78. Ibid., 394–95.

deals.[79] Piattoli tried to convince the Jewish delegates that the king was serious about reforming the Jews in the spirit of mercantilism in order to strengthen his rule and to accelerate the development of the Polish economy. The opinion common among the Jews and others was that Stanisław Poniatowski was primarily interested in raising money to pay his debts. The Jews also tried to lobby members of the commission, such as Bernowicz, complaining about Piattoli's extortion of money. During these negotiations specific Polish localities indicated interest in making special agreements with the Jews. But through charm, threats, and vain assurances, Piattoli tried to make the Jews as dependent on the King as possible so as not to reduce the king's potential profits from extortion.

Complaints began to arrive from local Jewish communities about anti-Jewish action prompted by the new Law of the Towns and the new constitution. These Jewish petitioners indicated that privileges that had existed for centuries were being contravened in the name of public law. Kołłątaj recommended that anti-Jewish action be stopped until the Sejm decided the status of Polish Jewry, but his recommendations were largely ignored. Still, the commission continued to meet, augmented now by several town representatives who offered proposals that were prompted, according to Piattoli, by bias and hatred toward the Jews.

The controversy that finally and irreversibly undermined the committee's report was over the settlement of the sizable debts accumulated by local Jewish communities resulting from heavy taxation and other obligations. No consensus could emerge over who would be authorized to assess this debt.[80] This failure brought to a conclusion efforts taking place in the parliament and political center to deal with the Jewish problem.

In early 1792 the Warsaw municipality renewed its attempts to expel the Jews based on the 1790 decision that Jews would not have the residential rights that they usually enjoy when the Sejm convenes during this extraordinarily long Sejm session. Jewish representatives asked the king to exercise his influence for the postponement of this decree until reform measures on behalf of the Jews were promulgated.[81] On the advice of Piattoli, they accompanied this request with a forty-thousand florin gift—to no avail. On February 8, 1792, a decree was issued expelling the Jews from Warsaw; the decree was executed fifteen days later.[82]

Last Efforts

At about the same time, on January 2, 1792, the final report of the commission, entitled "The Arrangement of the Jewish Population in the Whole Polish Nation," was published. A second draft was submitted to the Sejm on May 29,

79. Gelber, *Mendel Lefin Satanower,* 431.
80. Reform measures for Jews in France during the French Revolution were likewise thwarted over the issue of communal debts. Hertzberg, *French Enlightenment and the Jews,* 364–65; Malino, *Sephardic Jews of Bordeaux,* 61–64.
81. Eisenbach, *Materiały,* 460.
82. Gutterman, "Proposals," 93.

1792, with a handwritten note signed by Kołłątaj: "I set this settled motion before the deputies for a *pluralitate votorum.*"[83] The king tried to press Marshal Mała-chowski, the Sejm chairman, to support the proposal. Jezierski made the motion that it be read to the Sejm, but this was promptly turned down. Between the issuance of the first and second drafts Lefin likely appeared before the commission and sought to soften its harsher provisions, such as the one forbidding Jews the right to wear beards.

In the second draft, freedom of worship and religious rights were guaranteed, and the ridicule of Jews was prohibited. Jews were ordered to abandon traditional Jewish clothing within a specified period, and to wear the clothes of their particular class. Rabbis, however, would be allowed to retain their rabbinic garb. Jews would be permitted to make agreements with local authorities in regard to trade, crafts, and industrial activity and the manufacture of spirits. The distillation of alcohol in free towns and in towns of the gentry was to be allowed for only seven years. This point provoked a good deal of controversy, with a final amendment made by several deputies to permit innkeeping only at the discretion of local authorities. The Jews would not receive formal civic rights. They could not own estates or inherit land, but they could have lifelong leases.[84]

Jews would be protected by law and permitted to settle in towns and villages of the crown by special agreement with the officials, the gentry, and the clergy; in free towns permission would be granted by the municipal authorities and the police commission. The kehilla would be allowed to organize and oversee its traditional functions in education, religion, and welfare. Decisions in important matters such as contributions and payments to the kehilla were to be made by a majority vote, but only with the approval of the police commissioner, town officials, and in the countryside the gentry landlords as well. Litigation involving religious matters, including all cases involving only Jews, would be decided by Jewish courts. Appeals in these cases would go to the town court. Cases involving Jews and Christians would be tried before district courts. In gentry towns the landlord's court would be the final tribunal, with no right of appeal. The proposal concluded by specifying the amount of money that the Jews must pay for these privileges.

The Jewish representatives were distraught over this proposal. The consequences of the commission report, rendering Jews subject to local authority and increasing the intervention into their religious and communal lives, would be contrary to everything that those representatives had sought. Because they believed that their chances for obtaining privileges from the Sejm were slim, they now turned to the police committee. Some time before June 9, 1792, delegates from three provinces submitted a proposal to that committee requesting the right

83. Eisenbach, *Materiały*, 491–515. A noticeable difference between the two drafts is the role accorded to Jewish self-governance. The second draft often deletes the word *kehilla* where it was mentioned in the first.
84. Ibid., 493–95.

to maintain Jewish courts. In cases where the landlord was the arbiter, and in general cases involving Jews and Christians, they sought the right to appeal to district courts. They further requested that the imposition of taxes by municipal authorities be done in consultation with the kehilla leaders and that cash payment be allowed in lieu of conscription. No decisions were made on this proposal.[85]

Two likely participants in the intrigues surrounding the last years of the Polish republic were Dr. Jacques Calmansohn and Tadeusz Czacki. Calmansohn, from the Zamość area, studied medicine in Germany and France and traveled to Turkey and Russia. Upon returning to Poland, he worked as both doctor and translator for the king and the police commission. There is reason to believe that he was not reluctant to benefit from his connections with the court, even to the detriment of his coreligionists.[86] During the Four-Year Sejm he was actively involved in the schemes of the king and Piattoli to extort money from the Jews. His own proposals were published in French in 1796 and submitted to a Prussian minister in charge of areas annexed from Poland. They were subsequently translated into Polish. They were also submitted to Tsar Paul I. Calmansohn attributed the repulsion and antagonism expressed by Gentiles toward Jews to "miserable egoism" of Jews.[87] Their "strange appearance," their insistence on wearing special attire, and their refusal to remove such outer signs as the beard "is a reason why Jews are detested."[88] He spoke positively of the intentions of the Polish enlighteners and the reformers at the Four-Year Sejm. But Poland's Jews merely increased their indifference to the "people of genius . . . inspired with pure public spirit . . . who could lend a helping hand to the Jews."[89] Despite this obstinacy of the Jews, "they should be slightly corrected, slowly adapted to the life of the nation they entered." He proposed the usual array of religious, administrative, and economic reforms for which the radical Maskilim became known. "This," he underscored, "is the true way of converting them."[90] In view of the fact that there is no record of Calmansohn himself converting, despite the obstacles that his Jewishness posed to his professional career, it is not clear what he was advocating in this regard.

Czacki, also of the Polish gentry, was close to royal circles and served on the financial committee of the Four-Year Sejm. His reform proposals were not published until 1807.[91] Czacki paints a gloomy portrait of Polish Jews, noting their increasing population, indigence, infant mortality, ignorance, and bankruptcy. He says that Jews are prominent among forgers, though the general crime rate among

85. Ibid., 515–17.
86. Gutterman, "Proposals," 36–38.
87. Ibid., 9.
88. Ibid., 57–58. The wearing of the beard by Jewish men, Calmansohn comments, was originally incorporated into their religion to make them feel more secure with the bearded Asiatics among whom they resided.
89. Ibid., 11.
90. Ibid., 8.
91. Ibid., 25.

them is lower than among Christians. He declares them to be intolerant of other religions because they lack Enlightenment. Czacki unambiguously asserts the rights of Jews as free people to reside and to obtain property, including land, and emphasizes that they are not to be treated as serfs. As in the edict that Catherine the Great tried to promulgate in the late 1780s (without success), Czacki proposes that Jews be given municipal representation proportionate to their numbers in the local population. At the same time, they are to be completely eliminated from the propinacja for at least fifty years. In the spirit of Joseph II, Czacki advocates government intervention and oversight in virtually every area of the religious and communal lives of Jews in which heretofore they had enjoyed autonomy.

From "False Pretence" to Partitions

By the first anniversary of the May Constitution, and with the Sejm drawing to a close, the political clouds over Poland began to thicken. It would take more than parliamentary debates and proclamations to save the country at this dire moment. The rhetoric of reform resounded with growing intensity from the time of the first partition of Poland, nearly two decades earlier. Publicistic tracts, parliamentary debate, and what Świtkowski in 1786 called sagacious legislation now reached a crescendo in the chambers of the Four-Year Sejm. The problems of Poland's Jews were among many vexing issues calling for sagacity.[92] Some of the proposals registered concern for the Jews, but most did not; in the end, none of the reform proposals effectively and enduringly improved the Jewish situation.[93] The leaders of Poland, having lost this last initiative to shape their country's fate, were again buffeted by external forces. Public discourse soon degenerated into civil war, futile revolution, and the total annexation of Poland by foreign powers. Saving an unacknowledged order of feudal autarky through inadequate measures of reform proved to be impossible.

There is some evidence of Jewish celebration on that first anniversary of the constitution. "A New Song" was composed, flowery and effusive, with text in Hebrew, Polish, French, and German versions.[94] In this ode of praise to Stanisław Poniatowski, to his wisdom and fairness, the king is declared to be a gift from God. Like the sun, he brings morning to a land once shrouded in darkness. He strengthens himself, but not with human blood and the ruins of cities: his power rests on a bedrock of truth and reason. Both townspeople and villagers can rejoice, for their King rules by virtue. The king's ministers are also to be praised. The king sweetens the fate of his people, and like an angel, he cures them. The supplicant proceeds to

92. Vereté, "Polish Proposals," 148–55, 201–13. Vereté contends that the publicists could not avoid dealing with the Jewish question in terms of their agenda for shaping the future of Poland.
93. Jedlicki, "State Industrial Economy," 96.
94. Eisenbach, *Materiały*, 480–83.

note that the people had forgotten that Poland's Jews, too, were human. But the king knows how to value people, and so the Jews place their trust in him: "At dawn you established good laws on their behalf. You ordered not to distinguish between blood and blood. The tear from all faces you wiped away." Jews, the song continues, hope that other citizens will share the same fate under Stanisław that they enjoy. They swear their loyalty to the fatherland and to the king. The degree to which this "New Song" expressed the genuine patriotism or the sense of real anticipation of any sector of Polish Jewry is not clear. More likely, it was a stock and banal expression, a demonstration of politeness to be presented as an adornment to the bribes offered by Jewish negotiators.

A more forthright assessment of the May Constitution was presented by the enigmatic British lord George Gordon. Gordon's ardent anti-Catholic rhetoric was alleged to have incited the so-called Gordon riot, for which he was tried for treason. He subsequently converted to Judaism.[95] In a letter to W. P. Smith, a member of Parliament, accompanying his regrets for not attending a "Meeting in Support of the People of Poland, at the London Tavern," which was convened on that first anniversary, Gordon writes:

> There has been something not sincere in the Polish Revolution, a sort of false pretence in favour of Liberty, which is now too apparent, and they [the Poles] themselves are suffering the fatal consequences of the deception. The Jews, you must be well acquainted, are above One Million in number in Poland. Can you declare to this meeting what advantages have already been granted to them by the New Constitution, or whether any promises of being advanced to an immediate participation of Citizenship are assured to them by the present Diet? The Assembly of France, you know, has prudently admitted the Nation to the equal rights of Citizens. The Jews in France were soon penetrated with admiration and respect, on beholding the multiplied acts of Justice, which proceeded from that Assembly; and they deposited in the midst of them the solemn testimony of their patriotism and devotedness: their solemn oath to sacrifice, in every instance, *their lives and fortunes* for the public good; for the glory of the nation and the king. One sole object rules and animates all their thoughts, the good of their country, and a desire of dedicating to it all their strength. In that respect they will not yield to any inhabitants of France; they will dispute the palm with all the citizens for zeal, courage and patriotism. . . . But what encouragement does the present Diet hold out to the Polish Jews which they did not enjoy under the old Republican Government? None at all. Is it natural then to suppose that their monied brethren and friends in England, France, and Holland will be very ready to subscribe voluntarily to the support of the New Constitution of Poland, where the equal Rights of Citizens are still withheld from them?[96]

95. Solomons, "Gordon's Conversion to Judaism," 222–71.
96. Ibid., 257.

In this perspicacious refusal to celebrate, Gordon anticipated the attitude of those historians who paid scant attention to the so-called Jewish question at the Four-Year Sejm, disregarding its paper trail and archival legacy; who dismissed the Sejm as being merely of historical interest, rather than truly of historical significance; who treated it as an ephemeral episode of antiquarian interest rather than a watershed event that determined the course of future developments for Jews in the modern world. Whether the reforms proposed for Poland and Polish Jews may have succeeded under different circumstances is a question that still inflames passions, and it is ultimately irresolvable.

Catherine II exploited the opposition to the May Constitution expressed by some members of the Polish gentry, using it to justify military intervention. In 1793 Poland was partitioned for a second time, and there followed an insurrection led by Tadeusz Kościuszko (1746–1817), a veteran of the American Revolutionary War.[97] Kościuszko "found it expedient to make some slight concessions to the peasants," but offered little more than inspiring appeals to Jews. He did not redress their legal status. A Jewish cavalry troop made up of five hundred volunteers and "idlers" was actually established under the leadership of Berek Joselowicz and other Jewish officers. Notwithstanding the pride that Polish Jews in later years felt in this Jewish legion, its military accomplishments remain unclear.[98] Jews in war-torn Poland were caught in the quandary of lending support to the familiar but oppressive armies of the partitioning countries or to the altogether-unknown but popular forces of revolution and Polish nationalism whose success could lead to worse oppression: many Jews were caught in the crossfire and suffered a great deal of brutality.[99] Following the third partition in 1795, "independent Poland disappeared from the map of Europe."[100]

But the effect of the Four-Year Sejm on visions of the Jewish future was not wholly ephemeral. The precedent was established by which the status of the Jews, heretofore defined by charters and agreements, was radically changed through constitutional reform. Jews as a specific corporate group were excluded from public law, in contrast with their situation in other countries of Central Europe, where their privileges but also their disabilities may have been preserved by new legislation.[101] But Jews as individuals in Poland did not receive the rights guaranteed to other Poles nor the rights guaranteed to individuals, including Jews,

97. Lord, *Second Partition of Poland,* 274–81.
98. Mahler, *History of Modern Jewry,* 311.
99. Polish-Jewish historiography emphasizes, perhaps to an exaggerated degree, the enthusiasm of the Jewish masses for Kościuszko and the insurrection. See the fascinating story about Shemuel Zbitkower, a purveyor of war matériel at various times to both the Polish and the Russian armies, who used his sizable fortune to bribe Russian officers to allow the burial of Jews slaughtered in the Warsaw suburb of Praga. Ringelblum, "Shemuel Zbitkower," 246–66, 337–55.
100. Wandycz, *Lands of Partitioned Poland,* 10–11.
101. Dinur, *Bemifne Haddorot,* 334.

through successful constitutional reforms in Western countries. This left Poland's Jews, even more than before the May Constitution subject to the whims of petty local tyrants. Vis-à-vis the larger collectivity, the Polish nation, Jews were now defined administratively as nonpersons. For Jews on the brink of the modern period, a period that would witness the mightiest effort to define the Jew as a nonperson and thereby to eliminate Jews from European society, the legacy of Poland's "bloodless revolution" was insidious.

But even in the immediate future of the Four-Year Sejm, the content of many written proposals and public speeches—the rhetoric of reform—constituted not just a literary debate. A direct line can be traced from characterizations of the Jews and prescriptions for their future to a plethora of edicts, ordinances, reform measures, and laws that would harass and undermine Jews. In this period the foundations for a third serfdom were adumbrated, which, as envisioned by some Polish publicists, could at one and the same time solve Poland's labor problems and resolve the "Jewish question."[102] The final partition of Poland did not put an end to such schemes, including resettlement proposals that would reduce Jewish farmers approximately to the condition of serfs. The officials of the well-ordered police states that annexed Poland never lacked imagination in exploring the administrative implications of the anomalous legal status of Polish Jews; Russian state officials in particular—often provincial, xenophobic, and incompetent— from their initial contact with Jews following the first partition of Poland, demonstrated independent talent and alacrity in these matters. Generations of Jews would endure humiliating commissions, erratic policies, expulsions, conscription, and forced migrations. Gottlober's comment about traps that were evaded once but nevertheless persisted as future dangers proved to be tragically accurate.[103]

Against this background we begin to understand how the reforms accompanying Poland's efforts to modernize, which were seen by some Poles and poorly informed observers as sagacious legislation, to many Jews appeared to be little more than wicked decrees. It is against this background that we have a better understanding of the legend of Levi Yizhak of Berditchev, which portrays him escaping the "impurity" surrounding the big city, representative of the modern world. And against this background we discern the change of heart that takes place in a man like Menahem Mendel Lefin, who portrays himself as harshly criticizing the Hasidim and others during the Four-Year Sejm for not taking collective worldly action in response to the problems of the day. Yet a few years later, this same Lefin eschewed political action on behalf of Jews in favor of ardent and systematic educational efforts to be made among his coreligionists, attempting to

102. Czacki, *Rozprawa o żydach i karaitach* (Lwów, 1807), 220; Gelber, "Program for a Jewish State," 291–320, and "Jewish Question in Poland, 106–43; Vereté, "Polish Proposals," 148–55, 203–13; Mahler, *History of Modern Jewry,* 304.
103. For a comparison of the policies of Polish and Russian officialdom toward the Jews, see Levine, "Between Polish Autarky and Russian Autocracy." 27 (1982), Part I.

transform them spiritually and intellectually and thereby to make them better prepared as Jews to confront the modern world. The position of the cautious modernizer, of the moderate Maskil, becomes increasingly shaky as the masses of Jews in fact confront the limits of reform. It is against this background of failed modernization and its very equivocal terms that we must understand the intellectual and spiritual history of what came to be called Eastern European Jewry, the Jews of the partitioned lands of Poland.

For many Jews in Eastern Europe at the end of the eighteenth century, and even a century and more later, the very word *reform* took on threatening overtones. They responded unenthusiastically, and with a justified measure of wariness, to state-promulgated reforms expressed in "harsh tongues" and having more of a disruptive effect upon their inner and communal lives than the church-inspired decrees with which their ancestors had to cope for centuries. They understood, intuitively perhaps, that modernization results in more possibilities than success or failure; modernization, as we now know, sows the seeds of its own opposition in forms that are often virulent. And although antimodernization movements often take a dim view of changes that are under way, favoring as they do the restoration of a golden age, these same movements in actuality forge a different path to the future. For Jews, that path proved to be unimaginably devastating.

Conclusion

The Broken Bridge Revisited:
The Politics of Productivity

This analysis of Poland and Polish Jews in the early modern period has led us back to the questions with which we began: Why did the French and Polish revolutions differ in their responses to the problem of the rights and status of Jews? And to what different futures did each hint for the Jews of Western and Eastern Europe in the modern period? In order to assess what have been thought to be the dramatic moments of the late eighteenth century, we have had to step back two centuries. The disparities that develop between different regions of Europe, I have suggested, are a consequence of human choices, contemplated responses to "small changes" and not merely reflexive reactions of the dependency of one region upon the other. The awareness of backwardness where modernization failed, the intense look over the shoulder with admiration and envy at the accomplishments of others, leads to a deprecated sense of self and of one's people. The all-too-human needs to explain and to blame are the results, the "other side" of those successful processes that transformed the West in the eighteenth century.

Historians of the Polish Jews often view abiding anti-Jewish sentiments in Poland as explanations rather than as results, as causes rather than as effects. By locating these antagonisms on something of a metaphysical level, they make them inaccessible to analysis. By placing the relations between Polish Christians and Jews in the deeper context of East-West relations, I have tried to suggest a more complicated relationship between cooperation and conflict, between the pragmatic interests that Jews represented and the religious emotions that they evoked. Poland, the home of nearly half of world Jewry on the eve of the modern era, emerges as an instructive and historically significant case study of the failed modernization of Eastern Europe and of its reaction to the West. What do we learn about the modernization of polities and economies and the entry of Jews into the modern world from the singular failure of Jews to be integrated as citizens and entrepreneurs into early modern Poland?

The century of religious wars precipitated by the Protestant Reformation had a powerful but somewhat equivocal influence on European Jewry. Under medieval Christendom the terms of Jewish involvement and toleration had been religious. Jews had been kept in a lowly and precarious status but otherwise had been preserved because they were deemed useful. In the most remote localities Jews symbolized on behalf of emperor and pope the claims of Christianity to truth and the "plenitude of apostolic power." Their degradation and humiliation provided a useful social spectacle through which a premodern society could interpret itself, mapping its social boundaries and lines of power. By the mid-seventeenth century, following the stalemate of devastating wars, there was growing recognition (particularly in northwestern Europe) of the dangers of sectarianism, seemingly with the effect of reducing the influence of religion on the polity. Moreover, the devastation itself led to a new concern for capital and population. Efforts at reconstruction opened the door to more significant Jewish participation. In the commercial centers of Europe, such as Protestant Holland and England, where trade was expanding and its accumulated profits were being transferred into the development of early industrial enterprises, new Jewish residents, in alliance with princes, burghers, monarchs, and lords, were readily able to demonstrate "how useful are the Jewes." Sefardim, including the descendants of Marranos and newly escaped Marranos, some of whom settled in France, Holland, and England, as well as a growing stream of Ashkenazim, largely from Poland, maximized the benefit of "small changes" and took important initiatives in the international commerce that created the increasingly unbridgeable gap between Western and Eastern Europe.[1]

In 1740 and 1750 in England, between 1789 and 1791 in France, in 1798 in Holland, and in 1750 and 1793 in Prussia, the question of Jewish rights surfaced in public discourse. These publicistic and parliamentary debates coincided with the agricultural, commercial, industrial, scientific, political, religious, and social transformations that at least in retrospect we causally relate to successful modernization. The parliamentary debates resulted in the granting of rights to Jews that were by no means irrevocable, sufficient for full citizenship, or transformative of all facets of their daily lives. But by the end of the eighteenth century, particularly in the more urban areas of northwestern Europe, the prominence and integration of Jews in national economies settled any questions of their usefulness. Those philosophes of the Enlightenment favorably disposed toward Jews provided arguments, and generated models other than conversion, for Jewish participation in the larger society. And these arguments, rather than precipitate new trends, largely legitimated the existing realities of Jewish economic integra-

1. Bloom, *Economic Activity of the Jews of Amsterdam*; Yogev, *Diamonds and Coral*; Swetschinski, "Portuguese Jews of Seventeenth-Century Amsterdam."

tion. In a relatively short period many Jews in these countries became more fully involved in the larger society and felt a deeper and more positive interest in the reference to non-Jewish society. But none of these developments led to the high drama of emancipation.[2] The countervailing forces to this new tolerance based on economic and political utility became palpable. Even in the more secular Protestant countries, the wedge between religion and the polity was not as deep as it first appeared. Faith, even fervor, was not eliminated by science and the Enlightenment but was supported by new syntheses. The state now assumed the responsibility of maintaining Christian morality and Christian sensibilities independently of the church. This impeded Jewish entry into semineutral European society and culture.[3] Insofar as Jews' identification with their homeland and with Christian fellow citizens was not always reciprocated, here the tragedy of the Jew in the modern world began.

The failure of the Protestant Reformation in Poland to bring about the religious transformations and other changes in society and consciousness that we associate with the Reformation in the West did not lead to a restoration of the status quo ante. The Counter-Reformation strengthened, rather than weakened, the nexus between Catholicism and the Polish state, generating in early modern Poland the types of nationalistic ideologies and political faiths, such as Sarmatianism, prevalent elsewhere in Europe only in the nineteenth and twentieth centuries. Within the institutionalization of the second serfdom, pervaded as it was by Counter-Reformation Catholicism and Sarmatianism, Jews served new and important symbolic and practical roles. They were continually needed to symbolize and demonstrate, through their denigration and their precarious status, the claims to truth of Sarmatian chosenness, the higher utility of Poland's lack of order, and the feasibility of the gentry's frivolous "golden freedom." Bridge theories and messianism may have provided Polish traditionalists and even Polish modernizers with fantasized solutions to Poland's problems; resentment against Jews, however, offered more immediate emotional compensation for, and a symbolic resolution of, Poland's domestic failures. The existence of a readily identifiable subgroup, constituting (through much of the eighteenth century) 10 percent of Poland's population, could serve as an explanation for disunities and conflict whose social, political, and economic dimensions were difficult to fathom and even more difficult to resolve. The agreement on the pernicious role of the Jews in the Polish tragedy achieved among a motley bunch of ideologues—ranging from devotees of Sarmatianism trying to legitimate their claims to serf labor, to fellow travelers of the Enlightenment trying to popularize new concepts of productivity—provided a rare opportunity for the development of a national consensus.

On the practical level, in Catholic Poland, the most anticommercial country of Europe, Jewish commercial activities had reconciled the contradiction, im-

2. Katz, "The Term 'Jewish Emancipation,'" 1–25.
3. Katz, *Out of the Ghetto*, 42–56.

plicit to the feudal economy, between the lords' idealized autarky and their real need for goods that could not possibly be generated on the estate. Thus, with the help of Jewish merchants, agents, and arendars, members of the gentry could enjoy their principled condemnation of trade without sacrificing their luxuries. The Jews, who had been used for two centuries to overcome the economic and organizational problems of feudal agriculture and the inefficiencies of guild-regulated burgher crafts and trade, now were blamed for economic failures. The indignation against Jewish involvement in the propinacja mounted with particular viciousness and self-righteousness, at the same moment that this ingenious device by which the Jews had helped the gentry to "save the system" of single-crop agriculture against rebellion from within, and market forces from without, had lost its economic function.

It is against this background that we must understand the politics of "productivization." The call for tolerance of Jews based on their productivity did not imply any objective economic standard. The call for Jewish productivity was generally a call for Jews to accept the state's definition of what was useful and what was harmful, to integrate their economic activities into the activities of the larger economy, and to initiate large-scale economic activity, rationalizing the management of personnel, the use of supplies, and the application of technologies. All of this was to be accomplished with little regard for market forces. The recurrent criticism of Jews in Poland, and later in Russia, for not participating in agricultural production illustrates the mixed motives and wishful thinking involved in the call for Jewish productivization. The ideological impetus for this mode of Jewish reform, as we have seen, may have come from French physiocracy and its emphasis on agricultural production as well as from the economic realities of a faltering and unreliable serf labor supply. Given the nonexistence of a land and labor market, agriculture could only be a code word for exile to remote areas and marginal lands whose productivity would require of Jews an unreasonable capital outlay, enserfment, or both. Traditional Jews who resisted this call for reform demonstrated a more perceptive and rational understanding of what these terms of productivization were about than did many Jewish enlighteners with bucolic visions of Jewish productivity. It was not only innate conservatism that led Jews at the turn of the nineteenth century to resist what might have become a third serfdom.

Whereas in Western Europe in the early modern period there was an increasing tendency to view Jews, among other citizens, as a source of productivity, in Poland they were looked upon as a source of revenue, with little concern for the long-range implications of how that revenue was to be produced or extorted. Jews in the West demonstrated resourcefulness in optimizing the effects of "small changes." In Poland they made similar adjustments to erratic economic conditions. These Jews, in the service of the lords, often demonstrated the same initiative, business acumen, and calculated risk taking for which their cousins in the West became legendary. However unfettered their economic thinking and activity, Polish Jews had to function within a highly controlled economy, one based on reconciling contradictions rather than taking advantage of market forces; they had to profit from decline rather than expansion. Their economic surplus was being siphoned off by the gentry through their profitable leasing agreements, on the one hand, and by the monarchy through the heavy taxation supporting the feeble central institutions, on the other. Moreover, the legal and political context provided a climate for capital investment that was particularly unfavorable to the Jews. The uncertainties of daily life for Jews in Poland, along with the general stagnation and the gentry's idealization of backwardness, did not encourage Jewish entrepreneurs to engage in either long-range risk taking or innovative managerial techniques. So the broken bridge remained broken. Solomon Maimon's grandfather, in refusing to fix it, even in reorganizing his life and that of his family for short-term reaction to the negative consequences rather than long-term remedies through capital investment, may have been demonstrating more of a capacity for rational cost-benefit analyses than we initially thought.

Other broken bridges likewise remained broken. The possibility for a minority, even a resourceful and well-connected one, to transform this economy was far from great. Nevertheless, as Poland stood on the brink of disaster, and the gentry persisted in profiteering from economic decline, the Jews were blamed. Their productivity was increasingly called into question. With greater frequency Polish Jews were compared negatively to their cousins, those great bridge builders the West European Jews; the difficulties in effecting changes in Poland in accordance with the Western pattern were largely ignored; and the Jews in the West, for their own reasons, were not reluctant to distance themselves from Polish Jews by embellishing the stereotype of the *Ostjuden.* It is perhaps because of Moses Mendelssohn's clear understanding of the political and economic problems that would plague East European Jews in trying to emulate West European Jews that he dismissed his disciples' recommendations for the education of Polish Jews as being of little use.

In contrast with the experience of an increasing number of West European Jews, the Jews of Poland did not identify with the larger society. Thousands of Jews put down roots on feudal estates across Poland and became integrated into the dual economies of Polish feudalism—the wheat field and the market; they were involved not only with intermediate trade but also with management and primary production. But as much as they were not strangers to day-to-day life, they continued, then and through the twentieth century, to be strangers to Polish society.[4] The ideologically motivated assimilation of Polish Jews was much delayed and was limited in comparison with assimilation movements among French or German Jews. This mode of isolation contributed to the intensity of Polish

4. Simmel, *Philosophy of Money,* 225. Ruth Wisse aptly described this tendency of "turning citizens into sojourners as if all the time the Jews had only been passing through." "Poland without Jews," *Commentary* 66, no. 2 (August 1978): 67. The tendency had tragic consequences in less than two decades after the reestablishment of a Polish state following World War I. See Wynot, Jr., "A Necessary Cruelty"; Grynberg, "Is Polish Anti-Semitism Special?"

Jewish culture and the wide variety of Jewish renewal movements that in Poland found fertile ground for recruitment; these movements ranged from Zionism to socialism, from Yiddish and Hebrew literary movements to the popular and vital Hasidism—and various combinations of these. Skepticism regarding the true intentions of reform, amplified by historical events in the nineteenth and twentieth century, may have encouraged the descendants of early modern Polish Jews to see their security more in self-reliance than in alliances with Gentiles.

Whereas in the West in the seventeenth and eighteenth centuries Jews were moving more and more toward the status of citizens, in Poland their status both as serfs of the royal chamber and serfs of many chambers was increasingly undermined, leading them to the legal status of nonpersons. The last partitions of Poland may have rendered that status, along with the entire Polish constitution, moot. But with Polish nationalism going largely underground from 1795 until the reestablishment of a Polish state after World War I, the Catholic church continued to be the custodian of national consciousness, more than in other countries experiencing successful or even failed modernization, where secular modes of national identity developed. Demography notwithstanding, there continued to be something anomalous about a non-Catholic Pole. The citizenship of Polish Jews continued to be tenuous in Poland between the world wars even though the rights of national minorities, in the wake of the Treaty of Versailles, were formally recognized by the renewed Polish state. With different concerns, both antisemites and Zionists continued to question those Jews' productivity.

The Jewish presence in Poland points to a different type of dependency, lending itself again to the confusion of cause and effect and raising more general questions in regard to tragic results in the conflicts between the nation-state and its minority ethnic groups. To this day these conflicts account for a large measure of global violence. What in the American context have come to be called the "unmeltables," sizable and unassimilable minorities, by their very existence impede that hegemony based on homogeneity often sought by nation-states. Members of these minority groups are severely restricted to roles of ambiguous utility deemed by some members of the majority as harmful. From Moses Mendelssohn to Malcolm X, leaders of such unassimilable minorities have expressed the perverse logic of this situation in similar terms: they poke out our eyes and blame us for not seeing.

The short-term benefit to the Jews indeed may have had longer-range, unanticipated consequences that were harmful—though in ways different from those that their enemies foresaw. The participation of Polish Jewry in the second serfdom, which was by no means planned or fully expected, may have abetted the Polish gentry not only in cruelly exploiting and enserfing the peasants but also in transcending without really resolving the conflicting political and economic forces that threatened the gentry's position. Jewish activities in Poland from the sixteenth through eighteenth centuries, which saved a declining system and propped up a failing order, may have enabled the Polish nobles to delude themselves into thinking of their sense of disorder as ultimately functional and truly viable. The Jews' new role, particularly during the last century and a half of the Polish state in managing the propinacja, masked the strains engendered by the economic failures of feudalism, as well as the conflicts between different sectors of Polish society that accompanied those failures. This postponed but did not avert the crisis. And if the Polish lords had confronted the crisis at an early date, if they had understood the limits of a single-crop economy, the unreliability of serf labor, and their own ambivalence to commerce and currency, would they have been able to make more adequate responses to small changes? And insofar as they did not, what responsibility does this ethnic minority share for Poland's failed modernization? And how do we assess the claim, "how useful are the Jewes"?

Here we find the frightening outlines of old resentments expressed in new forms. In observing the failures in incipient modernization and the growing awareness, at least among some Poles, of backwardness, we have had the opportunity to examine a reaction that occurs in other countries where economic development is thwarted. From the second half of the eighteenth century there is an upsurge in the allegations that Jews are unproductive and therefore parasitic, impeding development for other members of the society; or conversely, that they are too enterprising, standing at the avant-garde, disrespectful of the traditional ways "we" insiders do things, that they pose unfair competition to other members of the society or appropriate an excessive proportion of the profits through activities that are not socially useful, are even harmful, and benefit only themselves. These allegations were made separately and in combination, at times blending even contradictory insinuations, animated by primordial sentiments and medieval images and even distorted applications of Western Enlightenment thinking. They received what is not necessarily their earliest but is certainly their fullest, harshest, most sustained, and most virulent formulations in eighteenth-century discussions of how to "reform" Polish Jews. And they became most insidious at that beginning of the end of Poland, when—for however long a moment—Jews were legislatively defined as nonpersons.

What does this meeting of gentry lack of order and Jewish order reveal about the politics and economics of productivization, and the functions that might have been served by contradictory assessments of Jewish productivity? In their disturbing essay *Dialektik des Aufklärung*, written shortly after World War II, Max Horkheimer and Theodore Adorno of the Frankfurt school remind us that resentment against the Jews is often an effective mode of concealing the domination of one class by another in production.[5] Whether this points to the economic origins of antisemitism inciting the rise of national socialism in a country characterized by reactionary modernism, it does make provocative suggestions about the country of failed modernization. In the second serfdom, the early modern Polish institution of production and domination, and in the devices that the Polish gentry developed to mask their own domination and their failures to project their blame and their shame, we might begin to understand this source of Jewish

5. Horkheimer and Adorno, *Dialectic of Enlightenment,* 173.

resentment without resorting to vague, ahistorical, even metaphysical notions of a special Polish antisemitism.

Economic antisemitism expresses itself differently from the age-old hatred whose theological presuppositions, though still able to stir the mob, were losing plausibility in an increasingly secular world, and from the political antisemitism that would develop in Germany in the late 1870s.[6] The matrix of this resentment toward Jews can be more clearly identified, not so much in the competition of international trade or industrialization in the West, but in the failed modernization of Poland. Economic antisemitism traveled both east and west, finding different modes of expression in more- and less-developed countries in the nineteenth and twentieth centuries, with the new virulence of that industrialized and bureaucratized age. Is it not chillingly ironic that its roads converged at that German-made institution erected on Polish soil with its cynical welcome, "Arbeit Macht Frei"?

6. Katz, *From Prejudice to Destruction.*

Bibliography

Albeck, Shalom. *Dinei Hammamonot Battalmud.* Tel Aviv, 1976.

Alon, Menaḥem. *Hammishpat Haivri.* vol. 1, 2d ed. Jerusalem, 1978.

Altmann, Alexander. *Moses Mendelssohn: A Biographical Study.* University, Ala., 1973.

Anderson, Perry. *Lineages of the Absolutist State.* London, 1974.

Arendt, Hannah. *The Origins of Totalitarianism.* Cleveland, 1964.

Aschheim, Steven. *Brothers and Strangers: The East European Jew in Germany and German Jewish Consciousness, 1800–1923.* Madison, Wisc., 1982.

Ashcroft, Richard. *Locke's Two Treatises of Government.* London, 1987.

Assaf, Simḥa. "On Jews and the Mint in Egypt" (Hebrew). *Zion,* n.s., 1 (1936).

———. *Mekorot Letoledot Haḥinnukh Beyisrael.* 4 vols. Tel Aviv, 1984.

Attman, Artur. *The Bullion Flow between Europe and the East, 1000 to 1750.* Translated by Eva Green and Allan Green. Göteborg, 1981.

The Babylonian Talmud. 20 vols. Jerusalem, 1957.

Bain, R. Nisbet. *The Last King of Poland and His Contemporaries.* New York, 1971.

Bałaban, Mayer. *Historja żydów w Krakowie i na Kazimierzu 1304–1868.* 2 vols. Kraków, 1931–1936.

———. *Letoledot Hattenua Hafrankit.* Part 1. Tel Aviv, 1934.

Banfield, Edward. *The Moral Basis of a Backward Society.* Glencoe, Ill., 1958.

Barfield, Owen. *Saving the Appearances: A Study in Idolatry.* New York, 1965.

Barkai, Ron. *Madda, Magya, Umitologya Bimei Habbeinayim.* Jerusalem, 1987.

Barkun, Michael. *Disaster and the Millennium.* New Haven, 1974.

Baron, Salo. "The Economic Views of Maimonides." In *Essays on Maimonides: Octocentennial Volume*, edited by Salo Baron. New York, 1941.

———. *The Jewish Community, Its History and Structure to the American Revolution*. 3 vols. Philadelphia, 1942.

———. "Modern Capitalism and Jewish Fate." *Menorah Journal* 30 no. 2 (Summer 1942).

———. *A Social and Religious History of the Jews*. 16 vols. 2d ed., rev. New York, London, and Philadelphia, 1952–1983.

———. "Plenitude of Apostolic Power and Medieval Jewish Serfdom." In *Yizḥak Baer Jubilee Volume*, edited by Salo Baron et al. Jerusalem, 1960.

———. *History and Jewish Historians*. Philadelphia, 1964.

———. *The Russian Jew under Tsars and Soviets*. 2d ed., rev. New York, 1976.

Bellah, Robert. "Meaning and Modernisation." *Religious Studies* 4 (1968).

Ben-Sasson, Hayyim Hillel. *Hagut Vehanhaga: Hashkafoteihem Haḥevratiyyot Shel Yehudei Polin Beshilehei Yemei Habbeinayim*. Jerusalem, 1959.

———. "The Reformation in Contemporary Jewish Eyes." *Proceedings: The Israel Academy of Sciences and Humanities* 4 no. 12 (1970).

———. "Jews and Christian Sectarians: Existential Similarity and Dialectical Tensions in Sixteenth-Century Moravia and Poland-Lithuania." *Viator* 4 (1973).

Ben-Sasson, Yonah. *Mishnato Haiyyunit Shel Harama*. Jerusalem, 1984.

Ben Shlomo, Joseph. *Torat Haelohut Shel R. Moshe Cordovero*. Jerusalem, 1965.

Benish, Ḥayyim. *Middot Veshiurei Tora*. Benei Berak, 1987.

Berger, Peter. *The Sacred Canopy: Elements of a Sociological Theory of Religion*. Garden City, N.Y., 1967.

Berger, Peter, Brigitte Berger, and Hansfried Kellner. *The Homeless Mind: Modernization and Consciousness*. (New York, 1973.

Bernard, Paul P. "Joseph II and the Jews: The Origins of the Toleration Patent of 1782." *Austrian History Yearbook* 4–5 (1968–1969).

Bialik, Hayyim Naḥman. *Kol Shirei Bialik*. Tel Aviv, 1953.

Bieńkowska, Barbara. "The Heliocentric Controversy in European Culture." In *The Scientific World of Copernicus*, edited by Barbara Bieńkowska. Dordrecht, Holland, 1973.

Bloch, Marc. "The Problem of Gold in the Middle Ages" (1933). In *Land and Work in Medieval Europe: Selected Papers*, translated by J. E. Anderson. Berkeley and Los Angeles, 1967).

Bloom, Herbert. *Economic Activity of the Jews of Amsterdam in the Seventeenth and Eighteenth Centuries*. New York, 1987.

Bogucka, Maria. *Nicholas Copernicus, the Country and Times*. Wrocław, 1973.

———. "The Monetary Crisis of the Eighteenth Century and Its Social and Psychological Consequences in Poland." *Journal of European Economic History* 4, no. 1 (Spring 1975).

————. "L'attrait de la culture nobiliaire (Sarmatisation de la bourgeoisie polonaise au XVIIe siècle." *Acta Poloniae Historica,* no. 33 (1976).

————. "Towns in Poland and the Reformation: Analogies and Differences with Other Countries." *Acta Poloniae Historica,* no. 40 (1979).

Boss, Valentin. *Newton and Russia: The Early Influence, 1698–1796.* Cambridge, Mass., 1972.

Braudel, Fernand. *Capitalism and Material Life, 1400–1800.* New York, 1973.

————. *The Wheels of Commerce: Civilization and Capitalism, 15th–18th Century.* New York, 1979.

————. *The Perspective of the World.* New York, 1984.

Braudel, Fernand, and F. C. Spooner. "Prices in Europe from 1450–1750." In *The Cambridge Economic History of Europe,* vol. 4. Cambridge, 1967.

Bravo Sierra, Restituto. *El pensamiento social y económico de la escolástica desde sus orígines al comienzo del catolicismo social.* Madrid, 1975.

Breger, Marcus. *Zur Handelsgeschichte den Juden in Polen während des 17 Jahrhunderts.* Berlin, 1932.

Breuer, Mordekhai. "The Rise of 'Pilpul' and 'Hillukim' in the Yeshivot of Ashkenaz" (Hebrew). In *Sefer Hazzikkaron Lihiel Yaakov Weinberg.* Jerusalem, 1969.

Brodrick, J. *The Economic Morals of the Jesuits.* London, 1934.

Burke, Kenneth. *The Rhetoric of Religion.* Boston 1961.

Calhoun, George. *The Ancient Greeks and the Evolution of Standards in Business.* Boston and New York, 1926.

————. *Business Life of Ancient Athens.* Chicago, 1926.

Calmansohn, Jacques. *Essai sur l'état actuel des juifs de Pologne et leur perfectibilité.* Warsaw, 1796.

Carsten, Francis. "The Court Jews: A Prelude to Emancipation." *Leo Baeck International Year Book* 3 (1958).

Chafuen, Alejandro. *Christians for Freedom: Late Scholastic Economics.* San Francisco, 1986.

Cherniavski, Michael. "The Old Believers and the New Religion." *Slavic Review* 25 no. 1 (March 1966).

Cipolla, Carlo M. *Money, Prices and Civilization in the Mediterranean World, 5th to 17th Century.* New York, 1967.

Cohn, Norman. *Warrant for Genocide: The Myth of the Jewish World and the Protocols of the Elders of Zion.* New York, 1967.

Cooperman, Bernard, ed. *Jewish Thought in the Sixteenth Century.* Cambridge, Mass., 1983.

Courtenay, William J. "The King and the Leaden Coin: The Economic Background of 'Sine Qua Non' Causality." *Traditio* 28 (1972).

————. "The Critique of Natural Causality in the Mutakallimun and Nominalism." *Harvard Theological Review* 66 (1973).

————. "Nominalism and Late Medieval Religion." In *The Pursuit of Holiness in Late Medieval and Renaissance Religion,* edited by Charles Trinkhaus. Leiden, 1974.

————. *Covenant and Causality in Medieval Thought.* London, 1984.

Cox, William. *Travels into Poland, Russia, Sweden and Denmark.* London, 1785. Reprint. New York, 1971.

Craig, Sir John. *Newton at the Mint.* Cambridge, 1946.

Cynarski, Stanisław. "The Shape of Sarmatian Ideology in Poland." *Acta Poloniae Historica,* no. 19 (1968).

Czacki, Tadeusz. *Rozprawa o żydach i karaitach.* Lwów, 1807.

Czartoryski, Adam. *Memoirs of Prince Adam Czartoryski and His Correspondence with Alexander I.* Edited by Adam Gielgud. 2 vols. London, 1888.

Dan, Joseph. "'No Evil Descends from Heaven': Sixteenth Century Jewish Concepts of Evil." In *Jewish Thought in the Sixteenth Century,* edited by Bernard Cooperman. Cambridge, Mass., 1983.

Darowski, Roman S. I. *État actuel des recherches sur l'enseignement de la philosophie dans les collèges des jésuites de Pologne du XVIe au XVIIIe siècle. Archivum Historicum Societatis Iesu* 46 (1977).

Davidson, Herbert. "Medieval Jewish Philosophy in the Sixteenth Century." In *Jewish Thought in the Sixteenth Century,* edited by Bernard Cooperman. Cambridge, Mass., 1983.

Davies, Norman. *God's Playground: A History of Poland.* 2 vols. New York, 1982.

Dawidowicz, Lucy. *The Golden Tradition: Jewish Life and Thought in Eastern Europe.* New York and Chicago, 1967.

de Roover, Ramon. *Money, Banking and Credit in Medieval Bruges: Italian Merchant Bankers, Lombards and Moneychangers, a Study in the Origins of Banking.* Cambridge, Mass., 1948.

————. "Scholastic Economics: Survival and Lasting Influence from the Sixteenth Century to Adam Smith." *Quarterly Journal of Economics* 69 no. 2 (May 1955).

Demian, J. A. *Darstellung der Oesterreichischen Monarchie,* 4 vols. Vienna, 1804.

Dempsey, B. W. *Interest and Usury.* Washington, D.C., 1943.

Dienstag, Jacob, ed. *Studies in Maimonides and St. Thomas Aquinas.* New York, 1975.

Dinur, Ben Zion. *Bemifne Haddorot.* Jerusalem, 1955.

Dobbs, Betty Jo Teeter. *The Foundation of Newton's Alchemy.* Cambridge, 1975.

Douglas, Mary. *Purity and Danger: An Analysis of Concepts of Pollution and Taboo.* London, 1966.

Dov Ber of Bolechow. *The Memoirs of Dov Ber of Bolechow.* Edited by M. Wischnitzer. Berlin, 1922.

Dubnow, Simon. "The 'Council of Four Lands' and Its Relationship with the Local Councils" (Hebrew). In *Sefer Hayyovel Likhvod Naḥum Sokolov.* Warsaw, 1904.

————. *History of the Jews in Russia and Poland.* Translated by I. Friedlander. 3 vols. Philadelphia, 1916–1920.

————. *Pinkas Hammedina.* Berlin, 1925.

————. *Divrei Yemei Am Yisrael.* Translated by Barukh Kero. 10 vols. 2d ed. Tel Aviv, 1948.

————. *Toledot Haḥasidut.* Tel Aviv, 1975.

Duhem, Pierre. *To Save the Phenomena: An Essay on Physical Theory from Plato to Galileo.* Translated by Edmund Doland and Chaninah Mascher. Chicago, 1969.

Dumont, Louis. *Homo Hierarchicus: The Caste System and Its Implications.* Chicago, 1970.

————. *From Mandeville to Marx: The Genesis and Triumph of Economic Ideology.* Chicago, 1977.

Duncan, Hugh. *Symbols and Social Theory.* New York, 1969.

Eilat, Moshe. *Kishrei Kalkala Bein Arẓot Hammikra Bimei Bayit Rishon.* Jerusalem, 1977.

Eisenbach, Artur. *Materiały do dziejów Sejmu Czteroletniego.* Vol. 6. Wrocław, 1969.

Eisenstadt, S. N. "The Protestant Ethnic Thesis." In *Sociology of Religion,* edited by Roland Robertson. Baltimore, 1969.

Elbaum, Jacob. "Currents in Sixteenth Century Ethical Literature." Ph.D. diss., Hebrew University, 1977.

————. "Aspects of Hebrew Ethical Literature in Sixteenth Century Poland." In *Jewish Thought in the Sixteenth Century,* edited by Bernard Cooperman. Cambridge, Mass., 1983.

Eliade, Mircea. *The Forge and the Crucible.* Chicago, 1956.

Encyclopedia Judaica. Jerusalem, 1972.

Encyklopedja powszechna. Warsaw, 1898–1912. Reprint. Warsaw, 1985.

Ettinger, Shemuel. "The Muscovite State and Its Attitudes toward the Jews" (Hebrew). *Zion* 18 (1953).

————. "The Legal and Social Status of Ukrainian Jews in the 15th through the 17th Century" (Hebrew). *Zion* 20 (1955).

————. "Jewish Influence on the Religious Ferment in Eastern Europe at the End of the Fifteenth Century" (Hebrew). In *Yiẓḥak Baer Jubilee Volume,* edited by Salo Baron et al. Jerusalem, 1960.

————. "The Ideological Background to the Appearance of the Antisemitic Literature in the New Russia" (Hebrew). *Zion* 35 (1970).

————. "Jews and Judaism in the Eyes of the English Deists in the 18th Century" (Hebrew). *Zion* 29 (1964).

————. "The Bases and Goals in the Shaping of the Russian Government's Policy in Regard to Jews with the Partition of Poland" (Hebrew). *Heavar* 19 (1972).

Evans, R. J. W. *The Making of the Habsburg Monarchy, 1550–1700: An Interpretation.* Oxford, 1979.

————. *Rudolph II and His World: A Study in Intellectual History, 1576–1612.* New York, 1984.

Ezrahi, Sidra. *By Words Alone: The Holocaust in Literature.* Chicago, 1980.

Falk, Joshua. *Sefer Meirat Einayim.* Prague, 1692.

Falk, Ze'ev. "Jewish Law and Medieval Canon Law." In *Jewish Law in Legal History and the Modern World,* edited by Bernard Jackson. Jewish Law Annual, Supplement 2. Leiden, 1980.

Fedorowicz, J. K. *England's Baltic Trade in the Early Seventeenth Century: A Study in Anglo-Polish Commercial Diplomacy.* Cambridge, 1980.

Fedorowicz, J. K., ed. and trans. *A Republic of Nobles: Studies in Polish History to 1864.* Cambridge, 1982.

Finkelstein, Louis. *Jewish Self-Government in the Middle Ages.* New York, 1924.

————. *The Pharisees: The Sociological Background of Their Faith.* 2 vols. 3d ed. Philadelphia, 1966.

Fishman, David. "Rabbi Moshe Isserles and the Study of Science among Polish Jews." Paper presented at the Conference, "Tradition and Crisis Revisited," Harvard University, Cambridge, Mass., October 10–12, 1988.

Foucault, Michel. *The Order of Things: An Archeology of the Human Sciences.* New York, 1973.

————. *The Birth of the Clinic: The Archeology of Medical Perception.* New York, 1975.

Fox, Marvin. "Maimonides and Aquinas on Natural Law." In *Studies in Maimonides and St. Thomas Aquinas,* edited by Jacob Dienstag. New York, 1975.

Fox, P. "The Reformation in Poland." In *The Cambridge History of Poland.* Vol. 1. Cambridge, 1950.

Frenk, A. N. *Yehudei Polin Bimei Milḥamot Napoleon.* Warsaw, 1913.

————. *Haironim Vehayyehudim Befolin.* Warsaw, 1921.

Friedberg, Ch. *Bet Eked Sepharim.* Tel Aviv, 1952.

Friedlaender, David. *Aktenstücke die Reform der jüdischen Kolonien in den preussischen Staaten betreffend.* Berlin, 1793.

————. *Über die Verbesserung der Israeliten im Königreich Polen.* Berlin, 1819.

Frydman, S. "French Reports on the Jews in Poland and Russia from the Fifteenth to the Beginning of the Nineteenth Century" (Yiddish). In *Yidn in Frankraykh,* edited by E. Tcherikover. Vol. 1. New York, 1942.

Funkenstein, Amos. *Theology and the Scientific Imagination from the Middle Ages to the Seventeenth Century.* Princeton, 1986.

Fuss, Abraham. "The Eastern European Shetar Mamran Re-examined." *Dine Yisrael* 4 (1973).

Fustel de Coulange. *The Ancient City.* Garden City, N.Y., 1956.

Gay, Peter. *The Enlightenment: An Interpretation—the Rise of Modern Paganism.* 2 vols. New York, 1966, 1969.

————. *Freud, Jews and Other Germans.* New York, 1978.

Geertz, Clifford. *Islam Observed.* Chicago, 1971.

————. "Thick Description: Toward an Interpretive Theory of Culture." In *The Interpretation of Cultures: Selected Essays.* New York, 1973.

Gelber, N. "The Program for a Jewish State" (Hebrew). *Keneset* 3 (1939).

————. "The Jewish Question in Poland in the Years 1815–1830" (Hebrew). *Zion* 13 (1948).

Gierowski, J. *Rzeczpospolita w dobie upadku 1700–1740.* Wrocław, 1955.

Gieysztor, Aleksander, et al. *History of Poland.* Warsaw, 1979.

Gieysztor, I. "Research into the Demographic History of Poland: A Provisional Summing-up." *Acta Poloniae Historica,* no. 18 (1968).

————. "La Démographie historique polonaise (XVIIe–XVIIIe s.): Sources, méthodes, résultats et perspectives." *Acta Poloniae Historica,* no. 27 (1973).

Girard, René. *Violence and the Sacred.* Translated by Patrick Gregory. Baltimore, 1977.

Glamann, Kristof. "European Trade, 1500–1750." In *The Fontana Economic History of Europe: The Sixteenth and Seventeenth Centuries,* edited by Carlo Cipolla. New York 1974.

Goetz, Walter. "Jesuits." In *Encyclopedia of Social Sciences.* Vol. 6. New York, 1937.

Goldberg, Jacob. "Between Freedom and Bondage: Forms of Feudal Dependency of the Jews in Poland in the Sixteenth to Eighteenth Centuries" (Hebrew). In *Proceedings of the Fifth World Congress of Jewish Studies.* Vol. 2. Jerusalem, 1969.

————. "Poles and Jews in the Seventeenth and Eighteenth Centuries: Rejection or Acceptance." *Jahrbücher für Geschichte Osteuropas,* n.s. 22 (1974).

————. *Jewish Privileges in the Polish Commonwealth: Charters of Rights Granted to Jewish Communities in Poland-Lithuania in the 16th–18th Centuries.* Jerusalem, 1985.

Górski, Janusz. *Poglądy merkantylistyczne w polskiej myśli ekonomicznej XVI i XVII wieku.* Wrocław, 1958.

Gottlober, Abraham Baer. *Zikhronot Umassaot.* Edited by Rubin Goldberg. 2 vols. Jerusalem, 1976.

Goudsblom, Johan. *Dutch Society.* New York, 1967.

Graetz, Heinrich. *History of the Jews.* 6 vols. Philadelphia, 1891–1898.

Greenberg, Louis. *The Jews in Russia: The Struggle for Emancipation.* Edited by Mark Wischnitzer. New Haven, 1965.

Grice-Hutchinson, Marjorie. *Early Economic Thought in Spain, 1177–1740.* London, 1978.

Gross, Naḥum, ed. *Economic History of the Jews.* New York, 1975.

Grünwalde, Kurt. "Three Chapters of German Jewish Banking History." *Leo Baeck International Year Book* 22 (1977).

Grynberg, Henryk. "Is Polish Anti-Semitism Special?" *Midstream* 29, no. 7 (August-September 1983).

Gulak, Asher. *Oẓar Hashetarot Hannehugim Beyisrael.* Jerusalem, 1926.

Gutterman, Alexander. "Proposals of Polish Jews for Reform of Their Legal, Economic, and Social and Cultural Status, in the Period of the Great Sejm, 1788–1792" (Hebrew). Ph.D. diss. Hebrew University, Jerusalem, 1975.

Haber, Adolf. "Jewish Innkeepers in the Polish Publicistics of the 'Grand *Sejm,*' 1788– 1792" (Hebrew). *Gal-Ed: On the History of Jews in Poland.* Vol. 2. Tel Aviv, 1975.

Haberman, Jacob. *Maimonides and Aquinas: A Contemporary Appraisal.* New York, 1979.

Hagen, William W. *Germans, Poles and Jews: The Nationality Conflict in the Prussian East, 1772–1914.* Chicago, 1980.

Haiman, C. M. *The Fall of Poland in Contemporary American Opinion.* Chicago, 1935.

Halpern, Israel. *Beit Yisrael Befolin.* 2 vols. Jerusalem, 1948, 1953.

———. *Yehudim Veyahadut Bemizraḥ Eiropa.* Jerusalem, 1968.

Halpern, Israel, ed. *Pinkas Vaad Arba Araẓot.* Jerusalem, 1945.

Hamilton, E. J. "American Treasure and the Rise of Capitalism." *Economica* 27 (1929).

Hans, H. "Polish Protestants and Their Connections in England in the Seventeenth and Eighteenth Centuries." *Slavonic and East European Review* 37 (1958).

Hanson, Elizabeth de G. E. "'Overlaying' in Nineteenth Century England: Infant Mortality or Infanticide?" *Human Ecology* 7, no. 4 (1979).

Harris, R. W. *Absolutism and Enlightenment.* London, 1967.

Hay, Malcolm. *Europe and the Jews.* Boston, 1961.

Heckscher, Eli F. *Mercantilism.* Translated by Mendel Shapiro. London, 1935.

Heineman, Yiẓhak. *Taamei Hammiẓvot Besifrut Yisrael.* Jerusalem, 1959.

Herf, Jeffrey. *Reactionary Modernism: Technology, Culture, and Politics in Weimar and the Third Reich.* Cambridge, 1984.

Hertzberg, Arthur. *The French Enlightenment and the Jews.* New York, 1968.

Herzog, Isaac. *The Main Institutions of Jewish Law.* London, 1936.

Higgs, Henry. *The Physiocrats.* London, 1897.

Hinz, Henryk, and Adam Sikosa. *Polska myśl filozoficzna.* Warsaw, 1964.

Hirschman, Albert. *The Passions and the Interests: Political Arguments for Capitalism before Its Triumph.* Princeton, 1977.

Horkheimer, Max, and Theodore Adorno. *Dialectic of Enlightenment.* Translated by John Cumming. New York, 1972.

Horn, Maurycy. *Regesty dokumentów i ekscerpty z metryki koronnej do historii żydów w Polsce, 1697–1795.* Vol. 1. Wrocław, 1984.

Hoszowski, Stanisław. "The Baltic Trade in the Fifteenth to Eighteenth Centuries." In *Poland at the Eleventh International Conference of Historical Sciences in Stockholm.* Warsaw, 1960.

———. "The Revolution of Prices in Poland in the Sixteenth and Seventeenth Centuries." *Acta Poloniae Historica,* no. 2 (1959).

————. "Central Europe and the Sixteenth and Seventeenth Century Price Revolution." In *Economy and Society in Early Modern Europe,* edited by Peter Burke. New York, 1972.

Hsia, R. Po-Chia. *The Myth of Ritual Murder: Jews and Magic in Reformation Germany.* New Haven, 1988.

Hughes, Everett. "Good People and Dirty Work." *Social Problems* 10 (1962).

Hundert, Gershon. "Security and Dependence: Perspectives on Seventeenth Century Polish Jewish Society Gained through a Study of Jewish Merchants in Little Poland." Ph.D. diss. Columbia University, 1980.

————. "An Advantage to Peculiarity? The Case of the Polish Commonwealth." *Association for Jewish Studies Review* 6 (1981).

————. "Jews, Money and Society in the Seventeenth Century Polish Commonwealth: The Case of Kraków." *Association for Jewish Studies Review* 43 (1981).

————. "On the Jewish Community in Poland during the Seventeenth Century: Some Comparative Perspectives." *Revue des études juives* 142 (July–December 1983).

————. "The Role of the Jews in Commerce in Early Modern Poland-Lithuania." *Journal of European Economic History* 16, no. 2 (Fall 1987).

Hundert, Gershon, and Gershon Bacon. *The Jews in Poland and Russia: Bibliographical Essays.* Bloomington, 1984.

Huntington, Samuel. *Political Order in Changing Society.* New Haven, 1968.

Idel, Moshe. "Sitre Arayot in Maimonides' Thought." In *Maimonides and Philosophy,* edited by S. Pines and Y. Yovel. Dordrecht, 1986.

————. *Kabbalah: New Perspectives.* New Haven, 1988.

————. "'Deus Sive Natura': The Metamorphosis of a Dictum from Maimonides to Spinoza." In *Maimonides and the Sciences,* edited by Robert Cohen and Hillel Levine. Forthcoming.

Inkeles, Alex, and David Smith. *Becoming Modern: Individual Change in Six Developing Countries.* Cambridge, Mass., 1974.

Israel, Jonathan. *European Jewry in the Age of Mercantilism.* Oxford, 1985.

Isserles, Moses. *Torat Haola.* Prague, 1570.

Jacob, Margaret. *The Newtonians and the English Revolution, 1689–1720.* Ithaca, N.Y., 1976.

Jedlicki, Jerzy. "Social Ideas and Economic Attitudes of Polish Eighteenth-Century Nobility: Their Approach to Industrial Policy." In *History of Economic Thought.* Fifth International Congress of Economic History Papers, vol. 1. Leningrad, 1970.

————. "Native Culture and Western Civilization: Essay from the History of Polish Social Thought of the Years 1764–1863." *Acta Poloniae Historica,* no. 28 (1973).

Jedruch, Jacek. *Constitutions, Elections and Legislatures of Poland, 1493–1977: A Guide to Their History.* Washington, D.C., 1982.

The Jewish Encyclopedia. New York and London, 1902.

Kahan, Arcadius. "The Costs of 'Westernization' in Russia: The Gentry and the Economy in the Eighteenth Century." *Slavic Review* 25, no. 1 (March 1966).

————. "Notes on Serfdom in Western and Eastern Europe." *Journal of Economic History* 33, no. 1 (March 1973).

Kahana, Yizhak. *Mehkarim Besifrut Hatteshuvot.* Jerusalem, 1973.

Kamiński, Andrzej. "Neo-Serfdom in Poland-Lithuania." *Slavic Review* 34 (June 1975).

Kantrowicz, Ernest. *The King's Two Bodies: A Study in Medieval Political Theology.* Princeton, 1967.

Kaplan, Lawrence. "Rabbi Mordekhai Jaffe and the Evolution of Jewish Culture in Poland in the Sixteenth Century." In *Jewish Thought in the Sixteenth Century,* edited by Bernard Cooperman. Cambridge, Mass., 1983.

Karo, Joseph. *Shulhan Arukh.* 8 vols. New York, 1954.

Katz, Jacob. *Tradition and Crisis: Jewish Society at the End of the Middle Ages.* Glencoe, Ill., 1961.

————. *Exclusiveness and Tolerance: Jewish and Gentile Relations in Medieval and Modern Times.* New York, 1962.

————. "The Term 'Jewish Emancipation': Its Origin and Historical Impact." In *Studies in Nineteenth-Century Jewish Intellectual History,* edited by Alexander Altmann. Cambridge, Mass., 1964.

————. "The Base of Interest and Its Licence in the Period of the Mishna and Talmud" (Hebrew). In *Hakkongres Haolami Hashelishi Lemaddaei Hayyahadut: Din Veheshbon.* Jerusalem, 1965.

————. *Jews and Freemasons in Europe, 1723–1939.* Cambridge, Mass., 1970.

————. "'A State within a State': The History of an Anti-Semitic Slogan." Israel Academy of Sciences and Humanities Proceedings, vol. 4. Jerusalem, 1971.

————. *Out of the Ghetto: The Social Background of Jewish Emancipation, 1770–1880.* New York, 1978.

————. *From Prejudice to Destruction: Anti-Semitism 1700–1933.* Cambridge, Mass., 1980.

————. *Goy Shel Shabbat.* Jerusalem, 1983.

————. *Halakha Vekabbala.* Jerusalem, 1984.

————. *Toward Modernity.* New Brunswick, N.J., 1987.

Kesten, Hermann. *Copernicus and His World.* New York, 1945.

Kieniewicz, Stefan. *The Emancipation of the Polish Peasantry.* Chicago, 1969.

Klausner, Israel. *Toledot Hakkehila Haivrit Bevilna.* Vilna, 1938.

————. "The Inner Struggle in Jewish Communities in Russia and Lithuania at the End of the Eighteenth Century" (Hebrew). *Heavar* 19 (1972).

Klier, John. *Russia Gathers Her Jews: The Origins of the "Jewish Question" in Russia, 1772–1825.* DeKalb, Ill., 1986.

Kot, Stanisław. *Socinianism in Poland: The Social and Political Ideas of the Polish Antitrinitarians in the Sixteenth and Seventeenth Centuries.* Boston, 1957.

Koyré, Alexander. *From the Closed World to the Infinite Universe.* New York, 1958.

Kremer, Moshe. "Towards the Study of Labor and the Artisan Guilds among Polish Jews (16th–18th Centuries)" (Hebrew). *Zion* 3–4 (1937).

Kuhn, Thomas. *The Copernican Revolution.* Cambridge, Mass., 1957.

Kukiel, Marian. *Czartoryski and European Unity, 1770–1861.* Princeton, 1955.

Kula, Witold. *Problemy i metody historii gospodarczej.* Warsaw, 1963.

———. *An Economic Theory of the Feudal System: Towards a Model of the Polish Economy.* London, 1976.

Kupfer, Ephraim. "The Cultural Image of Ashkenaz Jewry and Its Scholars in the 14th–15th Centuries" (Hebrew). *Tarbiz* 42, nos. 1–2 (1973).

Lamb, Charles. "Imperfect Sympathies." In *Essays of Elia.* Boston, 1892.

Landes, David S. *The Unbound Prometheus.* Cambridge, 1969.

———. "To Have and Have Not." *New York Review of Books,* May 28, 1986.

Lane, Robert. *Political Ideology: Why the American Common Man Believes What He Does.* New York, 1962.

Langer, William. "Checks on Population Growth: 1750–1850." *Scientific American* 226, no. 2 (1972).

John LeDonne, "Indirect Taxes in Catherine's Russia. II: The Liquor Monopoly." *Jahrbücher für Geschichte Osteuropas* 24 (1976).

Lefin, Menaḥem Mendel. "Essai d'un plan réforme ayant pour objet d'éclairer la nation juive en Pologne et de redresser par la fes moers." Warsaw, 1792.

———. *Teshuva Beinyenei Haddat.* Unpublished manuscript, fol. 72, Joseph Pearl Archives, Makhon Lekitvei Yad, National and University Library, Jerusalem, Israel.

———. *Refuat Haam.* Zolkava, 1794.

———. *Heshbon Hannefesh.* Lvov, 1809.

———. *Likkutei Kelalim.* Reproduced in part in N. M. Gelber, "Mendel Lefin Satanower" (Hebrew). In *Abraham Weiss Jubilee Volume.* New York, 1964.

Leskiewicz, J. "Le montant et les composants du revenu des biens fonciers en Pologne aux XVIe–XVIIIe siècles." In *Première Conférence Internationale d'Histoire Économique.* Stockholm, 1960.

Lesnodorski, B. *Les Jacobins Polonais.* Paris, 1965.

Lestchinsky, Yaakov. "The Economic Background of the Jewish Pale of Settlement" (Hebrew). *Heavar* 1 (1952).

Letwin, William. *The Origins of Scientific Economics.* Garden City, N.Y., 1964.

Levenson, Joseph. *Confucian China and Its Modern Fate: A Trilogy.* Berkeley and Los Angeles, 1965.

Levin, Mordechai. *Erkhei Hevra Vekalkala Baideologya Shel Tekufat Hahaskala.* Jerusalem, 1975.

Levine, Hillel. "Between Hasidism and Haskala: On a Hidden Anti-Hasidic Polemic" (Hebrew). In *Studies in the History of Jewish Society in the Middle Ages and in the Modern Period: Presented to Jacob Katz,* edited by E. Etkes and Y. Salmon. Jerusalem, 1980.

————. "Gentry, Jews and Serfs: The Rise of Polish Vodka." *Review* 4, no. 2 (Fall 1980).

————. "On the Debanalization of Evil." In *Sociology and Human Destiny: Essays on Sociology, Religion and Society,* edited by Gregory Baum. New York, 1980.

————. "Between Polish Autarky and Russian Autocracy: The Jews, the *Propinacja* and the Rhetoric of Reform." *International Review of Social History* 27, pt. 1 (1982).

————. "Paradise Not Surrendered: Jewish Reactions to Copernicus and the Growth of Modern Science." In *Boston Studies in the Philosophy of Science,* edited by Robert Cohen and Max Wartofsky. Boston, 1983.

————. *Ha'khronika'—Teuda Letoledot Yaakov Frank Utenuato.* Jerusalem, 1984.

————. "Judaism and Mercantilism" (Hebrew). *Zion* 53, no. 1 (1988).

Levitats, Isaac. *The Jewish Community in Russia, 1772–1844.* New York, 1943.

Lewin, Isaac. "The Protection of Jewish Religious Rights by Royal Edicts in Ancient Poland." In *Polish Civilization: Essays and Studies,* edited by M. Giergielewicz. New York, 1979.

Libiszowska, Z. "American Thought in Polish Political Writings of the Great Diet (1789–1792)." *Polish-American Studies* 1 (1976).

Liebermann, Yehoshua. *Taharut Iskit Bahalakha.* Ramat Gan, 1989.

Lipiński, Edward. "Fezjokraci w Polsce." *Ekonomista,* 1951, no. 1.

————. *Studies on the History of Polish Economic Thought.* Warsaw, 1956.

————. "Copernicus as Economist." In *The Scientific World of Copernicus,* edited by Barbara Bieńkowska. Dordrecht, 1973.

————. *Historia polskiej myśli społeczno-ekonomicznej do końca XVIII wieku.* Wrocław, 1975.

Litak, S. "The Parochial School Network of Poland prior to the Establishment of the Commission of National Education." *Acta Poloniae Historica,* no. 27 (1973).

Little, David. *Religion, Order and Law: A Study in Prerevolutionary England.* New York, 1969.

Locke, John. *The Philosophical Works of John Locke.* 8th ed. London, 1777.

Lord, Robert. *The Second Partition of Poland: A Study in Diplomatic History.* Cambridge, Mass., 1915.

Lorence-Kot, Bogna. *Child-Rearing and Reform: A Study of the Nobility in Eighteenth Century Poland.* Westport, Conn., 1985.

Lovejoy, Arthur. *The Great Chain of Being.* Cambridge, Mass., 1973.

Luria, Solomon. *Yam Shel Shelomo* (on *Bava Kama*). Jessnitz, 1723.

————. *Sheelot Uteshuvot Maharshal.* Jerusalem, 1969.

————. *Hokhmat Shelomo* (on *Pesahim*). Cracow 1581 or 1587. Photoreprint. Jerusalem, 1972.

Lüthy, Herbert. *La Banque Protestante en France* (Paris, 1959–1961).

————. *From Calvin to Rousseau: Tradition and Modernity in Socio-political Thought from the Reformation to the French Revolution.* Translated by Salvator Attanasio. New York, 1970.

Luzzatto, Simone. *Maamar al Yehudei Venezya.* Edited by A. Z. Aeskoly. Jerusalem, 1950.

Mably, Gabriel Bonnot [Abbé] de. "Du gouvernement et des lois de la Pologne." In *Oeuvres,* vol. 8. Paris, 1795.

Macartney, C. A., ed. *The Habsburg and Hohenzollern Dynasties in the Seventeenth and Eighteenth Centuries.* New York, 1970.

McClaine, James J. *The Economic Writings of Dupont de Nemours.* Newark, 1977.

McNeill, John. *A History of the Cure of Souls.* New York, 1951.

Mączak, Antoni. "Export of Grain and the Problem of Distribution of National Income in the Years 1550–1650." *Acta Poloniae Historica,* no. 18 (1968).

——. "Money and Society in Poland and Lithuania in the Sixteenth and Seventeenth Centuries." *European Economic History* 5 (1976).

——. "The Structure of Power in the Commonwealth of the Sixteenth and Seventeenth Centuries." In J. K. Fedorowicz, *A Republic of Nobles: Studies in Polish History to 1864.* Cambridge, 1982.

Mahler, Raphael. *Toledot Hayyehudim Befolin.* Merhavya, 1946.

——. *Yidn in amolikn Poiln in likht fun tsifern.* Warsaw, 1958.

——. *A History of Modern Jewry, 1780–1815.* London, 1971.

Maimon, Solomon. "A Dedication to the Polish King" (Hebrew). *Moznayim* 2 (1940–1941).

——. *Sefer Hayyei Shelomo Maimon.* Translated by Y. K. Barukh. Tel Aviv, 1953.

Maimonides, Moses. *Guide of the Perplexed.* Translated by Shlomo Pines. 2 vols. Chicago, 1963.

——. *Mishne Tora.* 5 vols. Jerusalem, 1976.

Maine, Henry Sumner. *Ancient Law: Its Connection with the Early History of Society and Its Relation to Modern Ideas.* Boston, 1963.

Makkai, L. "Neo-Serfdom: Its Origin and Nature in East Central Europe." *Slavic Review* 34 (June 1975).

Malino, Frances. *The Sephardic Jews of Bordeaux: Assimilation and Emancipation in Revolutionary and Napoleonic France.* University, Ala., 1978.

——. "Attitudes toward Jewish Communal Autonomy in Prerevolutionary France." In *Essays in Modern Jewish History: A Tribute to Ben Halpern,* edited by Frances Malino and Phyllis Cohen Albert. East Brunswick, N.J., 1982.

Manuel, Frank. *The Religion of Isaac Newton,* Oxford, 1974.

Maor, Yizhak. "The Pale of Jewish Settlement" [Hebrew]. *Heavar* 19 (1972).

Meir of Lublin. *Sheelot Uteshuvot Maharam Lublin.* Venice, 1615.

Merton, Robert. "Puritanism, Pietism and Science." In *Social Theory and Social Structure.* Glencoe, Ill., 1964.

Meyer, Michael. *The Origins of the Modern Jew: Jewish Identity and European Culture in Germany, 1749–1824.* Detroit, 1967.

Michalski, Jerzy. "Sarmatyzm a europeizacja Polski w XVIII wieku." In *Swojskość i cudzoziemszczyzna w dziejach kultury polskiej,* edited by Zofia Stefanowska. Warsaw, 1973.

————. *Rousseau i sarmacki republikanizm.* Warsaw, 1977.

Miller, Perry. *The New England Mind: The Seventeenth Century.* New York, 1939.

Mintz, Alan. *Ḥurbran: Responses to Catastrophe in Hebrew Literature.* New York, 1984.

Miskimin, Harry. *The Economy of Later Renaissance Europe, 1460–1600.* Cambridge, 1977.

Moody, E. A. "Ockham, Buridan and Nicholas of Autrecourt: The Parisian Statutes of 1339 and 1340." *Franciscan Studies* 7 (1947).

————. "Ockham and Aegidius of Rome." *Franciscan Studies* 9 (1949).

Mun, Thomas. *England's Treasure by Forraign Trade.* London, 1664.

Nadav, M. "Rabbi Avigdor ben Ḥayyim and His Battle against Hasidism in Pinsk and Lithuania" (Hebrew). *Zion* 36 (1971).

Nathan of Hanover. *Yeven Mezula.* Venice, 1653.

————. *Megillat Eifa.* Edited by M. Weiner. Hanover, 1855.

Nef, J. U. "Prices and Industrial Capitalism in France and England, 1540–1640." *Economic History Review* 7 (1937).

Nelson, Benjamin. *The Idea of Usury: From Tribal Brotherhood to Universal Otherhood.* Chicago, 1969.

————. *On the Roads to Modernity: Conscience, Science and Civilizations: Selected Writings.* Edited by Toby Huff. Totowa, N.J., 1981.

The New Cambridge Modern History. G. Elton and F. Carsten, eds. Vols. 2 and 5. Cambridge, 1958, 1964.

North, Douglass C., and Robert Paul Thomas. "An Economic Theory of the Growth of the Western World." In *Economic History Review,* 2d ser., 23 no. 1 (1970).

O'Brien, Charles H. "Ideas of Religious Toleration at the Time of Joseph II: A Study of the Enlightenment among Catholics in Austria." *Transactions of the American Philosophical Society,* new ser., 59, pt. 7 (1969).

Ogonowski, Zbigniew. *Filozofia i myśl społeczna XVII wieku.* Warsaw, 1979.

Opaliński, E. "Great Poland's Power Elite under Sigismund III, 1587–1632." *Acta Poloniae Historica,* no. 42 (1980).

Opalski, Magdalena. *The Jewish Tavern-Keeper and His Tavern in Nineteenth Century Polish Literature.* Jerusalem, 1986.

Pach, Zs. P. "Business Mentality and Hungarian National Character." *Etudes Historiques Hongroises* (1985).

Pachter, Henry. *Paracelsus: Magic into Science.* New York, 1951.

Palmer, R. R. *The Age of Democratic Revolution: A Political History of Europe and America, 1760–1800.* Princeton, 1959.

————. *The Age of Democratic Revolution: The Struggle.* Princeton, 1964.

————. "At the Sources of Jewish Liberty and Equality." *Christianity in Crisis,* October 28, 1968.

Pines, Shelomo, and Yirmiyahu Yovel, eds. *Maimonides and Philosophy.* Dordrecht, 1986.

Pinto. *Traité de la circulation et du crédit.* Amsterdam, 1771.

Pipes, Richard. "Catherine II and the Jews: The Origins of the Pale of Settlement." *Soviet Jewish Affairs* 5, no. 2 (1975).

Plato. *Laws.* Edited by E. B. England. Manchester, 1974.

Pocock, J. *The Machiavellian Moment: Florentine Political Thought and the Atlantic Republican Tradition.* Princeton, 1975.

Polak, A. "Jews and the Mint in Egypt in the Mameluk Period and in the Early Reign of the Turks" (Hebrew). *Zion* 3 (1937).

Polanyi, Karl. *Primitive, Archaic and Modern Economics: Essays.* Edited by George Dalton. Garden City, N.Y., 1968.

Polanyi, Karl, Conrad Arensberg, and Harry Pearson, eds. *Trade and Markets in the Early Empires: History and Theory.* Glencoe, Ill., 1957.

Polgár, László, ed. *Bibliographie sur l'histoire de la Compagnie de Jésus, 1901–1980.* Vols. 1 and 2. Rome, Institutum Historicum S.I., 1981, 1983.

Poliakov, Leon. *The History of Anti-Semitism: From the Time of Christ to the Court Jews.* New York, 1965.

Pospiech, A., and W. Tygielski. "The Social Role of Magnate Courts in Poland from the End of the Sixteenth up to the Eighteenth Centuries." *Acta Poloniae Historica,* no. 43 (1981).

Pribram, Karl. *Conflicting Patterns of Thought.* Washington, D.C., 1949.

———. *A History of Economic Reasoning.* Baltimore, 1983.

Pyszka, Stanisław. *Professori di Vilna in defesa dei diritti umani dei contadini negli anna dal 1607 al 1657.* Rome, 1987.

Rabb, Theodore K., and Robert Rotberg, eds. *The New History: The 1980's and Beyond.* Princeton, 1982.

Raeff, Marc. *The Well-Ordered Police State: Social and Institutional Change through Law in the Germanies and Russia, 1600–1800.* New Haven, 1983.

Ravid, Benjamin. "How Profitable the Nation of the Jews Are: The Humble Addresses of Menasseh ben Israel and the Discorso of Simone Luzzatto." In *Mystics, Philosophers and Politicians: Essays in Jewish Intellectual History in Honor of Alexander Attmann,* edited by Jehuda Reinharz and Daniel Swetschinski. Durham, N.C., 1982.

Ringelblum, E. "Shemuel Zbitkower" (Hebrew). *Zion* 3 (1938).

———. "Hasidism and Haskala in Warsaw in the Eighteenth Century" (Yiddish). In *Wachstein-Bukh.* Vilna, 1939.

———. *Kapitelen geshikhte fun amoliken yidishen leben in Poilen.* Edited by Jacob Shatzky. Buenos Aires, 1953.

Rivkin, Ellis. *The Shaping of Jewish History: A Radical New Interpretation.* New York, 1971.

Robertson, Hector. *Aspects of the Rise of Economic Individualism: A Criticism of Max Weber and His School.* Cambridge, 1933.

Rorabaugh, W. J. *The Alcoholic Republic: An American Tradition.* New York, 1979.

Rosen, Edward. *Copernicus and the Scientific Revolution.* Malabar, Fla., 1984.

Rosenberg, Nathan, and L. E. Birdzell. *How the West Grew Rich: The Economic Transformation of the Industrial World.* New York, 1985.

Roskies, David. *Against the Apocalypse: Responses to Catastrophe in Modern Jewish Culture.* Cambridge, Mass., 1984.

Rosman, Murray [Moshe]. "The Image of Poland as a Center of Torah Learning after the 1648 Persecutions" (Hebrew). *Zion* 51, no. 4 (1986).

———. "The Polish Magnates and the Jews: Jews in the Sieniawski-Czartoryski Territories, 1686–1731." Ph.D. diss., Jewish Theological Seminary of America, 1982.

Rostworowski, E. "La Grande Diète (1788–1792): Réformes et perspectives." *Annales historiques de la révolution française* 36 (1964).

Roth, Guenther, and Wolfgang Schluchter. *Max Weber's Vision of History.* Berkeley and Los Angeles, 1979.

Rousseau, Jean-Jacques. *The Government of Poland.* Edited and translated by Willmoore Kendall. Indianapolis, 1972.

Rubinstein, Avraham. "The Besht's Epistle to Reb Gershon of Kitov" (Hebrew). *Sinai* 67 (1970).

Rudé, George. *Revolutionary Europe, 1783–1815.* New York, 1967.

Rutkowski, J. *Badania nad podziałem dochodów w Polsce w czasach nowożytnych.* Vol. 1. Kraków, 1938.

Schama, Simon. *The Embarrassment of Riches: An Interpretation of Dutch Culture in the Golden Age.* New York, 1987.

Schatz-Uffenheimer, Rivka. "Rabbi Moses Cordovero and the Ari: Between Nominalism and Realism (Hebrew). *Jerusalem Studies in Jewish Thought* 3 (1982).

Schepers, H. "Holkot contra dicta Crathorn," *Philosophisches Jahrbuch* 77 (1970), 79 (1972).

Schipper, Ignacy. *Der Anteil der Juden am europeischen Grosshandel mit dem Orient.* Chernowitz, 1912.

———. *Dzieje handlu żydowskiego na ziemach polskich.* Warsaw, 1937.

Schipper, Isaac. "Economic History of the Jews in Poland-Lithuania from the Earliest Times and to the Partition of the State" (Hebrew). In *Beit Yisrael Befolin,* edited by Israel Halpern. Vol. 1. Jerusalem, 1948.

Schnee, Heinrich. *Die Hoffinanz und der moderne Staat.* 2 vols. Berlin, 1953–1963.

Schumpeter, Joseph. *History of Economic Analysis.* New York, 1966.

Schwartz, Benjamin. *In Search of Wealth and Power: Yen Fu and the West.* Cambridge, 1964.

Scriven, Michael. "Maximizing the Power of Causal Investigations: The Modus Operandi Method." In *Evaluation in Education: Current Applications,* edited by W. James Popham. Berkeley and Los Angeles, 1974.

Shatzky, Jacob. *Die Geschikhte fun Yidn in Varshe.* 3 vols. New York, 1947.

Shell, Marc. *Money, Language and Thought: Literary and Philosophical Economies from the Medieval to the Modern Era.* Berkeley and Los Angeles, 1982.

Shilo, Shemuel. *Dina Demalekhuta Dina.* Jerusalem, 1974.

Shklar, Judith. *Men and Citizens: A Study of Rousseau's Social Theory.* Cambridge, 1969.

Shmeruk, Hone. "Moses Marcuse of Slonim and the Source of His Book *Ezer Yisrael*" (Yiddish). In *Sefer Dov Sadan.* Jerusalem, 1977.

———. "Yiddish Literature in Poland" (Hebrew). *Tarbiz* 46 (1977).

Shohet, Azriel. *Im Hilufei Tekufot.* Jerusalem, 1960.

Shulvass, Moses. *From East to West.* Detroit, 1971.

———. *Jewish Culture in Eastern Europe: The Classical Period.* New York, 1975.

Shusberg, Gabriel, *Petah Teshuva.* Amsterdam, 1651.

Simmel, Georg. *The Sociology of Georg Simmel.* Edited and translated by Kurt H. Wolff. New York, 1950.

———. *The Philosophy of Money.* Translated by Tom Bottomore and David Frisby. London, 1978.

Sirkes, Joel. *Sheelot Uteshuvot Bayit Hadash.* Frankfurt-am-Main, 1697.

———. *Sheelot Uteshuvot Bayit Hadash Hahadashot.* Koretz, 1785.

———. *Sheelot Uteshuvot Bayit Hadash Hayyeshanot.* Ostrog, 1834.

Slutsky, Yehuda, and M. Buba. "The History of the Jews in Russia in the Eighteenth Century (Three Documents)" (Hebrew). *Heavar* 19 (1971).

Small, Albion. *Cameralism.* Chicago, 1909.

Smith, R. E. F., and David Christian. *Bread and Salt: The Social and Economic History of Food and Drink in Russia.* Cambridge, 1984.

Smoleński, W. *Stan i sprawa żydów polskich w XVIII w.* Warsaw, 1876.

———. *Ostatni rok Sejmu Wielkiego.* Cracow, 1897.

Solomons, Israel. "Lord George Gordon's Conversion to Judaism." *Jewish Historical Society of England: Transactions* 7 1911–1917.

Soloveitchik, Haym. *Halakha, Kalkala, Vedimmuy Azmi: Hammashkantaot Biemei Habbeinayim.* Jerusalem, 1985.

Sombart, Werner. *The Jews and Modern Capitalism.* Translated by M. Epstein. New York, 1913.

Southern, R. W. *The Making of the Middle Ages.* London, 1953.

Sperber, Daniel. "The Sale of Makhpela Cave and the Economic Condition in the Land of Israel in the Fourth Century" (Hebrew). *Tarbiz* 42 (1972).

———. *Roman Palestine: Money and Prices.* Ramat Gan, 1974.

Spinoza, Benedict. *A Theologico-Political Treatise and a Political Treatise.* Translated by R. H. M. Elwes. New York, 1951.

Sprecht, Rainer. "Zur Kontroverse von Suárez und Vázquez über den Grund der Verbindlichkeit des Naturrechtes." *Archiv für Rechts und Sozialphilosophie* 45 (1959).

Springer, Arnold. "Gavriil Derzhavin's Jewish Reform Project of 1800." *Canadian-American Slavic Studies* 10 (Spring 1976).

Stampfer, Shaul. "Reading and Writing among East European Jewry in the Early Modern Period" (Hebrew). In *Temurot Bahistoriya Hayyehudit Hahadasha: Kovez Maamarim Shay Lishmuel Ettinger,* edited by Shemuel Almog et al. Jerusalem, 1988.

Stein, S. "The Development of the Jewish Law on Interest from the Biblical Period to the Expulsion of the Jews from England." *Historia Judaica* 17 (1955).

Stephens, John Lloyd. *Incidents of Travel in Greece, Turkey, Russia and Poland.* Vol. 2. New York, 1838.

Stern, Fritz. *The Politics of Cultural Despair: A Study in the Rise of the Germanic Ideology.* Garden City, N.Y., 1965.

Stern, Selma. *The Court Jew.* Philadelphia, 1950.

Stone, Lawrence. *The Causes of the English Revolution.* New York, 1972.

Strack, Hermann L. *The Jew and Human Sacrifice. Human Blood and Jewish Ritual: An Historical and Sociological Inquiry.* Translated from the 8th German edition. New York, 1909.

Supple, B. "The Nature of Enterprise." In *The Cambridge Economic History of Europe,* edited by E. E. Rich and C. H. Wilson. Vol. 5. Cambridge, 1977.

Swanson, Guy. *Religion and Regime: A Sociological Account of the Reformation.* Ann Arbor, 1967.

Swetschinski, Daniel. "The Portuguese Jews of Seventeenth-Century Amsterdam: A Social Profile." Ph.D. diss., Brandeis University, 1979.

Szelągowski, Adam. *Pieniądz i przewrót cen w XVI i XVII wieku w Polsce.* Lwów, 1902.

Talbot, C. H., ed., *Relations of the State of Polonia and the United Provinces of That Crown Anno 1598: Elementa ad Pontium Editiones XIII.* Rome, 1965.

Talmon, Jacob. *The Rise of Totalitarian Democracy.* Boston, 1952.

Tartakower, A. "Polish Jewry in the Eighteenth Century." *Jewish Journal of Sociology* 2 (1959–1960).

Tawney, R. H. *Religion and the Rise of Capitalism.* 1926. Reprint. New York, 1954.

Taylor, Henry. *The Classical Heritage of the Middle Ages.* New York, 1957.

———. *Thought and Expression in the Sixteenth Century.* 2 vols. New York, 1959.

———. *The Medieval Mind.* 2 vols. Cambridge, Mass., 1966.

Tazbir, Janusz. *Piotr Skarga.* Warsaw, 1962.

———. *Literatura antyjezuicka w Polsce, 1578–1625. Antologia.* Warsaw, 1963.

———. *A State without Stakes.* Translated by A. T. Jordan. New York, 1972.

———. "La culture nobiliaire en Pologne aux XVIe–XVIIIe siècles." *Acta Poloniae Historica* 40 (1979).

———. "The Fate of Polish Protestants in the Seventeenth Century." In *A Republic of Nobles: Studies in Polish History to 1864,* edited and translated by J. K. Fedorowicz. Cambridge, 1982.

———. "Die Reformation in Polen und das Judentum." *Jahrbücher für Geschichte Osteuropas* 31 (1983).

Thackeray, Frank W. *Antecedents of Revolution: Alexander I and the Polish Kingdom.* Boulder, Colo., 1980.

Thane, Pat, Geoffrey Crossick, and Roderick Floud, eds. *The Power of the Past: Essays for Eric Hobsbawm.* Cambridge, 1984.

Thomas, Keith. *Religion and the Decline of Magic.* New York, 1971.

Tirosh-Rothchild, Hava, "The Concept of Tora in the Study of Rabbi David Mesir Leon" (Hebrew). *Jerusalem Studies in Jewish Thought* 1 (1981).

Tishbi, Isaiah. *Mishnat Hazzohar.* 2 vols. Jerusalem, 1957.

———. *Netivei Emuna Uminut.* Jerusalem, 1982.

Tönnies, Ferdinand. *Community and Society.* Edited and translated by Charles P. Loomis. East Lansing, Mich., 1957.

Topolski, Jerzy. "Causes of Dualism in the Economic Development of the Modern Age." *Studia Historiae Oeconomicae* 3 (1968).

———. "Economic Decline in Poland from the Sixteenth to the Eighteenth Centuries." In *Essays in European Economic History,* edited by P. Earle. Oxford, 1974.

———. "Sixteenth Century Poland and the Turning Point in European Economic Development." In *A Republic of Nobles: Studies in Polish History to 1864,* edited and translated by J. K. Fedorowicz. Cambridge, 1982.

Topolski, Jerzy, and Jan Rutkowski. "La genèse du régime de la corvée de l'Europe Centrale depuis la fin du Moyen Age." In *La Pologne a VIe Congrès International des Sciences Historiques.* Oslo, 1928.

Trachtenberg, Joshua. *The Devil and the Jews.* New York, 1966.

Trevor-Roper, H. R. *The European Witch-Craze of the Sixteenth and Seventeenth Centuries and Other Essays.* New York and Evanston, 1969.

Troeltsch, Ernst. *Protestantism and Progress: A Historical Study of the Relation of Protestantism to the Modern World.* Boston, 1966.

Troyat, Henri. *Catherine the Great.* Translated by Joan Pinkham. New York, 1980.

Trunk, Isaiah. "Letoledot Hahistoriografya Hayehudit-Polonit (Sekira)." *Gal Ed* 3 (1976).

Turner, Victor. *The Ritual Process: Structure and Anti-Structure.* Chicago, 1969.

Twersky, Isadore. *Introduction to the Code of Maimonides* (Mishne Tora). Yale Judaica Series, vol. 22. New Haven, 1980.

Uminski, J. "The Counter Reformation in Poland." In *The Cambridge History of Poland.* Vol. 1. Cambridge, 1950.

Urbach, Ephraim. *Baalei Hattosafot.* Jerusalem, 1968.

Usher, Abbott Payson. *The Early History of Deposit Banking in Mediterranean Europe.* New York, 1943.

Vereté, M. "Polish Proposals for a Territorial Solution to the 'Jewish Question,' 1788–1850" (Hebrew). *Zion* 6 (1940–1941).

Viner, Jacob. *The Role of Providence in the Social Order.* Philadelphia, 1966.

Voegelin, Eric. *Order and History.* Vol. 1. Baton Rouge, La., 1956.

Wallerstein, Immanuel. "From Feudalism to Capitalism: Transition or Transitions?" *Social Forces* 55, no. 2 (December 1976).

———. *The Modern World-System. Capitalist Agriculture and the Origins of the European World-Economy in the Sixteenth Century.* New York, 1974.

Walzer, Michael. "On the Role of Symbolism in Political Thought." *Political Science Quarterly* 82, no. 2 (June 1967).

———. *The Revolution of the Saints.* New York, 1969.

Wandycz, Piotr S. *The Lands of Partitioned Poland, 1795–1918.* Seattle, 1974.

Weber, Max. *The Protestant Ethic and the Spirit of Capitalism.* Translated by T. Parsons (New York, 1958).

———. *The Sociology of Religion.* Translated by Ephraim Fischoff. Boston, 1964.

———. *On Law in Economy and Society.* Edited by Max Rheinstein. New York, 1967.

———. *Economy and Society.* Edited by Guenther Roth and Claus Wittich. Vol. 1. Berkeley and Los Angeles, 1978.

Weinryb, Bernard Dov. *Neuste Wirtschaftsgeschichte der Juden in Russland und Polen.* Breslau, 1934.

———. "The Problems of the Economic and Social History of the Jews of Germany" (Hebrew). *Zion,* n.s., 2, no. 2 (1936).

———. *Meḥkarim Betoledot Hakkalkala Vehaḥevra Shel Yehudei Polin.* Jerusalem, 1939.

———. *The Jews of Poland: A Social and Economic History of the Jewish Community in Poland from 1100–1800.* Philadelphia, 1973.

Weiss, Jacob. *Middot Umishkalot Shel Tora.* Jerusalem, 1984.

Wertheimer, Jack. *German Policy and Jewish Politics: The Absorption of East European Jewry in Germany, 1868–1914.* Oxford, 1987.

Wiener, Martin. *British Culture and the Decline of the Industrial Spirit, 1850–1980.* Cambridge, 1981.

Wilenski, Mordecai. *Ḥasidim Umitnaggedim.* 2 vols. Jerusalem, 1970.

Wischnitzer, Mark. *A History of Jewish Crafts and Guilds.* New York, 1965.

Wisse, Ruth. "Poland without Jews." *Commentary* 66, no. 2 (August 1978).

Wójcik, Zbigniew. "Poland and Russia in the Seventeenth Century: Problems of Internal Development." In *Poland at the Fourteenth International Congress of Historical Sciences in San Francisco: Studies in Comparative History.* Wrocław, 1975.

Wolf, Lucien, ed., *Menasse ben Israel's Mission to Oliver Cromwell.* London, 1901.

Wolfson, Harry. *Philosophy of Kalam.* Cambridge, Mass., 1976.

Woliński, I. J., J. Michalski, and E. Rostworowski, eds. *Materiały do dziejów Sejmu Czteroletniego.* 5 vols. Wrocław, 1955–1969.

Worseley, Peter. *The Trumpet Shall Sound: A Study of "Cargo" Cults in Melanesia.* New York, 1970.

Wyczański, Andrzej. "The Problem of Authority in Sixteenth Century Poland: An Essay in Reinterpretation." In *A Republic of Nobles: Studies in Polish History to 1864,* edited and translated by J. K. Fedorowicz. Cambridge, 1982.

Yates, Francis. *The Rosicrucian Enlightenment.* London, 1972.

Yeḥiel of Pisa. *Hayyei Olam.* In *Minḥat Kenaot,* edited by D. Kaufman. Berlin, 1898.

Yerushalmi, Yosef. *From Spanish Inquisition to Italian Ghetto: Isaac Cardoso, A Study in Seventeenth Century Marranism and Jewish Apologetics.* New York, 1971.

Yisakhar Ber of Kramnitz. *Yesh Sakhar.* 1609. Reprint. Jerusalem, 1961.

Yogev, Gedalia. *Diamonds and Coral: Anglo-Dutch Jews and Eighteenth-Century Trade.* Leicester, 1978.

Zagorin, Perez. *The Court and the Country: The Beginning of the English Revolution.* New York, 1970.

Zaret, David. *The Heavenly Contract: Ideology and Organization in Pre-Revolutionary Puritanism.* Chicago, 1985.

Index